BUSINESS PLANNING AND POLICY FORMULATION

Other books by Robert J. Mockler

*The Business Management Process: A Situational Approach

Circulation Planning and Development for the National Observer: A Research Study on Business Applications of Management Planning and Control Principles

Guidelines for More Effective Planning and Management of Franchise Systems (with Harrison Easop)

*The Management Control Process

New Profit Opportunities in Business Publishing (editor and contributing author)

Putting Computers to Work More Effectively in Business Publishing (editor and contributing author)

*Readings in Business Planning and Policy Formulation (editor and contributing author)

*Readings in Management Control (editor and contributing author)

*published by Appleton-Century-Crofts

BUSINESS PLANNING AND POLICY FORMULATION

ROBERT J. MOCKLER
St. John's University

New York
APPLETON-CENTURY-CROFTS
Educational Division
MEREDITH CORPORATION

72 73 74 75 76/10 9 8 7 6 5 4 3 2 1

Library of Congress Card Number: 78-154408

PRINTED IN THE UNITED STATES OF AMERICA

390-64435-8

Dedicated to A. J. Lerager

CONTENTS

PREFACE

The purpose of *Business Planning and Policy Formulation* is to provide a comprehensive outline of what planning and policy development are and how they are carried out in a business enterprise.

Most schools of business offer courses in business policy. A sampling of these courses indicates that many of them cover strategic planning. This is understandable, since policies are based on overall planning objectives and strategies and policy development is sometimes considered part of strategic planning.

What is difficult to understand, however, is why these courses so often carry the vague title "Business Policy" which fails to identify precisely the conceptual basis of the subject, and creates confusion as to the intended purpose and content of the course. Because of this lack of a clear conceptual focus, and because they are primarily taught by the case method, these courses are often turned into general decision-making courses or follow the personal interests of the instructor, and fail to give the student a clearly defined approach to planning and policy development which he can subsequently use in business.

Similar problems are encountered in business. The term "policy development" is used to describe a wide range of different planning activities, from developing corporate objectives, philosophies, and strategies to creating policy and procedural manuals. This has led to some confusion among business managers as to exactly what planning and policy development are and how they are performed. And because the relation between policy development and planning has not been adequately defined, specific policies are often not developed and reviewed as part of a company's planning effort, as they should be, and so are not effectively integrated with overall company objectives and strategies.

While there are many fine books on planning and on policy development, at present there is no one book which gives a concise but comprehensive summary of business planning theory, a step-by-step approach to all levels and kinds of business planning, methods for applying the approach in various business situations, and guidelines for developing policies within this planning framework. This book attempts to meet the needs for a concise, practical, unifying text on business planning and policy development.

Business Planning and Policy Formulation focuses on a number of aspects of planning which are important to successful management:

1. A business planning process or model is developed, which is applicable to all levels and kinds of planning situations. The relation of the planning process to the problem-solving/decision-making process is described as are the many complexities of the intellectual process involved in doing planning effectively.
2. Two kinds of business planning are distinguished and discussed: strategic planning, which establishes overall planning directions; and implementation planning, which spells out the action steps designed to carry out these overall directions.
3. Guidelines are developed for using the business planning process at different management levels—from the planning done for the corporation as a whole to the planning done at the lower management levels for the different operations within a company.
4. The interrelationships among the various levels and kinds of business planning within the framework of the business planning process are examined in a variety of business situations.
5. The place of policy development within the planning process is defined and guidelines are given for developing policies based on planning directions.

Business Planning and Policy Formulation covers the steps in the planning process. Chapter 1 discusses the nature of business planning: its definition, the various levels and kinds of business plans and planning, the planning process and its relation to the problem-solving/decision-making process, and the complexities of the planning process at work. The following chapters deal with different phases of the planning process. Chapter 2 concerns organizing the planning effort, Chapter 3 planning premises, Chapter 4 objectives, Chapter 5 overall policies, Chapter 6 implementation planning, Chapter 7 specific operating and staff plans, Chapter 8 implementation policies and procedures, and Chapter 9 coordinating and controlling planning. Chapters 10 and 11 outline some of the scientific tools used in coordinating and controlling planning, such as operations research, information systems and electronic data processing. Chapter 12 deals with organization planning, an integral part of the planning process. Chapter 13 discusses some of the special problems encountered in small business planning. The conclusion summarizes other studies done in business planning and policy development, as well as the major planning concepts developed in this book.

Case studies are given in the Appendix. These studies are designed both to illustrate material in the text and provide the instructor with supplemental classroom exercises. Suggestions on ways to use these cases in conjunction with the text material are given in the questions at the end of each chapter.

Because of its broad scope and concise practical treatment of the subject, this book can be used by anyone—whether in school or in business—who wishes to increase his grasp of business planning and to develop a framework for further study of the subject. The book is designed primarily as the main text in courses in business policy or business planning, as a supplemental text in courses on basic management principles, economic planning or decision making, and for use in middle management reading programs.

I wish to thank David W. Ewing for reading preliminary versions of the book and suggesting ways to improve it. I am also indebted to my students at St. John's University for their commentaries, to my research assistants, Thomas Deely and John Daly, for their contributions to the book, and to Mrs. Katherine Kelly for her patience in preparing the many drafts of the book. Finally, I want to thank my wife, without whom the book would never have come into print.

R. J. M.

BUSINESS PLANNING AND POLICY FORMULATION

CHAPTER 1

THE NATURE OF THE BUSINESS PLANNING PROCESS

Planning first of all is an intellectual process which each of us follows in getting any job done. For example, the housewife studies her family's household needs, determines the alternative ways in which these needs can be fulfilled within her limited resources, decides which way is best, allocates time and money for getting her jobs done, and makes up such detailed plans as her shopping list, meal schedules, and transportation arrangements. In the same way, every business manager sizes up the requirements of his job, the opportunities open to him and his available resources, and then plans his course of action.

This general planning process is only one aspect of business planning, however. Business planning also includes a variety of specific activities within a company. It can be the scheduling done by a production supervisor to meet his daily or weekly quotas. It can be the steps taken by a marketing manager to determine the overall marketing strategy for his company for the coming year. Or, it can be the formal system set up by a corporation to develop its overall five-year growth plan.

The purpose of this chapter is to outline overall business planning concepts. The discussion covers the definition of planning, the various levels and kinds of planning, the planning process and its relation to the problem-solving/decision-making process, and the complexities of the planning process at work.

THE DEFINITION OF BUSINESS PLANNING

Business planning is an intellectual process which requires analyzing anticipated future circumstances, both external (environmental) and internal (company), and developing within the context of that future a company objective, guidelines for action (policies), implementation plans, an organization, and controls designed to achieve the objective.[1] The purpose of business planning is to determine the most profitable way to allocate limited company resources among competing alternative profit opportunities. It is always done within the framework of a business' long-term future, although the plan itself may be either long-term or short-term, may be either for a company as a whole or for only one of its operations, and may be done either by an individual manager for his own operations, or by a corporate planning department for an entire company.[2]

This definition is a broad one, covering both what planning is and the general steps involved in making a plan. A number of authorities cover these steps in their definitions of business planning.[3] Brian Scott, for example, spells out major steps in the planning process in a definition which relates the planning process very closely to the problem-solving/decision-making process:

> Planning is an analytical process which encompasses an assessment of the future, the determination of desired objectives in the context of the future, the determination of alternative courses of action to achieve such objectives, and the selection of a course (or courses) of action from among these alternatives.[4]

Such definitions are essentially extensions of Henri Fayol's definition of planning, "to assess the future and make provision for it," and the plan of action, "the result envisaged, the line of action to be followed, the stages to go through, and methods to use."[5] They differ from Fayol's, however, in that they also try to indicate the steps involved in planning.

Not everyone agrees exactly on the definition of business planning. Peter Drucker, for example, defines planning as "the continuous process of making *present entrepreneurial (risk-taking) decisions* systematically and with the best possible knowledge of their futurity, organizing systematically *the efforts* needed to carry out these decisions, and measuring the results of these decisions against the expectation through *organized, systematic*

[1]This discussion is limited to business planning, although such planning has much in common with public planning (city planning, government planning, and international planning) and military planning. The relationship between corporate planning and planning in other areas is discussed by Neil Chamberlain, *Public and Private Planning* (New York: McGraw-Hill Book Company, 1965), and Melville C. Branch, *Planning: Aspects and Applications* (New York: John Wiley and Sons, 1966).

[2]This definition of planning is based upon the work of many authorities on planning. The works of these authorities are reviewed in the Conclusion to this book.

[3]See, for example, Preston P. LeBreton and Dale A. Henning, *Planning Theory* (Englewood Cliffs, N.J.: Prentice-Hall, Inc., 1961), p. 7, and Brian W. Scott, *Long-Range Planning in American Industry* (New York: American Management Association, 1965), p. 21.

[4]Scott, *Long-Range Planning in American Industry*, p. 21.

[5]Henri Fayol, *General and Industrial Management* (New York: Pitman Publishing Corporation, 1949), p. 43.

feedback."[6] His definition differs from those given above in that he concentrates on the process involved in carrying out plans and assuring their effectiveness, not on the process involved in creating the plans.

Other authorities focus only on what planning is, and not how it is done, in their definitions. According to Stewart Thompson, for example, "a business plan states what results are to be achieved and states things that people can and should do to achieve them."[7] And E. Kirby Warren describes planning as a "process directed toward making today's decisions with tomorrow in mind and a means of preparing for future decisions so that they may be made rapidly, economically, and with as little disruption of the business as possible."[8]

These shorter definitions of planning are useful, because they crystalize the essence of planning in a few easy to remember words. However, they are incomplete, for business planning is an applied science and these definitions do not give a sense of how planning is done. The longer definitions given at the beginning of this section attempt to provide a more comprehensive, practical guideline.

VARIOUS LEVELS AND KINDS OF BUSINESS PLANNING

Figure 1.1 outlines the various levels and kinds of business planning discussed in this study.

At the corporate management level, there is the company's overall long-range plan, that is, the plan that covers the general strategic directions for all company operations (including the company's objective, philosophy, strategy, and major policies), the overall profitability projections, and the highlights of the company's major operating plans. This kind of planning is called "comprehensive" planning, and includes corporate "strategic" planning and overall "implementation" planning.[9] The comprehensive plan is the master plan for a business' operations and covers as many years into the future as management feels are required by the business. Normally this is not less than five years, although it will vary according to the needs of the business. Indian Head Mills, for example, recognizes in their policy manual that long-range planning normally covers at least five years; however, the nature of their industry, textiles, makes long-range

[6]Peter Drucker, "Long-Range Planning," *Management Science*, April 1959, p. 240.

[7]Stewart Thompson, *How Companies Plan* ("AMA Research Study, No. 54," New York: American Management Association, 1962), p. 14.

[8]E. Kirby Warren, *Long-Range Planning: The Executive Viewpoint* (Englewood Cliffs, N.J.: Prentice-Hall, Inc., 1966), p. 18.

[9]Melville C. Branch, *The Corporate Planning Process* (New York: American Management Association, 1962), p. 26; Franklyn H. Sweet, *Strategic Planning . . . A Conceptual Study* ("Research Monograph No. 26;" Austin, Texas; Bureau of Business Research, The University of Texas, 1964), p. 1; Anthony, *Planning and Control Systems*, p. 24; Scott, *Long-Range Planning in American Industry*, pp. 31-32.

Figure 1.1

VARIOUS LEVELS AND KINDS OF BUSINESS PLANS

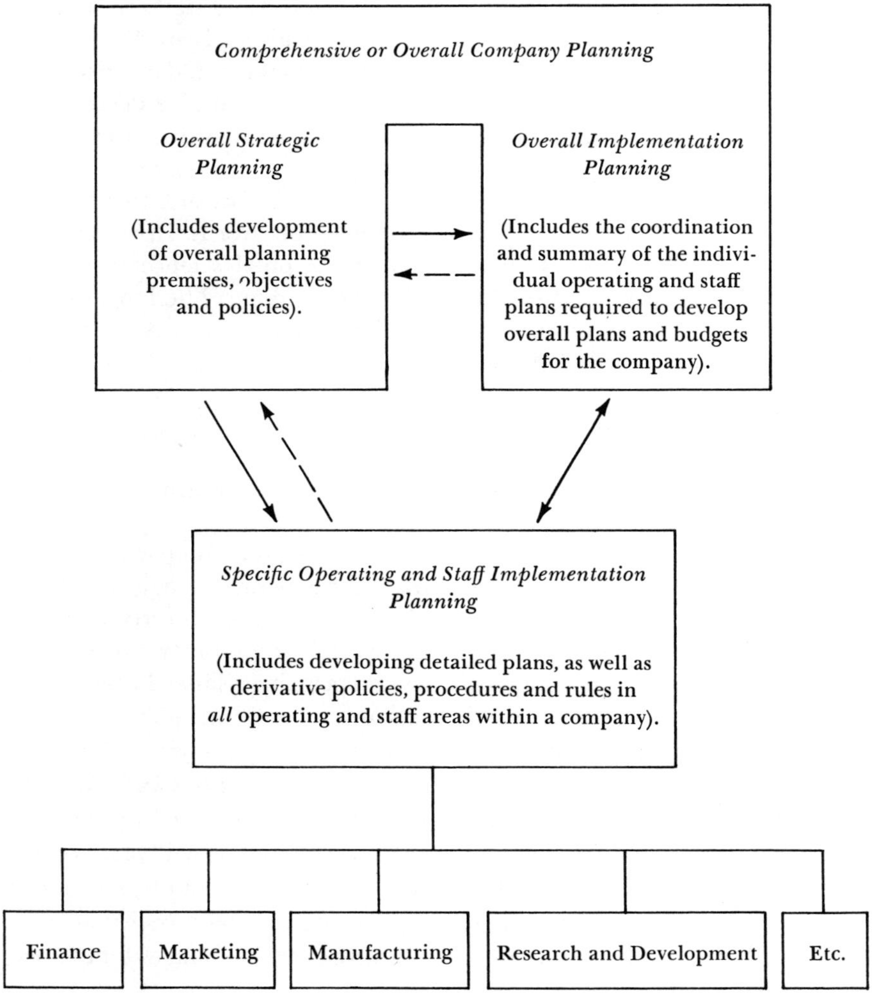

planning difficult, sometimes impossible, and as a result, "Indian Head Mills has been built on plans rarely looking more than six months into the future."[10]

[10] *Indian Head Mills Policy Manual,* in Audrey T. Sproat and E. P. Learned, *Indian Head Mills,* A case prepared for the Harvard Graduate School of Business Administration and copyrighted by the President and Fellows of Harvard College, 1961, p. 31. See Appendix C.

All business planning begins with the development (either formally or informally) of a strategic plan for a company. Once overall strategic directions for a company have been established, more detailed plans are developed. These plans, which spell out specific steps to be taken to achieve company objectives, are called "implementation", "functional", "tactical", or "operational" plans. They cover all the staff and operating areas of a business, such as marketing, manufacturing, finance, organization, and information and control systems. They can be broad enough to be incorporated into the overall comprehensive plan, or they can take the form of detailed operating and staff plans and budgets.

A large part of implementation planning is done at the lower management levels within a company. Implementation planning generally starts with the marketing operations, that is, with the customer.[12] The needs of the marketplace are what the company serves, and it is only through fulfilling market needs effectively that a company can survive over the long-term. For this reason, marketing plans are normally the basis of other company implementation plans. The planning in other areas will affect marketing planning, for facilities, manpower, financial, systems and control resources and requirements all set limits on what marketing management can realistically hope to accomplish. And on occasion, as David Ewing points out, the availability of resources will lead a company to ignore perceived market opportunities and concentrate on business areas in which it has the most experience.[13] Even in these situations, however, the marketing plan will be the basis of company action planning, for the marketplace is where the ultimate success of all plans is determined. Once marketing plans (including sales goals) have been set, final plans in other operating and staff areas designed to meet sales expectations can be developed.

While much implementation planning is done at the individual operating and staff management levels, implementation planning is also an integral part of comprehensive corporate planning, for it provides information for refining overall strategic plans and developing overall company operating plans and budgets. For example, once preliminary overall strategic directions were established each year at a major communications company with which the author worker, division managers began developing operating plans while at the same time helping corporate

[11]Scott, *Long-Range Planning in American Industry*, pp. 31-32; Branch, *The Corporate Planning Process*, p. 26; Charles E. St. Thomas, *Practical Business Planning: A Manager's Guide* (New York: American Management Association, 1965), Chapter 10.

[12]Bruce Payne, *Planning for Company Growth: The Executive's Guide to Effective Long-Range Planning* (New York: McGraw-Hill Book Company, Inc., 1963), pp. 97-98; St. Thomas, *Practical Business Planning*, p. 46; Robert W. Ferrell, *Customer-Oriented Planning* (New York: American Management Association, 1964), pp. 26-28.

[13]David W. Ewing, "Corporate Planning at a Crossroads," *Harvard Business Review*, July-August 1967, pp. 84-85.

planners refine and amplify company strategy. The highlights of these operating plans were then incorporated into two preliminary overall operating plans, a one-year and a five-year plan.

These preliminary plans were prepared by the corporate planning department and checked by the corporate control department. They were then sent down to operating managers who developed their final operating plans in further detail or fed back up information that could be used to refine overall operating plans. At the same time, strategic plans were reexamined in the light of information in the preliminary operating and staff plans. This back-and-forth process continued until final plans were developed. Implementation planning thus occurs at both the corporate level and lower management levels and is closely linked with strategic planning.

As can be seen from the above example, the relationships among the various levels and kinds of business planning are dynamic, not static. Preliminary strategic plans are developed, individual operating and staff plans are then created within this strategic planning framework, and the effects of these plans on overall company operations and profits studied. The planning cycle then begins again, as strategic plans are refined, specific operating and staff plans revised, and so forth, based on information gathered during the preceding steps in the planning cycle. In practice, there is a constant exchange of information between operating and corporate planners as strategic plans are tested against the practical realities of the marketplace, and as operating and staff plans are adjusted to meet more effectively the strategic planning and overall company profit objectives.

While it is possible in theory to distinguish two kinds of planning (strategic and implementation) and two levels of planning (comprehensive and operating), in practice these distinctions become blurred, for all levels and kinds of planning are parts of a single, dynamic business planning process. This unifying business planning process is described in the following section.

THE BUSINESS PLANNING PROCESS

The steps in the overall corporate planning process are:[14]

1. *Planning and organizing the planning effort*: Define specifically what the

[14]Many of the books on planning theory and practice summarize and discuss the planning process: Branch, *The Corporate Planning Process*, Chapter II; Ferrell, *Customer-Oriented Planning*, Part II; Harold Koontz and Cyril O'Donnell, *Principles of Management: An Analysis of Management Function* (4th ed.: New York: McGraw-Hill Book Company, Inc., 1968), Chapter V; LeBreton and Henning, *Planning Theory*, Part III; Payne, *Planning for Company Growth*, Chapter I; Scott, *Long-Range Planning in American Industry*, Part II; Sweet, *Strategic Planning*, entire book; George Steiner, *Top Management Planning* (New York: Macmillan, 1969), Chapter II. See also George Steiner, "Long-Range Planning: Concept and Implementation," *Financial Executive*, July 1966, p. 56 (chart).

planning effort is expected to achieve, and to what use the plans will be put; develop an approach to carrying out the planning function (including how it is to be organized and the policies that will guide the planning effort), and a timetable for developing the plans.

2. *Defining planning premises*: Determine the key factors which will have a major influence on planning, through a study of environmental factors (the economy, society, public policy, industry and market) related to the plan being developed, as well as available company resources, stockholder goals, and past and present company operations and profitability. Since this step develops the basis upon which specific plans are built, wherever possible assumptions about the future should be quantified and given in the form of forecasts.

3. *Determining the company objective*: In the light of the planning premises, develop and evaluate alternative directions that the company might follow. Based on this evaluation, select the corporate objective (that is, kind of company) that will most profitably exploit the market opportunities identified during the premising stage of planning. In addition, state the principles of action, general philosophy, and overall strategy that will guide and control all phases of planning.

4. *Developing policies or guidelines for action*: After developing and evaluating alternatives that will achieve the objective, select the overall policies that best fulfill the corporate objective and still meet market, industry, and company criteria (premises).

5. *Developing implementation plans*: After developing and evaluating alternatives:

   —Select implementation or operating plans including subsidiary objectives for all functional areas. All implementation plans should be consistent with the overall planning premises, objectives, and policies established above; and they should be within the capabilities of the organization under study. Wherever possible, plans should be quantified. The sales forecast is one of the most important sub-objectives at this stage of the planning process.

   —Specify needed derivative policies, procedures, and rules in all planning areas.

6. *Coordinating and controlling planning*: After implementation plans are completed, review and coordinate them, and develop controls for measuring performance against plans. Most often these controls will be in the form of budgets. Management information systems and other scientific decision-making tools are used extensively in developing plans and their control systems.

7. *Organization Planning*: Develop a suitable organization and staff and establish adequate administrative procedures to implement the plan.

8. *Review*: Review and refine the plan periodically.

The above outline, like the outline of the problem-solving/decision-making process discussed later in this chapter, organizes into a systematic process the planning activities. It is not a hypothetical ideal, but a working model designed to show others how successful executives work.

This process is the perspective within which all company planning is done. Even though the marketing manager, for example, may not have been exposed to every step in the process followed by higher management in developing the overall company plan, he needs to understand what the process is, for his yearly operating plans are an integral part of a larger planning process. He needs to know what planning has gone on around him, for his objectives grow out of overall company objectives and his mission is to fulfill them. His plans are affected by the environmental and corporate resource limitations within which the entire corporation must work, and his policies are in large part dictated by overall company directions.

Corporate success depends on maintaining this perspective, for operating managers are the vital links between the overall company objective and and its realization. It is they who daily translate company strategy into action, see that all plans are carried out, and take action to correct deviations of performance from plans.

The specific process followed in implementation planning at the various operating management levels is a sub process of the overall business planning process and follows the same basic outline of the overall process:

1. Define what the planning effort is to accomplish.
2. Isolate the key factors that will affect development of the plans. These will include overall company planning factors as well as those factors uncovered that relate directly to the planning situation under study.
3. Determine the objective to be achieved by the plan. This could range anywhere from meeting a specified sales or production goal to developing a new transportation and distribution system. Implementation strategies, which are consistent with overall company strategy, are also formulated, as are implementation policies, procedures, and rules.
4. Develop step-by-step plans of action for achieving the objective, including controls and organization plans. These action plans should be coordinated with the plans being developed in related operating and staff areas, and with company comprehensive plans.
5. Carry out the plans, and review and refine them periodically.

As can be seen from an examination of the implementation planning subprocess and the overall company planning process, there is a basic planning process applicable to all types of planning situations: define the purpose of the planning effort; isolate planning premises; determine objectives and overall directions; develop policies and other guidelines for action; develop action plans, including budgets, controls and organization plans; carry out the plan, and review and refine it periodically. For the average business manager, the above process is probably no more than a systematic restatement of the process he goes through daily. However, many managers admit that in fast-moving operational situations the daily pressures of immediate problems sometimes cause them to lose sight of business fundamentals. A restatement of the process thus helps to give perspective to complex and demanding operating problems, and so simplify their solution.

THE COMPLEXITIES OF THE PLANNING PROCESS AT WORK

The outline of the business planning process describes only one aspect of the actual planning process—the ideal mental disciplines and the ideal methods for preparing a formal plan. This process model, however, is only a starting point in planning.

The statement of the planning process is in reality no more than a descriptive model, an artificial breakdown of the process into its components. While this model is useful for understanding the process, it should not be mistaken for the complex intellectual activities that are actually gone through in making a plan.

The complexities of the planning process are evident from the moment one starts to work on a planning problem. The planner discovers that in practice the "steps" in the planning process given earlier in this chapter are not steps at all, but merely the areas that are covered in making plans. Rather than being an orderly and sequential series of steps, the first of which is completed before the second is begun, the process of planning, involves much back-and-forth movement among the different parts of the outline. Many of the steps are, in fact, performed simultaneously; most often some work is done on all the steps before the first is finalized. The planner also learns that to plan well requires considerable ingenuity and practice.

A detailed examination of how objectives are formulated illustrates the complexities of the planning process. Contrary to what is implied by the outline of the planning process, phase three, the development of company objectives, is not necessarily completed before policies and implementation plans are developed. The determination of an objective is stated as a preliminary step to developing policies and implementation plans merely because it ultimately controls that development, and so is best presented there in a final report which details the plan.

At first, when developing a long-range plan, the corporate planner is likely to form some vague and generalized ideas of purpose, normally containing ideas about growth, profitability, survival, and stability. He knows what kind of company he is now dealing with, and he has some general ideas about what the company would like to become over the coming years. These ideas provide a useful point of departure in that they give the planner something to work with. However, they require considerable development.

Next, as planning analysis proceeds, as key factors are examined, and as tentative operating plans are developed, the planner formulates tentative working objectives to guide and assist him in testing and checking the feasibility of certain courses of action.

As the analysis progresses further, revised objectives are developed. At this point, the planner has the opportunity to correct, adjust, or confirm the earlier objectives in the light of his subsequent analysis and evaluation.

Last, final objectives are developed. This is the stage during which the objectives are stated in the formal written plan presented to management.

This same process is at work in the premising stage of the planning process, when the corporate planner is probing, defining, and quantifying the overall economic, political, social, industry, and market planning premises. The process is repeated again in developing policies, implementation plans, controls, and the like. And nothing can be done to bypass or simplify this continuing process of investigation and evaluation so necessary for successful planning.

Because no two planning situations are identical, applying the planning process in a specific situation is also not a simple task. Each industry has its own peculiar set of planning assumptions, and in our fast-changing economic and political environment the interrelationships of environmental factors are constantly changing. No two corporations have the same strengths and weaknesses, the same resources, the same objective. Considerable judgment and experience is, therefore, needed to determine the most important planning factors and the ways in which they will influence a particular company's future action, as well as to evaluate alternative courses of action.

Considerable creativity is also needed to devise solutions to planning problems and to develop alternative courses of action. Planning is more than just sitting back and picking the "best" plan. Devising the alternatives to pick from, developing them to suit a specific company's needs, and shaping them into practical money makers, are far more demanding and challenging tasks.

There are also many practical organizational roadblocks encountered in applying planning theory to practice in a corporation. There is *never* enough time or manpower to do the planning job properly, so that compromises are inevitable. The intellectual limitations of some managers and planners will also contribute to errors, false starts, and poor planning practices. Objectives and policies, no matter how clearly stated, will be misinterpreted by some managers, leading to further headaches. And occasionally, an executive will deliberately undermine a planning effort for personal reasons.

One area in which practical problems frequently arise is in establishing and administering the planning department for larger corporations. While this is a single specialized area of business planning, it is nonetheless a crucial one, because it is frequently the mechanism through which the overall corporate plan is developed. The wide range of political, personal, and business problems encountered in this area of business planning are discussed in the next chapter.

The existence of all these difficulties and complexities does not mean that planning is not a science, for underlying the intellectual searching just described is the systematic process of defining and organizing the planning effort, premising, developing strategic plans, and the like. What these complexities do mean is that knowing planning theory is only a small beginning. Adapting that systematic body of planning theory to solving the problem at hand is the art of planning, which complements the science, and this aspect of planning is learned principally by doing.

THE PLANNING PROCESS AND THE PROBLEM-SOLVING/DECISION-MAKING PROCESS

The basic concepts of the business planning process and the problem-solving/decision-making process are very similar. This similarity can be seen from the following juxtaposition of the problem-solving/decision-making process[15] and a simplified outline of the planning process:

Problem-Solving/ Decision-Making Process	*Business Planning Process*
1. Find and define the problem.	1. Define the purpose of the planning effort.
2. Diagnose the problem to find the key factors affecting the problem and its solution. This step is sometimes referred to as premising.	2. Develop planning premises.
3. Develop alternative solutions.	3. Develop possible courses of action in the area of company objectives.
4. Test and evaluate the alternatives to determine the best solution.	4. Evaluate these alternative objectives.
5. Construct a clear statement of the solution selected, and convert the decision into action.	5. Select the most promising objective and develop plans for carrying it out. (Steps 3, 4 and 5 are repeated in developing corporate philosophy, over-all policies, implementation plans, procedures, rules, programs, sub-plans, etc.).

[15]These steps are given in Peter Drucker's *The Practice of Management* (New York: Harper and Row, Publishers, 1954), pp. 351-359; H. Igor Ansoff's *Corporate Strategy: An Analytic Approach to Business Policy for Growth and Expansion* (New York: McGraw-Hill Book Company, 1965), pp. 1-11; and C. William Emory and Powell Niland, *Making Management Decisions* (Boston: Houghton Mifflin Company, 1968), p. 9.

Problem-solving/decision-making cannot be equated with planning, however. The two processes are distinct, for one can make decisions all day without doing any planning. Nonetheless, they are closely related. Planning requires a series of decisions, first about what are the most relevant planning premises, then the best objective, then the most effective policy statements in each policy area, and so on. In other words, the corporate planner goes through the problem-solving/decision-making process at each step in the planning process. Planning, therefore, depends on good decision making and is in essence one kind of decision making, namely "anticipatory decision making."[16]

BUSINESS PLANNING AND THE OTHER MANAGEMENT FUNCTIONS

In *Principles of Management,* Harold Koontz and Cyril O'Donnell describe the basic management functions as "planning, organizing, staffing, directing and controlling."[17] Although other management theorists vary in their descriptions of these functions, they all consider planning as one of the basic management functions and include some discussion of business planning in their studies of general management theory and practice.

Planning is closely related to the other management functions. Management control, for example, is an extension of the corporate planning process, for a good plan should have controls built into it. Management control can be defined as a systematic effort to set performance standards consistent with planning objectives, to design information feedback systems, to compare actual performance with these predetermined standards, to determine whether there are any deviations and to measure their significance, and to take any action required to assure that all corporate resources are being used in the most effective and efficient way possible in achieving corporate objectives. Not only does management control provide the planner with the tools he needs to coordinate planning and insure that operations conform with plans, but its feedback systems also give him the information he needs to review and revise his plans.

Business planning also relies on the other management functions. When plans are being developed and performance goals set, the planning manager must deal with those who are doing the planning, as well as with those who will eventually be carrying out the plans. Effective planning thus depends on knowing how to manage human resources effectively—in selecting staff, in dealing with human error, in introducing organization

[16] Russell L. Ackoff, "The Meaning of Strategic Planning," *McKinsey Quarterly,* Summer 1966, p. 48.

[17] Harold Koontz & Cyril O'Donnell, *Principles of Management* (4th edition; New York: McGraw-Hill Book Company, 1968), pp. 48-50.

changes, in motivating persons to better efforts, and in training and guiding people. Ultimately, the success of any plan or planning effort depends on the abilities of the people carrying out the plan, for people who do not have basic skills or psychological and emotional attitudes required for successful job performance will always be ineffective. It is, however, too easy to say that getting the right people solves *all* planning problems, for even qualified people need to be managed well if their potential is to be realized.

A plan is also affected by the organization set up to carry it out. Organization planning is, therefore, an important part of the planning process, and a good plan will always specify any changes in organization structure needed to implement the plan effectively.

BUSINESS PLANNING AND NEW TECHNOLOGY

Business planning also makes use of tools drawn from many other areas of management science. These areas include systems theory, PERT/CPM, operations research, decision theory, economic forecasting, and electronic data processing.

Systems theory guides the development of information systems for planning; PERT and CPM both aid the planning and control of specific programs and projects; decision theory and operations research provide tools that can be applied to situations ranging from inventory and distribution planning to production, manpower and resource planning; economic forecasting is a means of translating plans into specific sales and output forecasts, which can in turn be used as performance standards; and electronic data processing provides more elaborate and economical means of storing and processing planning information.

Admittedly, no manager could be expected to master all these highly technical fields. It is, however, possible to learn enough about these areas to understand their role in planning and so put these tools to work in developing better business plans.

CONCLUSION

Business planning can be examined from two viewpoints: first, as a general management function, performed by any manager in any operating or staff area; second, as a job performed by a specific department or executive in developing overall long-range corporate plans. Both kinds of planning, although distinct, are very closely related in practice. First, the basic process followed in doing all types of planning is essentially the same, whether it is done by a small-company president for his entire business, or by the director of a corporate planning department, or by the marketing or production manager at one of the lower echelons in a large company. Second, in all instances the planning done by an individual manager for any part of a company's operation is always done within the framework of the overall corporate plan, because his plans carry out the overall corporate plan.

Business planning theory provides the scientific discipline for doing all types of planning in business, for it defines what planning is and outlines the processes followed in doing planning at all management levels and in all types of business. As all planning practitioners know, however, theory is only a beginning. Being able to put theory into practice is the key to success in planning.

Successful planning requires more than simply the decision to plan. Planning in today's competitive business world requires the patience to live with the gradual adaptation of company personnel to long-range thinking, the skill to develop a viable organization for doing planning, the persistence to maintain performance standards, the ability to get along well with people, the physical and mental discipline to put aside operational problems and find time for planning, the courage to live with reduced short-term profits, many compromises, and a good deal of luck.

The remaining chapters of this book discuss the different phases of the planning process in detail, explore the problems encountered in doing planning, individually and corporately, and provide guidelines for overcoming these problems.

DISCUSSION QUESTIONS

1. What are the major differences between the definition of business planning given in this book and those given by two other writers on the subject?
2. Describe the various levels and kinds of business planning discussed in this study.
3. What are the distinctions and interrelationships between strategic planning and implementation planning? Between overall company comprehensive planning and specific operating and staff plans?
4. Outline the corporate business planning process and implementation planning subprocess. What is the basic planning process underlying both these processes?
5. Discuss the complexities of the business planning process. Why do you think these complexities are a necessary part of the planning process?
6. What are the distinctions and interrelationships between the business planning process and the problem-solving/decision-making process?
7. Describe the mental processes you go through in solving a problem and making a decision, and any personal techniques you may use as aids in solving problems and making decisions. Compare the process you follow with that described in this chapter.
8. Planning involves looking into the future and determining as well as one can what will happen. How far do you think a manager can ever go in developing a "perfect" plan? What limitations will he always face?

9. Look up the definition of a "science" in your dictionary. In what way has or has not this chapter outlined the first parts of a science of business planning?
10. Business planning has been called a developing science. Discuss those aspects of the concept of business planning which you feel need further development.
11. Why do you think that authorities like Fayol have divided the management function into five parts—planning, control, administration, organization and staffing? Are these divisions valid? What are the distinctions and interrelationships among these functions?
12. In the Blakeston and Wilson study in the Appendix, the President has obviously done a considerable amount of planning, in order to have developed the business as successfully as he has. Can you describe the steps in the planning process he followed, and how he followed them? What are the potential pitfalls you can see if he continues to follow such an undisciplined, informal approach to planning?
13. What are the factors which you feel make business planning such a difficult discipline to master?

CHAPTER 2

SETTING THE STAGE FOR SUCCESSFUL PLANNING

This chapter concerns the first phase of the planning process, planning and organizing the planning effort at both the overall corporate level and lower management levels.

The discussion begins with a review of the preliminary questions which need answering before undertaking this phase. Next, the chapter surveys the various ways in which larger companies have said they formally organize their planning departments. This survey does not tell the whole story, however, since in practice there are many roadblocks to successful planning which reduce the effectiveness of ideal planning systems. The practical roadblocks at both the corporate and lower management levels are discussed in detail, and guidelines for overcoming them are developed. The chapter concludes with a discussion of the special skills and perspective the planner needs to carry out the planning function.

SOME PRELIMINARY QUESTIONS

Before any planning can be undertaken, a planner first answers the question, "What kind of plan is required here?" For example, is the plan to be for just one operation, one division, or the corporation as a whole? Is the plan to be for one year, two years, five years or longer? Is the plan to give complete and detailed guidelines, including policies, sub-objectives, implementation plans, programs, and the like? Or, is it to provide only a general framework for action?

During this phase a planner also analyzes the use that will be made of the plans. What level of management will be using the plans, and how will they use them? Will managers actually use these plans as specific action guidelines and will they be held accountable by higher levels of management for meeting planned goals? Or, is the planning effort merely designed as an integrating exercise and as a means of helping focus executive attention on the future? Frequently, the anticipated use of a plan proves under careful scrutiny to be too small to justify the planning effort, or to be quite different from the initially stated purpose. Sometimes, a review reveals that too much is expected from the planning effort, and either expectations must be lowered or more resources allocated to planning.

A third area studied is the availability of resources for planning. How much time, money, and manpower will be needed to do the planning? Have sufficient amounts of each been allocated to accomplish the stated purpose? In addition, information sources should be examined to determine the availability of information upon which to base the planning. Often limited availability of information will change the whole character of the planning effort.

A fourth question examined is "What are the specific requirements of the corporation and people involved with the plans?" Answering this question usually involves analyzing the present corporate business and the personal objectives of the stockholders. Such an analysis gives the planner a starting point, for he can begin his industry and market survey with areas presently served by the company, and then later extend his study into related markets. Such an analysis will also give him the general limits within which to work, for he will not investigate areas the corporation hasn't the finances to exploit or the owners or managers haven't the desire to enter, unless they show extremely promising potential.

The fifth question concerns who will head the planning effort and how it will be organized. If the planning to be done is relatively narrow in scope, the organizing and staffing stages are relatively simple. An operating manager starting his planning may be faced only with organizing his own time or his own job, in order to leave time for planning. The complications grow as the size of the project grows. As a result, the corporate planner's job is quite different from that of the operating manager's planning job, even though the two levels of planning are interdependent and each planner makes use of the same overall planning process. The corporate planner frequently becomes involved in formally organizing a department or corporate function. He also becomes enmeshed in the many political and personal management problems encountered in getting others to do planning and in setting a favorable climate for developing plans and carrying out plans at the operating level. The human problems are thus extremely important in planning, and to ignore them may spell disaster for any planning effort.[1]

The sixth question to be answered is how to adapt the planning process to the specific company under study, and the people doing the

[1]David W. Ewing, "Corporate Planning at a Crossroads," *Harvard Business Review*, July-August 1967, pp. 77-86; and David W. Ewing, *The Human Side of Planning* (New York: The Macmillan Company, 1969).

planning. While guidelines for doing planning are given in Chapter 1, they deal with only one dimension of planning, the ideal approach. Knowing how to adapt these guidelines to individual situations is equally important. As Charles St. Thomas points out in his *Practical Business Planning*:

> The manager who successfully undertakes his planning work must begin by recognizing that the primary key to his effectiveness lies in his capability to adapt. His fundamental challenge is to learn to adapt the knowledge and methods of business planning to *his* company, *his* products. and to do this in a way that will enable *his* planning to be effective with *his* people.[2]

ORGANIZATION OF THE PLANNING FUNCTION AT THE CORPORATE LEVEL

Considerable information is available on how large companies have tried to organize their planning efforts.

David Ewing's and George Steiner's collections of readings both contain studies of how specific companies organized and carried out their planning efforts.[3] In 1967 Harold Henry studied the "formal" long-range planning practices of forty-five industrial concerns.[4] There are a number of articles which describe the experiences of such companies as Motorola in this area,[5] and this author has worked with planning groups at a number of companies who have provided additional material for this chapter.[6]

Experience has shown that no single planning organization will suit every company and that each company must develop the form most appropriate to its requirements. However, three basic patterns can be identified:

1. The president or his executive can do planning as part of their basic duties, with no other formal planning organization.

[2]Charles E. St. Thomas, *Practical Business Planning: A Manager's Guide*, (New York: American Management Association, 1965), pp. 9-10.

[3]David W. Ewing, ed., *Long-Range Planning for Management* (Rev. ed.; New York: Harper and Row, Publishers, 1964); George A. Steiner, ed., *Managerial Long-Range Planning* (New York: McGraw-Hill Book Company, 1963); George A. Steiner and Warren M. Cannon, eds., *Multinational Corporate Planning* (New York: The Macmillan Company, 1966).

[4]Harold W. Henry, *Long-Range Planning Practices in 45 Industrial Companies* (Englewood Cliffs, N.J.: Prentice-Hall, Inc., 1967).

[5]For example, John T. Hickey, "Guidelines to Successful Future Planning," *Financial Executive*, November 1966, pp. 32-40.

[6]Robert J. Mockler, *Circulation Planning and Development for The National Observer: A Research Study on Business Applications of Management Planning and Control Principles* (Atlanta, Georgia: Georgia State College, 1967); Robert J. Mockler and Harrison Easop, *Guidelines for More Effective Planning and Management of Franchise Systems* (Atlanta, Georgia: Georgia State College, 1968).

2. A planning function can be organized within an existing function. Customarily, such efforts take place in the control, finance, or marketing department, where the cost and product planning systems serve as a common, formal thread for all corporate planning.
3. A separate planning department can be organized at the corporate level. In addition, each division may also have a planning director or planning organization which works with the corporate planning department in developing plans.

The trend among larger companies seems to be towards treating planning as a separate and distinct functional area comparable to control, finance, and marketing.[7]

This trend towards more formal organization of the planning effort is evident in Henry's study in 1967 of the forty-five companies, for only seven of the forty-five companies had no formal planning organization. As Table 2.1 indicates,[8] in twenty-six of the thirty-eight companies with planning organizations, planning was a separate and distinct function with its own full-time director. Only six organized the planning function within the existing finance and control group, and only six assigned planning functions to executives who also performed other duties. All companies assigned the planning responsibility to a higher echelon executive.

Table 2.1

RESPONSIBILITY ASSIGNMENTS FOR COMPANY PLANNING IN 45 COMPANIES

Major Planning Responsibility Assigned to:	Number of Companies
Vice President Planning (or equivalent title)	16
Executive Vice President or Group Vice President	3
Vice President-Finance or Controller	6
Director of Forward Planning who reported to the Chairman of the Board of Directors	1
Director of Planning (or equivalent title) who reported to the President	5
Vice President (limited planning functions)	3
Specific Planning Units (responsible executive undetermined)	4
Companies Having Formal Planning Assignments	38
Companies Having No Formal Planning	7
All Companies Studied	45

Note: In 22 of these companies, a committee of top executives had important long-range planning responsibilities. In 26 companies, planning assignments were made to staff personnel in operating units, in addition to corporate staff assignments.

7Francis J. Aguilar, "Organization for Corporate Strategic Planning: Western Europe and the United States," in *Multinational Corporate Planning*, eds. Steiner and Cannon, pp. 47-59.

8Henry, *Long-Range Planning Practices*, p. 36.

In the majority of companies studied there is a fairly consistent division of planning responsibility between a corporate staff group or executive who develops overall strategic plans, coordinates planning, analyzes proposed new ventures, and the managers of staff and operating (or line) units who are responsible for developing short- and long-range operating plans for their respective departments or divisions. In Henry's study, for example, twenty-six of the companies gave planning assignments to both operating personnel and the corporate planning staff. In a few instances—steel companies, for example—companies did have completely centralized planning (that is, all planning was done by the corporate planning staff), but these were the exception rather than the rule.[9]

The duties of a corporate planning director can vary considerably. The following is a description of the job of one company's planning director:[10]

1. Formulate corporate objectives and policies (for approval of the President).
2. Develop action programs (for approval of the President).
3. Direct the planning staff in activities of market research, economic and business analysis, and planning for products, facilities, and acquisitions.
4. Evaluate market growth potential.
5. Coordinate overall company marketing strategy.
6. Coordinate and integrate divisional planning activities.
7. Direct and participate in a search for opportunities for business growth and developments.
8. Evaluate possible mergers or acquisitions and negotiate desired ones.
9. Direct the corporate handling of proposed new processes and products.
10. Develop priorities for major new products and projects, recommend special research projects to the President, and audit the progress of projects.
11. Provide an information service to other executives.
12. Review major capital expenditures in relation to corporate objectives.
13. Recommend short-term and long-term budgets.

The scope of this planning director's job is somewhat broader than that of many planning executives, but it gives an idea of the wide range of duties that fall within the planning area. Generally, the corporate planning director is responsible for at least the following functions: first, administering all planning activities; second, specifying overall company strategic directions (including company objectives); third, insuring the quality of individual operating plans; fourth, coordinating and balancing all individual plans within the overall corporate plan, which the planning director prepares; fifth, performing planning activities not covered by individual operating units, such as diversification, mergers and acquisitions.

[9]Henry, *Long-Range Planning Practices*, pp. 65-66.
[10]Henry, *Long-Range Planning Practices*, p. 38.

In many companies, the corporate planner has a staff to assist him in performing his duties. One of the major jobs of his staff is to supply the operating managers with the environmental information needed to prepare plans. This information covers such areas as general economic forecasts, total product demand, the share of that demand the company can expect to sell, and projected potential company sales by product and by major market. The staff would also supply operating managers with strategic planning information (overall company objectives, policies, and other strategic factors limiting planning), as well as information on available resources. In addition, the corporate planning staff develops procedures for preparing plans. These procedures can be very thorough, such as those given in American Machine and Foundry's 17-page planning manual, or they can be simple and limited to a single-page document which only spells out overall guidelines for planning.[11]

In those companies where the author was involved in the actual planning job, there was considerable variation in how operating managers and corporate staff planners worked together in developing plans. In some instances, the operating managers working with the corporate planning group developed long-term strategy for their operations, and then created short- and long-term implementation plans which the planning group coordinated and put into a final comprehensive plan for top management. In other instances, the role of operating managers was limited to preparing short-term plans for their operations, while the staff planning group handled all other tasks, including the development of strategic plans. In almost all companies examined for this study, specific operating planning was done for the most part by operating managers. Sometimes they would do it themselves, sometimes they would have their own staff prepare the plan under their guidance, and sometimes the corporate planning staff would provide the staff assistance needed to work out the plan. In general, the success of the overall planning effort seemed to depend more on the nature of the interaction between the planning director (and his staff) and the operating managers, than on the formal planning procedures.

Final approval for comprehensive plans usually rests with the chairman of the board, president, or executive vice-president. Overall comprehensive plans are, therefore, always reviewed by one of these executives or an executive committee appointed by them. Generally these reviews are made once a year, although in one company studied they are reviewed quarterly and at another semi-annually. The majority of comprehensive plans are for five years, and so cover both long- and short-term plans.

As for the content of formal comprehensive plans, all comprehensive plans contain projections of sales and net income, usually in the form of

[11]Ewing, ed., *Long-Range Planning for Management,* Chapters 26 and 27.

proforma profit and loss statements, as well as the highlights of implementation plans. Other information concerning the strategic factors (objectives, strategies, policies, and premises) upon which the figures and action plans are based is included in varying degrees in the comprehensive plans surveyed, although emphasis is generally placed on the figures. Capital expenditures, cash flow, proforma balance sheets, prices, and other information essential to the individual company's operations are also included, as necessary. A typical outline of the comprehensive plans surveyed by Henry is given in Table 2.2.

Table 2.2

OUTLINE OF A "FIVE-YEAR BUSINESS PLAN"
PREPARED FOR ONE CORPORATION[12]

Section	*Topic*
I	Business Results Summary
	Operations
	Business Indices
	Marketing
	Product
	Cost and Productivity
	Facilities
	Personnel
	Product Line Performance
II	Business Environment
III	Division Guidelines
IV	Most Important Problems and Opportunities
V	Business Strategy
VI	Major Business Plans and Programs
VII	Business Results
Appendix I	Product Line Analyses and Plans
Appendix II	Cost Analyses and Plans

The size of the comprehensive plan varies by level of management, with the plan for top management being the shortest and having the least detail. As one vice-president put it, a long-range plan "might be six file cases of material in total, a two- or three-inch thick book at the Vice-Presidential level, and then only 30 minutes worth of slides and charts at the Board of Directors' level."[13]

Companies, evidently, are slow in introducing formal planning organizations. At least three years seems to be needed before such an organization can function effectively, since considerable time is required to demonstrate the advantages of strategic planning to the operating managers, to enlist their cooperation, in coordinating their individual planning

[12]Henry, *Long-Range Planning Practices*, p. 72.
[13]Henry, *Long-Range Planning Practices*, p. 70.

activities, and to train them in planning techniques. Except for indications that strong and active support by a company's president will hasten introduction of a planning organization, very little information is available on how to actually introduce and run a planning department.

Work is also being done on ways to help smaller companies improve their overall planning. These studies concentrate on developing a systematic approach to strategic planning which the manager of a small business can follow, even to the point of providing the forms and charts he can use for his planning.[14] A sample of one of these studies is described in Chapter 13 of this book.

Even though published accounts of how companies plan are naturally biased, since management is rarely willing to talk about problems or failures, the above survey of company case histories does give some idea of the general approach used in organization for planning in various size companies. By no means, however, does this kind of review tell the whole story.

ROADBLOCKS TO SUCCESSFUL BUSINESS PLANNING

As can be seen from the preceding discussion, there is no doubt that leading corporations believe that formal planning is essential to corporate survival.[15] Besides the companies discussed above, there is a long list of companies that have written about their planning efforts, including such major corporations as American Airlines, Ford Motor Company, Lockheed, Continental Oil Company, Aerojet-General, American Machine and

[14]Roger A. Golde, "Practical Planning for Small Business," *Harvard Business Review*, September-October, 1964, pp. 147-161; Raymond M. Haas, Richard T. Hartman, John H. James and Robert R. Milroy, *Long-Range Planning for Small Business* (Bloomington, Indiana: Bureau of Business Research, Graduate School of Business, Indiana University, 1964).

[15]E. Kirby Warren, *Long-Range Planning: The Executive Viewpoint* (Englewood Cliffs, N.J.: Prentice-Hall, Inc., 1966), pp. 29-31, lists a number of reasons why corporations consider planning important: 1) Providing a clearer understanding of likely future impacts on present decisions; 2) Anticipating areas requiring future decisions; 3) Increasing the speed of the flow of relevant information; and 4) Providing a faster and less disruptive implementation of future decisions.

Discussions of the importance of planning also appear in: Donald M. Bowman and Francis M. Fillerup, eds., *Management: Organization and Planning* (New York: McGraw-Hill Book Company, 1963), pp. 66-67; Melville C. Branch, *The Corporate Planning Process* (New York: American Management Association, 1962), Chapter I; Preston R. LeBreton and Dale A. Henning, *Planning Theory* (Englewood Cliffs, N.J.: Prentice-Hall, Inc., 1961), Chapter I; National Association of Accountants, *Long-Range Profit Planning*, Research Report No. 42 (New York: National Association of Accountants, 1964), pp. 6-8; Bruce Payne, *Planning for Company Growth* (New York: McGraw-Hill Book Company, 1963), Chapter I; Brian W. Scott, *Long-Range Planning in American Industry* (New York: American Management Association, 1965), p. 27; Charles E. St. Thomas, *Practical Business Planning*, Chapter I; Franklyn H. Sweet, *Strategic Planning: A Conceptual Study*, ("Research Monograph No. 26;" Austin, Texas: Bureau of Business Research, The University of Texas, 1964), pp. 6-7.

Foundry, IBM, Bell and Howell,[16] and General Electric.[17] And a close relation of corporate success to long-range planning is implied in a recent study which showed that companies which gave high priority to long-range planning outperformed those who did not.[18]

On the surface, therefore, it would appear that American industry endorses the concept of planning. Probing beneath the surface, however, one finds major weaknesses in planning practices. E. Kirby Warren's study of fifteen large United States corporations showed that with few notable exceptions corporate executives are unwilling to commit a significant part of their own energy or company resources to developing long-range planning[19]—in spite of what is officially written about these corporations' planning efforts.

According to Warren's survey, the reason for this is that management performance is still measured by the current year's profits, and promotions are based on such performance. Because of this and because of high turnover among divisional line managers, there is little incentive for managers to think long-term, for they are not likely to have to live with tomorrow's problems. In other words, most managers believe in long-range planning as an ideal, but practical considerations, such as available time and personal goals, have made it difficult for them to practice what they believe.

Another major problem uncovered in Warren's study was that at most larger companies plans were usually reduced to just figures by the time top management saw them. This occurred because the control sections ordinarily participated in planning in the companies he studied. In those few companies where planning was successful, the planner and his staff reviewed and reported to the president on both the quantitative and non-quantitative duplication sections of the long-range plans. These non-quantitative (or narrative) portions included such items as key economic and environmental assumptions on which projections were based, basic objectives and strategies, a description of the steps planned to be taken by each unit to reach its objectives within the planning assumptions (premises), and a definition of those problems not within the unit's ability to solve.

[16]Descriptions of the planning efforts of these companies are given in Ewing, *Long-Range Planning for Management*, and George A. Steiner, ed., *Managerial Long-Range Planning*.

[17]Controllership Foundation, *Planning, Managing and Measuring the Business* (New York: Financial Executives Institute, 1955), a case study of business planning and control at General Electric Company.

[18]Stanley S. Thune & Robert J. House, "Where Long-Range Planning Pays Off," *Business Horizons*, August 1970, pp. 81-87.

[19]Warren, *Long-Range Planning: The Executive Viewpoint*, pp. x-xi. The companies studied by Warren were ACF Industries, American Cyanamid, American Machine and Foundry, American Radiator and Standard Sanitary, Colgate-Palmolive, E. I. duPont de Nemours, General Electric, General Foods, International Business Machines, International Telephone and Telegraph, New York Central Railroad, Stauffer Chemical, Sylvania Electric Company, and Union Carbide.

A number of additional roadblocks to setting the stage for successful corporate planning are described in a study of a planning program developed for Dow Jones' newest publication, *The National Observer*.[20]

Dow Jones launched *The National Observer*, a national weekly newspaper, in early 1962. After one year of publication circulation had declined from 240,000 to 140,000.

An initial analysis revealed the basic sources of *The Oberver's* problems were threefold:

1. *Insufficient Background Research and Management Staffing.* *The Observer's* marketing management was not sufficiently centralized or staffed to gather together and interpret all available market information, and to build integrated strategic plans based on these findings. As a result, there was little specific researched information available to operating managers on the size of the product's potential market, or on the nature of its primary competition.
2. *Insufficient Planning and Management Coordination.* Since all *The Observer's* marketing operations had been placed under existing Dow Jones departments, the methods which had been so successful for Dow Jones' major publication, *The Wall Street Journal,* were used in marketing the new publication and *The Observer* did not have the coordinated management guidance required to develop marketing objectives, policies, and programs tailored to its specific marketing needs.
3. *Resistance to Change.* Dow Jones relied heavily on past corporate experience in designing the product and in establishing marketing objectives, policies, and programs; even though the company's corporate experience was mainly in financial markets, not in the general consumer market which *The Observer* served. As a result, there was a tendency to move slowly in accepting innovations, and to do very little forward planning based on a realistic appraisal of the product's market.

In 1963 a plan for solving *The Observer*'s problems was developed in a relatively short period of time. However, major problems and delays were encountered in gaining acceptance of the new plan and in developing an internal organization for continuing planning and program development after the initial study was completed.

At Dow Jones, management initially tended to rely on information such as "talks with other publishers" or "a feel for the market." When presented with plans based upon extensive market and industry information, management had no frame of reference to judge the plans' value. As a result, they felt more comfortable following old patterns of action, no matter how inappropriate they might be to *The Observer*'s operation. The operating departments were equally suspicious of any innovations which might lead to changes in their traditional ways of doing business. Carrying

[20]Robert J. Mockler, "How To Avoid Costly Mistakes When Introducing a New Product," *Advanced Management Journal,* July 1966, pp. 45-52; and *The National Observer*, a case study prepared for the Harvard Business School by Stephen A. Greyser and Philip R. McDonald, 1965.

out plans was further hampered by the organization of *The Observer's* operations. Since there was no brand or product coordinator for *The Observer*, it was difficult to coordinate either planning or implementation of plans for the publication. In this instance, a reorganization of operations was needed before plans could be effectively carried out.

In *The Observer* situation, knowing planning theory and developing a plan was a very small part of the solution to the problem. The major roadblocks were finding ways to overcome resistance to change and innovation at all management levels, working out methods for effectively introducing the plan in the operating areas, and developing adequate staffing and management coordination of the planning effort.

ADJUSTING PLANS TO MEET INTERNAL PRESSURES

A planner must be prepared to face and solve a wide variety of internal company problems in carrying out the planning function. A successful planning effort conducted recently at a major corporation illustrates the kinds of internal pressures which a planner might expect to encounter.

The plan being developed was for a large division of a billion dollar corporation. The division, which will be referred to as a XYZ division, was engaged in three different businesses, all of them interrelated: product line "A" produced most of the division's sales; product lines "B" and "C" were relatively new and represented only a small portion of the division's sales.

The XYZ division's business depended mainly on marketing expertise, so that the division's marketing vice-president was given the task of heading the planning effort. Both one-year and five-year plans were to be developed. The marketing vice-president was assigned financial analysts from the controller's section to help in the planning effort and assist in developing the profit estimates within the plan. The corporation's economic section provided him with environmental information needed for planning, and the statistical section was assigned to do the forecasts and projections of division sales within the plan. Outside consultants were also employed to assist in the preparation of the plan in such areas as economic analysis and new product development. He also worked very closely with the operations and customer-service managers, to be certain the overall plan would take into account company capabilities in these areas and that complete subsidiary plans were developed for these operations. However, it was made quite clear that the marketing vice-president directed the planning effort and had the last word as to the shape of the final plan to be presented to the president.

Once a staff had been designated, the planning mission defined, and authority and responsibility fixed, the XYZ division's marketing manager spent considerable time with each of his own subordinate managers in the marketing area. He explained the nature and purpose of the planning effort. He explored potential areas of opportunities with them and studied the present and planned capabilities for exploiting these opportunities. And he started them working on preliminary plans for their operations.

As part of the planning effort, the market research department analyzed the present and future market for product line A. They came to the conclusion that the total market for product line A, a specific age group in the U.S. population, would be growing very slowly over the next five years, and that A's share of this market would shrink, because a major competitor was expanding and for the first time would offer a competitive product line. These premises were based on economic forecasts of the growth of disposable income, Gross National Product, and population by age group; as well as on studies of market competition. In the light of these environmental planning premises, a product strategy was developed for product A to exploit the changing age patterns in the market, and sales projections were adjusted to take into account competitors' growing strength and the slow growth of the total market.

While the analysis and evaluation of the environment revealed that A's growth potential was limited, the study also showed that the markets for product lines B and C were growing rapidly. The B operation was fairly well established, and expansion into new marketing areas could be plotted with a high degree of certainty. The C operation, on the other hand, was relatively new and its expansion depended on developing successful marketing strategies. Since management knew a market of some size existed for product line C and were confident a strategy for reaching that market profitably would one day be found, they were able to develop a probable growth curve.

Market and economic studies revealed other areas of growth potential in markets related to the XYZ division's present line of business. Acquisition and new product development plans were then made, and the division's sales forecasts were increased proportionately on the basis of beliefs in probable success in some of these areas.

A reasonable forecast of growth in all of these areas led to the conclusion that the XYZ division could expect overall sales growth in excess of 50% within five years, although the growth would not be consistent throughout all product lines. Plans were then made to expand service and production facilities in specific product areas.

Up to this point, the planning effort was well conceived and well executed. Before the final sales forecasts could be made, however, a number of other factors had to be considered:

1. The XYZ division was in a business entirely foreign to that of the parent corporation, so that corporate management did not fully understand the division's problems and special ways of doing business. Each presentation of the overall plan, therefore, had to begin with a lengthy explanation of the basic principles governing the division's business.

2. The parent corporation's other operations were high-margin, high-capital investment businesses, so that the XYZ division was saddled with a goal of 10% minimum return on sales, even though it was engaged in a low-margin, low-capital investment business.
3. The parent corporation was a growth company, and so assigned a five-year growth goal to the XYZ division.
4. There were a number of management personality problems.

In the light of these other considerations, the initial realistic sales and profit forecasts by product and marketing area were revised before the final plan was submitted to the parent corporation.

The XYZ division's manager calculated that the parent corporation was mainly interested in his division's total profit. His final plan, therefore, showed the same total dollar profit as was shown in his internal division forecasts. But for the final plan he lowered his sales forecast to the point where he showed a 10% profit on sales. While the XYZ division manager would have preferred a more straight-forward approach, based on his past experience he knew that it would not have been possible to explain to the parent corporation the marketing strategy necessary for success in the division. He candidly made the adjustments for management survival reasons.

Internally, the forecasts given to the XYZ division's operational managers were realistic. The marketing managers were a young, energetic, ambitious, and honest group, so that it was not necessary to give them inflated or adjusted forecast and budget figures. The economic and financial analysts involved in planning did not at first agree to making two forecasts, one for the division's operating managers and one for the parent company management; eventually, however, they did see the wisdom of having the dual forecasts and they developed them.

Although the adjusted forecasts solved the problems the XYZ division encountered in dealing with corporate management, the adjusted forecasts created major problems in the area of facilities expansion. Since the sales forecasts given corporate management were below realistic expectations, forecasts of facilities needed (based on sales forecasts) were also below anticipated needs. This meant that the XYZ division was constantly understaffed and underequipped, especially in the areas of computers, servicing facilities and marketing manpower. This was something the division simply had to live with, in view of the attitude and atmosphere of the parent corporation. However frustrating such a situation may seem to a management theoretician, this kind of corporate maneouvering is regrettably typical—and so must be taken into account when doing planning.

While the case of the XYZ division may be an extreme example, it illustrates a major practical consideration in developing plans. Accurate plans and forecasts of likely events can be made, but they may be used only as a basis for the final plans and forecasts, which must also take into account the realities of corporate life. Adjustments and compromises in final plans are almost always needed to meet the conditions of other planning premises, though usually not to the degree they were at the XYZ division. For example, if a major stockholder wishes to satisfy a personal goal through his business, the plan must achieve this goal, even though it may be at the expense of profit opportunities. This will probably continue to be the case as long as companies are run by human beings.

The final form of plans and their forecasts must always be shaped to suit the purpose for which they will be used. Different levels of management require different kinds of planning forecasts. For example, if the sales forecast is to be given to salesmen, it may be inflated to provide an incentive for the sales effort. If the sales forecast is to be used for calculating the profit to be reported to corporate management, it may be lowered in order to present a conservative picture to management. This does not mean that the initial, unadjusted plan is not valuable and necessary. Nor does it mean that plans should be arbitrarily played with to suit personal whims and expedients. It is simply that the ideal plan is only a starting point, and other factors, such as how the plan is going to be used and what level of management will be using it, must also be considered in making the final plan.

SOME GUIDELINES FOR OVERCOMING ROADBLOCKS TO PLANNING

The above studies of corporate long-range practices indicate that managers do not seem to need to be convinced that planning is important, nor do they need more lessons in the theory and principles of planning. What business managers need to know is how to improve planning practices in a working corporate situation.

Some planning theorists have gone so far as to say that practical guidelines cannot be developed in this area. For example, in *The Corporate Planning Process* Melville Branch says, "Some readers would undoubtedly prefer more precise prescriptions than are provided in this chapter: exact procedures, categorical do's and don'ts, or administrative recipes guaranteeing results. . . This managerial discernment precludes precise prescription."[21] While results cannot be guaranteed, systematic guidelines can be developed for adapting planning theory to individual corporate situations. Without them, the science of planning would be incomplete and theories of planning mere platitudes, for the key to successful planning is knowing how to put it to work in a corporation. As Peter Drucker says, "Planning and doing . . . are parts of the same job."[22]

[21]Branch, *The Corporate Planning Process*, p. 213.

[22]Peter Drucker, *The Practice of Management* (New York: Harper and Row, 1954), p. 284.

Because of the problems corporations have encountered in carrying out planning efforts, increased attention is now being paid to defining the practical problems that hinder successful corporate planning efforts, and to developing guidelines for a systematic approach to planning administration.[23] For example, in late 1966 John T. Hickey presented a study of Motorola's corporate planning experiences,[24] and in late 1967 an even more detailed study of Dow Jones' experience with *The National Observer* was published.[25] E. Kirby Warren's *Long-Range Planning: The Executive Viewpoint* published in 1966 is the most comprehensive attempt to date to develop some practical guidelines for overcoming roadblocks to successful corporate planning.[26] The following guidelines for organizing and administering planning activities were developed from the successful experience of the companies analyzed above, from the author's own planning experience, and from the work of other authorities in the field.

First, a statement of what the planning effort is to accomplish and what uses the plans will serve is needed, in order to coordinate the efforts of the planners and to isolate and overcome any management resistance to either doing the planning or implementing recommended changes. This statement should be communicated to everyone affected by the planning and should be understood by them. This step is a necessary one in obtaining management support for the planning group, its efforts and its proposals.

Second, adequate staff assistance and facilities are needed. The primary role of staff is to facilitate, support, coordinate, and encourage adequate planning by line management. In fulfilling this role, the staff must be prepared to give technical assistance in such areas as economic analysis, systems development, EDP applications, and planning theory. In addition, the staff provides useful planning premise information and assistance in developing overall directions for the planning activities and in quantifying the plans.

Third, operating managers should do the actual job of creating specific implementation plans, though staff planners may provide assistance in

[23]Very little information is available on actual corporate planning practices. Part of the problem has been the difficulty of getting corporations to tell an honest story, including the pitfalls, false steps, and mistakes. For example, at a recent magazine seminar at Harvard University, one major publishing company presented a case written solely from a public relations viewpoint, praising successful steps, hiding the problems, and distorting the facts. In the area of company case studies, *Indian Head Mills, Inc.*, prepared for Harvard Business School by Milton P. Brown, *et al.* in 1962, is an outstanding example of useful and honest presentation of actual business conditions—good and bad.

[24]Hickey, "Guidelines to Successful Future Planning," pp. 32-40. This work is in sharp contrast to that of planning theoreticians such as LeBreton and Henning. For example, on page 14 of *Planning Theory*, these authors outline a planning procedure which gives only passing consideration to the practical problems involved in performing the planning job.

[25]Mockler, *Circulation Planning and Development for The National Observer*.

[26]Warren, *Long-Range Planning: The Executive Viewpoint*.

developing and coordinating these plans. Staff planners will usually develop overall strategic plans, with the assistance of operating managers. Corporate planning is thus a job requiring the coordinated efforts of both line management and staff.

Fourth, because the planning activities extend into almost every part of a company's operations and require considerable skill in coordinating and handling people, a top management man, who has the authority and the administration skills needed to get the job done, should be chosen for planning director. Normally, only a manager with line experience has the background to build operational reality into long- and short-range corporate plans. For daily he has had to adjust to market, operational and internal corporate influences and translate them into effective and profitable operating programs. His viewpoint will be the practical viewpoint, and he will bring to the planning effort judgment matured by experience.

Fifth, procedures are needed to enable all line and staff managers to work out mutually agreeable plans. This balance between line and staff participation and responsibility must be maintained so that on the one hand line management retains a profit responsibility and is not forced to accept staff plans, while on the other hand corporate planning review staffs are given adequate freedom to make recommendations without punitive recourse by line managers.

Sixth, the discipline of some formality is necessary in strategic planning, a formality such as writing down all the assumptions upon which the plan is based and the specific policies which are essential to the plan's success—and including them in the final plan, instead of only presenting forecasts and budgets in the final plan, as is often the case.

Seventh, planning should include action steps assigned to individuals, within a timetable of accomplishment. Managers must be allowed a realistic amount of time to do planning, and not be expected to do planning in addition to other regular operating duties. This sometimes means relieving them from specific operating duties.

Eighth, top management is responsible for creating an atmosphere favorable to planning. At Pennsalt Chemical Company, for example, the president attributes the success of their planning effort to the fact that each month he personally reviews results in relation to plans and so demonstrates his strong interest in planning.[27]

Ninth, those who will be carrying out the plan should participate in the planning, so that they will better understand what the plan is and what it is designed to achieve, identify more closely with the plan (and so have a greater interest in seeing that it is successful), and more quickly communicate to management any flaws existing in the plan.

Last, in judging the usefulness and success of the planning effort, it should be remembered that the plan is both an important end and a means

[27] J. D. Baxter, "Budget Guides Profit Growth," *The Iron Age* October 28, 1965, pp. 44-46.

of structuring thinking and action. The act of planning is often as important as the actual plan produced, for planning focuses the attention of line management on the future, improves coordination and provides a measure of achievement.

GUIDELINES FOR THE MIDDLE MANAGER

Planning goes on at all levels of a business enterprise, as the manager of each segment of the business develops functional plans for his particular area of responsibility. However, most middle managers, for example the manager of a company's advertising department, obviously do not encounter all these complex organizational problems when preparing to do planning for their department. The scope of their plan is much smaller, very few resources must be marshalled to do the planning, and their demands on the corporate organization will be much less. The steps a middle manager takes in planning and organizing his planning effort will, therefore, differ in many ways from what occurs in overall comprehensive corporate planning.

An operating planner would first study the larger planning context within which the planning is done. Simply stated, he answers such questions as: What is the company's strategic plan? What was last year's overall comprehensive plan? What other plans have been developed by higher levels of management which will affect my planning? What is the company's overall sales goal? And the like.

The operating planner would then define the scope and purpose of his planning within the framework of higher levels of planning. If there is no fully developed formal plan or planning organization, he may not have clearly defined guidelines as to what his planning is to accomplish. In this case, he would take the initiative in seeing to it that the purpose of his planning effort is established in accordance with management's view of his planning task.

Where there is no formal planning organization the operating manager may also have difficulty assembling the planning premises critical to his planning problem. Foremost among his premises, of course, will be the overall corporate objective. In most instances he will also need pertinent information about the economic, social, and political environment. Obtaining this information can be a time-consuming job, and frequently requires the help of trained staff assistants such as economists, forecasters, operations researchers, financial analysts, and systems analysts. Determining available information sources and their reliability in these areas, and obtaining access to these sources, can thus be major roadblocks at this level of planning.

Where overall corporate planning is not highly developed, the middle manager may initially be given only a vague idea of the financial, material, and human resources available to him. Frequently, it will be necessary for him to propose a possible plan of action and define its earnings potential before higher management indicates precisely what resources will be made available. In planning the time needed to develop final plans in these circumstances, therefore, the middle manager should allot ample time for a considerable amount of back-and-forth questioning and probing.

Naturally, the smaller the planning problem and the lower the level of the plan within the corporation, the less likelihood there is that this problem will arise. For example, the plans for weekly or monthly production operations are normally based on adjusted historical premises. Any major changes in the premises at the lowest operational levels are usually made quite explicit.

The problems of obtaining information seem to be most acute at those middle management levels where overall functional or divisional plans are developed—where overall product and functional responsibility is fixed and profits calculated. For example, in the case of the XYZ Company described above, very little information on economic or industry trends was provided to the division manager. The corporate economist did provide information on share of market, consumer motivation, and general economic trends. But no one was assigned to the very time-consuming job of relating these trends to the division's product lines.

In *The National Observer* study, cursory consumer preference studies were conducted, but no definition was made of critical economic and industry trends affecting the product. As a result, *The Observer*'s marketing manager had no basis upon which to build plans, except his own experience in the field. At another company with which this author worked, a correspondence school, such market studies were done only after two million dollars had been spent on a new product. These studies led to major changes in market strategy, product pricing and promotion plans.

While great strides are being made in improving *overall* corporate planning practices, very little work has been done on how to solve the critical planning problems faced at the *middle* management level, where detailed implementation plans are made. It does not appear that the solutions to these problems will come entirely from top management. Rather, they must come from the middle managers themselves.

Middle managers thus will often need to take the initiative in developing specific procedures for the planning done at their level, even though it is not an easy way or the best way. If overall corporate plans are not clearly spelled out, an operating manager should help shape them before large sums of money are committed to programs for which he is responsible. If planning premises are not spelled out, and adequate information on available corporate resources and environmental influences is not provided, he should define the information that is needed and ask for it specifically.

Naturally, he cannot bend a corporate operation at will to satisfy all his requests, since other demands may supercede his. In these circumstances, however, he can make clear the consequences of building a plan on an insufficient base. And he can quantify some of the risks involved in acting on inadequate plans. If the corporation wishes to take these risks, then he has performed his job; and when failures do arise, it is much easier to determine their causes.

By following these guidelines the middle manager can become a catalyst for improving planning practices within a business enterprise as a whole, while at the same time protecting himself from weak planning practices at the overall management level. The greatest preparatory step any manager can take is to develop a firm grasp of scientific business planning, and to use every available opportunity to experiment with putting its principles into practice.

THE BEHAVIORAL SCIENCES AND BUSINESS PLANNING

As can be seen from the above discussions, effective leadership, organization, and staffing are important to successful planning.

Planning is a participative job. And in those companies with successful planning efforts, the actual job of planning is for the most part done by those managers who will be carrying out the plans. In the XYZ study discussed above, the planner involved a considerable number of people in the planning effort. A planning director thus needs to be able to motivate operating managers to do planning. Sometimes this will be easy, especially where the chief executive is firmly behind the planning effort. At other times, however, skillful use of motivational & leadership tools is needed to motivate managers to initiate the planning effort at the operating level.

Once it is initiated, the planner must administer the planning effort. Since all company planning should be done within the boundaries laid down by the planning director, the better the planning director is able to communicate these overall guidelines to the operating managers, the more likely they are to work within them. As planning progresses, the planning director reconciles differences, revises specific plans where necessary, corrects errors, integrates and coordinates all individual planning efforts, and sees that the quality of planning is maintained consistently in all areas. Additional administrative skills are also required in dealing with higher management, in reviewing performance, in initiating corrective action where deviations from plan have occurred, and in introducing organization changes—all important aspects of the planning function. The behavioral sciences are again important in these direction phases of the planner's job, for they provide methods for motivating people to more effective performance, for better guiding and controlling their efforts, and for more easily introducing change and corrective action.

An organization is needed to carry out most plans. In addition to the various operating and staff plans required as part of the comprehensive corporate plan, therefore, organization plans are also needed. An organization structure has to be developed and charted. Jobs must be defined, their interrelationships and hierarchy specified, and responsibility for getting the jobs done assigned to individuals. As is shown in Chapter 12, in developing such an organization plan behavioral science considerations need to be taken into account in planning the framework within which people's efforts can best be directed towards achieving the corporate objective.

Staffing plans are also needed in an overall company plan. Sufficient manpower resources of the right kind have to be planned for, just as adequate financial resources and manufacturing and marketing facilities must be arranged. Policies providing guidance for administration, for replenishing the staff, and for adequate training may also thus be part of overall company plans.

Within the long-range plan there should also be statements of employee rights and obligations, and of management's attitude toward its personnel. These statements should be consistent with the overall corporate philosophy. Corporate philosophy varies with each company. Indian Head Mills, for example, is an entrepreneurial corporation, and the rugged individualism of its managers and owners is reflected in its personnel policy:

> The company will not take a paternalistic point of view towards its employees. Employees will be compensated well, in return for which their full support and cooperation is expected. If terms of employment are not satisfactory, any employee is free to look elsewhere for more satisfactory arrangements.
>
> The company wants superior personnel and will not settle for mediocrity. Length of service is of importance but not as important at Indian Head as is quality of performance. Results, not effort count.

Northern Illinois Gas Company, on the other hand, is more paternalistic, and this paternalism is reflected in such overall guidelines as "The company will provide: Job security to the greatest extent possible; a comprehensive, modern benefit program; and safe, and as far as possible, pleasant working conditions and practices."[29]

[28]*Indian Head Mills Policy Manual,* quoted in Audrey T. Sproat and E. P. Learned, "Indian Head Mills, Inc. (E)," a case prepared for the Harvard Graduate School of Business Administration and copyrighted by the President and Fellows of Harvard College, 1961, p. 27.

[29]M. Valliant Higginson, *Management Policies, Vol. II: Sourcebook of Statements,* AMA Research Study No. 78 (New York: American Management Association, 1966), p. 49.

During this phase the planning process, setting the stage for successful planning, the administration, organization, and staffing functions are especially important to effective performance of the planning job. The behavioral sciences provide tools for performing these functions and thus are an indispensable aid in carrying out this step in planning. The behavioral science tools useful in planning are discussed in detail in Chapter 12.

CONCLUSION

Specific steps are taken in setting the stage for an effective planning effort.

First, the planner answers some basic questions about what the planning effort is to accomplish, the kinds of plans that are to be developed, who will be using them, the use to which they will be put, and the resources needed to perform the planning job successfully.

Second, a planner or planning director is selected. This man should possess a combination of conceptual and practical skills and be provided with adequate staff, time, and other resources to get the job done.

Third, the planning director organizes the planning activities. If the planner faces an overall corporate planning situation, he will have available considerable information on how companies organize their corporate planning departments—the structure, reporting relationships, general functions, and the like—to guide him at this stage. If the planner is developing a specific operating plan at a lower management level, he must adapt this general approach to the requirements of his specific situation.

Fourth, the planner establishes a procedure for doing planning and following up to see that planning is done. The management control techniques used in setting up a means of measuring the effectiveness of plans are discussed at length in Chapter 9.

Fifth, top management support of the planning effort is needed, in order to provide continuity and follow-through in the planning effort.

As Warren's study showed, there is evidently a wide gap between what companies say is done in their planning operations and what actually occurs. While it is possible to develop principles of action at both the overall corporate level and at lower management levels, putting these principles to work is no simple task. Planning has only recently found a place among the management sciences, and it is not yet widely understood and practiced in business. Since its benefits are rarely immediately visible to a manager, it is difficult to stir his interest in it. Moreover, when systematic approaches to planning are introduced into a company, there is a natural resistance to it within the organization, as there is to almost every change or innovation.

All of these factors create roadblocks to planning. These roadblocks are not insurmountable, however. This chapter has attempted to give guidelines for overcoming roadblocks to planning and for more effectively administering the planning effort.

Gradually companies are introducing planning departments and improving their planning practices. For example, a study of company planning practices done by the Stanford Research Institute in 1962 concluded that the number of companies in the United States with fully developed and staffed long-range planning programs was "tiny."[30] By 1967, when Harold Henry made his study of just 45 major industrial companies, over half appeared to have had such departments.

The trend is clear. Industry is increasingly recognizing the importance of the planning function. Improved techniques for administering the planning effort are, however, needed. These techniques will be developed only through experience, as more companies undertake the arduous task of setting up formal planning functions, as companies which now have planning departments discover new ways to increase the effectiveness of their planning operations, and as these companies communicate their experiences in planning to others.

DISCUSSION QUESTIONS

1. What are some of the preliminary questions which must be answered before beginning planning?
2. Outline the various methods generally followed by larger companies in organizing the planning function. How do these differ from those followed by lower level managers?
3. Outline a typical comprehensive plan at a large company. Why are the figures usually placed first in most comprehensive plans? What problems does this emphasis on figures create?
4. What are some of the problems which are encountered in administering a planning effort? How can they be overcome?
5. How would you go about organizing the planning function in the Blakeston and Wilson Company and Superb Biscuits Company studies given in Appendix of this book?
6. What special problem does the middle manager face in carrying out the planning function?
7. In what areas can the behavioral sciences be helpful in performing the planning function in a business?

[30] Robert N. Anthony, *Planning and Control Systems: A Framework for Analysis* (Boston: Division of Research, Graduate School of Business Administration, Harvard University, 1965), p. 38, footnote: "Stanford Research Institute estimates that the number of manufacturing companies with a fully developed and staffed 'long-range planning program' does not exceed 25. (Stanford Research Institute, *Conference on Long-Range Planning*, 1962). Although any of the attempts to count the companies that follow a given practice (out of many tens of thousands of companies in all) is suspect, there is general agreement in this case that the number is tiny."

8. Why do you think it so difficult to get truly accurate information about company planning practices?
9. Why is handling the relationship between the staff planner and operating manager such a challenging and difficult job?
10. What kind of person would you look for to fill the job of Corporate Planning Director at the Superb Biscuits Company?
11. What special planning problems does a small company face?

CHAPTER 3

BUILDING THE BASE FOR A BUSINESS PLAN: PLANNING PREMISES

This chapter concerns the next phase of the planning process, developing planning premises. Planning is based on assumptions or forecasts about what the planner expects to occur within the company's environment. In addition to isolating these external factors, company resources are studied to see what steps can be taken to meet the requirements of the environmental situation and to exploit company strengths. This chapter discusses how the manager involved in the planning effort can effectively develop both external and internal planning premises at all management levels.

EXTERNAL PLANNING PREMISES: DEVELOPING MEANINGFUL INFORMATION ABOUT THE ENVIRONMENT

All planning is done within the context of external planning premises—that is, specific stated assumptions about economic, social, political, industry and market factors that will affect the company's future profitability. This is true no matter what level of planning is being done, for all corporate activities focus ultimately on the movement of goods or services at a profit to some areas of the company's external environment.

In all cases, therefore, planning requires on examination of the external environment within which the company is or will be operating.[1] In large companies, an economist can play an important role in this stage of comprehensive planning, for he is the specialist trained in providing useful environmental information.

In scanning the environment the planner finds that not all of the future events in the social, political, economic, and market environment

[1]Murray L. Weidenbaum, "The Role of Economics in Business Planning," *Business Topics*, Summer 1962, p. 47.

will affect every company; nor will they affect each company in the same way. What the planner needs to determine is the economic, industry, and market information related to his specific planning needs. This is a challenging area, since in most cases economic, industry, and market information is not compiled in a way *directly* related to the corporation's business. The planner's first task in premising, therefore, is to isolate those areas in which premises are to be developed.

A comparison of the approaches of a major oil company, American Machine and Foundry, Lockheed, American Airlines, and A-D-M Company shows that although each began by studying external factors that would affect their futures, there was considerable variation in the kind of information developed.

For example, a major oil company had long used a limited number of market forecasts, which upon review were found to be inadequate planning premises. As a result of this review, the company developed much more detailed forecasts of environmental and competitive factors related specifically to its own marketing problems. Ten-year projections were made by state or trading area of car registrations, population, and new road construction—all major factors influencing the sale of petroleum products. Internal factors influencing planning were also examined more carefully, and specific performance standards—such as market share by state, sales and profit contribution by product, and capital budgets by district—were developed in much greater detail, thus enabling more effective business planning. Figure 3-1 illustrates the kinds of planning premises initially formulated, and those developed when the company's planning became more sophisticated.[2]

In its attempt to improve corporate planning, American Machine and Foundry developed even more specific market and industry information and forecasts in their planning premises. The degree of refinement developed in AMF's planning effort can be seen from the following checklist of some of the environmental information gathered and forecasts made for planning by the company:[3]

1. The market.
    a. Present major production lines and proposed new major product lines.
    b. Total industry volume and unit sales volume in each.
2. The competition.
    a. Present major product lines and proposed new major product lines.
    b. Total industry volume and unit sales volume in each.

[2] D. R. Daniel, "Management Information Crisis," *Harvard Business Review*, September-October 1961, p. 118.

[3] Stewart Thompson, "Planning at American Machine and Foundry Company," in *Long-Range Planning for Management*, ed. David Ewing (Rev. ed.; New York: Harper & Row, Publishers, 1964), pp. 266-272.

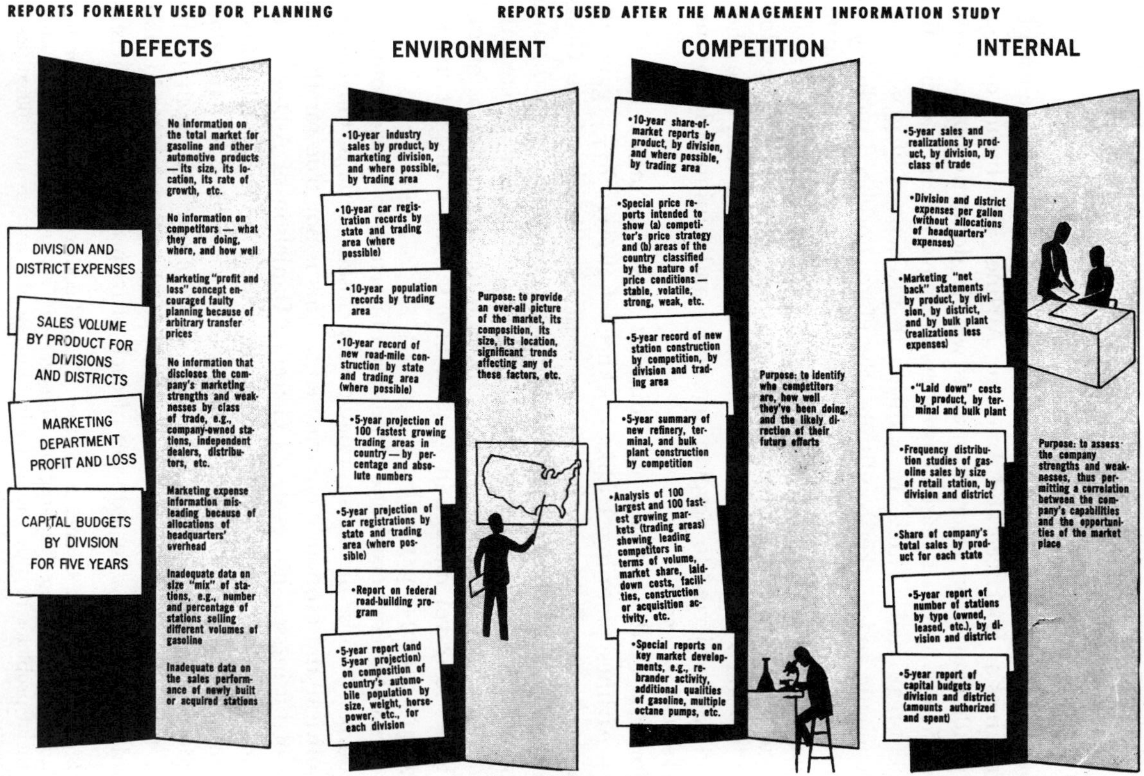

Figure 3.1

COMPARATIVE ANALYSIS OF MARKETING PLANNING INFORMATION NEEDED BY A MAJOR OIL COMPANY

3. Factors affecting unit performance.
    a. Future price structure for products.
    b. Direct and indirect labor costs.
    c. Market strategy.
    d. Trends within the industry.
    e. Technological changes affecting product cost and use.
    f. Market penetration (percent and dollar volume).

Broader economic, political and social planning premises are used by such companies as Lockheed and American Airlines. The future of Lockheed depends heavily on international as well as domestic political and economic factors, since its major customers are government agencies and government-regulated airlines. In addition to projections of general domestic economic and market conditions, therefore, Lockheed included in its planning premises such factors as the international political situation and projected Cold War conditions, the United States Government's attitudes towards air power and missiles, and possible technological developments. The effects of changes in these conditions on sales were then quantified and projected to develop maximum and minimum long-range potential sales forecasts.[4]

A forecast of the external environment was also the first step in American Airlines' planning. Unlike Lockheed, however, they began with projections of overall factors in the domestic economy, such as Gross National Product, disposable personal income, population growth, and then isolated those additional economic indicators which affected the domestic transportation market specifically, in order to develop a forecast of the domestic travel market in general and the air transport market (passenger and cargo) in particular.[5]

Forecasts of overall economic trends are important to a large company or to a company whose business is related very closely to major movements in the political and economic environment. This is not true for the vast majority of businesses, however. As Clarence Danielson of A-D-M Company points out, "few companies are fortunate enough to have well-defined arithmetical relationships of sales and major external factors."[6] In developing its comprehensive plans, A-D-M Company found that such major economic trends as Gross National Product, total industrial production, and population growth affected sales of each of its products in a different

[4]L. Eugene Root and George A. Steiner, "The Lockheed Aircraft Corporation Master Plan," in *Long-Range Planning for Management*, ed Ewing, pp. 239-259. Lockheed's financial problems in 1971 dramatically illustrate the hazards and difficulties of corporate planning.

[5]C. N. Oursler, "Long-Range Planning at American Airlines," in *Managerial Long-Range Planning*, ed. Steiner, pp. 115-126. TWA's approach is described in Clark and Elgers, "Evaluating the Sales Forecast," *Michigan Business Review*, May 1968, pp. 14-19.

[6]Clarence A. Danielson, "How We Took Hold of Long-Range Planning at A-D-M," in *Long-Range Planning for Management*, ed. Ewing, p. 259.

way and were not specific enough to be useful in planning for A-D-M's product lines. Instead, A-D-M directed its attention to isolating specific industry indices, such as machine tool orders, which might be reasonably related to their specific product lines.[7]

In smaller companies and industries, it is sometimes difficult to develop very much relevant industry and market information. For example, a leading paper company for which this author worked needed planning information for a proposed expansion into envelope manufacturing. Since at the time most envelope manufacturing companies were privately held, practically no information was available on the size or composition of the market or on the competition within it. Neither envelope or paper associations nor government statistical sources had much information related to the specific type of expansion proposed—even though the envelope group is a sizeable segment of the paper industry. An extended, round-about search of such diverse information sources as banks, suppliers, and company financial reports yielded the semblance of background information upon which decisions could be made. Although this information on past and future industry trends in the envelope industry was hardly an adequate basis for a major investment decision, it was all the information that could be found and a major decision was made on the basis of it—evidently a fairly common business practice.

More recently the author was involved in planning for a mail-order marketing operation. Total retail sales had some relevance in developing a comprehensive plan for the operation, as did trends and forecasts of population, disposable income, and selected product-group sales. But none of these were directly related to mailorder sales and so were of no real help when developing detailed product and marketing plans. Since adequate breakdowns of sales trends within the mail-order industry were not available, plans had to be based largely on premises other than economic forecasts, such as probable developments in postal rates and services, in marketing concepts and media, in consumer attitudes and mail-order buying habits, in the actions of competitors, and the like.

The Blakeston and Wilson Company described in Appendix A was faced with a similar situation, where very little overall economic information was available that was directly relevant to the company's planning problems. Relevant environmental information was thus gathered principally in the specific industry and marketing areas directly affecting company operations: the trend towards manufacturer-retailer tie-ins which bypassed the wholesalers, specific candy product growth trends, price trends in the wholesale market versus price trends at the manufacturing and retail level, competitors' plans, competing product lines and outlets, available advertising media, industry regulations on advertising, and the

[7]Danielson, "How We Took Hold of Long-Range Planning at A-D-M," pp. 259-266.

like. Overall economic and political factors such as the coming end of rationing, the potential increase in disposable income, and the recent end of the war, were among the few broader environmental factors of importance that were relevant. The ways in which these environmental factors affected the development of strategic plans at the Blakeston and Wilson Company are discussed in the next chapter.

Once the environmental areas in which premises are needed and the kind of information desired have been determined, the next job is to develop specific information within each area. As is seen from the above examples sometimes these external planning premises are general prose statements of possible or likely events and general trends. In other instances, they are forecasts or predictions which quantify trends, risks, or the impact of likely events.

SOURCES AND METHODS FOR OBTAINING ENVIRONMENTAL INFORMATION

Many sources are used to obtain information about a company's environment. Among the most common, according to one study,[8] are:

1. Personal Experience
2. Professional Journals
3. Reports
4. Books
5. Professional Meetings
6. Industrial Conferences and Associate Publications
7. Colleagues
8. Board Members
9. Friends
10. Employees
11. Suppliers and Customers
12. Government Statistical Publications

According to the same survey, the kind of information most often sought is:[9]

	Category	General Content
1.	Market potential	Supply and demand considerations for market areas of current or potential interest: for example, capacity, consumption, imports, exports.
2.	Structural change	Mergers, acquisitions, and joint ventures involving competitors; new entries into the industry.
3.	Competitors and industry	General information about a competitor, industry policy, concerted actions in the industry, and so forth.

[8]Francis F. Aquilar, *Scanning the Business Environment* (New York: The Macmillan Company, 1967).

[9]Aquilar, *Scanning the Business Environment*, p. 40.

4. Pricing	Effective and proposed prices for products of current and potential interest.
5. Sales negotiations	Information relating to a specific current or potential sale or contract for the firm.
6. Customers	General information about current or near-potential customers, their markets, their problems.
7. Leads for mergers, joint ventures, or acquisitions	Information concerning possibilities for the manager's own company.
8. Suppliers and raw materials	Purchasing considerations for products of current or potential interest.
9. New products, processes, and technology	Technical information relatively new and unknown to the company.
10. Product problems	Problems involving existing products.
11. Costs	Costs for processing, operations, and so forth for current and potential competitors, suppliers and customers, and for proposed company activities.
12. Licensing and patents	Products and processes.
13. General conditions	Events of a general nature: political, demographic, national, and so forth.
14. Government actions and policies	Governmental decisions affecting the industry.
15. Resources available	Persons, land, and other resources possibly available for the company.
16. Miscellaneous	Items not elsewhere classified.

Not all companies, nor all levels or types of managers, need the same kind of information or obtain it from the same sources.[10] For example, small companies and lower level managers tend to use more personal and less formal sources for obtaining information, while large companies and higher level managers tend to use more formal procedures for obtaining information. On the one hand, marketing managers will most often seek out industry and market information; on the other hand, financial managers are more interested in broader economic information. And lower level managers tend to get more unsolicited information, whereas higher level managers tend to solicit and seek out environmental information more aggressively. In brief, each company and each manager must determine their particular information needs, the specific sources that will provide this information, and the best way to get it.

[10]Aquilar, *Scanning the Business Environment,* Chapters Five and Six.

Obtaining information about competitors is one of the most perplexing problems facing a manager. Many executives find that a company's suppliers and customers are a good current source of information on competitors. This is especially true for smaller companies.

While larger companies tend to be more fully integrated and are more likely to do exploratory work internally, smaller companies are not, and so need to consult and use suppliers more heavily when exploring new products and services. Since suppliers serve many customers, they tend to be channels of information about new projects being considered. Smaller companies are also forced to use outside market research and testing facilities more than larger companies, for smaller companies are less likely to have internal testing and research facilities, thus making these outside facilities an independent source of information on new developments. Information on the new operations of larger, fully integrated companies is harder to come by during the early stages of development, except through direct hiring of a competitor's personnel or through corporate espionage.

Specific information on competitor profitability and efficiency by product line is practically impossible to come by.

EXTERNAL PLANNING PREMISES: ECONOMIC AND MARKET FORECASTING

Planning and forecasting can and should be distinguished. Forecasting predicts quantitatively what will happen under a given set of circumstances; planning specifies the steps that will be or should be taken to achieve a designated objective. Although distinct, the two processes are closely related, for economic and market forecasting provides specific quantitative premises for use in building plans and developing sales forecasts.

In comprehensive planning, overall economic forecasts—projections of what will happen in the overall economy—are first made. Wherever possible forecasts are then made of trends within the industry and market served by the company, including what the total market for a company's products will be and what share of that market the company can realistically expect to obtain. Forecasts within specific market segments which will affect operating planning are also made, where possible. These environmental forecasts are then combined with internal company factors to come up with a sales forecast.

Some of the more commonly used long-term economic forecasts are:[11] projections of the Gross National Product; projections of disposable per-

[11]Carl A. Dauten, *Business Cycles and Forecasting* (2nd ed.; Cincinnati: South-Western Publishing Company, 1961), pp. 353-358; Adolph G. Abramson, "Techniques of Forecasting," in *Business Forecasting in Practice*, eds. Adolph G. Abramson and Russell H. Mack (New York: John Wiley and Sons, Inc., 1956), p. 75; Harry Deane Wolfe, *Business Forecasting Methods* (New York: Holt, Rinehart and Winston, 1966), p. 133.

sonal income; full-employment models; and long-term economic series. Some of the more commonly used short-term economic forecasts are:[12] short-range forecasts of the GNP; industrial production models; leading, coincident, and lagging series; and econometric models of the economy.

The forecasts of the overall economic environment form the background within which industry and market forecasts are made in areas more closely related to a company's business. In the majority of companies, these specific industry and market forecasts (where they can be developed) are the ones which have the most relevance to planning, for they are the basis upon which actual company sales forecasts are developed. An example of how a market forecast was developed for a large telephone company is given later in this chapter to illustrate how market forecasts are developed and used to build company sales forecasts. Before describing this study, however, the following sections review some of the statistical techniques used in making economic and market forecasts.

There are various statistical techniques which can be used in forecasting. Three of the major ones—time series analysis (including trend development), regression analysis and adaptive forecasting, as well as the data formulation process, are discussed in this section.

The Data Formulation Process

Before a forecast or prediction can be made, the data must first be formulated; that is it must be collected, analyzed, interpreted, and presented.

In the *collection* phase, data can be obtained from existing published or unpulblished source such as government agencies, trade associations, research bureaus, magazines, individual research workers, and others mentioned earlier in this chapter. In addition to these data sources, the investigator may find it necessary to collect his own information by physically going to the originating sources and compiling it. Although a person may never have to collect data, it is essential that he have a working knowledge of the processes of collection and be able to evaluate the reliability of data he uses.

In the *analysis* phase, data must be classified into useful and logical categories. The four important bases of classification of statistical data are: 1) qualitative, 2) quantitative, 3) chronological, and 4) geographical.[13] For example, in doing a forecast of telephone usage, classifying telephones

[12]Elmer Clark Bratt, *Business Cycles and Forecasting,* (5th ed.; Homewood, Illinois: Richard D. Irwin, Inc. 1961), pp. 408, 438-439; Dauten, *Business Cycles and Forecasting,* pp. 388-415; Geoffrey H. Moore, *Business Cycles Indicators* (Princeton, N.J.: Princeton University Press, 1961), Vol. I; Norman N. Barish, *Economic Analysis for Engineering and Managerial Decision-Making* (New York: McGraw-Hill Book Company, 1962), p. 561.

[13]Frederick E. Croxton, Dudley J. Cowden, and Sidney Klein, *Applied General Statistics* (3rd ed.; Englewood Cliffs, N.J.: Prentice-Hall, Inc., 1967), p. 3.

as rotary or touchtone gives a qualitative differentiation, for the distinction is one of a kind rather than of amount. When items vary in respect to some measurable characteristic, a quantitative classification is appropriate. For example, families may be classified according to the number of children and individuals may be classified according to the amount of income tax they pay. Chronological data, or time series classification, shows information about continuing series of events at various specified times. For example, one may chart daily stock prices over a period of months or years. Geographical classifications present data arranged by geographical region. For example, one can show the number and kinds of telephone users for each of the counties in New York City.

The *interpretation* phase of the data formulation process consists of drawing conclusions based on the analysis. In doing this step, the limitations of the original data must be studied carefully, so that the investigator can discover and clarify all the useful and applicable meanings present in his data.

Finally, the data must be *presented* in some suitable form either for one's own use or for the use of others. Usually the figures are arranged in a table or represented by various graphic devices.

This four-step procedure for formulating data is a prerequisite to developing a significant forecast.

Time Series Analysis

The first major forecasting technique to be discussed in this section is time series analysis. All data reported at regular intervals of time are referred to as time series. This includes data reported daily, weekly, monthly, and annually.

There are four kinds of movements which can be examined in any time series: trend, cyclical, seasonal and irregular. In order to study the influences that affect a particular series, it is necessary to isolate these four factors.

1. *Trend* is the basic tendency of an activity to either increase or decrease over a long period of time. The Gross National Product is in a rising trend. A declining trend is found in the number of candlestick manufacturers. It is important to describe the trend of a series for a number of reasons. First, this description gives one an idea of the general direction of the activity being studied and avoids the confusion which may be introduced by random fluctuations. Second, once an historical trend has been established, it enables one to project the future behavior of the trend. Third, trend development enables the planner to compare one trend against another more easily—for example, the trend of his company's sales against the sales of the industry in general.

   The simplest method of developing a trend graphically is by inspection. If the trend is a straight line, or linear, it may be drawn with a straight edge (see Figure 3.2). If the trend is non-linear, it may be drawn freehand or with a curvilinear ruler (see Figure 3.3). The straight line is the simplest type of trend line. For short periods of time a straight line may provide a reasonably good description of the trend of a series, but for longer periods a curved or nonlinear line may be called for. It is also possible to represent trends by mathematical formulas.[14]

2. *Cyclical* movements are successive phases of expansion and contraction above and below the trend. Turning points occur with little advance warning and usually for different reasons. Recession and recovery in overall business conditions are the primary causes of cyclical movements.
3. *Seasonal* variations are distinct from cyclical ones, because they recur regularly and last one year or less. A seasonal pattern could be man made, or it could be the result of weather conditions, holidays, social traditions and customs, or other recurring developments.
4. *Irregular* movements are those fluctuations caused by such unusual events as strikes, storms, assassinations and the like.

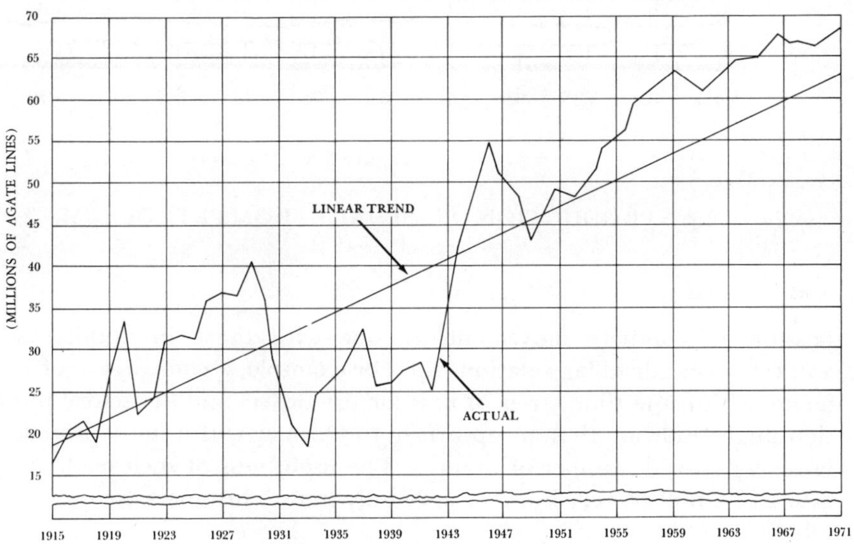

Figure 3.2

MAGAZINE ADVERTISING IN THE U.S.
1915-1971

Isolating the various kinds of movements within a time series and going beyond merely looking at the trend of the series enables one to project into the future the variations that can be expected within a trend over a short term. When several time series are being studied, it may be

[14]Croxton, Cowden and Klein, *Applied General Statistics*, Chapters 11 and 12.

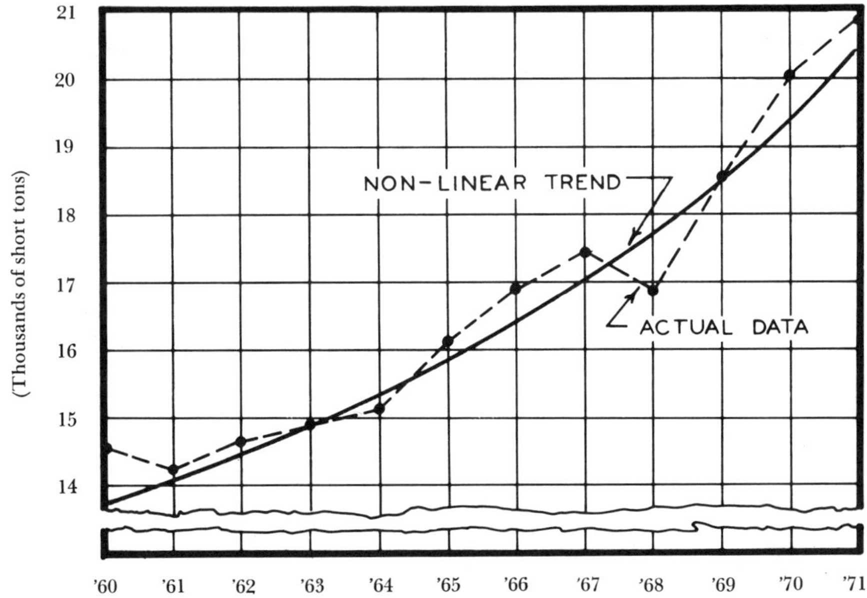

Figure 3.3

PRODUCTION OF ASPHALT FROM PETROLEUM
1941-1971

possible to compare movements in one with those in another series and establish a lead-lag relationship. For example, a comparison of movements within the time series of new factory orders and of factory production might indicate that an upturn in the former will usually precede the latter by a fixed number of months. The usefulness of such leading indicators is, however, very limited, since only in rare instances are they highly reliable.[15]

The time series method is not recommended for long-term projections. It is best suited for one-year or two-year month-to-month forecasts.[16]

Regression Analysis

The econometrician's standard analytical tool in business cycle research is regression and correlation analysis.[17] The regression and cor-

[15]Wolfe, *Business Forecasting Methods*, pp. 48-51.

[16]"New Horizons in Telephone Forecasting," *Telephony*, November 7, 1964, p. 60.

[17]William F. Butler and Robert A. Kavesh, *How Business Economists Forecast* (Englewood Cliffs, N.J.: Prentice-Hall, Inc., 1966), p. 8.

relation approach is based on the fact that elements of the economy are interrelated and that many of these interrelationships are relatively constant. If two variables are related, then a knowledge of one, the independent variable, will make possible an estimate of the other variable, the dependent variable. For example, if one can predict the number of marriages that will occur over the coming years, one can predict the number of new houses or apartments which will be needed during those years, since marriages normally create the need for new homes.

There are three measurements which must be made in conjunction with simple *linear regression analysis.*

1. A mathematical regression equation which describes the relationship between the two variables.
2. A measure of the possible divergence of the actual values of the dependent variable from their estimated or computed values. For example, if one projects a GNP of $1.45 trillion for 1975, one must also specify how much the actual results might vary from the projections. This measure is called the standard error of estimate.
3. A measure of the degree of relationship or correlation (r) between the variables.[18]

The term linear describes those relationships which when plotted, independent variable vs. dependent variable, approximate a straight-line relationship. For example, if one were to plot temperature on the X-axis and cricket chirps per minute on the Y-axis you would find scatter points lying on an almost straight line, since cricket chirping increases with the temperature. By determining the regression equation, it would then be possible to forecast the dependent variable, chirps per minute, of one could forecast the temperature, the independent variable.

An example of the use of regression analysis in business might be to determine if there is a relationship between furniture sales and personal income. If the relationship is significant enough, it is then possible to forecast one event, furniture sales, knowing the value of the other, personal income.

The statistical term used for measuring the degree of relationship between two factors is correlation. The correlation coefficient is a figure which measures the degree to which two variables correlate. It is usually accepted that an 80 per cent correlation coefficient is significant.

Exactly the same principles are involved in *multiple linear regression analysis* as in simple linear regression analysis. The procedure for computing measures of relationship is also essentially the same, although it is more laborious in multiple linear regression analysis, since there is more than one independent variable.

[18]Croxton, Cowden and Klein, *Applied General Statistics,* p. 393.

Adaptive Forecasting

Adaptive or exponential forecasting deals with forecasting of individual products for inventory control and for production scheduling.[19] The need for adaptive forecasts of individual product lines most frequently arises when a company has an inventory control system or a production scheduling system with predetermined decision rules which specify when to produce or order more of a particular item. These decision rules are based in part on a prediction of sales or usage of each item in the near future.

Certain desirable characteristics of these forecasts are implied by their use: they must be made quickly, cheaply, easily, and in such a manner that they can be followed routinely. In its simplest form, the adaptive or exponential forecasting system makes a forecast of expected sales in the next period by a weighted average of sales in the current period, and the forecast of sales for the current period made during the previous period.[20] Such a method has the characteristics desired in a prediction method: current sales information is easily introduced, the forecast calculation is fast, and only a limited amount of information need be maintained. For products with stable sales rates and little seasonal fluctuations, this simple exponential model proves quite satisfactory.

It is usually worthwhile to extend the adaptive forecasting system to take into account long-range trends and seasonal effects. While more information is required with this more complete model, the accuracy of prediction is also substantially increased for most kinds of products.

A CASE STUDY IN MARKET FORECASTING FOR PLANNING

A major telephone company recently completed a study of ways to improve forecasting of new telephone demand, which illustrates how planning premises are defined and forecasting techniques used for planning. The technique used in the study was multiple regression, a technique which is commonly used in economic and business forecasting.

The purpose of the study was to develop a way to forecast telephone usage a year in advance, so that the company could develop manufacturing and service facilities to make, install, and maintain new telephones. The study was confined to one geographical area.

It was first necessary to examine the factors that appeared to affect station or telephone demand, which in this case was the dependent variable. Two factors were initially examined: live births, and marriage licenses issued. These factors were selected because marriages create house-

[19]Peter R. Winters, "Forecasting Sales by Exponentially Weighted Moving Averages," *Management Science*, April 1960, pp. 324-342.

[20]H. Theil and S. Wage, "Some Observations on Adaptive Forecasting," *Management Science*, January 1964, p. 198.

holds, which are potentially new telephone users, and these marriages could be shown to be the result of births 22 years earlier in the geographic area under study.

The lead time of 22 years was determined through a computer program. The number of marriages was shown to relate very closely to births 22 years earlier, which in statistical terms meant there was an extremely high index of determination.

The problem was then to forecast marriages, using births as the controlling independent variable. A computer was used for this, although longhand or manual methods could have been used.

Once a projection of the marriages expected in any given year was made, then information was developed on the housing that would be available to accomodate these potential telephone users. Since in the area being studied it usually took one full year from the issuance of the permit to the completion of a building, data from the F. W. Dodge Corporation regarding building permits issued and building contracts awarded was analyzed. The data was then projected one year to provide meaningful forecast information. This information was then compared with the projections of marriages and with new telephone demand over the years, in order to determine the degree of correlation, if any, that existed among the three variables.

A computer program was used to perform the multiple linear regression of these three variables. This program fits the linear regression equation $Y = A + B(X_1) + C(X_2)$, where Y = station demand, X_1 = marriage licenses issued, X_2 = building contracts awarded, and A, B, and C were the regression coefficients. The index of determination was 0.998776, indicating that movements in the three variables were consistently very closely related. Since one could forecast marriages and new homes for the coming year, then, one could also forecast new telephone demand, by projecting the past relationship (or correlation) into the future.

The forecasts proved to be very accurate. For example, for 1970 the company had previously forecast 51,000 installations. In contrast, the new forecasting method predicted 48,700. The actual figure proved to be 47,000.

This case is a very simple example of how forecasting techniques can be used to predict events within a company's environment, and so help develop more precise external planning premises. A simple example was selected in order to illustrate the basic approach to using forecasting techniques. Since the telephone company in this case was the only one serving the market, the company proceeded to develop sales forecasts and plans to produce and service the new telephones expected to be sold.

This is an exceptional situation, however, for normally more than one company competes in a market. If the market had been served by more than one telephone company, subsequent studies would have been needed to determine the expected share of the market for each company before a sales forecast could be made.

Under normal circumstances, therefore, once the economic forecaster has studied the environmental factors and established what the overall market for a company's product line will be, he must predict the share of the market his company might expect to achieve profitably. This he can do partially through analysis of historical industry, economic, and company data. These ideal projections must then be studied in the light of the company's available resources and the sales the operating managers feel can be achieved through these resources.[21]

COMPANY PLANNING PREMISES

The information developed during the economic analysis stage only tells the manager what sales he might reasonably expect under various circumstances. Whatever conclusions are drawn from an analysis of external factors, these conclusions must be tempered by what the company realistically can do and the owners want to do. Normally, a company's planning is influenced as much by internal company factors as it is by environmental factors.

Company planning premises are all the internal company factors which must be taken into account when developing corporate plans. Company planning premises may concern the amount of available financing, manpower, and facilities; the areas in which the company has experience (including marketing expertise, present product line, and production knowhow); and the kind and sophistication of internal, automated information and control systems. These premises may also concern the internal "character" of the organization, and how much and how soon it can be adapted to growth and change. And they may include the needs and desires of company stockholders and the aspirations, values, and prejudices of company managers (as in the XYZ Company study described in the last chapter).

The review of company factors usually begins with a thorough examination of past operating results and major planning decisions. Such a review is not only a good introduction to company operations; it also helps uncover a company's strengths and weaknesses.

More than just an analysis of figures is needed, however. An intense corporate self-appraisal is needed to determine the relevance of internal strengths and weaknesses to planning. The expansion of facilities will always be limited by the availability of funds and management resources. For example, in the Blakeston and Wilson case given in Appendix A, the number of retail stores which could be opened was limited because the company was small, had limited cash, and was basically run by one man.

[21] Wolfe, *Business Forecasting Methods,* Chapters Seven and Eight.

Entry into new markets will always be affected by the strengths and weaknesses of a company's production and marketing experience: if the company has a strong distribution system for selling toiletries in drug stores, for example, it may be able to expand most easily by adding new products which can be sold through the same channels.

In some instances, as David Ewing has pointed out, a study of internal corporate resources (especially in the area of marketing and production experience) has caused management to go against conclusions drawn from a study of industry opportunities and to choose to concentrate on seemingly less dynamic portions of a market.[22] For example, both Franklin Life Insurance Company in the 1940's and AMP Inc. in the 1950's successfully did this. By concentrating on their areas of expertise, they were able to build very strong businesses in face of what appeared to be unfavourable market indicators. In contrast, Joseph E. Seagrams and Sons, Inc. used the "market opportunity" approach. They foresaw expanding markets for a wider range of expensive beverages and expanded their product line. Unfortunately, the same approach was used by competitors, and severe competition resulted.

What were the lessons learned from these experiences? First, success depends on doing a job better than the competition, so that companies are *sometimes* better off concentrating on what they know how to do best, in spite of perceived potential market opportunities in new fields. Second, while forecasts of market potential are useful, they have their limitations. No matter how clairvoyant an economic forecaster may be, there is no way of fully anticipating what the competition will do.

Successful past experience in a given area does not, however, always guarantee success in a closely related area. For example, Famous Schools, a leader in the correspondence school field, had been extremely successful in starting art and writing schools and had the industry's most highly developed field-sales system. In the early 1960's management decided to introduce a photography school, which they felt could be successfully marketed in the same way as the art and writing schools, and they proceeded to follow the same marketing and product patterns for the photography school that they had used in their art and writing schools. Unfortunately, the photographers' market was distinct enough from the writers' and artists' market to require different marketing techniques, a different price for the product, and different student services, so that many changes had to be made after the product was introduced, and much time and money was needlessly lost. In the end, the photography school failed to live up to management expectations and at best seemed destined to make only a marginal contribution to company profits.

22David W. Ewing, "Corporate Planning at the Crossroads," *Harvard Business Review*, July-August 1967, pp. 77-86.

Dow Jones had a similar experience with its new publication, *The National Observer.* When Dow Jones introduced the new publication (a weekly newspaper), they used the marketing techniques they had used in marketing *The Wall Street Journal* (a daily business and financial paper), which was highly successful. As is shown in the discussion of *The National Observer* in Chapters 2 and 7, this marketing experience was not transferable and so was not a sound basis upon which to build a marketing program for the new publication.

The lack of adequate automated information and control systems is another limiting factor which is having an ever-increasing impact on planning today. For example, one major corporation in the entertainment field has been forced to wait indefinitely to develop a $25,000,000 business because, even though marketing plans and programs are tested and ready and adequate financial resources are available, the company's computerized order-servicing operation and its manpower resources are inadequate to handle even current business.

The effect of the personal biases and the desires of chief executives or major stockholders on a company's planning is well known. Ideally, the distortions resulting from emotional and personal biases should be eliminated in planning for a business. In practice they cannot be, and they frequently have a major impact on the utimate choice of what direction a company follows or how the company plans to get there.

Many clues to the overall direction a company can follow may be found while studying company planning premises. First, the company must answer the question of what business it is now in. Is an oil company in the "fuel" business or the "energy" business? Is a leather suitcase manufacturer in the "leather" business, the "travel accessory" business, or just the "suitcase" business? Is a candy company in the "boxed chocolate" business, or is its field the entire "confectionary" business? By abandoning familiar product or process definitions, by examining the market needs served, and by giving a broader definition to the kind of business it is in, a company can sometimes open the way to new growth. For example, a motion picture company which saw itself only as a producer of movies for local theatres was slow in exploiting the opportunities for making films for TV, whereas a movie company that saw itself as being in the "entertainment" field would be more likely to seize upon opportunities in fields closely allied to its present area of business, such as packaging shows for TV, or managing cable TV networks.

Second, in taking a hard look at its strengths, a company frequently finds that it has certain built-in strengths, which could give it an advantage over competitors in a new field. A well recognized brand name, such as A & P, can be applied to a whole line of products, and as in the case of A & P can open up an entirely new area of business growth, private label merchandise. Investigation of other strengths, such as special equipment, manpower skills, relations with customers, merchandising techniques and the like frequently unearth new avenues of growth.

Third, a probe of management and stockholder experience and interests can sometimes uncover new opportunities. At a major communications company, for example, a division marketing manager who was friendly with the corporate planning director heard by chance that one of the new areas of development being considered was correspondence schools. As it turned out, this manager had experience in the correspondence school field, was interested in it, and was able to help in developing plans for expanding company operations into that area.

The company planning premise stage thus often uncovers factors which not only set limits on company plans, but also open up new areas of opportunity and suggest new ways to grow. For this reason, this phase of the planning process is a necessary preliminary step to developing a corporate objective, and it must be thoroughly investigated before a final objective can be established.

THE SALES FORECAST

The sales forecast is the basis of most company implementation plans. Marketing, production, manpower, financial and other operating plans are based on this forecast, as is overall corporate profit planning.

Wherever possible, external economic, industry, and market forecasts are first made to arrive at an estimate of the sales the company should achieve under ideal circumstances. These forecasts are then adjusted on the basis of information gathered from operating managers, salesmen, and other sources,[23] as well as information on the limitations set by company planning premises.

For example, in the oil company case described earlier in this chapter, economic forecasts of total demand, and of the company's potential share of that demand, were first made. Internal factors were then examined to determine what proportion of these potential sales the company could get with its present and planned facilities and manpower, before a final sales forecast was made. The initial forecasts were then adjusted on the basis of executive judgment, and on information gathered from the operating managers on the plans of major customers, and on other local market factors affecting major segments of the company's sales.

In larger companies overall industry and market forecasts can have a major impact on company sales forecasting: first, a large company normally has a significant share of the market, so that changes in its sales are more likely to coincide with changes in total industry sales; second, large companies are more likely to have adequate resources to meet major increases in demand, so that they do not necessarily have to adjust sales forecasts

[23] Wolfe, *Business Forecasting Methods*, Chapters Seven and Eight, describes the various methods used to make sales forecasts for a company.

downward because of limited resources. The smaller the company, the more important internal company factors and specific market factors are likely to be in developing the sales forecast, since the company's resources are more limited and its share of market smaller.

Overall sales forecasts are refined and broken down into major product and market categories. These specific sales forecasts in turn are used as quantified marketing goals for each marketing division. Marketing, manpower, production, and financial plans are next developed, along with budgets to meet these sales goals. Overall profit and expense goals are also developed as part of this process, thus producing a whole fabric of sub-objectives and implementation plans for all the operating and staff areas in a company. Sales forecasts are thus extremely important to business planning and control, for they are the origin of sub-objectives, implementation plans, and performance standards for all profit center segments of a company's operation.

As can be seen from the above discussion, developing company sales forecasts is not always a simple process of economic analysis. The market can be studied, and the ideal share of that market a company should reasonably expect to achieve can be determined. But normally a company's business is influenced by special market factors, and its resources are limited (especially in the case of medium-size and small companies), so that except in very large companies ideal forecasts of sales and profits must always be tempered by what operating managers feel can be achieved with their available resources in the light of special market factors, and a balance must be struck between the ideal economic and pragmatic operating points of view.

Sometimes it may be necessary to insist that an operating manager set higher goals for his operation, when he appears to be overly conservative or merely trying to make his job a little easier. At the same time, an economic forecaster is not omniscient, so that his projection may be unrealistically high and must be tempered. Considerable executive judgment is needed to reconcile these two points of view.

Presumably, the two points of view act as controls on each other, and temper shortcomings or excesses at either the operating management or economic analysis level. Having these two points of view does not, of course, guarantee that one will come up with an accurate sales forecast, but they can help a manager come closer to the right answer.

The sales forecast, then, is in a sense the catalyst through which the effects of internal and external planning premises are reconciled. The sales forecast is also the bridge between comprehensive planning and implementation planning in a company. The sales forecast is both the basis upon which specified overall company profit plans are developed, as well as the basis for establishing sales goals for all the operations of a company, which in turn are the base upon which specific implementation plans are built.

HOW ACCURATE SHOULD FORECASTS BE?

For the most part economic and company forecasts are not much different from non-quantitative or qualitative planning premises, since they are basically refined estimates, translated into numbers, of probable future circumstances.

Since forecasts are basically estimates and so can never be considered 100 per cent accurate, it is important in planning to know the possible range of deviations of actual performance from forecast, the probability of their occurrence, and the magnitude of the effect of such deviations on corporate operations in quantitative terms. What management needs to know is what margin of error in the forecast he should plan for. The manager's job is then to create alternative operational plans to meet and exploit various possible future occurrences. The sooner a manager knows that performance could possibly deviate by 20% or 10% or 50% from forecast, the sooner he can develop alternative operational plans to meet these possible future circumstances.

For example, in a retail sales operation, it is impossible to predict exactly how much of each product will be sold. The astute merchandiser, therefore, develops outlets through which he can dispose of a specific amount of excess inventory, or arranges with the manufacturer to carry back-up inventory for him, or spaces his promotions in such a way as to limit his risk and his investment in inventory. The planning information that the merchandiser needs is a forecast of the maximum and minimum amount of merchandise that he is likely to have to dispose of in this way, or how much he must ask the manufacturer to provide in back-up inventory of the product, or the degree to which he should stagger his promotions.

The manager can never expect to have exact predictions or forecasts of future events, and the forecaster is not expected to produce them. The most a manager will ever know is the likelihood and probable range of future events, their impact on his operation, and the risks involved in various courses of action. This is the information the forecaster should provide. With this information in hand, the planner can prepare to meet each probable turn of events.

PLANNING PREMISES FOR DEVELOPING IMPLEMENTATION PLANS

The lower the level of planning in the corporate structure, the less concerned the planner is with broad environmental planning premises, since they have less direct influence on his planning premises. A marketing manager's operation, for example, may be affected generally by overall economic factors, but his immediate plans may be affected more by specific trends within the industry and market, such as the plans of his major customers. As a result, he will probably have to develop many planning premises which are unique to his operation.

In every planning situation, a large number of a lower level manager's planning premises will come from the overall company strategic plan. For example, the marketing manager cited above would be striving to achieve the overall company objective and would be working within the overall policies set by the company. And he would use the overall economic, industry, and market planning premises, where they are available, as guidelines for action. In a large company, he might even find his sales goal given as part of the overall plan. His planning is also affected by available company resources, plans in other operating areas, and the planning done at the next higher management level.

Within a company's planning structure, therefore, each level of plans becomes the framework, or in a sense the "premises," upon which the next lower level of planning is based. It is important to recognize the hierarchical nature of planning within a company, for not only does it give focus and prespective to business planning, but it also explains some of the confusion which exists in business planning terminology. For example, the comprehensive plan will have an objective which guides all sub-planning; at the next lower level of planning, however, this same "objective" becomes a "planning premise."

The terminology is not important. What is important is that the manager understands that the planning done at his level should be done within the framework of overall company strategic planning and the next higher level of planning above him, that he recognizes and understands the directions and guidelines dictated by the higher planning levels, and that he bases his plans upon them. His planning premises will be a combination of overall industry planning premises, the overall corporate objective and policies, the planning done in other areas affecting his operation, and whatever additional information he has gathered relevant to his specific market and his internal resources.

While these additional factors will vary with each situation, the process by which they are uncovered is in theory the same, no matter what the level of planning: critical areas affecting the future are identified; information is gathered in each area; present and future trends within the area are developed and projected; wherever possible quantifications of these trends are made; and a summary statement is prepared of the assumptions upon which these projections are made.

DETERMINING THE IMPLICATIONS OF PLANNING PREMISES

An important step in the premising stage of planning is determining what the implications of the planning premises are and what plans should be developed based on them. For example, a company planning manager may isolate what appears to be an industry growth area. One executive may conclude that the company should move strongly into that area to take advantage of the perceived growth potential. Another executive may conclude that the area is so obviously a growth area that other companies will be rushing in and competition will be severe. Information on what competitors are thinking about is always sketchy, so ultimately there is no completely rational basis upon which to make such a decision.

In most instances within the author's experience, top management ultimately relied on their own intuitive feeling for their company and the market in making final planning decisions. While the information developed and recommendations made as a result of the planning effort were essential in making the final decision, the ultimate decision was based on executive judgment. And this is as it should be, for the creative genius of a company's top managers is a major factor in any company's success. The science of planning can only support and help improve executive judgment; it cannot replace it.

CONCLUSION

In developing business plans, the planner starts by studying the environment within which he will be working. Different kinds of information will be sought and different methods and sources will be used, depending on the kind of plan and the level at which the planning is done. Forecasts are often made during this phase of planning, and the planner may have to use sophisticated forecasting techniques to develop as accurate a basis as possible upon which to build his plan. The planner must not mistake forecasts for facts, however, for they are only quantifications of assumptions about what may happen in the future. This point was dramatically illustrated by the experiences of Lockheed in 1971, when the company encountered severe financial difficulties.

Company planning premises are also developed and examined. During this step, the planner will not only specify those factors which limit his plan. He would also search for new ideas, new areas for expansion, and company strengths he can build upon in his planning.

The sales forecast is a natural extension of the premising phase in planning, for it is built on potentials seen in the market-place and is tempered by a company's ability to realize that potential. The sales forecast also serves as the first step in implementation planning, for it is the basis upon which operating managers begin to build their implementation plans.

Before implementation plans can be developed, however, company objectives and overall policies are established in order to give strategic direction to the development of specific operating plans. The following chapters discuss developing strategic directions.

DISCUSSION QUESTIONS

1. What are the major steps in developing planning premises? What are the major differences between developing premises for an overall company strategic plan and for operating plans?
2. What is the role of forecasting in the premising phase of the planning process?
3. Harry Deane Wolfe, in *Business Forecasting Methods* (Chapters 7 and 8), lists the many ways in which a company's sales forecast can be developed. Starting with a forecast of the economy, the industry and the market, the economic forecaster can use historical information to predict the percentage of that market (and the total sales) that the company should attain. This must be balanced with internally generated information from the operating personnel. Discuss the problems which may be encountered in reconciling these two points of view.
4. Once overall company sales have been predicted, it is necessary to predict sales by product category. This is extremely difficult in the case, for example, of a department store, which carries many thousands of items. Discuss the methods you would use to arrive at detailed forecasts by product. How much weight would you give to a buyer's estimate of volume for the next six months in the refrigerator and stove department, for example? What economic indicators might you use as a cross check against the buyer's forecast?
5. Discuss the ways in which economic forecasting is important to setting goals for a toy manufacturer's marketing department. What overall economic trends would affect this department's sales? How important are seasonal variations in forecasting these sales?
6. What is the difference between planning and forecasting?
7. In *The National Observer* case described in Chapters 2 and 7, what economic indicators might be helpful in predicting new subscription sales and circulation growth? Do you feel the economic forecaster would be of much help in predicting sales? Or, do you feel the forecast depends almost entirely on the money available for advertising and advertising cost of obtaining new subscribers?
8. In the Superb Biscuits Company study given in the Appendix, very little industry information for planning was available to the president at the time the case was written, because of the size of the company and the nature of the industry it served. What would you consider to be the most important external and internal factors affecting the company's planning? In what ways would each factor affect the company's overall corporate plan? Can you think of any additional sources the company might use to obtain more information?

CHAPTER 4

AN OVERALL STRATEGIC DIRECTION: DEVELOPING AN OBJECTIVE

Before undertaking a task, the objective or purpose which the task is aiming to achieve should be established. For example, as we pointed out in the discussion of step one in the planning process, before undertaking any planning effort a clear definition of what the effort is supposed to accomplish should be established.

The same is true of any activity within the corporation, at any level. The individual manager who is responsible for specific production, marketing, or product activities must define (based on a study of the planning premises) what purpose his operations are to serve, or what goals he is supposed to reach. Similarly, the corporate president is responsible for deciding exactly what the overall direction of his company is to be.

The following discussion explores the nature of an overall corporate objective and its strategic amplifications; the basic elements of such an objective; and the method by which one develops these objectives from planning premises, refines them, and comes to a decision as to which objective is best for a company. The discussion also covers the nature of subobjectives, the purpose these objectives are designed to serve, and the hierarchy and interrelationships of these objectives.

WHAT IS AN OVERALL CORPORATE OBJECTIVE?

The overall corporate objective defines the kind of company the owners, usually through their representatives, the board of directors, have determined will most profitably put their resources to use in exploiting available market opportunities over the long term.

Many objectives are established within a company. Marketing will have sales goals, market mix goals and market penetration goals. Finance will have return-on-investment goals, and personnel will have manpower and staffing goals. In other words, all the operating & staff activities within the business enterprise have their own objectives or goals.

Such goals are, however, only sub-objectives within the larger context of the overall corporate objective. These sub-objectives are intermediate goals. They support and further the corporate objective, and are the means of achieving a corporate objective—making maximum profits within a well-defined area of business activity, and within certain limitations established by the owners or by their representatives, the board of directors. All operating planning and all development of sub-objectives is based on the overall corporate objective.

The specific format in which an objective is stated will vary according to the requirements of the company involved. In many companies, for example, the overall objective is amplified by statements which embody the guiding philosophy of the company and the overall company strategy. In other companies, the statement of the overall objective is supplemented by a summary of the planning premises on which that objective is based. The following sections attempt to give some idea of the basic components of an overall company objective and the ways in which they are presented—before beginning a discussion of how company objectives are developed.

SOME EXAMPLES OF CORPORATE OBJECTIVES

As can be seen from the following examples, the overall corporate objective varies in many ways from company to company, according to the nature of the company's business, the availability of resources, the market and industry which it serves, and the aspirations of its owners and managers. The examples also show how the format for presenting objectives can vary. The complete statement of each company's objective is given in the appendices to this book.

The objective of the Northern Illinois Gas Company, for example, reads in part as follows:

> *Basic Purpose*: The basic purpose of Northern Illinois Gas Company is to perpetuate an investor-owned, free enterprise company, rendering a needed, satisfactory service and earning optimum, long-range profits.
>
> *What We Do*: The principal business of the company is the provision of gaseous energy through a pipe system to meet the needs of ultimate consumers.
>
> The company not only will provide the gas itself but also will encourage and help consumers to utilize the gas widely and in the safest, most efficient manner. All such service, research, supply, promotional, market development, financing, and similar activities for consumers are regarded as the company's principal business.
>
> In order to accomplish the company's basic purpose, it may be necessary or desirable for the company to provide other products or services which

supplement, complement, and enhance its principal business. Any such activities should be consistent with its responsibilities to its investors, customers, employees and others.

Where We Do It: The utility service area of the company is shown in the lastest Annual Report to Stockholders or in other publications. Service will be offered to everyone who can be served profitably, in accordance with the requirements of the Illinois Commerce Commission. Service will also be offered in this area subject to Illinois Commerce Commission approval, if indications are that a fair return on investment will be earned over the long-term, or if the competitive conditions warrant. . . .

How We Do It: The company will conduct its business in full recognition of its responsibilities, as set forth hereafter, to the several elements of the community upon which its operations have an impact. The company believes that in general, over the long run, the interests of all these elements are compatible.[1]

In this statement the company spells out in very specific terms the exact nature of its business. The objective defines the level of ownership and profitability desired, the industry served, the product and services offered, the functions performed, the customer and market served, and the social obligations of the company.

In contrast, Indian Head Mills established a much simpler and more investor-oriented objective for itself:

Objective: The objective of this company is to increase the intrinsic value of the common stock.

It is not to grow bigger for the sake of size, nor to become more diversified, nor to make the most or best of anything, nor to provide jobs, have the most modern plants, the happiest customers, lead in new product development, or to achieve any other status which has no relationship to the economic use of capital.

Any or all of these may be, from time to time, a means to our objective, but means and ends must never be confused. Indian Head Mills is in business solely to improve the inherent value of the common stockholder's equity in the company.

Scope: The present basis of the company's earning power is a diversified textile business. Continued growth within the textile and related industries is contemplated, in part, because the nature of the industry at present seems to offer above average opportunities for expansion.

The company, however, is not committed irrevocably to this industry, particularly if the hazards to be overcome in achieving our objective outweigh the chances of success. There is no ultimate limit to the size of the corporation.[2]

[1]See Appendix D for a complete statement of the company's objective. Reprinted with permission of the company.

[2]See Appendix C for a complete statement of the company's objective. Reprinted with permission of the company.

Although this company was in the textile industry in 1960, the intent of the statement was clear: the company was to be an investment or conglomerate company first and an operating company second. This objective was established in the early 1960's, and true to its objective, the company has since diversified into other industries which management felt would bring in higher profits.

Varian Associates has published the following statement of objective:

> *Purpose*: The prime objective is to conduct a strong, well-balanced, stable, well-managed research, engineering, and manufacturing international enterprise organized to return maximum benefits to employees, customers, and stockholders.
>
> *Nature of Enterprise*: The company shall strive to be a highly competent, profit-minded, technically oriented enterprise engaging in research, engineering, and manufacturing to meet the needs of the world markets. The company shall operate in those fields in which its research and development talents are required for business success. The company shall endeavor to exploit its talents in establishing new techniques and, through them, new products for commercial, industrial and defense applications.
>
> *Fields of Interest*: The company shall be engaged in the fields of microwave tubes and components; vacuum systems, instruments, and components; in fields exploiting recent contributions to science, including radio-frequency spectroscopy and instrumentation resulting there-from; and other fields of science which may produce products useful for industrial, commercial, and defense needs.
>
> *Diversification*: In recognition of the usual business cycles, the company shall develop new products and enter new product areas of activities as may properly diversify, balance, and profitably strengthen the company's economic position.
>
> The company shall endeavor to broaden and strengthen its product lines or fields of interests by sponsoring research and engineering programs, by purchase of patent rights, or by acquisition in part or in whole of other companies.
>
> The diversification and growth of the company shall be tempered with full consideration of its impact upon those who form the company structure and careful consideration of financial stability and the dangers of over-extension.[3]

Like the Northern Illinois Gas Company's objective, Varian Associates' objective covers many areas: functions performed, kind of profit desired, markets served, products and services offered, limitations of resources, and scope of operations.

As can be seen from the above examples, the nature of an overall corporate objective can vary widely from company to company—from setting

[3]See Appendix E for a complete statement of the company's objective. Reprinted with permission of the company.

broad stockholder goals to defining a specific market, product, or service the company will engage in. The format in which the objectives are presented, as well as what is covered in the statement of the objective will also vary from company to company. Indian Head Mills' statement, for example does not cover all the factors covered in the other two statements.

All three overall corporate objectives, however, have a common design: they all strive to define the nature or essence of the enterprise; they try to present the personality of the enterprise to the reader; they strike a balance between what the company would like to be and what it realistically estimates it can be. They do not attempt to give quantitative profit or sales goals, for such quantitative goals as the desired return on investment or level of sales are covered in the sub-objectives of the financial and marketing plans. Rather, an overall corporate objective should define the stockholders' and managers' views of the kind of enterprise they wish to build with available resources. All these objectives thus serve as models of what an overall objective is.

AMPLIFYING THE OBJECTIVE: CORPORATE PHILOSOPHY, PRINCIPLES OF ACTION, AND STRATEGY

In almost all instances, companies have found that the simple statement of an objective does not give employees adequate guidance, and that some amplification is needed. These amplifications take many forms.

For example, Northern Illinois Gas Company's statement of its overall direction includes both the statement of the company's objective given above and principles for guiding action in each of the following areas: Investors, Customers, Employees, Public, Suppliers, Competitors, Government and Gas Industry. Each of these sections contains ten or more statements of corporate philosophy, such as the following:

> *Investors*: The company will provide for its stock a ready, convenient, and technically sound market to ensure optimum flexibility for its owners.
>
> *Customers*: The company will deliver its gas customers, safely and dependably, a gas of uniform heating value that will burn cleanly and efficiently.
>
> *Employees*: The company will pay fair and just compensation comparable to what others are paying for like work.
>
> *Public*: The company will maintain a safe system.
>
> *Suppliers*: The company will deal fairly with its suppliers.[4]

These statements spell out the philosophy of the company. They inform employees of management's general intent in each of the areas covered, and so provide overall direction for corporate activities. As such, they are extensions of the objective.

[4]See Appendix D.

Indian Head Mills supplements the simple statement of their objective with sections entitled "Principles of Growth" and "Summary." These sections, which follow a statement of industry problems, read as follows:

> *Principles of Growth*: Indian Head Mills has had to contend with these problems ever since its formation in 1953 and has grown in spite of them. This growth has been based on the following fundamental concepts the application of which has enabled us to meet and successfully overcome these problems:

1. *Management* Management must have the intelligence, imagination and authority to cope with the problems of this difficult situation. To assure the best possible profit results for the stockholders, we believe that the interest of management should be identified as completely as possible with the interest of the stockholders. Compensation policies are keyed to this end.
2. *Organization* We believe that the operation divisions of the company are inescapably the profit centers. The company must be organized so that full responsibility for the profitable utilization of each division's assets rests with the division's General Manager.
3. *Pursuit of Profit* Profit must be pursued vigorously and without let-up in every area of operation, from the procurement of raw materials through the manufacturing and merchandising of the company's products and in the company's financial and administrative activities. The object is to maintain and enlarge operating earning power since this is the source of earnings per common share, which, in turn, build up the stockholders' equity.

   It is a general company policy that no product, plant or program will be maintained which is clearly unable to produce a satisfactory return on the capital employed.
4. *Capital Turnover* Maximum turnover of capital is essential to the realization of a satisfactory return on investment. Idle assets, of whatever type and for whatever reason, must be put to profitable use or disposed of. The money involved in this company must work as hard as the people do. To apply this principle, it is necessary to seek the lowest investment consistent with sound operations, and to maintain the closest possible control of inventories.
5. *Leverage* The principle of leverage is utilized deliberately to maximize the growth of earnings per share and of stockholders' equity. Debt and preferred stock, in that order, are therefore the chosen instruments for financing the growth of the company. Borrowed funds, however, must earn enough to justify their cost and risk, because leverage works both ways.
6. *No Dilution of the Common Stock* It is a fundamental principle of the company not to dilute the common stock. The use of debt and preferred stock accomplishes this, in addition to providing leverage. Common stock will not be used to acquire other businesses. It is used, however, on a limited scale to complete the identification of management interests with those of the stockholders.

7. *Growth by Acquisition* The management of this company is convinced that it is too risky to expand operating earning power from within through major improvement programs for established operations or for new productive capacity. This conviction is based in part on the assessments of textile industry conditions cited earlier, and in part on the results of past efforts to set up new operations, through investment in inventories and personnel, to take volume away from competitors. The volume can be obtained, but not at cost or prices which permit reasonable profits. The growth potential from acquisitions is both more immediate and more certain, and opportunities for acquiring other businesses appear likely to exist indefinitely in the textile industry. This is due to the excess equity capital locked in at unreasonably low (often negative) rates of return. Unable to correct the problems from within, or to solve personal tax problems, the owners find the sale of the business is the most practical, and frequently the sole alternative if they are to preserve their capital.

Summary: Five cardinal rules have been developed out of the company's experience which, when applied to any specific situation, should lead to the realization of our objectives:

1. Avoid catastrophe—but do not strive for the extra margin of safety which it is human nature to seek. Practice "Brinkmanship."
2. Maintain current operations at a profitable level.
3. Improve earning power, after satisfying rules 1 and 2 in that order.
4. In every phase of operation seek maximum return on minimum investment.
5. Play it straight. Whether in contact with the public, customers, stockholders, employees or any other individuals or groups, the only right way to deal with people is forthrightly and honestly.
   If any mistakes are made—admit them and correct them. Contracts should be honored and Indian Head has the right to expect the same performance from those people with whom it does business.[5]

Management's desire here was to extend the statement of the objective, so that its intent or purpose in major areas of the business would be clarified for all company employees. In this sense, then, these principles of growth or of action are part of the company's objective, for they give a more precise definition of the "character" of the enterprise.

A similar extended statement of objective and corporate philosophy has been made by Lockhead Aircraft (See Figure 4.1),[6] though the company uses slightly different terminology from that used by the other companies. As was the case with the three companies discussed above, Lockheed felt that a general statement of overall corporate objective was not enough and chose to amplify it.

[5]See Appendix C.
[6]Adapted from various published company reports.

Figure 4.1

LOCKHEED COMPANY'S STATEMENT OF PLANNING DIRECTIONS

The success that all of us are seeking for Lockheed depends upon the strength and teamwork of our people, and to build this all of us must know where we are heading and what it is we want to accomplish. Fundamentally we are seeking growth—to provide more opportunity for our people, continuing health for our corporation, increased service to our customers, and adequate returns for our stockholders.

But this is an overall and general target, and I thought you would like to know more specifically and in detail the direction we think Lockheed should be taking.

In this memorandum I am describing for you the series of basic corporate purposes, corporate objectives, and sales and profit goals that I recently distributed to company presidents and corporate officers for their use. Some of you may have seen these purposes and objectives in one form or another, but I want to be sure all of our management people have them clearly in mind and available for future reference.

Lockheed's Basic Purposes

The basic purposes of Lockheed are:

1. To be the major company satisfying in the highest technical sense the national security needs of the United States and its allies in space, air, land, and sea.
2. To employ technical resources in meeting the nondefense needs of governments and the requirements of commercial markets.
3. To achieve continuous growth of profits at a rate needed to attract and retain stockholder investment.
4. To recognize and appropriately discharge our responsibilities for the welfare of our employees, the communities in which we do business, and society as a whole.
5. To maintain a large proportion of sales in advanced technical products bearing the Lockheed name.
6. To maintain continuity of the enterprise by holding relatively low rates of change of ownership, management, and employees.

Corporate Objectives and Goals

The objectives we have set, based upon these purposes, can be divided into several important general areas:

1. Sales growth—To achieve growth in sales through (a) expansion of present lines of business, (b) internal development of new lines of business, and (c) acquisition. After reviewing the various long range plans of the companies, we have set an over-all Lockheed sales goal of $4 billion by 1976. This is about twice our current level and represents an annual compound growth rate of 7.2%. We aim for 25% of our 1976 sales in areas outside U.S. government national security business.

2. Profits—to accompany our growing sales with a steady increase in profits year by year. Our net earning goal for 1976 is $120 million, twice the current yearly total and an improvement over our present earnings-to-sales ratio of 2.8%

3. Markets—To broaden our role as a developer, systems manager, and supplier in air, space, sea, and land aspects of our national security programs. This means we must maintain and expand our present Air Force and Navy markets and considerably enlarge our Army and NASA business.

Another market objective is to employ resources in three nondefense areas: (1) We want to develop new sales, as long as they are profitable, by providing solutions to nondefense technological problems in which significant governmental support will be provided. (2) We aim for important sales volume in commercial nonaircraft markets.

(3) And we want to develop and produce by the early 1970's commercial aircraft that will capture an important share of the market.

Still in the market area, we want to expand foreign sales of our products from the current level of about 5% of total sales to 10% in 1976.

4. Diversification—To make a major diversification by acquisition or internal development and evolve several important businesses from current internal diversification activities such as ocean systems, information technology, prefab housing, and land vehicles. And of course, we will continue development of past acquisitions into sound and profitable businesses.

5. Research and development—To be a leading developer and user of advanced technology and maintain the highest technical capability in these disciplines and facilition necessary to achieve our market objectives. We strive for a significant fraction of our research and development through government contracts.

6. Management—To achieve recognized leadership in effective management methods that utilize our talents, experience, and the best computer techniques.

7. Facilities—To continue developing production facilities as up to date and efficient as any in our industry. And to produce in-house all systems and subsystems to the maximum extent practicable.

Putting First Things First

All of us have demanding jobs and many things to do. This means we must establish priorities—to focus on those things of primary importance. An understanding of our purposes and objectives as I have set them forth here should help us in putting first things first. I hope you will find this to be true.

You will notice the absence of references to people on this list. Our objectives and plans in regard to people are so important that I intend to discuss them in depth in a separate Management Memo. By means of such Memos, I propose to discuss other corporate thoughts with you and enlist your suggestions and help. Please feel free to offer your comments on this and subsequent Memos, either to appropriate company or corporate management or directly to me.

A statement of company strategy also sometimes supplements the statement of the objective. Business strategies, according to J. Thomas Cannon, are "the directional action decisions which are required competitively to achieve the company purposes."[7] Strategies spell out company objectives, and the means through which objectives are to be achieved.[8] There are overall strategies and strategies for such major areas as market development, product development, finance and administration, and general management.

A strategy is very simply the link between a company and its environment. It articulates the interrelationships between different areas of a company's business and its environment and specifies the company's objective and the general steps designed to achieve the objective. In some instances, as in the Blakeston and Wilson case discussed later in this chapter, the statement of the overall objective and major policies gives a clear

[7]J. Thomas Cannon, *Business Strategy and Policy* (New York: Harcourt, Brace and World, Inc., 1968), p. 9.

[8]Robert L. Katz, *Management of the Total Enterprise* (Englewood Cliffs, New Jersey: Prentice-Hall, 1970), Chapter Four, "The Concept of Corporate Strategy."

indication of the company's overall strategy, so that additional clarification in a separate statement of overall strategy is not needed. In essence, in such companies as Blakeston and Wilson, the overall Corporate objective and policy is the Company strategy. Statements of strategy are, however, developed for specific operating areas, such as marketing, in the Blakeston and Wilson study.

Indian Head Mills also clearly spells out its overall strategy under "Principles of Growth"—growth through acquisitions and maintenance of a high return on invested capital. This overall strategy was supplemented by specific strategies, such as the one specifying that each product or product line should "occupy a specialized niche in the market it serves." According to the company, "some particular competitive advantage—a customer's franchise, a long-term customer relationship built on performance, or a special technical or marketing skill—is present or is being developed in most of our operating divisions."[9]

Corporate strategies then are defined during this phase of planning. Once defined they may be presented in a number of ways: within the statements of objective, principles of action, philosophy, and policies, or in separate statements. Charles St. Thomas recommends including a separate statement of "company strategy" as part of the definition of the overall nature and direction of the company.[10] At a planning project on which this author is presently working, a statement of overall company strategy was added to the overall company plan. This strategy described in simple terms such strategic areas as: how the company was going to operate in its environment, the relative importance of the different areas of a company's business, and the limitations of their basic business activity. In this situation, the statement of strategy proved to be a very ueful focal point in developing coordinated action plans. A separate statement of strategy was also developed in *The National Observer* study described in Chapter 7. Separate statements of overall strategy are not always needed, however, providing that a company's basic business strategy is covered in other statements of the company's overall direction.

It is because this phase of planning articulates strategic directions for a company that it is called strategic planning.

AMPLIFYING THE OBJECTIVE: PLANNING PREMISES

Along with the statement of the objective in the planning document, some companies also include a statement of the major planning premises upon which the entire plan (including the objective) is based, in order to show how they have sized-up their own strengths and weaknesses, the resources

[9]Cannon, *Business Strategy and Policy*, p. 35.

[10]Charles T. St. Thomas, *Practical Business Planning: A Manager's Guide* (New York: American Management Association, 1965), pp. 94-95.

at their disposal, and the potential opportunities in the marketplace. Indian Head Mills' Policy Manual summarizes the major planning premises affecting strategic planning in a section immediately following the statement of a company's objective:

Special Problems of the Textile Industry

The textile industry offers special problems which must be overcome in order to reach the company's objective. The definition of these problems and the basic concepts which have been developed for solving them are an essential part of Indian Head Mills management philosophy.

It is the considered view of management that the textile industry in the United States is, at best, a static one. Although the market for textile and related products will grow with the expansion of population, the domestic textile industry and its owners are not likely to participate in this growth to any significant degree and for the following reasons:

1. *Domestic productive capacity* is greater than the market can absorb at prices which provide a reasonable return on the capital employed in the industry.
2. *The equity capital invested* in the industry is undisciplined in that it is chronically employed at rates of return lower than those obtainable from prime debt securities.
3. *The rapidly expanding competitive power of foreign textile producers* cannot be held at bay by tariff and similar market restrictions against foreign goods. In addition, nontextile products, both domestic and foreign, are constantly encroaching upon American textile markets.
4. *An irrational public policy* with regard to the nation's agricultural problems aggravates these competitive problems by maintaining raw material cost (for cotton and wool) at greatly inflated levels related to world markets. Federal tax rates on corporate income severely limit the power of business enterprise to retain profits for reinvestment to expand earning power to create more profits.
5. *The persistent advance of industrial wages*, reinforced by minimum wage legislation, constantly forces employment costs up and is a factor in the steady advance of general operating costs.
6. *No Relief in Sight.* It is believed that these problems will continue to dominate the textile industry for the foreseeable future, and the probability favors their becoming worse rather than better. While these problems are not unique to the textile industry, the narrowness of the profit margins on which the industry operates accentuates their impact because there is so little room for error.[11]

These were the reasons management presented to explain why Indian Head Mills was not irrevocably committed to the textile industry and why the company had an "investment company" orientation, which led it to grow through acquisitions rather than internal expansion.

[11]See Appendix C.

All statements of overall company objectives should include some sort of summary of major planning premises. Such statements make the objectives more understandable, expose the assumptions to wider scrutiny and refinement, give meaning to policy development and operating planning, and in general make for more complete strategic plans. Very few companies, however, seem to include planning premises in their statements of objectives.

THE FORMAT FOR PRESENTING OVERALL STRATEGIC DIRECTIONS

While most companies follow a similar pattern in developing overall corporate objectives, philosophy, principles of action and strategy, there is little agreement on the format of presentation. Varian Associates, for example, states their corporate philosophy in a section entitled "Premises" and divides their objective into eleven different sections.[12] Indian Head Mills states their planning premises under the title "Special Problems of the Textile Industry" and gives a very brief statement of their objective. And, as can be seen in Figure 4.1, Lockheed states their overall objective in a section entitled "Basic Purpose," which is amplified by a section entitled "Objectives and Goals," which is in reality a summary of the subobjectives in each major functional area of the business. The lack of consistency in the approach to stating objectives results in part from the inconsistent way basic planning terms are defined, in part from the varying needs of each company, and in part from the lack of consistent and widely accepted guidelines for preparing and stating corporate objectives.

The following are some recommended guidelines for presenting corporate objectives. They are based on the planning experience of the companies researched for this study.

A company's overall strategic directions can be presented in a four part format, beginning with a section entitled "Company Objective." Whereever possible, the statement in this section should be limited to one to four paragraphs. The purpose of stating the objective is to provide a *concise* picture of the kind of enterprise desired, so it should be as short as possible. In addition, long statements generally tend to include policy guidelines, as does Varian Associates', and these guidelines rightfully belong later in the plan.

If amplifications of the objective are desired, they can be made in a separate section entitled "Company Philosophy" or "Overall Principles of Action," which would expand the objectives statement or explain the management philosophy behind the objectives.

[12]M. Valliant Higginson, *Management Policies, Vol II: Sourcebook of Statements,* AMA Research Study No. 78. (New York: American Management Association, 1966), pp. 53-54.

A third section would give a statement of "Company Strategy," if a separate statement would not repeat material contained in the other sections and in the statements of overall company policies.

These statements of the overall direction should be followed by a fourth section summarizing the external and internal planning premises upon which corporate planning has been based. This section would be entitled "Planning Premises" or "Environmental and Company Factors Affecting Planning."

Whatever management decides should be included in the statement of overall strategic directions, the statement should be concise—that is, two or three pages at most.

DETERMINING THE BASIC ELEMENTS OF A CORPORATE OBJECTIVE

The above sections attempted to clarify what a company's overall objective is and how it is presented. The following sections discuss how an objective is developed. The first step in developing an overall company objective is to determine what aspects of the company's business should be covered in the objective.

During the early premising stages of the planning process, the planner is constantly formulating generalized ideas of what direction the company might follow in the future. As the analytical process progresses, these ideas begin to crystalize into statements of tentative objectives within the many areas affecting the company's success. For example, sometimes these tentative objectives may concern the industry or market the company will serve, sometimes the service or product which the company will offer, sometimes the function it will perform, sometimes the geographic areas in which the company will operate, sometimes its growth and the return on investment expectations, and sometimes its attitude towards society and people.

At the same time that these tentative, partial objectives are being developed, the planner should also be questioning just how important each of the areas in which alternatives are formulated is to the company's success. This is a vital step in building a comprehensive statement of a company's objective. During the "objective development" phase of his study the planner strives to identify the critical areas of the present and future that will affect the overall company operations and so should be included in the final statement of the company's overall objective.

Four areas almost always affect a company's success and so should be covered in the statement of the objective: the service or product which will be offered; the kinds of manufacturing and marketing operations the company will perform; the market or customer the company will serve or the industry in which the company will operate; and the company's expectations for the size, scope and profitability of its future operations.

This list of four elements can be expanded, according to the needs of the company being planned for. For example, in the Northern Illinois Gas Company statement of objectives given previously, the company chose to cover six areas:

1. The industry in which the company operated.
2. The product and the service offered.
3. The various operations performed.
4. The geographical location of the company's operations.
5. Its attitude towards the public.
6. Its general expectations for profit and for ownership distribution.

These particular areas seem to have been chosen because of the nature of the market served and the service offered by Northern Illinois Gas, and because of the limitations imposed by the company's resources. The following traces the reasoning behind the selection of these six areas.

1. *Industry.* The objective spells out the major industry within which the company will operate, namely, the gas industry, in order to give focus to all company activities.
2. *Product or Service Offered.* The company's principal business was to be the distribution of gas. Having a sizeable investment in gas producing and distributing properties and possessing a public franchise, the company could hardly go out of the gas business. Wishing to concentrate the company's efforts and not dissipate its energies across a wide range of businesses, management also limited the company from going into any other business than the gas business.
3. *Functions Performed.* Recognizing the need to supply the customer with complete and efficient service, the objective directs the company to perform all the necessary production, marketing and finance functions needed to maintain an effective gas distribution system.
4. *Scope of Operations.* The limitations of the geographic scope of the operation which result from the nature of the business are also recognized in the objective.
5. *Public Responsibilities.* Because the company is regulated, the objective recognizes the added burden the company carries for public responsibility.
6. *Profitability and Ownership.* As in most instances, the statement of objective includes some mention of profit and growth expectations, and the scope of ownership.

These areas were chosen, therefore, because in developing planning premises management determined that these areas were the most critical ones to its success and so should be covered in the objective. This decision about which areas to include is a crucial one, and should be made before any extensive analysis and evaluation is made of alternative objectives.

The structure and content of Indian Head Mills' objective differs considerably from that of Northern Illinois Gas. Indian Head considers return on investment as the primary objective of the company. The Indian Head Mills' Statement of Objectives includes some mention of market and service, but in sharp contrast to Northern Illinois Gas, Indian Head does not limit its area of business to the one it is currently in, textiles, but declares its intention to go into *any* profitable business venture. As a result of this investment company orientation, Indian Head specifically de-emphasizes customer service and superior workmanship as an end in itself, but only as a means to an end. Indian Head can do this because, unlike Northern Illinois Gas, Indian Head is not a government regulated company. It is clear from its Statement of Objectives that stockholder interests had a much greater influence on the shape of Indian Head's objective than it did on Northern Illinois Gas' objective, probably because Indian Head's major stockholders managed the company.

Given the resources available to Indian Head Mills, the limitations inherent in its market, and its owner-manager organization, the company's objective makes sense. In the same way, Northern Illinois Gas' statement is ideal for that particular company. While the statements differ in form and content, they have a common base. In both instances, the planners identified those areas which were significant to the long-term success of their companies—a major step in the development of objectives.

The following is a checklist of possible areas which should be considered in developing an objective and the questions which might be raised in each.

1. *Industry.* Exactly what industries is the company presently competing in? Can and should the company expand into other industries?
2. *Market.* What market is the company presently serving? Is the market growing, and at what rate? What products best suit this market? Should the market be expanded or narrowed? What is the competition in the market? What changes are anticipated in the structure of the market?
3. *Product or Service Offered.* What products or services does the company presently offer? Should any be eliminated? What additional products or services should the company plan to offer? What price ranges are best? What competing products and services are there?
4. *Customers.* Who are our present customers? Are there any additional categories of customers the company might serve? What are the customer service requirements? Can the company provide expanded services, or should the company narrow the range of services offered?
5. *Functions Performed.* What functions must be performed to achieve success in our industry and what is their interrelationship? Which of these functions is the company presently performing? Should the company expand to perform all manufacturing and marketing functions? Should the company try for greater control of its supply sources? Is a major expansion of resources needed to exploit major marketing opportunities and to what degree will company growth plans have to be limited because of this? How far should the company expand existing plant and manufacturing facilities?

6. *Social and Political Responsibilities.* What degree of government regulation is the company subject to, and what is the company's dependence on local labor markets? Do these factors have a significant enough impact on company operations to warrant covering them in the overall corporate objective?
7. *Scope of Operations.* Will the company be limited in geographical growth in the future?
8. *Size.* What is realistic expectation for growth in assets sales?
9. *Profitability.* What is a realistic expectation for Return on Investment?
10. *Ownership.* What limits does the company want to put on distribution of ownership?

Using this checklist, the planner can begin to determine early in the planning process those areas which should be covered in his company's objectives. By using this approach the planner begins to focus on the concept of the objective, before moving ahead to develop the statements of available alternatives.

An example of how a planner might select those areas to be covered in a company objective is found in the Blakeston and Wilson Company study.[13] In the Blakeston and Wilson Company study, five areas can be isolated which significantly affect the company's future: function performed; product or service offered; market or customer served; ownership; and size and scope of operation. These five areas were isolated by examining the problems facing the company and the factors affecting its future.

The Blakeston and Wilson Company was a small but expanding candy manuafcturer, whose president held 51% of the company stock. The company sold relatively high quality, medium-priced, boxed chocolates. The company had just within the past year opened its first retail shops; formerly it had sold only to wholesalers, chains and institutions. The opening of retail shops (the company had seven at the time the study was written) changed the entire character of the company—from a manufacturer-wholesaler to a manufacturer-retailer. The company was now at a crossroads: should it open more retail stores, or should it concentrate on manufacturing? The first critical question to be answered by the company, therefore, was what functions should it concentrate on?

As for the product or service offered, the second area, the company presently sold a very limited line of boxed chocolates, under the brand name "Perfection." They were considered medium-priced chocolates. If the company expanded its retail shops, would it also have to expand its product line and produce and sell low and high-priced chocolates, candy bars, other types of candy, or even related products, such as nuts?

A third question facing the company involved its customers. Should it

[13]See Appendix A. Although a disguised case situation is used for illustrative purposes here and in other chapters of this book, the situation closely parallels one in which the author was involved and in which the Company wished to remain anonymous.

continue to sell to chains and wholesalers, either under its own brand name "Perfection" or another name? Or, because of its limited production facilities, should it concentrate on selling only through its retail stores?

As for ownership, the fourth area significantly affecting the company's future, the president had evidently determined that he wanted to retain full control of the company. He personally ran the operations and made most of the decisions. The president had also brought in his daughter and son to work for the company, clearly signalling his intention to have a "family" company. These attitudes severely limited the training and development of middle managers outside the family.

These attitudes would also limit the size and scope of the company, the last critical area considered, and hold back expansion of retail stores. Limited management personnel, combined with limited manufacturing and financial resources, severely restricted the growth potential of the company—not only beyond its own region, but also within its own region. This question was an especially critical one for Blakeston and Wilson. If, as seemed likely, retail expansion should be continued, then ownership might have to be spread more widely and much greater management resources developed. If ownership was not expanded, then expansion objectives would have to be curtailed accordingly.

As can be seen from the above discussion, not all ten areas listed on the checklist were considered important enough to be considered in developing Blakeston and Wilson's final objective. For example, the company was too small to consider social responsibility an area of *major* concern. Only those areas of the ten considered which were important to Blakeston and Wilson were selected.

Since in reviewing the situation five areas seemed to be critical in considering the kind of company Blakeston and Wilson would be five years from the date of the study, it is within these areas that the planner would begin looking for valid alternatives.

DEVELOPING ALTERNATIVE OBJECTIVES AND SELECTING THE MOST PROMISING

The next step is to develop alternative objectives within each of the major areas selected, based on the study of the external and internal planning premises. Following are some of the more obvious and reasonable alternatives in the five major areas affecting Blakeston and Wilson's future:

1. As for the *function to be performed,* the company may become a manufacturer-retailer, or go back to being only a manufacturer-wholesaler.
2. As for *product or service offered,* the company can offer only its present "Perfection" boxed candy line, or a wide line of boxed chocolates, or a wide line of all types of candies, or a wide line of candies and other confectionaries. It can also offer candy under a variety of brand names.

3. As for *market or customers served,* the company can sell to the public solely through its own retail shops, or it can sell to wholesalers, chains and institutions, or it can sell to any combination of the four.
4. As for *ownership,* the president can maintain ownership and operational control, or he can elect to grow more rapidly in sales and profits by bringing in and developing a stronger management group and by widening stock ownership—providing that financial, manufacturing, and marketing resources can also be expanded.
5. As for *scope of operations,* the company can continue to operate within the same geographic area, or it can expand into other regions and eventually sell nationally.

None of these five areas are independent of each other, for they are all related in some way to the decision on retail expansion. A decision to serve both the retail and wholesale markets would probably dictate expanding the number of products offered and the brands under which they were offered in any region. A decision to double the number of stores would require expansion of production facilities, or elimination of some present wholesale and chain accounts, in order to be able to supply candy to the new stores. A decision to maintain the present closely-held ownership control would slow expansion of retail outlets by limiting management and financial resources.

By studying thc intcrrclationships among each of the five areas and the reasonableness of the alternatives, the planner can begin to develop a comprehensive statement of valid alternative overall objectives for Blakeston and Wilson. These statements would combine the various areas and the related alternatives within each area. Some of the more feasible alternatives the planner might consider are:

1. The objective of the Blakeston and Wilson Company is to be a closely-held manufacturer-retailer of a wide line of candy and related products, selling to all types of customers nationally.
2. The objective of the Blakeston and Wilson Company is to be a publicly-held manufacturer-retailer of a wide line of candy and related products, selling to all types of customers nationally.
3. The objective of the Blakeston and Wilson Company is to be a closely-held manufacturer-retailer of high quality boxed chocolates, selling principally through its own retail outlets, but also serving wholesale, chain and institutional customers with non-Perfection brand chocolates to the degree permitted by available production capacity.
4. The objective of the Blakeston and Wilson Company is to be a closely-held regional manufacturer-retailer of high-quality boxed and other types of chocolate candy, selling principally through its own retail outlets, but also serving wholesale, chain and institutional customers to the degree permitted by production.
5. The objective of the Blakeston and Wilson Company is to be a closely-held manufacturer-wholesaler of high-quality boxed chocolates, selling to wholesale, chain and institutional customers.

These are by no means the only alternatives available to Blakeston and Wilson. However, they represent a wide range of possibilities and enable the planner to begin his evaluation and subsequent refinement of objectives. If the planner wished to consider more alternatives, he would merely expand the same process and develop as many alternatives as he felt were reasonable and necessary to develop a satisfactory objective. What is important at this point is to identify the major *feasible* alternatives, not to identify *every possible* alternative.

EVALUATING ALTERNATIVE OBJECTIVES

In selecting the number of alternatives to evaluate, the planner would limit himself to no more than five or six during this phase, to keep his evaluation from becoming unwieldy. Where more alternatives seem appropriate, the planner would examine these after completing the first evaluation phase.

Five of the more reasonable alternative objectives for Blakeston and Wilson were developed for evaluation in the last section. The next step is to study and evaluate the advantages and disadvantages of each alternative, in order to determine which alternative is best.

The evaluation process which was used here and is given below roughly parallels that given by Kenneth Schnelle in *Case Analysis and Business Problem Solving* for evaluating and refining alternative courses of action and making a decision:[14]

1. State the planning premises or pertinent factors.
2. Develop a wide range of alternative objectives.
3. List the advantages and disadvantages of each alternative.
4. Evaluate the true significance of each advantage and disadvantage.
5. Narrow the number of alternatives to the most reasonable and refine the final alternatives.
6. Repeat the above process with additional alternatives, as often as time permits.
7. Evaluate the final alternatives in the light of how well they fulfill the conditions set forth in the planning premises.
8. Select the best alternative.

The following is a summary of the results of the evaluation of objectives for Blakeston and Wilson.

Alternative One: The objective of the Blakeston and Wilson Company is to be a closely-held manufacturer-retailer of a wide line of candy and related products, selling to all types of customers nationally.

The first alternative must be eliminated. Limited company resources argue against it. Attempting national expansion while maintaining close

[14]Kenneth E. Schnelle, *Case Analysis and Business Problem Solving* (New York:, McGraw-Hill Book Company, 1967), p. 39. Also see, Manley Howe Jones, *Executive Decision Making* (Rev. ed., Homewood, Illinois: Richard D. Irwin, Inc., 1962), Chapter 3.

control would mean very slow growth, so slow that the president would probably have died before it could be realized.

Alternative Two: The objective of the Blakeston and Wilson Company is to be a publicly-held manufacturer-retailer of a wide line of candy and related products, selling to all types of customers nationally.

The second alternative is feasible, but only over the very long term, since present financial and production resources are limited. This alternative would require the president to give up some of his 51% control over the company by selling stock to the public. It would also require bringing in some strong new managers. From the facts given in the case it appears unlikely that the president would do this, although this alternative should certainly be explored with him.

Alternative Three: The objective of the Blakeston and Wilson Company is to be closely-held manufacturer-retailer of high-quality boxed chocolates, selling principally through its own retail outlets, but also serving wholesale, chain and institutional customers with non-Perfection brand chocolates to the degree permitted by available production capacity.

The third alternative continues the company's expansion into what appears to be a very profitable area, retail stores. It enables the company to maintain a balance of outlets for its product, and to avoid competition with itself by having different brand names. However, this alternative sets limits on the line of products which could be offered through its retail stores, and fails to exploit a large and growing industry segment, candy bars.

Alternative Four: The objective of the Blakeston and Wilson company is to be a closely-held regional manufacturer-retailer of high-quality boxed and other types of chocolate candy, selling principally through its own retail outlets, but also serving wholesale, chain and institutional customers to the degree permitted by production.

The fourth alternative overcomes the objection to the third, by expanding the company's line of chocolates to include such items as candy bars. It also enables the president to retain ownership, and the Company to maintain full production by serving a variety of markets, and to increase its potential volume per outlet by expanding its product line.

Alternative Five: The objective of the Blakeston and Wilson Company is to be a closely-held manufacturer-wholesaler of high-quality boxed chocolates, selling to wholesale, chain and institutional customers.

The fifth alternative would be a step backwards. Since present company resources can sustain a modest expansion into the retail area and this area appears to be one of the better market opportunities available to Blakeston and Wilson, there seems to be no reason to take this step.

REVIEW AND REFINEMENT

If the planner has already determined from his study of the planning premises that the market for candy, especially boxed candies, is expanding and will not be subjected to too severe competition, his next step is to select and refine one of the above alternatives. Alternative four seems to strike the best balance between available market opportunities and limited company resources. If the planner feels that there are more alternatives open to Blakeston and Wilson he would repeat the above evaluation process, comparing his new alternatives to alternative four. If the planner felt he had covered all the major alternatives, he would proceed to examine alternative four more closely.

While the fourth alternative may seem adequate at first glance, the planner's job is not finished. The alternative still needs refinement. Some of the questions the planner might explore in this refining phase are:

1. Should we specify more clearly what is meant by "closely held?" Should we retain "closely held" at all or instead allow for the eventuality of broader ownership control?
2. Should we specify exactly what is meant by "other types of chocolate candy?" Should we be even more general and say "all types of chocolate candy?" Should we go even further and say "all types of candy" or "all types of candy and related products?" Since it has retail outlets, should Blakeston and Wilson consider distributing confectionary products it does not manufacture?
3. Should we re-examine the scope of operations? Should the company strive to eventually become a national enterprise through a gradual region by region expansion, or should it remain a regional company? Would the president be willing eventually to give up control, if it were the only means to go national?
4. Should the company bother to produce a non-Perfection brand or sell to non-owned outlets?
5. Is a wholly-owned retail chain really the right direction for Blakeston and Wilson, or should other alternatives, such as franchising, be considered?

Some of these questions may seem to go over the same ground, but it is important to review the basic questions again after a tentative objective has been selected. If possible, other executives would be asked to assist in the review to provide a fresh viewpoint and greater insight. Such questioning helps both to reaffirm the appropriateness of the objective and so help refine (and perhaps even redirect) it.

After considerable soul-searching and review, and after answering the additional questions asked above, the planner settled on the following statement:

> The objective of Blakeston and Wilson is to be a closely held regional manufacturer-retailer of a wide-range of candy and related products, selling principally

through its own retail outlets, but also serving other outlets as production permits.

This statement would then be amplified by the following statements of corporate philosophy:

1. Ownership of the company will remain closely held by the president, but not restricted to 51% ownership, in order to leave open avenues for attracting money and manpower to the company, as needed for growth.
2. The company will concentrate its efforts in its present area of operations, but will not be limited to it. Any expansion beyond this region will be slow, with a new region being opened only when retail shop concentration in that region would be adequate to eventually support a new medium-sized production facility.
3. The company will make only chocolate products. It may, however, add related products to its line through contract arrangements with other manufacturers.
4. The company will not limit the kinds of customers its serves, providing adequate production facilities are available for serving these customers. Perfection brand products will be sold to these other outlets only in those areas where Blakeston and Wilson does not have retail stores. Otherwise, a non-Perfection name will be used.
5. The company will continue to manage, finance and control retail outlets. At this time no provision is made for joint ventures with outside parties or franchising as a means of expanding retail outlets.

In addition, a section summarizing major planning premises was drawn up. It did not appear that the overall direction needed to be amplified with a statement of strategy, since the above statements gave a clear sense of the basic company strategy: the company would remain in the candy business, expanding into the retail area with an expanded product line, as rapidly as company resources permitted.

The process has admittedly been oversimplified, in order to give the reader an outline of the specific phases the planner goes through in developing an objective. For example, the above statements of philosophy could be refined further and the implications of such factors as the personal feelings of the owner-president might be more fully explored.

Nor does the process of review and refinement end with the final draft of the corporate objective and philosophy. Environmental conditions change, as do internal company circumstances. As changes occur, a company's objective may also change. As in the premising phase of the planning process, therefore, review and refinement is a continuing process during this phase. Periodic review is mandatory, and over a five-year period it is an unusual company that does not find that the cumulative effect of each annual review and restatement of the overall corporate objective has led to a dramatically new direction for the company.

The above discussion covers what a company objective is and how it is developed. While the complexity of the process will vary according to the size of the company being studied, the fundamental process remains the same—no matter how large or how small the company.

The question is frequently raised, "How can I be certain that I have picked the right direction?" You can't. The fact is that there are probably a number of good objectives. For example, there will probably always be successful manufacturers of candy who *don't* go into the retail business. The job of the planner is to pick a direction which appears to him to put the company's assets to work in the most productive and profitable way possible. As seen in Lockheed's experience in 1971, there is no guarantee that planning will assure success . . . it only helps to improve the chances of success.

What is important is that planner, by his development of an overall strategy, establishes a single direction for his company and outlines the steps which must be taken to achieve this objective efficiently. In this way there is a direction and focus for all company activities—an important key to corporate success. If these guidelines and the reasoning behind them are communicated to employees, everyone will be made aware of the problems and opportunities of doing business in the chosen area. Individual efforts will thus be coordinated, wasted efforts in unimportant areas will be minimized, and maximum use will be made of resources in achieving a single, specific objective in the most profitable way.

FUNCTION OF THE OBJECTIVE IN THE PLANNING PROCESS

The corporate objective functions to give focus and direction to all the subsequent steps in the planning process. Once an overall strategic direction for a company has been established, more specific guidelines are needed, if all corporate activities are to be effectively concentrated on achieving the overall corporate objective. These more specific strategic guidelines are usually in the form of overall company policies.

Implementation plans are also needed in all the areas of a company's operations. Sales forecasts and departmental strategies must be developed. Production, marketing, and financial programs and sub-plans must be established, based on the sales forecast and departmental strategies. And effective controls, administrative practices, and organization must also be developed, if plans are to be effectively administered.

Planning thus occurs at all levels in the organization, as corporate managers establish overall strategic directions, as marketing managers make plans to achieve company objectives, as production managers develop plans for cutting costs and meeting sales goals, as corporate management pulls together all the sub-plans—or even as the individual manager plans his daily work. In other words, planning occurs everywhere within an effective business enterprise.

The kind of planning done at the lower echelons differs in many ways from planning for the corporation as a whole. The scope of overall corporate planning is broader, the process more complex, the time span further into the future, and the direct effect on day-to-day operations less immediate. The process followed in all kinds of business planning is the same, however. The manager making a sales plan must still study external factors and internal resources, establish his strategic directions, and evolve ways of achieving that objective. The same is true of the managers in all the operating and staff areas.

This sub-planning should always be done within the framework of the overall corporate strategic objective. The marketing manager, in developing his departmental sub-plans, should use the corporate objective as one of his major planning premises. The individual manager planning his daily work in turn operates within the framework of his department plans, as well as the overall corporate strategic plans, so that he has even more specific planning guidelines. While overall corporate objectives may at first seem remote at the lowest level of planning, they do control that planning and so should serve as an overall reference point even for daily planning.

SUB-OBJECTIVES

Subsequent to establishing an overall strategic direction for a company, objectives must be established for each of the areas of the company's operation. Marketing, for example, will have an objective detailing the kind and degree of expansion wanted, and production, personnel, finance, and accounting will also have their own objectives. Each of these sub-objectives need to be achieved if the overall company objective is to be achieved.

Sub-objectives differ in many ways from the overall objective. First, they are often (though not always) quantitative, whereas the overall objective is not. For example, an overall objective may state that company operations are to be "profitable," whereas the financial sub-objective will spell out the desired return on investment. The overall objective may state that the company is to "expand rapidly," whereas the marketing sub-objective will spell out the dollar and unit sales expected by year. Second, sub-objectives are more limited in scope, for they deal with only one area of a company's operation.

Like the overall company objective, the sub-objectives for each operating and staff area cover the direction and general strategy for the area being planned for. In *The National Observer* case, for example, a circulation marketing strategy was developed, which spelled out "how" new subscribers would be obtained and old ones renewed and upgraded to longer-term, higher priced subscriptions through a variety of promotions and prices. Such a statement was needed in addition to operating objectives in order to give general direction to circulation marketing operations.

Ideally, these sub-objectives will be established by the middle managers, working in conjunction with higher management. To enable middle managers to do this phase of planning, overall objectives and other overall strategic guidelines must be communicated to lower levels of management. The overall strategic directions should then be discussed to avoid possible misunderstandings about them. Effective communication of overall objectives to all concerned management levels cannot be overemphasized, for without it effective business planning cannot be performed.

One method used at Indian Head Mills was to distribute an early draft of the company policy manual, which contained the basic elements of its overall strategic plan—company planning premises, objectives, corporate philosophy and policies. Comments were solicited from executives and meetings were held to hammer out the final draft.[15] Such an interchange assures the dissemination of a clear picture of the company's overall strategic directions and gives lower levels of management a base upon which to develop implementational plans—each with their own sub-objectives and strategies.

CONCLUSION: UNDERSTANDING THE ESSENCE OF THE PLANNING PROCESS

This chapter has outlined the steps to be followed in developing objectives:

1. Study the planning premises to determine the basic areas which should be included in the objective.
2. Develop possible alternative courses of action within each area.
3. Select the most reasonable alternatives.
4. Study the interrelationships among these alternatives to develop comprehensive statements of five or six alternative overall corporate objectives.
5. Evaluate these alternatives to determine the best one for the company involved.
6. Repeat the same process for any additional alternatives.
7. Select a tentative overall objective.
8. Review, refine and retest the tentative objective and make a clear statement of the final objective.
9. Determine whether such amplifications as a statement of corporate philosophy, principles of action, and overall strategy are needed, and develop them as called for.

[15] See Appendix C.

10. Communicate the statement of overall strategic directions to all managers involved in planning. Revise as needed.
11. Develop sub-objectives and strategies.

The basic concepts involved in this phase of the planning process are fairly clear. The company-wide strategic objective spells out the long-term, overall goal of all corporate activities, for it defines the kind of company desired by the owners. The corporate philosophy, principles of action, and corporate strategy amplify this objective. Policies are strategic guidelines for achieving that objective. Implementational sub-objectives are further extensions of the corporate objective and are the means of carrying it out.

These definitions are deceptively simple, however, for in developing plans a manager stumbles onto a number of problems. How specific should the objective be? If it is too specific, won't it overlap with policy statements? What is the distinction between policies and corporate philosophy? Don't they too sometimes overlap? While an objective is a goal, isn't it also a guideline for action, since it guides the action of individuals within the corporation?

The precise definitions of such terms as objectives and policies are not as important to the manager as an understanding of the process involved in planning, and of the general interrelationships of the parts of the process. The process of planning is a method of guiding future action. The process begins with the most general guidelines and directions of all, the overall planning premises and the objective. Systematically, the planner then develops more and more specific strategic guidelines: the corporate philosophy and principles of action are attempts to amplify the objective more clearly and understandably; and policies provide more specific guidelines, usually in the various operating staff areas of the business.

These overall strategic directions are then translated into more specific plans for achieving the objective and carrying out the overall strategy: implementation plans are individual area plans, with their own sub-objectives and operating strategies; budgets are attempts to quantify plans; and programs are plans for specific projects designed to further the attainment of the corporate objective. The summary and coordination of these specific implementation plans is carried out in the implementation phase of comprehensive planning.

Thus the process goes from establishing the most general guidelines through different levels of guidelines, each of which in turn is more specific than the last, in order to give direction to developing individual operating and staff plans. The exact dividing line between each level is never entirely clear, so that at times what one manager includes in his policy another may include under corporate philosophy with slightly different wording to make it more general. Exactly where such a statement appears is not the most important question. What is important is that the statement is written down and communicated to employees as an overall guideline for action.

All planning is done within the framework of the central strategic focus of corporate activity—the overall planning premises and the overall corporate objective and policies. Where overall strategic directions guide all activities throughout a business, where the hierarchy of objectives and interrelation of them with other parts of the planning process is understood and permeates all planning activities, then the planning within an organization will be integrated and unity of action is more likely to exist.

DISCUSSION QUESTIONS

1. What steps are followed in developing overall company objectives?
2. What kind of amplifications of the overall objective are needed, and under what circumstances?
3. What are the basic areas covered in the overall objective in the Blakeston and Wilson study? Why were these areas chosen and why were others eliminated?
4. What areas do you think should be covered in the objective of the Superb Biscuits Company, which is described in Appendix B?
5. Develop alternative objectives for the Superb Biscuits Company.
6. What are the steps involved in evaluating alternative overall objectives? Why are the planning premises so important during this phase of the planning process? Do they provide adequate criteria for evaluation in the Superb Biscuits case?
7. Evaluate the alternative objectives you developed for the Superb Biscuits Company, and select the best one.
8. Review and refine the objective finally chosen for the Superb Biscuits Company and develop a clear statement of the objective.
9. Does the overall corporate objective for the Superb Biscuits Company need amplification? Should you add a corporate philosophy section? A principles of action section? A statement of corporate strategy?
10. Define overall business strategy. Give a summary statement of an overall strategy for the Superb Biscuits Company.
11. Define the place of overall strategic planning in the planning process and its relation to implementation planning.
12. What is the relation between the overall corporate objective and sub-objectives?
13. What is the process followed in developing sub-objectives for staff and operating areas within a business?
14. Discuss the kind of strategic planning done as part of implementation planning and its relation to overall company strategic planning.

CHAPTER 5

OVERALL STRATEGIC GUIDELINES FOR ACTION: DEVELOPING POLICIES

This chapter concerns the next phase in the business planning process, developing and implementing policies to achieve the overall corporate objective. The first half of the chapter covers the definition of policies and their distinction from other planning concepts, the different levels of policies, the steps followed in formulating and implementing policies, and the criteria for evaluating policies. The second half discusses two company studies in overall corporate policy development.

SOME BASIC DEFINITIONS AND DISTINCTIONS

Policies are strategic general guidelines for action, which spell out what can and what cannot be done in all areas of a company's operation. Overall policies thus are generally designed both to convey to each manager a sense of where the company is going and to set limits on how the company should get there. For this reason, overall policy development is considered part of strategic planning.

The following definitions of policy, which amplify the one given above, are given in M. Valliant Higginson's *Management Policies*:[1]

> A policy is a guide for *carrying out* action. It establishes a specific course of action that has been adopted as expedient in order to govern the operations of an organization. Thus it expresses the philosophy, principles, and purposes of the organization, as well as its values. A policy is also a declaration of intent about an

[1] M. Valliant Higginson, *Management Policies, Vol. I: Their Development as Corporate Guides*, AMA Research Study No. 76 (New York: American Management Association, 1966), pp. 21-22.

organization's obligations and responsibilities. Since it indicates the manner in which the company wants to perform its activities, a policy states how goals are to be reached.

A policy is basically a statement, either expressed or implied, of those principles and rules that are set up by executive leadership as guides and constraints for the organization's thought and action. Its principal purpose is to enable executive leadership to relate properly the organization's work to its objectives.

These definitions clearly distinguish between policies and objectives: policies are called guidelines for action, while objectives are the ends to be achieved by that action. The use of the phrase "guidelines for action" can, however, lead to some confusion in understanding the two concepts. As every business executive knows, in a working situation an objective also guides action, for as the end to be achieved it functions as an overall guideline for all actions within the company. In practice, then, policies differ from objectives mainly in that policies provide more specific directions or guidelines for action, and set more specific limitations on what can and should be done by managers within a company.

Like the corporate objectives, corporate philosophy also forms a basis for policy, for it helps to explain a firm's reason for existence. As with the corporate objective, the distinction between policies and corporate principles or philosophy is also not always clear-cut. For example, in the Northern Illinois Gas Company study cited in the last chapter, the statement of the principle, "the company will pay a fair and just compensation comparable to what others are paying for like work," would be changed by some to "it is the *policy* of this company to pay a fair and just compensation comparable to what others are paying for like work." In the opinion of many executives this change is all that would be needed to change a "principle of action" into a policy.

The second statement is not, however, a policy. It provides no specific guidance. The statement merely tells what the company believes should be done. To turn this "principle" into a policy, the planner would define what was meant by "comparable," "compensation" and "like work," for example, in a general policy statement such as: "it is the policy of this company to pay salaries and give fringe benefits at least equal to what is given by competitive firms in similar communities, for work requiring the same skills and responsibilities." Or, the policy statement might be made even more specific, spelling out the types of fringe benefits, the kinds of communities, the specific work skills and responsibilities, and the levels of workers and management to which this policy applies. Without these clarifications, the original statement is too general to be a policy.

Corporate strategy and individual policies can also be distinguished. A statement of strategy is more inclusive than a single policy statement because it interrelates various goals and policies within a single, unified approach to a task.[2]

While the above distinctions are generally accepted by management authorities, there is nonetheless some confusion among management theorists as to how the terms are defined.[3] The confusion among these basic planning concepts is even greater in practice. As was seen in the discussion in the preceding chapter, objectives, philosophy, principles of action, and strategies are generally not consistently defined by business managers.

THE DIFFERENT LEVELS AND KINDS OF POLICIES

Just as there are many levels and kinds of objectives, ranging from overall corporate objectives down to specific derivative sub-objectives, there are many levels and kinds of policies, ranging from those of an overall corporate nature to derivative policies used in specific operating and staff areas. There can, in short, be policies for all management levels and types of decision making within a company.

Like objectives, policies can be arranged in a hierarchy of importance. Thus, there are overall corporate policies which extend the overall corporate objective, operating policies which extend operating objectives at the same time that they amplify overall corporate policies, and department policies that guide the achievement of specific departmental objectives within the limitations of higher levels of policy. The policy hierarchy corresponds to that of objectives, since policies are oriented towards specific objectives.

The following discussion concentrates on developing overall policies for both large and small companies. Development of policy guidelines for specific operating and staff areas is discussed in Chapter 8.

[2]Seymour Tilles, "How to Evaluate Corporate Strategy," in *Business Policy: Cases, Incidents, and Readings*, eds. Francis J. Bridges and Kenneth W. Olm (Boston: Allyn and Bacon, Inc. 1966), pp. 455-458. Also see J. Thomas Cannon, *Business Strategy and Policy* (New York: Harcourt, Brace and World, Inc., 1968), Introduction and Chapter One.

[3]For example, Charles L. Jamison in *Business Policy* (New York: Prentice-Hall, Inc., 1953), pp. 11 and 103, draws no clear distinction between objective and policy, when he states that a company's objectives are its main policies. He also does not distinguish sufficiently between procedures and policies, for he believes that policies are objectives concretized into procedures for action. Similarly, Merwin M. Hargrove, Ike H. Harrison, and Eugene L. Swearington in *Business Policy Cases with Behavioral Science Implications*, (Rev. ed.; Homewood, Illinois: Richard D. Irwin, Inc., 1966), pp. 10-11, while recognizing the fact that policies may implement objectives, considers policies to be general statements of goals and objectives. Paul M. Dauten, Jr. in "The Policy Formulation Process," in *Business Policy*, eds. Bridges and Olm, pp. 393-395, also considers objectives to be nothing more than master policies. Raymond J. Ziegler in *Business Policies and Decision Making*, (New York: Appleton-Century-Crofts, 1966), pp. 1-2, does not distinguish between policy and procedure but uses them interchangeably to describe the means by which a company reaches its objectives. And J. Thomas Cannon in *Business Strategy and Policy*, (New York: Harcourt, Brace and World, Inc., 1968), p. 10, uses the terms policy and strategy interchangeably.

THE FORMAL STEPS FOLLOWED IN DEVELOPING COMPANY POLICIES

The approach to overall policy development, which parallels the planning process, involves the following steps:

1. Define the level and kind of policies that will be developed or reviewed and revised; who will be handling policy development and administration, who will be affected by the policies, and to what use the policies will be put.
2. Analyze the nature of the company, its objectives, and the premises upon which all company planning is based. This step involves a thorough review of all the comprehensive planning done by the company.
3. Based on this preliminary research, establish tentative policies or evaluate present and proposed policies and suggest revisions.
4. Discuss the policies with the appropriate personnel who will be using the policies. This step involves communicating the exact nature and operation of the policies to all those who will use it or be affected by it, and obtaining feedback information.
5. Revise the proposed policies where necessary, recheck them with policy users where appropriate, and review the revised policies with the appropriate level of company management.
6. Put the policies into effect and preserve the policies in writing in a policy manual.
7. Establish a two-way communication between policy formulators and users, and establish criteria for judging the effectiveness of the policies.

Before undertaking policy formulation, a manager must determine who will be developing policies. The formulation of overall company policies in larger companies is a job that line management and staff personnel share with top management. Any level of management may recognize the need for policy formulation and initiate policy development or review. Operating managers may sense a lack of direction in certain areas of their operation and suggest ways to define clearer guidelines for action. Or, top management may recognize certain problem areas where policy definition is needed. Once the need for policy formulation is recognized then various levels of management will interact to create or redefine policies.

Where possible, a staff member or group should be assigned responsibility for coordinating overall policy development and writing overall policy statements. These staff policy developers could be part of an existing corporate staff group, such as organization planning and development, or of a specially created policy review and development committee, or they could be part of the planning group, though this is not a common practice. Because a good deal of work is involved in developing policies, a designated staff member or group is desirable to handle the additional work. A separate staff group also assures that there will be a periodic review and updating of policies.

Top management working with the company's officers and the board of directors should make the final decision on overall policy definition. Top management, because of its position in the company's organizational structure, is uniquely situated to decide on policy matters, for it is above departmental pressure groups and has the authority to decide issues of a basic corporate nature. Top management participation is required not only in making final policy decisions, but also throughout the formulation process.

Line personnel affected by the policies should participate where possible in policy formulation by offering their views on proposed policies or by offering suggestions for additions to or changes in policy. Their participation is important both because they are the ones who will be using the policies and because they are familiar with the policy's intended area of application. Participation in the formulation process should also increase their acceptance of policies.

In smaller companies, top management would most likely be responsible for developing overall policy statements, where there is no staff group to assign to the job. At lower management levels, formulation and revision of derivative policies is often handled by those responsible for the use of the policies. In these instances, either the operating manager himself or a committee assigned the task would perform the work involved in policy formulation. The general approach remains the same, however, in these situations, even though the job is much less complex.

The second step in developing policies is to examine the company's planning premises, its objectives, its existing policies and practices, and other pertinent planning factors. These other factors might include: values of our society, government and industry regulations, standards set by professional groups, values and interests of top corporate managers and owners, climate and type of management, company administrative practices, past policies and plans, and anticipated needs in any of these areas. This review of all planning factors provides a preliminary basis for developing new policies and evaluating existing policies, for it indicates the kinds of policies needed to meet corporate objectives.

The third step is to draft initial or revised statements of the policies needed. The degree of care and formality used in policy formulation should fit the policy level in question. For example, derivative policies initiated by a foreman to regulate the lunch schedules for his men do not require the same consideration as a company-wide policy on customer relations. In all instances where policies are not developed by those using the policies, the policy developers should work with policy users during the development stage.

The fourth step is to review the preliminary drafts of policies with the operating personnel who will be using the policies. This step may be a formal one, as in the Indian Head Mills study described later in this chapter. At Indian Head, a preliminary draft of the overall policy manual was drawn up by a staff group. The President then distributed the draft to all corporate executives and division managers, and asked for their comments. In smaller companies and at lower management levels, this step may be very close to step two, if the policy statement is relatively simple. No matter what the level of policy development, however, the final written policy statement should always be reviewed by the user.

As for the fifth step, any revisions made based on this review would in turn be reviewed with those higher level managers ultimately responsible for policy development. In all cases involving overall policies and major operating policies this final review would be with top company management.

Step Six, policy implementation and enforcement, should be handled by those managers who are familiar with the intent of the policy developers. The best way to insure effective policy implementation by managers at any level is to have them participate wherever possible in the development of the policy, so that they will be familiar with what the policy is intended to achieve.

Because of the turnover in management personnel, however, it is unlikely that all managers will have participated in the development of all the policies governing action in their area. Effective implementation and enforcement, therefore, ultimately depends upon the way that policies are promulgated and presented on a continuing basis. Policies can be promulgated and reviewed with new managers through personal contact between managers and policy formulators at training seminars or meetings, as well as through memos, bulletins, and policy manuals.

Written policies offer the best method for transmitting corporate policy intentions and reducing misunderstanding, since they cannot be altered during transmission. Writing also forces management to think more deeply about each policy's meaning, content, and purpose. Since written policies are more permanent than verbal statements, they are especially useful for employee orientation and training. Finally, written policies promote good human relations, since they give employees a guideline for what is expected of them.

The most effective way of presenting a written policy is in a policy manual. It offers a framework within which many policy statements and their supporting rules and procedures can be organized. It permits the reader to review corporate policy as a whole or at least the complete section with which he is concerned. Policies presented in this way are easier to understand and are more accessible to employees.

The organization and contents of the policy manual are affected by the size, organization, and complexity of the company. There are a number of general guidelines for policy manual preparation:

1. The introduction to individual policy manuals or overall company policy manuals should contain who the policies are intended for, their purpose, the

subjects or areas covered, the date they are effective, who approved them, a list of superceded policies (where applicable) and an index (where the manual is a large one). The manual should also contain an index to company form numbers cross indexed to the applicable policy area.

2. Where possible, a summary of the overall strategic planning base should be presented in the same document as the policies themselves. Indian Head Mills did this in their overall policy manual (see Appendix C), and this should be the procedure at least wherever *overall company* policies are presented.
3. The policies should cover all major areas affecting company profits, and be in sufficient detail to meet the needs of the management level for which they are written. Deciding the degree of specific detail is probably the most difficult aspect of policy development, and frequently the final solution will be an arbitrary one.
4. A separate section or manual should be devoted to each major staff and operating area, such as marketing, finance, manufacturing, personnel, and the like. Each section or manual should have a summary of basic objectives and strategies in the area, preceding the statements of specific policies in all key sectors. Normally the policy areas most important to company operations will be placed first.
5. The number of levels of policy development should be suited to company needs. In large companies, such as Sears and Roebuck, there are overall company policies, backed up by many levels of derivative policies for each division and section within that division. In these cases the overall policies are very general, with specific details spelled out in the lower level policies. Only two levels of policy seem needed in medium-sized companies such as Indian Head Mills. At Indian Head, more detail is included in the overall policies, since there was only one level of derivative policies supplementing these overall policies. At a small company, such as Blakeston and Wilson, only one level of policies may be needed, which combines both overall and derivative operating and staff policies in a single policy manual.
6. The style of the manual should be geared to the level of the reader, in order to establish contact with him. Explanations are kept concise and to the point. The use of simple imperative and declarative sentences as well as charts and graphs is particularly effective in this regard. Care must be taken in constructing a manual covering foreign operations to avoid potential tax problems arising from implied direct contact. In such instances, policies are worded as requests rather than instructions.
7. Where appropriate, procedures and rules supporting each policy would be presented along with the policy statement and explanation.
8. The length of the manual should be geared to the level and purpose of the policies. A complete policy manual, covering overall and all implementation policies, might very well cover 100 pages. A statement of overall company policies, such as Indian Head Mills' given in Appendix C, runs only 17 pages.

The seventh and last step in the policy formulation process involves evaluation and revision of policies. Policies are effective to the extent that they efficiently and effectively guide action toward stated objectives. This effectiveness can be determined in a number of ways.

Policies can be evaluated from the viewpoint of consistency—do they form an integrated pattern for goal achievement? For example, a firm's recruitment policies should be consistent with its promotional policies. If the firm fills its top management positions from within its own ranks, it should recruit a more qualified type of person at lower management levels than the firm that depends upon outsiders to fill higher management positions. In other words, the firm's recruitment policies, that is, the type of person it hires, must be consistent with its promotion policies, that is, the replacement of top management executives with qualified men from lower management levels. In addition, policies should be evaluated in relation to their consistency with company objectives and planning premises.

Policies can be evaluated for their practicality, that is, have they taken into account the available resources and organization, as well as any external influences affecting the company's operation? The company must have the facilities, money, manpower, and organization necessary to carry out its policies; those responsible for policy administration must have the authority necessary to put them into practice; and the influence of environmental factors must be reflected in the policies. If, in evaluating the effectiveness of policies, any of these areas have not been adequately considered, then policy development needs improvement and the policies may need to be revised. For example, if a company has a policy of promoting from within and of hiring people qualified for promotion, it must have the resources to train middle managers for higher positions, it must be able to pay higher salaries in order to attract more qualified people, and it must be ready to delegate authority in order to keep better qualified people happy.

Policies can also be evaluated for their usefulness, that is, do they reflect actual company practices, and are they being followed. Do they contain specific enough guidance for the management level to which they are directed? Are they too specific for the management level to which they are directed?

The evaluation of policies occurs both when they are being developed, and periodically after they have been implemented. This evaluation is best performed both by those who use the policies, and by those responsible for formulating them. The users are close to actual operations and so know whether policy is being followed or circumvented, and whether the policy system is useful to operating managers. The formulators are in the best position to compare and evaluate whether policies are furthering the achievement of overall company objectives.

A continuing two-way communication between policy users and formulators must, therefore, be maintained. This is accomplished directly through meetings and written reports, supplemented by personal contact between the policy originators and those who use and are directly affected by the policies in question. Where the company or operation is too small to support a separate staff for policy formulation, the managers responsible for policy development would handle the presentation and review of policies with policy users.

Attempts have been made to measure the effectiveness of a policy quantitatively. This is possible only in isolated instances. The quantitative evaluation is done by comparing the costs of implementing the policy with the benefits gained from it.[4] For example, a retailer might have a policy of servicing the product that he sells, rather than having the repairs performed by the manufacturer's factory. To evaluate this policy quantitatively, the company would determine the costs of its repair facilities. This cost would then be compared to the revenue earned from repairs performed on a fee basis and an estimate of additional sales generated by the good will created by the repair facility, in order to determine whether or not the investment in service facilities pays off. When the policy was first instituted, the lack of factory repair facilities may have led to the development of a company repair operation. However, if the reevaluation shows that the costs have become exorbitant, management might consider establishing repair facilities through local repairmen or converting its existing facilities into a concession.

A periodic review is needed in all companies to determine if policies need to be changed to meet changing business conditions. Where a company is having problems, inadequate policies may be one of the causes of the trouble; while in a prospering company they may seriously inhibit realizing full profit potential. Wherever possible, a specific individual in the company should be assigned responsibility for policy revision, even though policy revision is everyone's concern: the staff who originate policy; the top managers who approve it; the operating managers who participate in policy development, implementation, and evaluation; and those who work within the policies.

DEVELOPMENT OF OVERALL POLICIES AT INDIAN HEAD MILLS COMPANY

The experience of Indian Head Mills Company in the policy area provides an example of how to put theory into practice effectively when developing overall company policies at a medium-sized company. A copy of the preliminary draft of Indian Head's policy manual is given in Appendix C.[5]

[4]Melvin Anshen, "Price Tags for Business Policy," in *Management and Organizational Behavior Theories An Interdisciplinary Approach*, ed. William T. Greenwood (Cincinnati, Ohio: South-Western Publishing Company, 1965), pp. 257-258.

[5]See Appendix C. Mr. Robison, president of Indian Head Mills, requested that the reader be made aware that policies change with business conditions and that what was true in 1961 for Indian Head does not necessarily represent company views today.

The policy manual at Indian Head Mills was conceived as a self-contained summary of the company's strategic planning. In addition to the overall policies, the manual also gives the planning basis for them: the overall company objective, corporate philosophy or principles of action, and major planning premises. Overall policy development at Indian Head Mills thus was based directly on overall objectives, was considered an integral part of the comprehensive strategic planning, and was communicated to operating managers with the comprehensive strategic plan.

The overall policies were developed along with the overall directions for the company by a staff group working closely with the president and chairman, the board of directors, and the chief operating officers. Once a preliminary draft of the policy manual had been prepared by the staff, it was distributed by the president to those affected by the policies, the operating managers, for comment and revision.

The manual covers only overall company policies. Indian Head Mills is a diversified company, which operates in many different areas of the textile industry. In addition, each division is an autonomous profit center. The policy manual is thus limited to spelling out broad, general guidelines for action, in order to give the operating managers the flexibility needed to respond to the intense competitive pressures in each of their markets, and so better control profitability.

The major areas management chose for policy definition were: acquisitions; finance; manufacturing; marketing, personnel; public relations; and planning and control. These areas were selected because they were the major ones affecting company profits.

As was seen in the review of Indian Head's statement of its overall objective in Chapter 4, management felt that because of the depressed state of the textile industry, the fastest and most profitable way to expand and increase stockholder equity was through acquisitions. Policies in the acquisition area were thus defined first. Since the company started with very little capital and was in need of cash, finance was designated as the second most important area in which policies were needed. Policies in the other functional areas were then developed. The manual concluded with guidelines for planning and control.

Because policies were an integral part of the comprehensive strategic planning at Indian Head Mills, they were closely related to the company's overall objective. For example, the following policies are clearly designed specifically to carry out the overall objective of increasing the intrinsic value of Indian Head's common stock, that is, its invested capital and earning power per share.

> *Acquisitions*: Acquisitions should be made as far as possible with cash or borrowed funds rather than stock, since the issuance of additional shares risks dilution of the earnings and equity value (of the stock).

Marketing: The company's general marketing policy is to make maximum use of men, money, machinery and time. This requires high velocity of turnover and the maintenance of optimum inventory—neither the smallest nor the largest, but the one that permits the most effective marketing to be done with the least utilization of capital.

No products are to be kept in the line which cannot be made to provide a profit. It is impossible to make enough on the winners to overcome losses on the losers. It is not the policy of the company to have a complete line in order to keep a customer happy or provide extra service or convenience. Let competitors have the losers.

Manufacturing: Do not accumulate inventories, even though to do so has the effect of reducing unit costs. Total costs are what count.

Public Relations: The policy with respect to contributions of money or goods to charitable organizations and activities is to limit them to the cities and towns in which the company operates plants. The company's contribution policy is like all other policies directed to the achievement of Indian Head goals.

Personnel: In order to focus profit responsibility in the operating division, incentive compensation programs will be established on a divisional basis to the fullest possible extent, so as not to dilute the return on investment which would occur if profit sharing and bonus programs were on a company-wide basis.

The policies are also closely related to the planning premises. For example, the financial policy covering capital expenditures relates directly to the depressed state of the textile industry:

In relation to market value of textile securities, the bulk of fixed assets in the industry is valued at zero. The route preferred by Indian Head Mills for improvement of plants and fixed assets is to acquire existing textile assets which can be purchased well below book value.

In all policy areas, Indian Head's management took care to see that policies provided clear and specific guidelines as to how to carry out overall corporate strategic directions—the company objective, principles of growth, and philosophy. The integration of policy development with other parts of the overall planning process was helped considerably because the policies were presented in conjunction with overall corporate objectives and planning premises. Wherever possible, this is the format in which policies should be presented.

At the same time, corporate planners recognized that each division would be developing derivative policies for each of their operating areas. Care was also taken, therefore, to cover in the overall policy manual only those areas considered critical by top management and to avoid including material which would be covered in divisional policy guidelines.

As good as the original draft of the policy manual was, during the review of the policy manual by operating executives several areas were found where the consistency, practicality, and usefulness of the policies could be improved. Not all of the policy sections started with a general statement of overall directions and strategy for that area. Marketing, acquisitions, public relations, and planning and control had such statements, but finance had no strategy statement, and personnel had no overall summary statement at all. There was insufficient detail in such policies as "more frequent inventorying," and "do not accumulate inventories." And the format of the planning section was confusing and needed revision. Through this review process by the managers who would be using the manual, these and many other weaknesses were caught and improvements introduced before producing the final draft.

The Indian Head Mills study provides a fine example of how policy theory can be put into practice to develop practical overall policy guidelines.

POLICY FORMULATION FOR BLAKESTON AND WILSON COMPANY

The Blakeston and Wilson Company provides an example of over-all policy development at a small company.[6] While the general approach was the same as at Indian Head, the actual form of the policy statements and the procedure followed in developing them differed in many ways.

Since Blakeston and Wilson was a small company, and its operation centralized, only one policy manual was needed—except in the area of retail operations. This area required a separate manual for two reasons: first, it was the only area located outside the main office and so the only area not subject to direct supervision; second, a large number of guidelines (both policies and procedures) were needed covering all facets of the operation in detail, so that it would have been cumbersome to include them within the overall policy manual. In other areas, however, its was convenient to combine the statements of overall and implementation policies within a single manual. Since there was no staff available for the job, a consultant was used for the actual preparation of the policy statements.

The purpose of the manual was to provide guidelines for all company managers in carrying out their responsibilities. Specific department policies were included along with overall policies wherever possible. The manual was supplemented by a policy and procedural manual for store managers and procedural memos in other staff and operating areas as needed. The areas selected to be covered by the policies were marketing, manufacturing, personnel and administration, and finance and accounting. All of this information was included in a short general introduction to the manual.

[6]See Appendix A. Although a disguised case situation is used for illustrative purposes here and in other chapters of this book, the situation closely parallels one in which the author was involved and in which the company wished to remain anonymous.

The format of the manual was kept simple:

1. General Introduction
2. Overall Company Objective
3. Major Planning Premises
4. Company Policies
    a) Marketing
    b) Manufacturing
    c) Personnel and Administration
    d) Finance and Accounting

The first step in developing overall policies was to review the planning base developed in Chapters 3 and 4. As at Indian Head Mills, the manual contained an abbreviated statement of the planning base upon which the policies were built.

The overall company objective was given as follows:

> The objective of Blakeston and Wilson is to be a closely held regional manufacturer-retailer of a wide-range of candy and related products, selling principally through its own retail outlets, but also serving other outlets as production permits.

The assumptions or planning premises which gave direction to development of the objective and policies were divided into two parts: Industry and Market Factors, and Company Factors.

Some of the more important Industry and Market Factors included were:

1. There is a trend towards fewer wholesalers: Some large retailers are beginning to build their own candy factories, while manufacturing companies, such as Blakeston and Wilson, are going into the retail business.
2. Rationing is about to end (the time of the study was 1945), signalling the possible beginning of more severe competition at the retail level.
3. Boxed candy has had a strong growth trend and relatively good price stability in the past, and it seems reasonable to assume that this trend would continue into the future.
4. Candy bars represent the largest segment of the candy market.
5. Variety and chain stores are the fastest growing segment of the retail market. They generally sell bulk candies, which are bought on the basis of price.
6. The candy business is a highly seasonal business, with major peaks and valleys in sales during the year.

Some of the more important Company Factors included were:

1. The company has superior manufacturing facilities for high-quality boxed chocolates due to innovations in both machines and manufacturing techniques developed by Mr. Wilson, which enabled hand-dipping at an economical cost.
2. The company has good success in retail store operation on a limited scale through their Retail Management Corporation division.
3. The company believes in keeping sales expenses at a minimum.

4. Company growth has to this point been neither better nor worse than the industry in general, though its recent expansion into retail stores might lead to accelerated expansion in the future.
5. Although the company is small, its finances are in good shape.
6. The present owners would like to retain effective if not actual voting control of the company.

A summary of the corporate philosophy was also included under company planning factors, since it was felt that these were also an important aspect of the company's strategic plan. The five statements of corporate philosophy were given in Chapter 4.

Each policy area began with a statement of the objective and strategy for the area. The marketing objective, for example, was:

> The company will market through independent wholesalers and its own retail outlets both a high quality, medium-priced Perfection boxed candy, as well as other candies, confectionaries, and lower priced non-Perfection boxed chocolates throughout the central United States.

The marketing strategy was:

> The company will continue to serve wholesale accounts only so long as production permits, since its own retail outlets should always have first call on production, and production facilities will be expanded to service wholesale demand only if projected profits from that area justify it.
>
> New wholesale accounts will be solicited in areas where the company plans to open stores, so that there will be exposure of the Perfection brand name in that area prior to expanding with shops there. Wholesalers will be sold Perfection chocolates only in situations where they will not compete with our own stores; other wholesalers will be sold a second, lower-priced line of chocolates carrying another label (for example, "Yum-Yum"), only if and so long as demand warrants it.

The policies were designed to cover major aspects of each operation. For example, in the marketing area policies were developed for product, pricing, packaging, customers, distribution channels, advertising, store expansion, store location, store management, and product research and development.

The following are some selections from the marketing portion of the preliminary draft of the manual:

1. The company's product line will include high-quality, hand-dipped boxed chocolates, lower-quality boxed chocolates, candy bars and other related confectionary products. The other products will include non-chocolate candies and related confectionaries, such as nuts, which will be purchased from other suppliers.
2. While the quality of our Perfection boxed chocolates is equivalent to the quality of other high priced chocolates, they will be priced at the high end of the medium-price range established by the candy manufacturers association.

The chocolate bars will be priced at least 25% higher than the price of the mass produced candy bars, such as those made by Hershey. Their quality, therefore, should be superior to the mass produced bars.

3. The Company will employ two channels of distribution: wholly-owned retail shops and wholesalers.
4. Boxed chocolates will be sold under two brand names: Perfection and Yum-Yum. The Perfection brand will be sold through our own retailers and non-competitive wholesalers in high density areas. Yum-Yum chocolates will be sold through wholesalers in areas where there are Perfection Chocolate Shops. All other products sold by the company will carry the Perfection brand.
5. New wholesale accounts will be taken on in areas now served by Perfection stores, but they will be sold only Yum-Yum chocolates.
6. New wholesale accounts will be aggressively solicited in neighboring areas in which the company eventually hopes to open up Perfection Chocolate Shops, and these accounts will be sold Perfection boxed chocolates and related Perfection products.
7. The retail shops will continue to be incorporated separately and managed by our Retail Management Corporation.
8. Expansion of Perfection Chocolate Shops will be limited to these neighboring areas which can be economically served by our present production facilities. They will be opened only in high traffic areas. No stores will be opened merely to promote the Perfection name or give the company coverage of an area, for each store must be profitable in its own right or it should be closed.

The same steps were followed in developing policies for the other three areas: first, the policy developers designated the major aspects of the operation for which policies would be developed; second, specific policy statements were written. The following are some of the types of policies developed in the other three policy areas for the preliminary draft.

Manufacturing

—Products to be made
—Outlets served by manufacturing
—Production scheduling
—Quality control
—Facilities
—Manpower
—Work measurement standards
—Purchasing
—Warehousing
—Cost control standards
—Maintenance
—Control reporting

Finance

—Accounting and record keeping
—Cash bank balances
—Funds transfers

Administrative and Personnel

—Salaries
—Salary review
—Promotion
—Vacations
—Sick leaves
—Health insurance
—Safety
—Grievances
—Employee suggestions
—Employee discounts
—Executive compensation, promotion, etc.

—Debt financing
—Dividends
—Depreciation
—Payments
—Stock issues
—Insurance

As in the marketing area, specific policies were then developed for all areas and presented in the same format as those given in the marketing area. The policies in these three other areas were closely related to the policies in the marketing area. For example, in manufacturing one of the policies stated—"The company will manufacture only boxed chocolates, and purchase other products on a contract basis"—a policy closely related to the product-line policies in the marketing section of the policy manual. And in all cases the policies were rechecked for completeness and consistency against the planning factors.

Once a preliminary draft of the manual had been drawn up by the consultant, it was reviewed by the Board of Directors, the president, the production manager, the chief accountant, and the manager of the retail store division. The review process was much simpler at Blakeston and Wilson than at Indian Head, since there was daily direct contact between the president and his subordinate managers. Many changes were made based on this review. For example, the president requested deletion of the company planning factors and corporate philosophy statements on ownership, since he felt he might one day want to go public. In addition, the policy on pricing was expanded to include other products sold, and the following statement added:

> The price of other confectionary and candy products sold by the company through its retail stores will be based on the delivered price from the manufacturer, plus a 50% markup to cover the cost of handling display, spoilage and selling and to provide a reasonable profit.

The situation faced at Blakeston and Wilson was considerably more limited than at Indian Head. Only one policy manual was developed by the consultant—the manual outlining store operating policies and procedures had been written the year before by the president himself. Since both derivative operating and overall company policies were covered in the manual, except in the retail store area, the policies were more specific than at Indian Head's.

After the first year of use, the policy manual was reviewed again for consistency, practicability and usefulness—based upon the experience of the company managers. Revisions were recommended in several areas during this review. For example, Yum-Yum chocolates proved to be popular enough that modest advertising of the Yum-Yum name was undertaken. Company policies were changed to reflect such changes in market factors.

Revisions were also needed because of changes in environmental conditions. For example, more and more variety and chain stores began carrying higher priced chocolates, and supermarket chains also began to sell boxed chocolates. The policy on distribution channels was thus revised to include variety and chain stores.

In general, however, the policy manual proved to be an effective management tool, principally because of the systematic and organized way in which it was developed.

CONCLUSION

This chapter has outlined the approach to developing and administering overall company policies.

The two company studies discussed in this chapter illustrate how the approach was adopted in two types of policy situations. At Indian Head Mills, overall policies were developed for a medium-sized company. In that instance, the overall policies were fairly general, for each division developed additional lower level derivative policy manuals covering specific operating and staff areas. Examples of how derivative policies are developed for specific operating and staff areas are discussed in the Sears and Roebuck Company study in Chapter 8. At Blakeston and Wilson, a small company situation was studied. In that study, the policy statements were more specific, since in most areas there was only one level of policies, and overall and operating policies were covered in a single manual.

Each situation has its own peculiar requirements, and each company's policy manual or manuals must be constructed to meet these individual needs. Although there are these variations, the pattern is consistent: overall policies and specific operating and staff policies are both needed. Whether they are combined into single document or into many levels of policy manuals depends upon the size of the company, the nature of its organization and its business, and the level of management for which the policies are written.

The discussion in this chapter has concentrated on overall policy development. Overall policy formulation follows directly from the development of overall corporate objectives and overall policies must be based on and relate directly to fulfillment of the corporate objective. As such overall policy formulation is part of corporate strategic planning.

In order to help insure the success of policies, operating managers must participate in their development, for it is they who use the policies. Final authority for approval of overall policies should, however, rest with top company management, in order to be certain that the policies are consistent with other parts of the comprehensive plan. Procedures are also needed for reviewing policies for consistency, practicability, and usefulness after they are in use—and for revising them where necessary.

With the development of overall policies, the strategic phase of corporate planning is complete. The next phase of the business planning process discussed is implementation planning: developing specific operating and staff plans, including sub-objectives, strategies, policies, procedures, rules, action programs, and budgets; and incorporating their highlights into the overall comprehensive company plan and developing overall budgets, controls and organization plans. These areas of business planning are discussed in the following chapters.

DISCUSSION QUESTIONS

1. What is the place of policy development in the planning process?
2. In what ways are overall policies different from the corporate objective, philosophy, and strategy? In what ways are policies an integral part of a company's strategic planning?
3. What steps are followed in developing policies, and in putting them to work in an actual business situation?
4. Why must policies be constantly reviewed?
5. Discuss the different levels of policies needed within a company and the circumstances under which separate policy manuals would be needed for each level.
6. What is the relation of derivative operating and staff policies and overall company policies?
7. How closely did Indian Head Mills follow the "theoretical" approach in developing their overall policies?
8. In what ways was the approach to developing policies adopted to Blakeston and Wilson's individual requirements?
9. Why do you think a separate manual was needed for retail store operations at Blakeston and Wilson?
10. Review the Superb Biscuits Company case in Appendix B and develop overall policies for each functional area you consider important to their operation.
11. Why is it so necessary to have those who will use policies participate in their development?

CHAPTER 6

IMPLEMENTATION PLANNING

In addition to making overall strategic plans, detailed plans are also developed for reaching corporate objectives and carrying out corporate strategy. Since these plans are designed to carry out or "implement," they are often called implementation plans. Implementation planning includes preparing individual staff and operating plans, as well as coordinating and summarizing these plans and their budgets within the overall corporate plan. This chapter discusses the nature of implementation planning and develops an overall approach to it. The following chapters (7 through 11) discuss how this general approach is carried out in specific operating and staff areas. As such, this chapter is an introduction to the next four chapters.

THE NATURE OF IMPLEMENTATION PLANS

Overall strategic planning and implementation planning are closely related in practice. For example, when Blakeston and Wilson's management was developing an overall company objective, it was necessary to test the feasibility of each objective under consideration by studying such "implementation" questions as:

—What steps would have to be taken to reach the objective?
—Were the steps realistic and practical, and what were the consequences of taking these steps?
—How much would these planned steps cost in general, and what sales and profits would they produce?

While this type of analysis was clearly a part of strategic planning, the answers to these questions were at the same time the first phase of implementation planning, for they concerned the steps required to implement the proposed objective. Once the final objective was determined, the Blakeston and Wilson planner began his implementation planning by expanding and refining the projections made while evaluating alternative company objectives. In practice, therefore, implementation planning begins during the strategic planning phase.

Implementation plans can be developed by almost any level of management. In the marketing area, for example, the marketing manager will develop or have developed overall marketing objectives, strategies, policies, action programs, budgets and the like. He or his subordinate managers, if he has them, will also develop supporting plans, and programs covering each area of the marketing operation—plans to get new customers, keep his old ones, build his sales force, advertise and promote his products, and the like These supporting plans will be integrated within an overall marketing plan, while the highlights of the overall marketing plan will in turn be incorporated into the company's overall comprehensive plan.

The corporate treasurer will also develop plans for implementing company strategy. His plans will range from financial plans to meet the corporation's cash needs for the next five years, to plans for such specific operations as the transfer of cash. The first plan is a broad one, and closely related to the company's overall strategic plan. The second is department plan for a specific operating area, and is much narrower in scope.

The diagram given in Figure 6.1 shows the relationships among the the various levels and kinds of business planning.

The integration and coordination of planning activities is done at many levels in a company. The marketing manager will coordinate the planning activities of all areas under him, while the advertising manager will in turn coordinate the detailed planning in his area. In a large company, operating and staff plans may be coordinated by successively higher levels of division managers. In all companies, however, as is seen in Figure 6.1, individual operating and staff plans are always directly or indirectly coordinated within an overall company implementation plan. This overall plan brings together the highlights of individual operating and staff plans, details those parts having the greatest impact on overall company operations, and shows the effect of these plans on profits over the current and subsequent years. This overall implementation plan (and its budgets), together with a company's strategic plan, form the company's overall comprehensive plan.

The nature of the implementation plans developed for each operating and staff area of a company will vary in scope and importance depending on how much of the operation is being planned for, the use to which the plans will be put, the kind of business the company is in, the size of the company, the company's organization structure, the qualification and training of its personnel, and the like. The way in which overall and operational planners work together in coordinating implementation plans

Figure 6.1

VARIOUS LEVELS AND KINDS OF BUSINESS PLANS

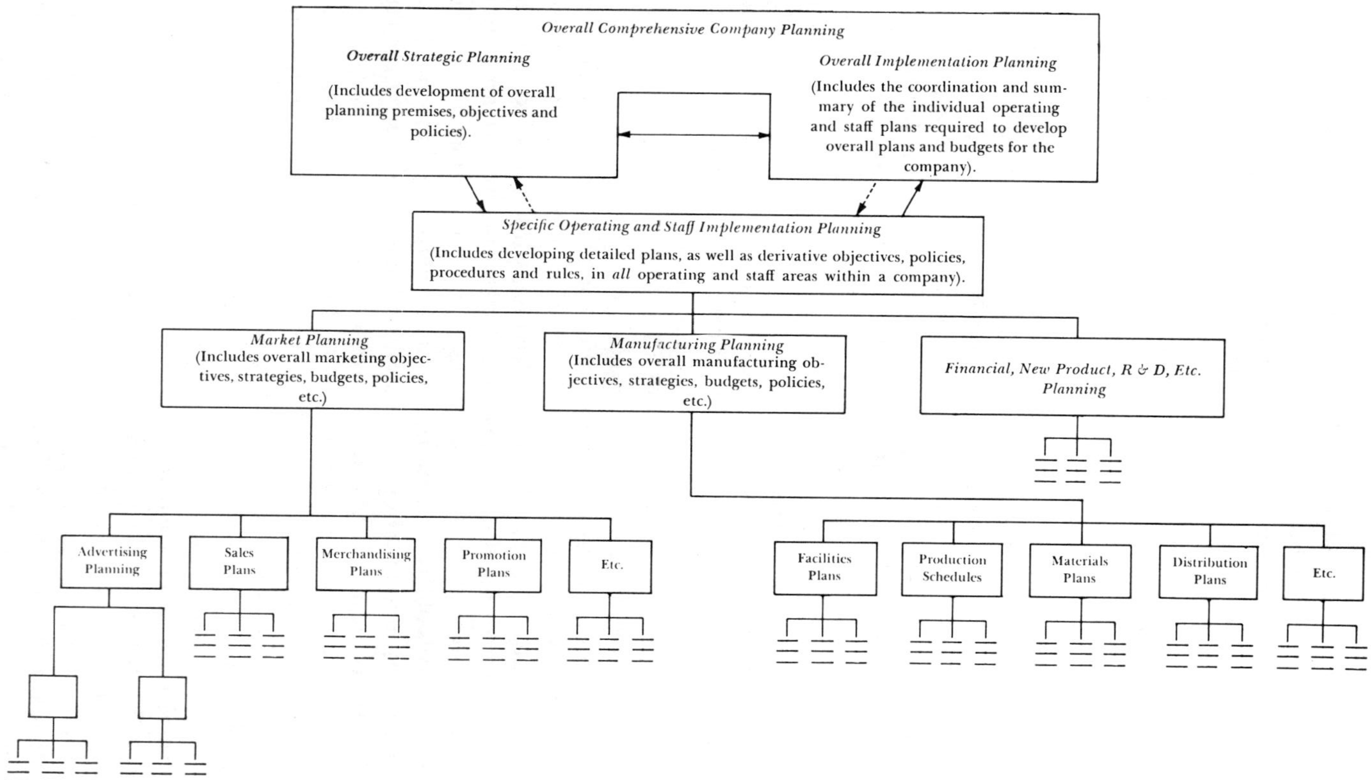

will also vary for the same reasons. The general approach to developing implementation plans is the same, however, no matter what the level or kind of implementation.

AN APPROACH TO IMPLEMENTATION PLANNING

In theory, the implementation phase of planning should flow directly from the strategic planning phase. In practice, however, this does not happen, for a company is a going concern whose operational patterns have already been established. In practice, the operating or staff manager models his current plans on previous plans. Using previous year's plans as a base, he will add some programs, cut costs where he can, increase sales by what he thinks is a percentage acceptable to management, and essentially do no more than adjust last year's plans to meet new strategic planning requirements. This is poor planning practice. While in doing his planning an operating or staff manager should draw information from last year's plans, he should at the same time look beyond them and where appropriate break old molds and patterns of thinking.

In addition to previous years' plans, an operating or staff manager may also be overly influenced by the "incentive" forecasts and budgets given him by higher management. Higher management has usually given him a goal or budget to meet, and in large measure he sees his job as devising the most efficient ways to reach that goal. While it would be naive to say that he should not keep a close eye on higher management's goals, he should also question and test their practicability. While he must work within the money and resources management allocates to his operation, he should also be alert to new areas where management could profitably spend more money, and to trouble spots where management may unknowingly be spending money unwisely.

In staff or operating planning, a conflict inevitably arises between the sales and profit forecasts which higher management believes realistically can be attained, and those which the managers believe can be attained. Frequently, this conflict increases current operating efficiency by forcing lower level managers to do more than they might have if not pushed. Just as frequently, however, it hinders effective planning; for it leads the manager to concentrate on developing expedient plans to meet management's forecasts or budgets, rather than on developing sound long-range plans which look beyond current operations and help fulfill overall company objectives.

Realistically, managers cannot ignore the dictates of higher management. In fulfilling these dictates, however, they can keep them in perspective by following a systematic approach to implementation planning which both focuses on long-term profits and satisfies management's short-term requirements.

The approach to implementation planning which was given in Chapter 1 closely parallels the overall planning process:

1. Define what the planning effort is to accomplish.
2. Isolate key factors.
3. Determine sub-objectives and derivative strategies, policies, procedures, and rules.
4. Develop a step-by-step plan of action.
5. Develop controls and coordinate planning.
6. Develop plans for organizing and administering the planned actions.
7. Carry out the plan, and review and refine the plan periodically.

The following sections discuss each of these steps.

Defining the Planning Effort

As in other kinds of planning, the implementation planner begins by determining what his planning effort is to accomplish and how it will be carried out. During this phase, he clarifies how the plans will be used, who will be using them, and in what ways they are related to other planning areas.

Isolating Key Factors

An implementation plan is designed to fulfill the corporate objective, using available corporate resources and working within the limitations and overall guidelines set forth in the corporate strategic plan. The first level of premises the implementation planner deals with, therefore, are the premises, objective, philosophy and general guidelines of the overall strategic plan. In most instances, the lower the level of the implementation plan, the less likely it is that the planner will automatically receive this information. He might, therefore, have to ask for what he needs—and preferably no more—and, if he does not get what he needs, learn to work with his own judgments of what the overall strategic directions are.

Working within the overall planning framework, the planner develops the premises applicable to his own specific planning problem. Higher management may spell out overall economic conditions and industry trends, but the planner determines which ones apply to his operation, and their impact on his operations. In addition, he goes beyond these premises to determine exactly what is going on in various segments of the markets he may be dealing with: what specific steps competitors are likely to take, what product improvements will be introduced, what his customers' plans are, whether the structure of the market is changing, whether new distribution channels are becoming available, and so on.

In most instances, higher management will tell the planner how much money and machinery is available for his operation, but he in turn will estimate how much money he can spend profitably. If this amount is more or less than that allocated, he would feed this information back to higher management, because it may lead to adjustments in the overall plans. Once final available resources have been settled, he will work out such specifics as how many salesmen can be hired with available funds or how soon new machinery will be available, in order to determine precisely what limitations he will have to work with in developing his plans.

Developing Sub-Objectives and Strategies

Each implementation planner determines specific objectives for the operation he is planning. Generally, there will be an overall objective related directly to his operation, backed up by a network of derivative objectives covering the various segments of his operation. Primary among his objectives will be specific sales or production forecasts and goals, profit forecasts, cost budgets, and other quantitative objectives either given to the planner by higher management or developed through his own investigations of what can reasonably be attained. These objectives should also cover the strategy guiding his operation, or be supplemented by a separate statement of strategy.

Developing Guidelines for Action

The individual manager refines, amplifies, and spells out the specific relationship of overall company policies to his operation. One example of such a development is given in the discussion of Sears Roebuck and Company in Chapter 8, where a general company policy involving customer service, "Satisfaction Guaranteed or Your Money Back," was amplified by four separate groups of derivative policies, each of which covered a different aspect of the service department's operations. Every overall corporate strategic plan should have general policies related to the major functional areas, such as marketing, finance and manufacturing, and these general policies have to be translated into more specific guidelines by each of the operating or staff managers.

Not only does the implementation planner translate corporate policies and the policies of such staff areas as personnel into policies for his operations. He also develops procedures (a prescribed step by step sequence of action) and rules (a prescribed action which should or should not be taken under specified circumstances) which are peculiar to his operations, and which he needs to guide and control his operation. This process is explained in some detail in Chapter 8.

Developing Action Plans

The heart of any implementation plan is the action steps which will be taken to achieve the objective. For example, in the marketing area, the manager develops promotion plans, advertising plans, salesman training plans, new product plans, and the like. Developing the details of these plans is discussed in the following chapter, Chapter 7.

Coordination and Control of Implementation Planning

Each level of implementation planning is coordinated and controlled by the next higher level of implementation planning, to be sure that individual plans have taken into account the planning in related areas. R & D planning, for example, is affected by maunfacturing, marketing, new product, and financial planning and in turn affects planning in those areas. Ultimately, all levels of implementation planning are coordinated within the overall company implementation plan. This process of coordination and control, which is done partially through the budgetary process, is discussed in Chapter 9.

Developing information for control and review of plans in today's business almost always involves the planner in systems development, electronic data processing, and the management sciences. These tools of planning, control, and coordination are discussed in Chapters 10 and 11.

Organization and Administration

Plans for organizing and administering action are also be developed as part of implementation planning. Reporting relationships must be established, responsibilities defined, staff hired, and communication channels established. Administrative procedures, particularly those establishing the ground-rules for inter-departmental dealings, are also needed. Organization planning, the last step in the business planning process, is discussed in Chapter 12.

Review and Refinement

The final step in the implementation planning process is to put the plan into operation, and review and refine the plan periodically.

CONCLUSION

This chapter has briefly outlined the nature of implementation plans and the steps involved in doing implementation planning. The following chapters, 7 through 12, give specific examples of how the general approach to implementation planning discussed in this chapter is carried out.

DISCUSSION QUESTIONS

1. Why is this phase of planning called implementation planning?
2. Discuss the ways in which implementation planning differs from overall strategic planning.

3. In what ways does overall strategic planning relate to and affect implementation planning?
4. Discuss the ways in which individual operating and staff planning affects overall company implementation planning and provides material for overall company plans.
5. List the various operating and staff areas which might be covered by implementation plans.
6. Outline the hierarchy of plans within a company.
7. Outline the process followed in developing implementation plans, and discuss its relationship to the overall business planning process.
8. Why does implementation planning always begin with an examination of the planning done at higher levels in the organization? What additional planning premises are needed in implementation planning in, for example, the marketing area?
9. What obstacles are sometimes encountered by lower level managers in studying the corporate strategic planning basis of implementation plans?
10. Describe the hierarchy of objectives which may be developed in marketing planning.
11. Discuss the problems involved in coordinating the various levels of implementation planning.
12. What are some of the more important tools used by the planner in coordinating and controlling his planning?

CHAPTER 7

PLANNING IN SPECIFIC OPERATING AND STAFF AREAS

This chapter discusses implementation planning in five important business areas: marketing; new products; research and development; manufacturing; and finance.

PLANNING FOR MARKETING

All implementation planning starts with the marketplace, for sales are what set into motion and support all other company operations. Such a customer orientation, according to St. Thomas, helps insure that "each critical decision is made with a foreknowledge of the impact of that decision upon its customers."[1] And Ferrell considers "customer orientation" to be "the fundamental concept which should direct the establishment and application of a business planning process with its related activities."[2] For these reasons, marketing planning is the area treated first in this chapter.

Planning for marketing begins with strategic company planning. For example, market factors are examined during the overall premising stage, and many basic questions about the marketing objectives are answered in establishing the final overall company objective. Thus, considerable groundwork for market planning has already been done and many major marketing questions have been answered *in general,* including:

1. What business are we in, and what business do we want to be in?
2. What services and/or products do we offer, and should we offer?

[1]Charles St. Thomas, *Practical Business Planning: A Manager's Guide* (New York: American Management Association, 1965), pp. 47.

[2]Robert W. Ferrell, *Customer-Oriented Planning* (New York: American Management Association, 1964), p. 6.

3. Who are our customers and what are their needs, now and in the future?
4. What are the characteristics of the industry and market and what are the significant trends within the industry and market?
5. What are our resources—such as money, manpower, research and development, sales and promotion experience and orientation, distribution systems, production capabilities—and what are our plans for strengthening our resources in each of these areas?
6. What are our overall marketing policies?

This preliminary information is only a start, however, and the planner should explore each of these questions as well as the entire marketing area in much greater depth, in order to have an adequate base upon which to build his marketing plan. The process used in doing this marketing planning follows the basic implementation planning process outlined in the preceding chapter.

First, the organization for marketing planning is established and the nature of the planning effort defined. While no two companies carry out this step in exactly the same way, there is a consistent pattern in the approach used by many companies. For example, in a recent study of planning in the marketing area in 126 U.S. companies,[3] responsibility for coordination of planning for marketing was assigned most often to product managers, marketing managers and vice presidents of marketing. In the majority of companies studied, individual marketing plans were prepared for each area of the marketing operation. Marketing planning was also done for all levels of operations—individual product lines, integrated marketing areas, company divisions or groups, and the corporation as a whole. Through this hierarchy of marketing plans, the highlights of individual marketing plans were successively incorporated into higher levels of planning and eventually into the overall company plan. Almost all of the companies developed an annual marketing plan in conjunction with a longer-term marketing plan (usually five years).

Second, planning premises are developed. Overall strategic planning provides basic premises for marketing planning. These premises include many factors covered in the earlier chapters of this book, such as: overall company objectives; relevant long- and short-term economic, political, social and technological trends; the company's financial, manufacturing, and distribution capabilities; and major company policies. As explained in Chapter 3, the overall industry and market information (especially the forecasts) would be broken down as much as possible by the market, geographic, and product areas served by the company.

These overall planning premises would then be supplemented by additional information on market segments within which the company

[3]Ernest C. Miller, *Marketing Planning: Approaches of Selected Companies*, AMA Research Study No. 81 (New York: American Management Association, 1967).

competed, including: anticipated competitive action; shifts in market structure and channels of distribution; price trends; and the legal and regulatory environment. Information is also needed on the characteristics of the existing marketing operation and its recent history, usually over the last five years. A checklist for this kind of information is given in Figure 7.1.[4] The checklist covers such areas as product, market, competition, financial results, and marketing operations. As can be seen from an examination of this list and the company studies described below, in planning for the future in the marketing area, such questions as who are the company's customers, what will be the customers' needs, what will they pay to satisfy them, and what products can be developed to fulfill these needs, are among the most important to be answered during this planning phase.

Figure 7.1

PRELIMINARY INFORMATION USED FOR MARKETING PLANNING

Product:

Models and sizes
Materials, workmanship, method of manufacture
Design
Quality
Unique characteristics
Packaging, material, size, shape, construction label, closure, competitive value
Brand-memory value, suggestiveness, line expansion, legal protection, goodwill value
Price by product: at factory
to wholesalers by type, size, territory
to retailers by type, size, territory
discounts—quality, cash, other allowances and deals
service charges
fair-trade position
Service—inspection, repair, refinishing
Delivery
Credit
Returned goods
Warranties
Complaints

Market:

Number of actual and potential consumers by territory
Characteristics of consumers—age, income, occupation, location, housing, sex, size of family, color, etc.
Place of purchase
Size of purchase
Time of purchase
Method of purchase—brand, impulse vs. planned, inspection, cash vs. credit
Purchase motivations and influences—decision maker

[4]Adapted from Bruce Payne, *Planning for Company Growth: The Executive's Guide to Effective Long-Range Planning* (New York: McGraw-Hill Book Company, 1963), pp. 122-126, Exhibit 5-2.

Favorable, unfavorable, and changing attitudes toward product—consumer and non-consumer
(Same data for retailers or wholesalers if relevant)
Shifts in importance of distribution channels

Competition:
Number and name of competitors—location and size
Number of brands—regional, local
Share of market by: product line
territory
Characteristics of products
Product differentiation
Estimates of competitive strength in terms of:

Knowledge of market
Coverage of market
Introduction of new products
Recognition of brand
Completeness of line
Quality
Style
Construction
Materials
Finish and color
Packaging
Credit policy
Pricing
Discounts
Advertising themes
Media used
Cooperative advertising
Aids for salesmen
Aids for dealers
Shows and exhibits
Publicity
Selective distribution
Warehousing
Delivery
Complaints
Warranties
Returned goods
Caliber of management
Caliber of salesmen
Dealer sales assistance
Salesmen's product knowledge
Salesmen's compensation
Sales reports
Salesmen's training
Recognition of sales performance

Financial: (last five years)
Total sales in dollars—
Total sales in units—
Total gross profit—
Per cent of sales for: personal selling/by territory
advertising
sales promotion
Dollar and unit sales by: months
product line
territory
type of outlet
number and size of orders
customer size
Gross profit by product line/territory/type of outlet
Per capita unit and dollar sales by market area
Share of market by total market, by territory
Relative profitability by: product
territory
customer
order size
salesmen/manufacturer representatives
Method of allocating costs

Marketing: (last five years)
- Total sales cost
- Cost per dollar of sales
  - unit of sales
  - customer
- Number of salesmen
- Calls per year by salesman—average per day
- Sales per call by salesman
- Recruiting and selection methods
- Training procedures
- Supervisory procedures—reports and controls
- Stimulation devices
- Compensation plan
- Administrative cost
- Total advertising cost
- Cost for trade and consumer media
- Advertising cost per dollar of sales, unit of sales, customer
- Media used—methods of selection and evaluation
- Schedules—size and frequency
- Appeals and themes—effectiveness
- Cost and methods of merchandising advertising—effectiveness
- Sales promotions cost per dollar, unit of sales and customer
- Types of activities—deals, premiums, bulletins, etc.—effectiveness
- Cooperative advertising—effectiveness
- Cost of publicity per dollar, unit, customer
- Volume of releases, etc.
- Media used
- Nature of releases—effectiveness
- Physical distribution facilities, size, nature, location
- Cost of shipping and delivery
- Time of shipping and delivery
- Inventory control procedures
- Warehouse and shipping volumes and costs by product/month

Third, the planner establishes marketing goals, policies, and strategies. The basic marketing objectives are closely related to overall company objectives. For example, the overall marketing objective developed for the Blakeston and Wilson Company in Chapter 5:

> The company will market through independent wholesalers and its own retail outlets both a high quality, medium priced Perfection boxed candy, as well as other candies, confectionaries, and lower priced non-Perfection boxed chocolates throughout the central United States.

is basically an extension into the marketing area of the company's overall corporate objective developed in Chapter 4:

> The objective of Blakeston and Wilson is to be a closely-held regional manufacturer-retailer of a wide-range of candy and related products, selling principally through it own retail outlets, but also serving other outlets with non-Perfection candies as production permits.

Marketing strategies are also usually developed at this point in the planning process. These strategies extend the prior steps in the process and are closely related to them. For example, Blakeston and Wilson's marketing strategy (given in Chapter 5) translates into more precise terms overall company and marketing directions within the limits set by overall company planning premises:

> The company will continue to serve wholesale accounts only so long as production permits, since its own retail outlets should always have first call on production, and production facilities will be expanded to service wholesale demand only if projected profits from that area justify it.
>
> New wholesale accounts will be solicited in areas where the company plans to open stores, so that there will be exposure of the Perfection brand name in that area prior to expanding with shops there. Wholesalers will be sold Perfection chocolates only in situations where they will not compete with our own stores; other wholesalers will be sold a second, lower-priced line of chocolates carrying another label (for example, "Yum-Yum"), only if and so long as demand warrants it.

A network of marketing sub-objectives is then created within this planning framework for significant aspects of the marketing operation. The marketing sub-objectives for Dow Chemical Company, for example, include "share of market, growth rate, planned capacity, image, field sales personnel deployment, manpower requirements, pricing, end-use patterns, advertising, promotion, and marketing budgets."[5] The network of sub-objectives will extend into as many areas and down to as many levels of the marketing operation as management feels is needed to adequately guide operating personnel.

As part of this step, marketing department policies and procedures are reviewed, and where necessary new policies are developed to supplement overall company policies. An example of marketing policies that were developed along with overall company policies for a small company was given in Chapter 5 in the discussion of the Blakeston and Wilson Company. An example of how a large company, Sears and Roebuck Company, carried out this phase of the planning process is given in Chapter 8.

The fourth step flows directly from the second and third, as specific marketing plans and programs are developed. A checklist of questions to be answered in developing marketing objectives, plans, and programs is given in Figure 7.2.[6] As can be seen from the list, basic definitions of objectives, marketing strategy, and financial objectives are first needed (sections I and II). Next, questions are answered as to what will be the company's products, product lines, markets, and competition over the period of the plan (sections III to V). Sections VI, VII and VIII cover specific marketing

[5]Miller, *Marketing Planning*, p. 16.
[6]Adapted from Payne, *Planning for Company Growth*, pp. 126-129, Exhibit 5-3.

plans, section IX plans for staffing, and section X the integration of marketing plans with other operations within the company.

Figure 7.2

QUESTIONS TO BE ANSWERED IN DEVELOPING A MARKETING PLAN

I. *Basic definition of business*
   - A. What is the best, brief definition of the nature of the business that the company should be in?
   - B. What should our basic marketing "philosophy" be?

II. *Financial*
   - A. What should be our objectives for profitability in this period?
   - B. What can we anticipate in terms of marketing cost-trends in this period?
   - C. What kind of a program or changes in our present program do we require to gain greater control over marketing costs?
   - D. What should our basic pricing policies be?
   - E. What should our basic objectives be in terms of financial stability, capital development, risk?
   - F. What changes or developments do we need in our methods of budgeting and cost control?

III. *Products*
   - A. What should our basic products be?
   - B. What are the particular strengths and weaknesses of our present product lines?
   - C. What products or product lines will be eliminated in this period?
   - D. What products or product lines will be modified and in what general direction in this period?
   - E. What new products will we have to develop and add to our product lines in this period?
   - F. What new technologies or manufacturing facilities will be required to accomplish the above?

IV. *Markets*
   - A. What broad markets should the company be serving, that is, consumer, institutional, government, etc.?
   - B. What specific segments of these markets should the company be serving?
   - C. What percentage of our total sales should be represented by each of these market segments?
   - D. What is the potential size and growth trend in each of these market sections?
   - E. What is the probable life of each market segment in terms of the company's products?
   - F. What are the particular advantages or disadvantages of these markets that will affect the company's future?
   - G. Who are the major customers in these markets that are important to the company?
   - H. What are the outstanding characteristics of these customers in terms of numbers, location, size, buying patterns, etc., related to the company's products?
   - I. What are the basic customer needs that the company is trying to serve in these markets?

V. *Competition*

A. What will be the nature of our primary competition in this period?
B. What should be our basic philosophy of competitive action?
C. What should our basic objectives be in terms of industry position, market share, product line matching, etc.?

VI. *Marketing planning and research*

A. What should be the basic objectives of our marketing planning?
B. What are the strengths and weaknesses of our present operations in terms of these objectives?
C. What kind of personnel or personnel skills will we require in order to accomplish these objectives?
D. What kind of a marketing research function or operation will we require to support the marketing planning and sales efforts?

VII. *Advertising and sales promotion*

A. What should be our basic objectives for advertising and sales promotion?
B. What are the strengths and weaknesses of our present operation in terms of these objectives?
C. What type and size of organization will we require to achieve these objectives?
D. What should be our basic strategy for the use of various promotion elements, such as space advertising, direct mail, sales and dealer aids, publicity, etc.?
E. What image of the company shall we attempt to create among customers, stockholders, employees, and others in the business and social community?
F. What, if any, changes or developments do we require in terms of our brand name and trademark policies, or in our brand management?
G. What can we anticipate in terms of our future relations with advertising agencies?

VIII. *Sales and distribution*

A. What will our basic strategy be in this period?
B. What are the strengths and weaknesses of our present sales and distribution operations?
C. What should our sales volume objectives be for the total company and for broad product lines?
D. What kind and size of a selling organization will be required?
E. What kind of a distribution system will be required?
F. What changes in existing sales and distribution organization will be required to accomplish the above?
G. What sales management personnel and skills will be required?
H. What kind of a compensation plan will we need?
I. What changes or development of our recruiting and training programs will be needed?
J. What kind of information system must be developed to give management a way to control and measure sales results?
K. What should our basic strategy for dealer development be?

IX. *Marketing organization and personnel*

A. What should be our basic "philosophy" of organization for marketing?
B. What should our major objectives be for marketing organization and personnel development in this period?

C. What kind of programs will we require in this period for recruiting, selection, training, supervision, compensation, simulation, and evaluation?
D. What kind of management development program will we require?

X. *Relationships with other functional groups*
A. What should and can marketing management contribute to the establishment of objectives for the new business developments, research and development, production, financial, legal, personnel, and corporate management groups?
B. What should marketing management's objectives be in terms of integrating its function with all of the above functions?
C. What particular strengths and weaknesses do we presently have in terms of the above?

In the marketing area specific plans are needed for all areas of the marketing operation: pricing, products, markets, market research and analysis, advertising and sales promotion, field sales, distribution, organization and staffing, and coordination with manufacturing and other operating divisions. The emphasis given each of these areas will, as is seen in the examples described below, depend on such variable factors as the size of the company and the nature of its business.

The fifth and last step in marketing planning would be to develop procedures for reviewing, controlling, and revising plans. This phase involves quantifying plans in the form of budgets.

Each company will adapt these steps to meet its own particular requirements. For example, the approach used by the General Electric Company is shown in Figure 7.3.[7] While the specific areas in which plans are developed at GE may differ from those of other companies, because of difference in the size and nature of the company's business, the general pattern of its planning for marketing is the same as the one described above: the customer and market are analyzed to determine market needs; other overall planning premises and objectives are isolated; product plans are developed, as are sales forecasts and master sales plans; plans are then created for each marketing operation; and finally, specific selling and distribution programs are evolved. GE's process, as can be seen from the chart, begins and ends with the customer. In addition to the above steps in marketing planning, GE also has a budgetary process to control the carrying out of the plans, and for making revisions in plans.

The market plan developed at International Paper Company for one of its product divisions, Business Forms, provides another illustration of how the planning process is adapted by individual companies to specific planning situations. The section of International Paper's market plan dealing with business forms is divided into four parts, as follows:[8]

[7] Miller, *Marketing Planning*, p. 20.

[8] Miller, *Marketing Planning*, pp. 33-34. For a description of the approach to marketing planning used by Hooker Chemical Corporation, see: William F. Christopher, "Marketing Planning that Gets Things Done," *Harvard Business Review*, September-October 1970, pp. 56-64.

Figure 7.3

GENERAL ELECTRIC: MARKETING PLANNING PROCESS*

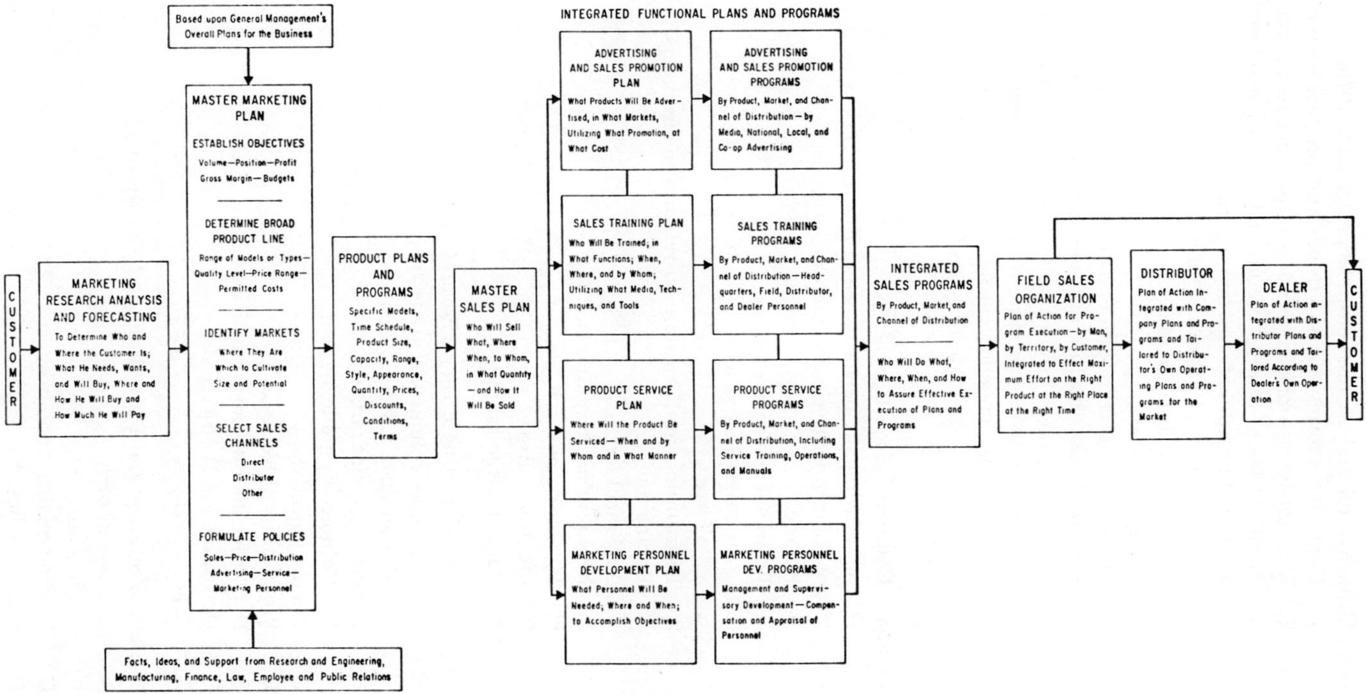

*Copyright by General Electric Company. Reprinted with permission of the General Electric Company.

I. Marketing Environment
  A. Growth of the end-use market—1958 projected to 1970:
    1. Continuous forms—market trends and product requirements.
    2. Unit set forms—market trends and product requirements.
    3. Manifold books—market trends and product requirements.
  B. Description of manifold forms manufacturing:
    1. Number and size of manufacturers.
    2. Geographical distribution.
    3. Foreign markets.
  C. Growth of the market for grades used in manifold forms—1958 to 1970:
    1. Register bond—product tonnage and physical requirements.
    2. Computer paper—product tonnage and physical requirements.
    3. Carbonizing tissue—product tonnage and physical requirements.
    4. Carbonless paper—effect on the markets for other grades.
  D. Demand analysis—estimate of manufacturers' requirements by grades to 1970.

II. Company Competitive Position
  A. History of company performance in this market—by grade.
  B. History of competitive performance—by grade.
    1. Pricing.
    2. Projected new market entries.
  C. Company strengths and weaknesses in this market:
    1. Sales force.
    2. Distribution—mill location in relation to customers.
    3. Pricing policy.
    4. Technical services.
    5. New product development.
    6. Marketing research.
    7. Quality control.
    8. Pulp and wood supply.

III. Objectives for Marketing Business Forms Grades
  A. Projected sales volume—by grade, by year:
    1. Market share.
  B. Projected account targets:
    1. Volume—by grade, by year.
  C. Pricing objectives.
  D. Profitability objectives.
  E. Derivative manufacturing policies.
  F. Derivative R & D objectives.
  G. Other objectives.

IV. Marketing Strategy and Plan (Long-and Short-Range)
  A. Account strategy.
  B. Product mix.
  C. Product quality standards.
  D. Pricing policy.
  E. Channels of distribution.

F. Sales force deployment.
G. Sales training and special sales techniques.
H. Sales promotion.
I. Advertising and publicity campaign:
 1. Product advertising.
 2. Promotion of the __________ mill.
J. Market surveillance and marketing research.
K. Research and product development direction.
L. Manufacturing aspects of the marketing plan.
M. Overall budget.
N. Timetable.
O. Measurement of performance versus plan.

The above planning process deals with only one product line within the company's marketing area, so that the focus of the plan is limited, and broad marketing planning factors are not specified in this particular segment of the company's master plan. The outline of the process, however, even in this fairly limited area is very close to the general approach to planning for marketing given above. The first two parts of the plan correspond to steps two and three in the planning process, dealing as they do with company and market background factors. Part Three develops specific objectives, the next step in the process, and Part Four spells out strategies and plans for specific marketing areas. As in the GE approach to planning, International Paper Company uses a separate budgetary process to control progress in meeting planned marketing goals and to review and revise plans.

These are only two examples, however, of how the marketing planning process is put to work. The situations to which the marketing planning process can be applied are legion, ranging from very small companies to very large companies, from overall marking plans to specific advertising and selling plans, from specialized single-product industrial companies to mass consumer-product companies and widely diversified multi-product companies. In order to show in detail how the planning process is carried out in the marketing area, the following sections describe a study done for a relatively small marketing operation. The study was made at Dow Jones and Company and involved their new publication, *The National Observer.*

Defining the Basic Problem

The National Observer, which was introduced by Dow Jones on February 4, 1962, was designed to be the first national family weekly newspaper in this country. Dow Jones seemed to be in an ideal position to publish *The Observer,* for the company was in the publishing business and had the printing, editorial, fulfillment, circulation, and sales operations needed to handle the new publication. It also had over $20,000,000 in uncommitted cash reserves available for developing new products which would help the company achieve its long-range objective of becoming a broad-based publishing company.

Figure 7.4

THE NATIONAL OBSERVER

Circulation 1962-1963

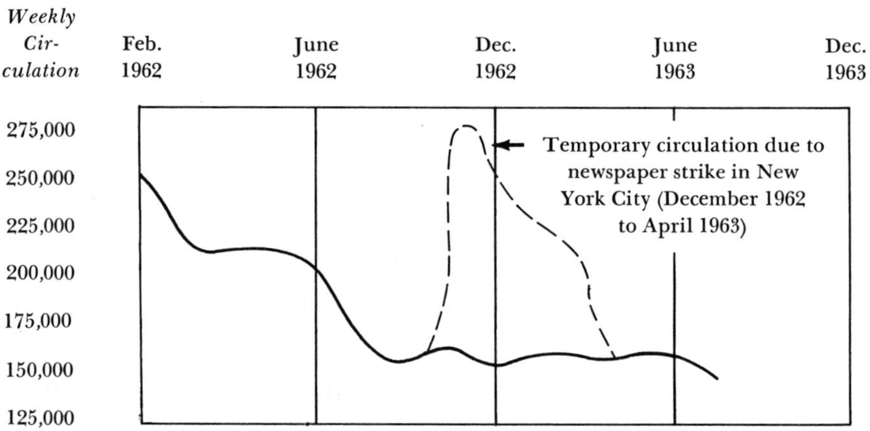

Even though after one year of publication the new paper was selling over 125,000 copies a week, circulation results (see Figure 7.4) made it clear that the paper was having marketing problems. By the end of 1962, Dow Jones realized that something had to be done, and done quickly, if the new publication was to be successful. The company decided to seek outside help with experience in marketing publications of general consumer interest, and early in March 1963 a consultant was engaged to develop a new marketing program for *The Observer*'s circulation operation.

One major cause of *The Observer*'s marketing troubles was the new publication's over-reliance on past corporate experience. Because of the operating savings involved, all *The Observer*'s marketing operations had been placed under existing Dow Jones departments. As a result of this integration of operations, the marketing methods which had been so successful for *The Wall Street Journal* (a daily financial-business newspaper) were used in marketing the new publication (a general consumer news weekly), and *The Observer*'s staff did not have the freedom to develop marketing programs tailored to the paper's own needs.

Once the paper's basic problem was recognized—that is, over-reliance on *The Journal*'s marketing approach—all those concerned agreed that new marketing objectives, policies, and programs independent of what

The Journal had done and would do, had to be developed for *The Observer* and put into operation.

Reappraising the Planning Premises and Establishing a New Direction

Through an analysis of the new publication's operations during 1962, it was possible to pinpoint what had gone wrong with the paper's initial marketing program, and what steps would have to be taken to reverse the declining circulation trend.

The Observer's market was first redefined. On the basis of their brief, initial analysis of the industry, Dow Jones had concluded that a large segment of the nation's readers was not reached by major local weekly newspapers and news magazines, or was dissatisfied with what it found in them. In attempting to fill that market gap, Dow Jones had concentrated on the newspaper market because of their past marketing experience in that area, and because they owned newspaper presses and so could produce the paper during free press time.

The Observer was unable, however, to compete effectively with Sunday newspapers for the following reasons:

1. Major regional Sunday newspapers—such as those in New York, Washington, and Los Angeles—had many more pages and covered essential local news not found in *The Observer*, yet they sold for about the same price.
2. The Sunday newspaper market is served mainly by single-copy newsstand sales. Because of transportation delays and because *The Observer* had to be printed on Saturday afternoon (if it was to use free press time), Sunday morning newsstand distribution on a national level outside major metropolitan centers was expensive and difficult. Competing local newspapers were, however, accustomed to fast delivery schedules, and were able to distribute more economically, because they had concentrated sales in a limited area.

Comments from readers and other newly-developed market research information showed that while there was a market for the new paper, this market was in reality much closer to that of the weekly news magazines than to that of the regional Sunday newspapers.

A new circulation marketing objective, based on this review of key factors affecting market planning, was then established: to compete aggressively in the national weekly news magazine market, and to exploit local newspaper markets only where economical.

Next, a number of new policy guidelines consistent with this objective were developed:

1. In contrast to the Sunday newspaper market, the weekly news magazine market is a national market which is served mainly by subscriptions delivered by mail. Under the new circulation program, therefore, sales efforts would be concentrated on subscription selling.

2. The major competing news weeklies, *Time, Newsweek,* and *U.S. News and World Report,* had color, convenient size, and broad editorial resources, all of which *The Observer* lacked. To overcome these disadvantages, *The Observer* needed new, more aggressive promotions, such as discount and credit inducements to new and old subscribers. Neither of these inducements had been used under the old program.
3. *The Observer*'s circulation operation now needed a staff skilled in mail-order subscription selling, a staff experienced in fathoming basic consumer motivation, in testing advertising scientifically, and in creating efficient national advertising programs. Under the old program *The Observer* had a circulation staff skilled in dealing with local newspaper wholesalers and retailers, and in selling single copies of a newspaper through retail outlets.
4. The dateline on the paper, which had initially been Sunday in order to be competitive with other Sunday newspapers, had to be moved forward, so that the publication would appear current to subscribers, who received their papers by mail on Monday or Tuesday.
5. The distribution and fulfillment departments now had to be prepared to handle a greater volume of subscription business. Their operations also had to be more closely coordinated with those of the circulation department, since extensive testing would be conducted and since superior subscriber service was essential to a strong, growing subscription circulation.

It was within these fundamental marketing guidelines that *The National Observer*'s new circulation marketing program was developed in 1963.

Building a New Action Plan for Circulation

A new selling strategy based on the reappraisal of *The Observer*'s market was then developed. The new strategy was similar to that used successfully by competing weekly news magazines, and quite different from that used by local newspapers.

Introductory subscriptions were sold to the public through advertising, direct-mail, and other sales programs. These subscriptions were generally sold on credit and at a discount, and were for at least five months duration. After a new subscription order was received, the subscriber was billed and delivery begun; if payment was not received within a reasonable period of time, the subscription was stopped. The public was also encouraged to buy the publication at newsstands in the hope that they would later order subscriptions.

When a trial subscription was about to end, or expire, direct mail promotions were sent urging the subscriber to renew. Normally, about 40% of these subscribers renewed their trial subscriptions for at least a year, if they were not offered shorter-term renewals and if they were offered a special discount. In subsequent years, about 75% of these established regular subscriptions would be renewed again for one year or more, if the publication was a good one and if the publication's price structure included longer-term discount offers.

Figure 7.5

THE NATIONAL OBSERVER

New Price Structure

Type of Offer	*Term*	*Price* *Original* (1962-3)	*New* (1964-5)
Regular and Renewal Subscriptions:	3 mos.	$ 3.50	—
	6 mos.	$ 6.00	—
	1 yr.	$10.00	$10.00
	2 yrs.	—	$15.00
	3 yrs.	—	$19.00
	5 yrs.	—	$25.00
Special Subscriptions:			
Introductory trial—	13 wks.	$ 2.67	—
(for new subscribers	20 wks.	$ 3.88	$ 1.97
only)	27 wks.	—	$ 2.67
	38 wks.	—	$ 3.88
Renewal—(made only to	1 yr.	—	$ 5.00
trial subscribers)	57 wks.	—	$ 5.67
Single Copy		$ .25	$ .25

A new price structure (see Figure 7.5) which carried out this strategy was established after extensive testing, and a new circulation sales and flow plan developed. This flow plan, which also served as the sales budget for the coming year, is shown in Table 7.1.

The new strategy, price structure, and circulation flow plan were designed to maintain a balanced circulation throughout the year, reduce selling costs, obtain a maximum of subscriber renewals, and keep subscriber turnover each year at a minimum.

Next, the circulation manager's job and his primary responsibilities were redefined, enabling him to carry out the new program. His new duties ranged from analyzing markets, through creating and implementing sales programs, to establishing controls and assuming responsibility for short-term circulation performance and long-range circulation planning.

Developing Sales Objectives and Improved Selling Methods

Once the new circulation flow plan was established, it was possible to review completely the paper's sales program for circulation.

New sales objectives were first established. They were to increase circulation to over 220,000 by December 1964, to concentrate promotions on subscription selling, to increase the number of methods used to sell

Table 7.1

THE NATIONAL OBSERVER—Circulation Department

*Estimated Subscription Sales and Circulation—1964**

	Jan.	Feb.	March	First Quarter	April	May	June	Second Quarter	July	August	Sept.	Third Quarter	Oct.	Nov.	Dec.	Fourth Quarter	Year
Subscription Circulation (Paid) Beginning of Period:	100,000	100,000	109,600	100,000	127,600	150,200	148,800	127,600	146,400	114,000	86,400	146,400	95,600	115,000	131,600	95,600	100,000
I. Additions:																	
Subscription Sales:																	
Direct Mail	26,200	35,600	39,000	100,800	12,800	2,000	2,000	16,800	4,000	14,000	32,400	50,400	25,200	18,000	12,400	55,600	223,600
Advertising	10,000	17,000	15,000	42,000	8,400	1,200	1,200	10,800	2,000	4,000	12,800	18,800	6,000	2,000	400	8,400	80,000
House Ads in DJ Publications	800	800	800	2,400	600	600	600	1,800	600	600	600	1,800	400	400	400	1,200	7,200
Development and Testing	1,200	3,600	2,200	7,000	200	200	200	600	200	1,600	3,600	5,400	3,600	1,200	200	5,000	18,000
Community and Phone	1,000	1,200	1,200	3,400	2,000	2,000	2,000	6,000	2,000	2,000	2,000	6,000	2,000	2,000	2,000	6,000	21,400
Subscription Agency	200	200	200	600	200	200	200	600	200	200	200	600	200	200	200	600	2,400
Education and Clergy	1,600	,200	600	3,400	-	-	-	-	-	-	1,000	1,000	6,000	3,000	1,000	10,000	14,400
Regular and Christmas Gift	200	200	200	600	200	200	200	600	200	200	200	600	200	200	5,800	6,200	8,000
Over the Counter, Employee and Institutional	1,800	1,800	1,800	5,400	1,200	1,200	1,200	3,600	1,400	1,400	1,400	4,200	1,400	1,200	200	2,800	16,000
Solicitation of Home Delivery Expires	2,000	-	-	2,000	-	-	-	-	-	-	-	-	-	-	-	-	2,000
Total Subscription Sales	45,000	61,600	61,000	167,600	25,600	7,600	7,600	40,800	10,600	24,000	54,200	88,800	45,000	28,200	22,600	95,800	393,000
Renewals: Long-term	8,000	10,000	4,000	22,000	4,000	10,000	14,000	28,000	8,000	6,000	6,000	20,000	8,000	6,000	6,000	20,000	90,000
Short-term	14,000	14,000	12,000	40,000	-	-	-	-	16,000	20,000	16,000	52,000	6,000	2,000	2,000	10,000	102,000
Total Additions	67,000	85,600	77,000	229,600	29,600	17,600	21,600	68,800	34,600	50,000	76,200	160,800	59,000	36,200	30,600	125,800	585,000
II. Losses: Long-term Expires	15,000	24,000	9,000	48,000	5,000	17,000	20,000	42,000	12,000	10,000	8,000	30,000	10,000	10,000	10,000	30,000	150,000
Short-term Expires	44,000	42,000	40,000	126,000	-	-	-	-	51,000	63,600	51,000	165,600	23,600	5,600	5,600	34,800	326,400
Education and Gift Expires	2,000	-	-	2,000	-	-	2,000	2,000	-	-	-	-	-	-	4,000	4,000	8,000
Credit Stops	6,000	10,000	10,000	26,000	2,000	2,000	2,000	6,000	4,000	4,000	8,000	16,000	6,000	4,000	2,000	12,000	60,000
Total Losses	67,000	76,000	59,000	202,000	7,000	19,000	24,000	50,000	67,000	77,600	67,000	211,600	39,600	19,600	21,600	80,800	544,400
Net Subscription Gain (or Loss) for Period	-	9,600	18,000	27,600	22,600	(1,400)	(2,400)	18,800	(32,400)	(27,600)	9,200	(50,800)	19,400	16,600	9,000	45,000	40,600
Subscription Circulation (Paid) End of Period	100,000	109,600	127,600	127,600	150,200	148,800	146,400	146,400	114,000	86,400	95,600	95,600	115,000	131,600	140,600	140,600	140,600
Unpaid Copies Delivered	12,000	10,000	6,000	6,000	6,000	6,000	4,000	4,000	6,000	6,000	6,000	6,000	6,000	6,000	6,000	6,000	6,000
Total ABC Subscription Circulation End of Period	112,000	129,600	133,600	133,600	156,200	154,800	150,400	150,400	120,000	92,400	101,600	101,600	121,000	137,600	146,600	146,600	146,600
Other ABC Circulation End of Period:																	
Newsstand and Home Delivery	16,000	16,000	16,000	16,000	16,000	16,000	16,000	16,000	16,000	17,000	17,000	17,000	17,000	18,000	18,000	18,000	18,000
Young Salesmen Program	3,600	3,800	4,000	4,000	4,200	4,400	4,700	4,700	4,800	5,000	5,200	5,200	5,600	5,800	6,000	6,000	6,000
Total ABC Circulation End of Period	131,600	149,400	153,600	153,600	176,400	175,200	171,100	171,100	140,800	114,400	123,800	123,800	143,600	161,400	170,600	170,600	170,600

*All figures have been disguised. However, the general relationships among the various components of the flow plan have been maintained to indicate the economics of circulation.

subscriptions, and to improve the efficiency of magazine advertising and direct-mail selling.

The last two objectives were most important. Prior to mid-1963, over 85% of *The Observer*'s subscription sales were made through direct-mail solicitations. This concentration on direct-mail selling, based on *The Wall Street Journal*'s successful experience, had created problems. First, circulation sales had become overly dependent on direct-mail solicitations. Second, excessive use of direct mail led to uneconomical saturation of mailing lists. Third, magazine advertising was not being used as effectively as it could be to obtain new subscribers.

Sales programs designed to overcome these problems and to achieve the new objectives were developed and tested in all selling areas. The major changes introduced in these programs were:

1. Concentration of subscription selling in the more productive seasons—winter, late summer and fall.
2. Use of advertising headlines emphasizing female and family appeals and incorporating strong emotional appeals which related *The Observer* to basic human needs and aspirations.
3. Introduction of proven mail-order advertising techniques, such as the use of insert cards, photographs, larger coupons, color, and the placing of ads near the front of a publication.
4. Concentration of advertising in mass circulation publications, more selective advertising in small circulation magazines, and less use of direct-mail solicitations.
5. Variation in the size of ads to suit the type of publications.
6. Exploitation of new outlets for selling subscriptions.

Under the new program, dependence on direct-mail selling was cut in half, print advertising efficiency was increased four-fold, and renewals were increased 25%.

Conclusion

The combined results of the new overall marketing program were most dramatic. From August 1963 to December 1964, circulation rose from 136,000 to over 300,000 (see Figure 7.6). In 1964 alone, the savings in circulation expenses exceeded $1,000,000.

The above admittedly is only a summary of what happened in market planning at Dow Jones and concentrates mainly on the advertising and promotion areas. A full description of how the steps in the marketing planning process were followed is given in the author's monograph on the subject.[9] The above discussion, however, provides a general idea how the

[9]Robert J. Mockler, *Circulation Planning and Development for The National Observer: A Research Study on Business Applications of Management Planning and Control Principles* (Atlanta, Georgia: Georgia State College, October 1967).

Figure 7.6

THE NATIONAL OBSERVER

Circulation 1963-1965

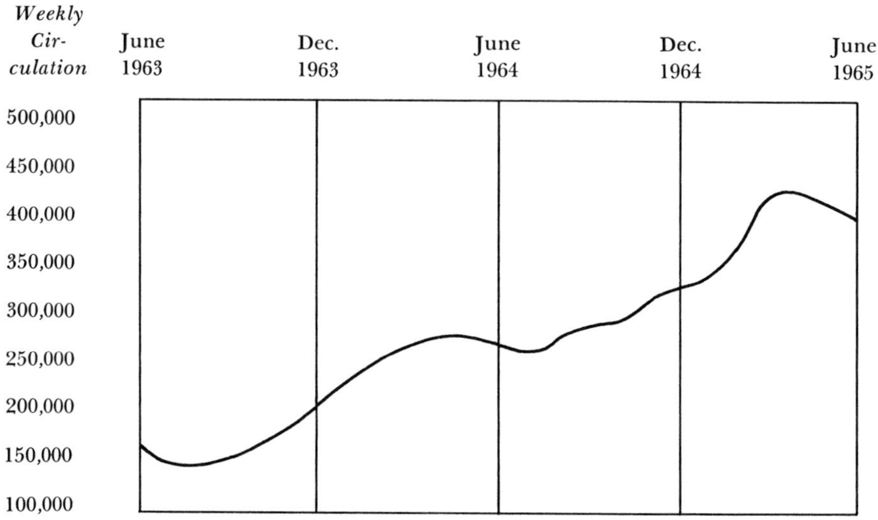

approach outlined at the beginning of this section was applied in an actual business situation.

PLANNING FOR NEW PRODUCTS

New product planning has become an increasingly important part of business operations as companies strive to stay ahead of changing customer requirements and preferences, to keep pace with fast-moving technology, and to match the new product entries of competitors.

The approach to new product planning is similar to the one used in other operational planning areas. First, the background factors are analyzed, new product objectives, policies, and strategies are formulated, and an organization created for new product planning. Then plans are made in those areas that significantly affect the success of the new product function. The discussion of how the planning process is carried out in the new product development area is divided into the following sections:

1. Organizing for new product planning and administration.
2. Analyzing the key factors affecting new product planning, and establishing new product objectives, policies, and strategy.
3. Planning the new product search and preliminary screening.
4. Analyzing and evaluating in detail the market potential, and estimated profitability of new products.
5. Product development and testing.
6. Production and exploitation.

Organizing for new product planning and administration

A wide range of new product planning organizations are possible. New product planning in small companies, for example, may be one of the president's jobs, and he may perform it personally. Larger companies have found that establishing new product planning managers or departments is an effective way of strengthening the coordination of new product planning with research and development, manufacturing, marketing, accounting, finance, and other business areas. Such an organization gives focus to new product activities, develops management incentives which will encourage new product development, stimulates and controls new product activities, and helps clear up communication problems among the related activities.

Because of its close links with marketing, responsibility for new product planning is sometimes placed within the marketing department. There is evidence, however, of a trend towards making new product planning a distinct function, whose manager reports directly to higher management. In a small company, of course, an elaborate organization for new product planning is not possible, and the job is handled by one of the company's top executives.

Whatever the organization, new product planning requires close coordination with other planning areas within a company. Because of this, new product planning must be centralized (see Figure 7.7) whether by assigning responsibility for it to the president, one of his executives, a

Figure 7.7

COORDINATION OF NEW PRODUCT PLANNING

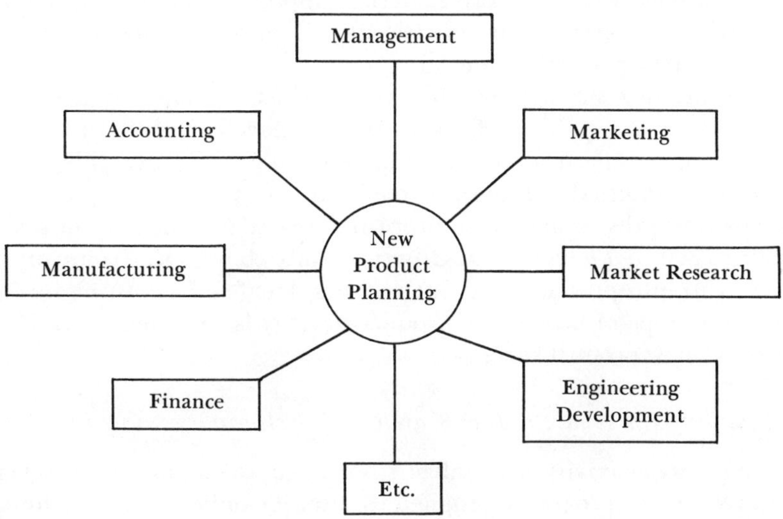

separate department reporting to top management, or a department or executive within the marketing department.

Analyzing Key Factors and Establishing New Product Objectives, Policies and Strategy

New product planning begins with an examination of overall company plans and marketing plans which define what areas of business the company wants to be in, what major product lines it will exploit, and the limitations of company resources. Based on this background study, new product objectives are formulated. These objectives would define the new product areas to be investigated, the intensity with which each area should be investigated, and the acceptance level (usually return-on-investment level) and other criteria to be used for judging the value of potential new products.

A company's new product strategy may be narrow. For example, a company may concentrate on products with the same physical and performance characteristics as its present products. This strategy could lead a company to focus on developing new markets for its present products, increasing product penetration within its present markets, or improving and modifying its present products. Or, this strategy might lead the company to concentrate on exploiting its existing distribution channels and to search for products which can be moved through these channels.

If a company chooses a broader new product strategy, it might seek products with physical and performance characteristics substantially different from those of its existing product lines. One strategy, such as that used by automobile manufacturers, involves vertical integration—that is, the company begins manufacturing sub-assemblies (such as spark plugs, batteries, etc.) or seeks to control raw material suppliers or marketing channels. The vertical integration strategy usually is pursued only for products which have strong growth potential.

New product strategy may be even broader. A company may search for new kinds of products. These products may be linked with present products (an outboard motor manufacturer might, for example, expand into making internal combustion engines), in order to exploit present company strengths. Some of the problems created by this kind of strategy were discussed in *The National Observer* study above. Or, a company may decide to go into product areas entirely unrelated to its existing business. This second type of broad new product strategy is sometimes called "conglomerate" new product strategy.

Planning the New Product Search and Preliminary Screening

The search activity may range from large-scale, continuing research and development programs designed to discover radically new techniques and products, to relatively informal, periodic efforts to uncover useful modifications of existing products. The exact form of the search activity will depend on the size and scope of a company's operation.

There are two basic methods of obtaining new products: first, through acquisition of a patent or another company that has developed a product; second, through development of a product within the company itself. The second method, which is discussed in this section, is usually more costly initially and involves a certain element of risk, although in the long run it is usually more profitable.[10]

New product ideas come from a variety of sources: marketing or sales management, the customer, the research and development department, outside consultants hired for new product search—in fact just about anyone inside or outside the company. A survey by Booz, Allen and Hamilton indicated that in 150 American companies 88% of the new product ideas came from within the company (60% from marketing and research and development) and only 12% from outside the company.[11]

As the planner reviews new product ideas or areas, a good deal of information is needed in order to initially screen each new idea. This information includes:[12]

1. Desired product attributes.
2. Applications and situations for which the new product might be used.
3. Identification of various types of users for the proposed product, and the specific needs of each.
4. Relative importance of proposed features and intended functions of the product to different classes of users.
5. Economic utility of the product to potential users and general evidence as to pricing possibilities.
6. Design parameters for the product.
7. Preliminary indications of potential sales volume.
8. Ways in which the product could best be marketed.
9. The current and future capacity of the market to absorb the product under consideration.

This information is supplemented by information on the internal capabilities of the company. In reviewing the internal information, the planner should ask such questions as:

1. Does our company have the technical equipment, competence, and engineering skills to manufacture a product of this type efficiently?

[10] J. Thomas Cannon, *Business Strategy and Policy* (New York: Harcourt, Brace, and World, Inc., 1968), p. 67.

[11] Elizabeth Marting, ed., *New Products, New Profits: Company Experiences in New Product Planning* (New York: American Management Association, 1964), p. 62.

[12] Morgan B. MacDonald, Jr., *Appraising the Market for New Industrial Products*, Studies in Business Policy, No. 123 (New York: National Industrial Conference Board, 1967), p. 33.

2. Does our company have the marketing and distribution skills to sell this type of product successfully?
3. Does this product enhance or detract from the reputation the firm has for excellence in a particular area?
4. Are we willing (and able) to devote the time and money necessary to market this type of product?

The next step is to make a rough estimate of the profitability of the new product: its cost, cash flow, and probability of success; the cost versus the return; and the eventual return on investment under varying circumstances.

Those product ideas which survive the initial screening are then subjected to a more thorough economic analysis.

Detailed Analysis and Evaluation

The first step in this phase of new product planning is to estimate more precisely the market potential for the new product. This phase is a detailed one, requiring considerable market research. It is the phase during which the planner examines the market segments to which the product will appeal (women-men, older-younger, eastern-western, upper income-lower income, retailer-manufacturer, and estimates within each segment the probable sales, pricing, share of market, life of product, and the like. In addition, the planner must identify within each market segment the pulling power of the product, the potential competition, customer motivation for buying, advertising and promotion channels, location and distribution of the market, and price-volume relationships. He must also develop pricing, distribution, and promotion strategies based on this investigation in order to test their feasibility.[13]

Once a coordinated review of the marketing and product aspects of the new product idea is completed, the next step is to estimate the product's potential for the company. In what ways does the new product exploit company strengths in such areas as: image with customers, distribution channels, research and development, marketing know-how, manpower, material position, manufacturing, customer service and technical know-how, and the like? What conflicts will arise with present product lines and customers? Are there any knowledge gaps which must be filled? What are the cost volume relationships, the probability of technical success, and the non-recurring expenses and investment? Are there any legal and safety problems? What kinds of patent protection are there? Are there any potential product substitutes? Lastly, a thorough examination is made of

[13]A form for doing this phase of new product planning is given in Edgar A. Pessemier, *New Product Decisions: An Analytical Approach* (New York: McGraw-Hill Book Company, 1966), pp. 86-91.

expenses, income, and return on investment under varying sets of assumptions.[14]

One more step is involved in this phase of new product planning. The results of the detailed analysis described above should be brought together in an evaluation report summarizing the risks and opportunities involved in introducing the new product. A form which can be used for this report is given in Figure 7.8.[15] The form covers: rate of return, class of proposal, planned time table, quantitative product-line effects, qualitative product-line effects, recommendations, budget, and risk.

Based on this intensive analysis and evaluation, management then makes a decision on whether to drop the new product idea or begin product development and testing.

Product Development and Testing

If the product appears promising, work then begins on development of product models, marketing plans, testing, redesign and reevaluation, retesting, etc. This circular process continues until a satisfactory new product and marketing formula is developed. The job of the planner is to develop schedules and control product development and testing.

At some point in the new product planning process, the actual product has to be designed, a model of it, and the product market tested. The economic realities of design and manufacture have a major impact on new product planning. While these realities are considered during the preliminary stage of new product planning, the specific costs, design problems, product limitations, and the like are not always uncovered until product development begins. A back-and-forth process then starts, during which the product is adjusted to meet customer and market needs, and its original cost estimates reevaluated in the light of new information.

Answers to many market and product questions are raised during this phase as the planner: tests user reaction to the product and its features; verifies prior estimates of the market potential; tests price possibilities; determines probable order patterns; identifies key purchasing influences; determines product acceptance, on all levels; tests the effectiveness of promotional materials and plans; and determines the most effective sales approach.[16] This information provides a basis for product reevaluations, as well as for marketing planning, if management decides to introduce the product.

Based upon the results of this phase, final marketing strategies are developed and final product specifications set.

[14]A form for doing this phase of new product planning is given in Pessemier, *New Product Decisions*, pp. 93-100.

[15]Pessemier, *New-Product Decisions*, pp. 102-106. Used with permission of the McGraw-Hill Book Company.

[16]MacDonald, *Appraising the Market for New Industrial Products*, pp. 99-100.

Figure 7.8

NEW PRODUCT EVALUATION FORM
SUMMARY SECTION

NEW PRODUCT PROPOSAL EVALUATION FORM

SUMMARY – PROPOSAL NO. ____________

EVALUATED BY ______________ DATE ___________ PAGE _1_

PRODUCT ____

RATE OF RETURN (1)

Estimated Rate of Return [ ] %
.01 Probability of Rate of Return Being Larger Than [ ] %
.01 Probability of Rate of Return Being Less Than [ ] %

CLASS OF PROPOSAL (2)
(circle one)

SPECIAL	REFORMULATION	REPLACEMENT
REMERCHANDISING	IMPROVED PROD.	PROD. LINE EXT.
NEW USES	MARKET EXT.	DIVERSIFICATION

if special, specify ____

PLANNED TIME TABLE (3)

	Start	Complete
Economic Analysis	x x x	_____
Development	_____	_____
Test Marketing	_____	_____
Sales Planning	_____	_____
Full-scale Introduction	_____	_____

QUANTITATIVE PRODUCT LINE EFFECTS (6)

1. If the product is added to the existing product line, will it <u>improve</u> the company's rate of return more than the marginal new product reviewed this <u>period</u>? Explain. ____________

2. If the product is added to the existing product line, will it <u>decrease</u> the variability (variance) of the product line's rate of return more than the marginal new product reviewed this period? Explain. ____________

SUMMARY
PAGE _2_

3. Will the combined effect on the product line be more desirable than the marginal new product reviewed this period? Explain. ____________

QUALITATIVE PRODUCT LINE EFFECTS (7) ____________

RECOMMENDATION (8)

[ ] Unconditional rejection of proposal.
[ ] Postpone action. Reconsider after ____________ months / years.

Gather the following additional information before reconsidering proposal

____________ Research Budget: $ ____________

[ ] Accept the proposal subject to the following modifications or conditions.

[ ] Unconditional acceptance

Figure 7.8 (continued)

SUMMARY
PAGE 3

BUDGET (4)

ESTIMATED NEW REVENUE

DESCRIPTION	TOTAL MARKET FACTORY SHIPMENTS	PRODUCT'S FACTORY SHIPMENTS	PRODUCT'S MARKET SHARE	UNIT PRICE	VARIABLE COST PER UNIT	A.T. PROFIT PER YEAR
Present Year	$	----	----	----	----	----
Year of Intro. ( )		$	%	$	$	$
" 2						
" 3						
" 4						
" 5						
" 6						
" 7						
" 8						
" 9.						
" 10						
Total	$	$	----	----	----	$
Annual Average	$	$	%	$	$	$

If the product will increase the sales of the other company products or reduce the sales of other company products, indicate the nature and extent of the effect. ______

ESTIMATED NEW INVESTMENT

DESCRIPTION	TOTAL	YEAR ENDING ____	YEAR ENDING ____	YEAR ENDING ____	YEAR ENDING ____	YEAR ENDING ____
Econ. Analysis	$	$	$	$	$	$
R and D						
Test Marketing						
Introduction						
New Capital Expenditures						
Recoverable Capital Required						
Total	$	$	$	$	$	$

If the product will require assets which can be used for other purposes or be liquidated, specify their character.

SUMMARY
PAGE 4

RISK (5)

	10% PROBABILITY OF LESS THAN	EXPECTED	10% PROBABILITY OF MORE THAN
Economic Life	Yr.	Yr.	Yr.
Average Annual Unit Sales:			
Price*$ ____			
Price**$ ____			
Price***$ ____			
Average Sales Price per Unit	$ *	$ **	$ ***
Average Variable Cost per Unit	$	$	$
Average Contribution Profit per Dollar Sales	%	%	%
Average After-tax Profit per Dollar Sales	%	%	%
Total New Investment Required	$	$	$
Total After-tax Profits	$	$	$
Payback Period	Yr.	Yr.	Yr.
Average Annual A.T. Profit / Aver. Net Investment = Unadjusted Rate of Return	%	%	%
Probability of Technical Success	____		____
Probability of Marketing Success	*	**	***

Rate company's overall experience with this type of product.

VERY EXTENSIVE — AVERAGE FOR EXISTING PRODUCTS — VERY SLIGHT

Rate company's relative advantage in handling this type of product with respect to

	OVERWHELMING ADVANTAGE			AVERAGE FOR EXISTING PRODUCTS			VERY SERIOUS DISADVANTAGE
R and D							
Production							
Marketing							

Figure 7.8 (continued)

SUMMARY

PAGE 5

Rate the extent that failure might be due to adverse developments with respect to

	VERY IMPORTANT			AVERAGE FOR EXISTING PRODUCTS			VERY UNIMPORTANT
Business cycle							
Competitive action							
General technology							
Market environment							
Sociopolitical environment							

If the product failed after introduction, what part of the investment could be converted to cash ____________? other uses ____________? cash or other uses ____________?

What would be the cost of postponing the product's scheduled introduction for six months ____________? one year ____________?

Note: Used with permission of McGraw-Hill Book Company.

Product Introduction and Exploitation

One of the planner's most useful tools in preparing for the introduction of a new product is a PERT chart. Samples of PERT planning charts used by one company for new product introduction are given in Chapter 10, Figures 3 and 4. The charts give the steps needed to get the product onto the market, the timing of the steps, and the slack time available. Modification of this PERT approach can be used by the planner in all new product situations.

Technically, the new product planning job ends at this point as market planning takes over to handle the sale of the new product on a continuing basis, and develops plans for all phases of marketing the product for the duration of its life.

PLANNING FOR RESEARCH AND DEVELOPMENT

Even the smallest company performs some research and development. To go into business, a company has to develop a product or service and a means of producing or rendering it. To stay in business, a company has to do additional R & D work, in order to meet the continuing threat of competitors developing better products or services, or more effective means of producing or rendering them. The rapid pace of change in today's competitive business environment has increased the importance of R & D to survival in business, and has had a profound impact on many companies' attitudes toward R & D.

This section discusses seven areas related to R & D planning: the definition of R & D; technological factors affecting overall company planning; overall R & D planning directors; and planning considerations in the four basic R & D areas.

What is R & D?

Four major types of research and development are discussed in this section: basic research; applied research; product development; and process development.

Basic or fundamental research is the broad study of natural phenomenon, which may or may not require an interdisciplinary approach—that is, an approach involving many disciplines such as physics, chemistry, biology, etc. Although knowledge is pursued as an end in itself in this type of research, it is usually undertaken in the hope that some useful applications will develop from it. While the commercial payoff may be remote, the long-term benefits of opening up entirely new fields, such as atomic physics or lasers, are potentially enormous. Because it has a less certain and less immediate payoff potential, this type of research is usually performed only by large companies, the government, and educational institutions.

Applied research differs from basic research in that it has specific product development goals and is usually limited to the study of fields closely related to a company's existing areas of business. This type of research may build on generally available knowledge, or new facts uncovered by a company's basic research. The more immediate payoff potential in this area makes it more feasible for commercial enterprises than basic research.

Product development involves the creation of new or improved marketable products, based on generally available information, on new information uncovered during earlier research, or on information from the new product planning area. Since this type of R & D usually requires a smaller investment and has a quicker payoff potential, it is open to smaller companies. Product development efforts may be directed towards improving existing products, finding new uses for existing products, or creating new products or services.

Process development concentrates on finding the most efficient means of production for new and old products. Where little product differentiation is possible, more efficient processes can give significant competitive advantages. The investment required is generally small and the payoff potential quick, making this area suitable for smaller companies.

Technological Factors Affecting Overall Company Planning

In the process of defining its overall objectives, a company explores the major technological areas affecting its business and the impact of technological change on the company's future. The following are some significant aspects of this technological impact that would be covered during the premising phase of overall planning and that affect R & D planning.[17]

First, a company would study the technological environment within which it operates. This environment includes not only the industries in which the company's products presently compete, but also parallel industries in which major substitute or competing products may be developed. As Igor Ansoff and John Stewart point out, sometimes "breakthroughs by immediate competitors are no serious threat; the danger is that breakthroughs in other industries and other technologies may obsolete the entire mature technology."[18] Thus a copper producer would evaluate the technological developments both within its industry and other metal industries, as well as in such related industries as plastics, where there are products which might perform functions similar to that of copper. Such research has led copper companies into aluminum alloys production in an effort to learn more about these potentially competitive areas and protect the position of their primary products.

Second, clearly-perceived demand tends to be the primary force stimulating technological innovation. Therefore, forecasting of potential demand and the ability of various future technologies to satisfy that demand economically can be very useful. Market research would thus try to uncover unsatisfied customer needs and the anticipated changes in customer requirements affecting the company's products or services, in order to give direction to company R & D efforts.

Third, potential threats and opportunities of current technological development work are also appraised. Areas that are receiving greatest research attention or show promise of breakthroughs are potentially more dangerous than areas that are, scientifically speaking, dormant. Although there are accidental major discoveries, such as penicillin, relatively few of these breakthroughs occur during one generation. A "breakthrough" is more often the organization of separate fragments of previously developed knowledge into an integrated framework. Accumulated past knowledge is thus often the basis of innovation.

Fourth, the marketing significance of potential or new technological

[17]For a further discussion of technological forecasting see: Brian W. Scott, *Long-Range Planning in American Industry* (New York: American Management Association, Inc., 1965), pp. 123-136; James Brian Quinn, "Technological Forecasting," *Harvard Business Review*, March-April 1967, pp. 89-106, and "Top Management Guides for Research Planning," in *Long-Range Planning for Management*, ed. David Ewing (Rev. ed.; New York: Harper and Row, Publishers, Inc., 1964), pp. 370-376; R. E. Gibson, "The Strategy of Corporate Research and Development," *California Management Review*, Fall 1966, pp. 35-42.

[18]H. Igor Ansoff and John M. Stewart, "Strategies for a Technology-Based Business," *Harvard Business Review*, November-December 1967, p. 80.

developments is determined. New developments should lead to improved product performance or lower costs, if they are to have an impact on company planning.[19]

These external premises are then weighed with other premises, such as the company's technological capabilities, in developing overall company objectives and specific R & D objectives. The present R & D facilities are first examined and their capabilities evaluated in order to determine if any additional investments appear needed, or if present expenditures are warranted. This investigation should be a thorough one and cover such questions as:

1. The number of scientists and engineers—their background and technical competence. How does this talent reservoir compare with that of the competition?
2. The R & D physical facility—the sophistication and age of equipment.
3. The size and quality of the research library.
4. The success of the R & D function in the past—projects successfully completed, and the time interval elapsed from concept to working model.
5. Profitability of R & D in the past based on the payout of developed products compared with expense of development. Comparison of these figures with payouts on other corporate investments over a similar period, that is, acquisition, or purchase of licenses to manufacture products developed in other laboratories.
6. A comparison of the R & D past results with the work and achievements of competition in this area. This can often be achieved by careful review of all publications, including annual reports and public relations releases of competition.
7. Appraisal of projects currently underway to determine how they fit the market research forecasts and projections as to technological trends in the industry.[20]

Other internal factors, such as available financial resources, are then examined. The company's ability to maintain or increase its R & D investment (in the light of projected profits and available funds) will in part dictate which markets the company will serve, the function it will perform, the products or services it will offer, and its potential profitability. Both technological developments and company R & D capabilities are thus important considerations in developing overall company objectives, as well as R & D objectives.

Overall R & D Planning Directions

The overall strategic plan should provide the answer to such questions as how much of the R & D effort should be directed towards protecting

[19]Leslie G. Cook "How to Make R & D More Productive," *Harvard Business Review*, July-August 1966, pp. 145-153.

[20]Payne, *Planning for Company Growth*, pp. 158-159.

present product lines, and how much towards exploring new product areas; the fields of R & D concentration, the type of research the company will pursue; and the size, scope and organization of the R & D effort. R & D planning thus begins with overall company planning, and overall R & D objectives are for the most part established during that planning phase.

If a company decides to engage in more than one type of R & D, the company's R & D strategy should spell out the balance which will be maintained among the different types. A company's R & D strategy would also specify whether a company will follow a "first to market" or "follow the leader" strategy. A "first to market" strategy requires heavy R & D expenditures, while a "follow the leader" strategy requires a smaller investment, since it places heavy emphasis on development instead of applied or basic research. The "first to market" strategy is best suited for industries with high rates of change. The "follow the leader" strategy emphasizes product and process development, carries the lowest costs, gives the quickest delivery, often requires no other R & D efforts, and is well suited for industries where the rates of change are low.

Once overall R & D directions have been established, plans are made for obtaining the facilities and manpower the company determined during the strategic planning phase were needed—providing, that is, that additional facilities and staff are needed. Plans are also needed for organizing the R & D effort and coordinating R & D planning with planning in other areas, such as marketing, manufacturing, and finance.

Since all planning starts with the marketplace, because sales are what set in motion and support all other company operations, marketing must be kept informed of all potential new products and services being worked on in R & D. It is up to marketing management to determine if the new product or service being created by R & D fills a real market need and can be successfully sold. Manufacturing management determines the potential production costs of the newly developed product. Even though a new product developed by R & D may fill a market need, if the product cannot be manufactured economically there can be no production and sale. Communication between the financial area of the company and the R & D function is also necessary, for financial analysis is needed to estimate potential product profitability, and financial management determines what funds the company can allocate to research and development.

A company's major input into R & D is money for manpower. If R & D is to be effective, a company should be able to commit whatever funds it has decided to expend on R & D for more than a year at a time,[21] since the investment in R & D usually does not product tangible results for several years and time is needed to train researchers. Even though the output of

[21]Otto L. Forchheimer, "Management's Role in R & D," *Advanced Management Journal,* April 1967, p. 61.

R & D is sometimes difficult to measure, a system of periodic reviews should none the less be built into all R & D planning, in order to determine if each project is proceeding as planned and to check on the current potential return-on-investment estimates for each R & D project.

In addition to the above overall R & D planning considerations, there are specific factors which affect planning in the individual R & D areas. The following discussion covers these factors.

Planning for Fundamental or Basic Research

Basic research is always undertaken by a company in the hope that commercially successful products will be developed, so that very little "pure" basic research is done by commercial enterprises. As Quinn points out, a company builds its plan in R & D in the hope that fundamental research in broad scientific areas will produce applicable technology.[22]

Industry is spending a considerable amount of money on basic research: "American industry is spending about $3-billion of its own money this year on a fundamental research, to find knowledge to spark ideas to improve or develop products and services that customers need and want and will pay for, permitting the company to grow and make a profit."[23] And these expenditures do pay off. For example, the present industrial uses of atomic energy originated with the study of the structure of matter (fundamental research), which led to the discovery of atomic fission. Atomic fission was then studied for potential use (applied research), which in turn led to the development of such commercial uses as electricity generation (product or service development) and efficient and safe material processing methods in such areas as mining and purification (process development).

A basic research breakthrough may yield substantial advantages over competitors, while at the same time the acquired store of knowledge can allow a company to take advantage of breakthroughs achieved elsewhere. As Quinn emphasizes, "the group supporting longer-term (fundamental) research will eventually control large areas of basic knowledge and can make business subject to royalty payments and/or specific controls if it uses such knowledge. Atomic energy is a case in point."[24]

Basic research requires a long-term commitment, mainly in money for manpower. Aside from such undertakings as atomic physics, which may require heavy equipment investments, basic research facilities tend to be fairly simple, because they are used in the analysis and evaluation of basic phenomena. For example, research into the basic structure and behavior

[22]Quinn, "Top-Management Guides for Research Planning," p. 388.

[23]Arthur M. Bueche, Vice-President R & D, General Electric Company, quoted in *Industrial Research*, November 1968, p. 30.

[24]Quinn, "Top-Management Guides for Research Planning," p. 382.

of cancer requires only simple chemical and microscopic equipment (the search for a direct cure would be applied research).

Basic research planning cannot be too highly organized, for the creative scientist works best under personal management direction, without extensive policy or procedural restrictions.[25] One large chemical company has developed the following approach to balancing creative freedom with planned control in the R & D area.[26] At this company, management expects the individual researcher to come up with project proposals within the area of his specialty. He discusses any new idea with his director, who screens it for feasibility to avoid efforts in a fruitless direction, guides the preliminary exploratory investigations for project approval, and then evaluates the subsequent progress. In this way, management selects and coordinates acceptable projects, and still provides a simple and direct management structure for research.

The economic benefits of basic research can be evaluated only from a long-term viewpoint. Since it is often difficult to measure precisely the benefits which may be gained from basic research, it is difficult to calculate a precise return on investment. In general, very large companies are more successful in doing basic research, for they have the financial resources to take advantage of unplanned discoveries, can bring a wider cross-section of expertise to bear on exploring complex areas, and can afford to finance somewhat loosely structured exploratory research, whose payoffs are uncertain.

Planning for Applied Research

The objective of applied research is to acquire technological knowledge with commercial potential in specific areas of interest to the company. The effort may be directed toward protecting existing markets or towards exploring new areas of growth and diversification, or toward both. It can attempt to provide product alternatives to satisfy specific present and projected customer needs, uncover entirely new applications of existing products or fill existing knowledge gaps—for example, by determining the ultimate characteristics of certain types of materials that will affect product development. Applied research can be based on generally available knowledge, or can concentrate on investigating the commercially significant aspects of the company's basic research efforts.

The need for applied research is greatest in industries with short product life-cycles and intense competition. Although mature industries, which are scientifically dormant or approaching saturation, may require

[25]M. R. Feinberg "14 Suggestions for Managing Scientific Creativity," *Research Management,* March 1968, pp. 83-92 and condensed in *Management Review,* December 1968, pp. 25-29.

[26]Quinn, "Top-Management Guides for Research Planning," pp. 388-392.

less research, management must also be aware of competitive technologies that may obsolete the entire industry and direct applied research to meet any perceived threats. Almost every company has a few products or processes which are its bread and butter and which must be defended with strong research commitments in the light of forecasted customer needs and competitive activity.

Each area of applied research is evaluated for its potential contribution to achieving company objectives in the light of its required investment, and in the light of the technological forecasts and the company's present capabilities. The critical variables of each proposed project are pinpointed, the probability of research success and the commercial application potential estimated, and project planned in line with the R & D goals.[27] Where there is presently not sufficient market feedback information for evaluating an R & D project's potential value to the company, an R & D concept under consideration should be market tested.[28]

The organization for applied research can be more clearly structured, as can its objectives and policies, than the organization for fundamental research. Everett Hughes has outlined a simple organization structure for applied research that combines the needed control with the essential creative environment, while reducing overhead.[29]

Planning for Product Development

Product development involves developing the actual product. The product concept may come from the company's applied research, its new product and market planning groups, or from outside idea sources.

Product development is closely linked with new product planning. In theory, product planning concentrates on product and marketing concepts, while product development concentrates on creating the actual product. In practice, the two are inseparable, for development works within areas designated by new product planning, while planning must work within the product limitations specified by the product development area. The requirements of the two areas thus must be continually reconciled.

Product development may concentrate on developing new products or improving existing ones. Unless a company's products are clearly obsolete, the producing company is usually forced to upgrade them to maintain

[27]Laurence D. McGlauchlin, "Long-Range Technical Planning," *Harvard Business Review*, July-August 1968, pp. 55-64; Leslie G. Cook, "How to Make R & D More Productive," *Harvard Business Review*, July-August 1966, pp. 145-153; Carl E. Barnes, "Get Inventions off the Shelf" *Harvard Business Review*, January-February 1966, pp. 138-139; and Milton F. Usry and John L. Hess, "Planning and Control of Research and Development Activities," *Journal of Accountancy*, November 1967, p. 43-48.

[28]Robert R. Kubick, "Concept Testing Made Easy," *Business Management*, July 1967, pp. 57-62.

[29]Everett C. Hughes, "Preserving Individualism on the R & D Team," *Harvard Business Review*, January-February 1968, pp. 72-82.

or expand their market demand. The amount of development, and perhaps research effort, that can be expended is determined by the added economic returns arising from any new investment in the product. Because basic technical, manufacturing, and marketing operations supporting the products are already in existence, accumulation of the basic cost data for decision-making and program implementation are relatively straightforward processes.

Because coordination is needed between new product development and other company activities—marketing, manufacturing, and finance, many companies create special groups drawn from all these areas and headed by a new product manager to appraise and coordinate new products. Such a separate organization is needed to create the wide perspective, initiative, drive to succeed, imagination, and top-management backing needed for success in new product development. The separation of new ventures is also desirable, because "the level of functional organization that is typically found running a going business breeds resistance to change. Key decisions . . . are made by persons . . . judged on other bases."[30] A proper balance must be achieved among the various functions, if optimum marketing characteristics are to be combined with technical soundness,[31] safety, and manufacturing efficiency considerations.

New product development is subject to more rigid planning and scheduling than either applied or basic research. New product development objectives and policies can be made specific and procedures established to guide the actions of the various groups involved. In view of the job—getting products onto the market—product development management requires a disciplined sequencing of tasks to minimize delays. Studies by McKinsey and Company indicate that management changes contribute more heavily to cost and schedule overruns as a rule, than do technical or engineering changes.[32] Not only are delays expensive, but they also give a competitor a greater chance to get to the market first and they can eat away a portion of the 17-year period of patent protection.[33] As is shown in Chapter 10, PERT/CPM is a useful tool for planning and scheduling the steps in new product development and reducing to a minimum the time lapse between research and new product sale.[34]

Another tool used in planning new product development is "value analysis." Value analysis strives to balance all factors influencing product

[30]Russell W. Peterson, "New Venture Management in a Large Company," *Harvard Business Review*, May-June 1967, p. 69.

[31]Joseph J. Hansen, "The Case of the Precarious Program," *Harvard Business Review*, January-February 1968, pp. 14-34, 170, gives an illustration of the effects of poor organization and control of development projects.

[32]Ansoff and Stewart, "Strategies for a Technology-Based Business," p. 74.

[33]Peterson, "New Venture Management in a Large Company," p. 74.

[34]"Pioneering with PERT: How to Speed Entry into a New Market," *Business Management*, September 1967, pp. 66-74.

design and production—marketing appeal, manufacturing efficiency, and technical functionality. For example, in one company the use of the "functional analysis system technique"[35] uncovered the critical mechanism operations and led to the reduction of parts from 59 in the prototype to 16 in the finished product and from 17 to 1 in a sub-assembly, through simplifying the design prior to production tool-up. The finished unit was easier and safer to fabricate, and was more rugged and easier to operate in service. When materials, components and subassemblies are purchased from outside sources, these sources should be consulted in the design stage, for they may have experience or expertise which will aid the value analysis. Different materials or processes uncovered in this way have resulted in substantial time and cost savings for many companies.[36]

Planning for new product development in a small company differs in many ways from that found in a large company. In a small company, the new product is most often an addition to the existing product line or an improvement in an existing product. Because of the size of the operation, communication between functional activities is also simpler and top management supervision and coordination more direct. The steps in planning for new product development are the same, however, in all size companies: the direction for new product development must be determined, based on research findings and market sensings; development must be coordinated with other functional areas, either by top management or an inter-functional group; the development must be scheduled and controlled to meet specified time and cost goals; continuing analysis is needed to simplify the product design, reduce costs, and improve marketability.

Planning for Process Development

Although often included with product development (because process development is necessary in developing a new product), process development can be undertaken separately to improve the processing of existing products. In industries with long product life-cycles, such as the steel industry, process development to reduce costs and expedite delivery can undercut companies with strong product development capabilities. Often entry into mature industries is accomplished through developing advanced processes.

Changing processing requirements may be triggered by new knowledge uncovered in applied research, changes in product specifications or in costs of elements of production, outside technological developments in available materials and equipment, the degree of vulnerability to disruption of outside sources of supply, or simply by the desire to improve

[35]"Benefits of Value Analysis are Keyed to its Timing," *Product Engineering*, August 28, 1967, pp. 112-115.

[36]" 'Save' Gets Buyers, Vendor into the Design Act," *Purchasing Week*, February 24, 1969, pp. 32-33.

efficiency periodically. In making changes, the systems approach can be used—that is, the whole production system is examined, from raw material and sub-component supplier, to warehousing and inventory, to production scheduling, to machinery capabilities and maintenance, to storing and shipping. The objective is to develop the optimum balance in the production system. Within this total systems perspective, individual processes are studied for improvement or for meeting changing requirements of different aspects of the production system.

PLANNING FOR MANUFACTURING

Manufacturing includes all the functions required to produce a company's products, and so includes such areas as facilities, production, material, distribution, and manpower. The following are the steps in manufacturing planning process:[37]

1. Study the overall corporate plan and define objectives.
2. Analyze the present manufacturing operations and the present and future environmental trends to determine company mannufacturing strengths and weaknesses, and to isolate environmental factors such as the manpower supply and new process and equipment developments, which significantly affect manufacturing operations.
3. Review the long- and short-term sales forecasts, and the marketing, new product, R & D and other plans, to determine if they are feasible from a manufacturing viewpoint, and recommend adjustments where necessary. Set specific manufacturing goals, based on this analysis.
4. Develop detailed policies and plans for manufacturing, covering such areas as facilities, production scheduling and control, materials, distribution, and manpower.

As in the other functional areas, manufacturing planning begins with the overall company objectives and planning premises. Based on a recent study, Wickham Skinner concluded that all too frequently a company's manufacturing planning is not closely coordinated with its strategic planning, and as a result the strategic plans do not adequately take into account major manufacturing limitations, and manufacturing plans do not carry out corporate objectives and strategies as fully as they should.[38] Examina-

[37]This approach and the discussion in this section is based in large part on the following books: Robert E. Finley and Henry R. Ziobro, eds., *The Manufacturing Man and His Job* (New York: American Management Association, 1966); Robert A. Pritzker and Robert A. Gring, eds., *Modern Approaches to Production Planning and Control* (New York: American Management Association, 1960); Management *Bulletin No. 18* (New York: American Management Association, 1962); *Successful Planning and Control: Special Report No. 5* (New York: American Management Association, 1955); *American Management Association: Manufacturing Series No. 206* (New York: American Management Association, 1953).

[38]Wickham Skinner "Manufacturing—Missing Link in Corporate Strategy," *Harvard Business Review*, May-June 1969, p. 136.

tion of overall company strategic planning not only provides overall directions for manufacturing, it also answers questions about overall economic, industry, market, and company factors which will limit and otherwise affect manufacturing planning. Within the framework of these overall planning factors, the planner establishes manufacturing objectives and definitions of the general product and process areas that manufacturing should concentrate in.

During the second step in manufacturing planning, the planner examines other planning premises affecting manufacturing planning specifically. The following is a checklist of some questions concerning the company's present operations which might be covered during this phase:

1. *Plant Location.*
   a. Percentage of plant capacity now being used effectively.
   b. Importance of plant location as it relates to key suppliers, and/or channels of distribution; appraisal of effectiveness of present location with respect to these channels.
   c. Economics of plant location in terms of labor costs and reservoir of labor skills—short-term and long-term.

2. *Equipment.*
   a. Age of present machinery.
   b. Depreciation.
   c. Comparison of quality and efficiency of plant with others in industry including competitors overseas.
   d. How many new equipment developments within the industry have we adopted: for example, use of computers for scheduling, automated warehouses, miniaturization, programmed equipment, etc?
   e. Schedule for replacement of machinery and cost of such replacement.

3. *Maintenance.*
   a. Availability of replacement parts.
   b. Are we anticipating trends in costs and skills required?
   c. Have we work standards to measure productivity?

4. *Production.*
   a. Downtime on machinery.
   b. Accuracy of scheduling.
   c. History of production delays, and reasons why they occurred.
   d. Effectiveness of quality control—record of customer complaints, repairs, replacements.
   e. How rapidly is the engineering department able to translate products from R & D into production? What is the engineering backlog?
   f. What methods changes have occurred over the past five years? What are anticipated?
   g. Have engineered work standards been set for each new method?
   h. Have standards been applied to new areas of indirect labor? What is the ratio of direct to indirect labor? What is the trend?

i. How much work is actually being produced?
j. Is the present cost accounting system sufficiently accurate to provide control of costs by individual products or jobs? What is the cost of maintaining the present cost accounting system?

5. *Materials.*
   a. What are purchasing requirements?
   b. Inventory controls—rate of inventory turnover.
   c. How often have out of stock materials caused production delays?
   d. In what condition is the material handling equipment?
   e. In what ways have we anticipated the future trends in this area?
   f. Are the facilities for storing and warehousing materials adequate?

6. *Distribution.*
   a. What are our present distribution requirements?
   b. What changes are planned to meet long- and short-term future requirements?
   c. What industry trends will significantly affect the company's operation?
   d. What are the present distribution facilities?
   e. In what ways do they fail to meet our present and anticipated requirements.

7. *Manpower.*
   a. Analysis of background, training and talents of present employees.
   b. Are we making provision for trends in skills required?
      - How strong is the trend from direct to indirect labor?
      - To what degree and at what rate is automated equipment replacing the present labor force?
      - What has been the shift in labor skills required to manufacture this firm's products over the past five years? What will it be over the five years?
      - Would present employee skills be an asset in manuafcturing goods other than those currently produced?
   c. Appraisal of labor and supervisory training programs in the light of labor trends. Are these programs developing skills that will be required in the years ahead?
   d. Wage rates.
      - Are they competitive with other domestic producers? With foreign manufacturers?
      - Trend in wage rates.
   e. Union relations.
   f. Quality of supervision.
   g. Rate of turnover estimated at each wage level.
   h. When was the company's incentive plan last reviewed?

Since planning in other areas affects manufacturing plans, the planner next examines the plans in these areas. Sales goals are the basis upon which specific implementation plans in manufacturing are built. Hopefully, manufacturing management will have participated in the development of these goals, so that the sales goals will not be beyond manufacturing capabilities. Where they are, sales goals would be reconciled with manufacturing limitations. Once settled, manufacturing plans can be developed to meet sales goals.

Manufacturing plans are affected by plans in other areas, such as R & D, new product, and marketing plans. The point has been made over and over again in the preceding sections of this chapter that plans in any one functional area cannot be made without consideration of their impact on other functional areas, such as manufacturing. Only if the plans made in these other areas have been coordinated with manufacturing can the planner proceed to develop intelligent manufacturing plans.

The last step in manufacturing planning is to develop specific plans for each of the manufacturing areas.

In a recent article, Skinner outlined an approach to manufacturing planning, which closely resembles the one given in this chapter. The steps in his approach, which are given in Figure 7.9, correspond to those given in this study: overall company and environmental planning factors, as well as company objectives and strategy, are examined first (Skinner's steps 1 to 3), in order to develop manufacturing objectives (step 4); specific environmental factors (steps 5 and 6) and company factors (step 7) are then studied, in order to develop manufacturing directions (step 8); next, implementation plans, programs, systems, and controls are developed (steps 9 to 12); last, information is fedback and used to review and refine plans (steps 13 to 15). The purpose of Skinner's process was to emphasize the importance of basing all manufacturing planning on overall company strategic planning, in order to give guidance to the technicians in the manufacturing area.

Since Skinner was discussing overall manufacturing planning, he did not give as much emphasis as is given in this chapter to the affect of implementation planning in other areas on manufacturing planning, and his process does not deal with planning in specific manufacturing areas. His approach is none the less clearly patterned on a fundamental planning approach similar to the one described in this study, and so provides a useful model (based on his experience) of how successful companies plan in the manufacturing area.

The following sections cover planning considerations in five major manufacturing areas.

Facilities.

Facilities planning covers plans for location, design, layout, selection, construction, and purchase of all plant, equipment, and related services.

[39]Skinner, "Manufacturing," p. 143.

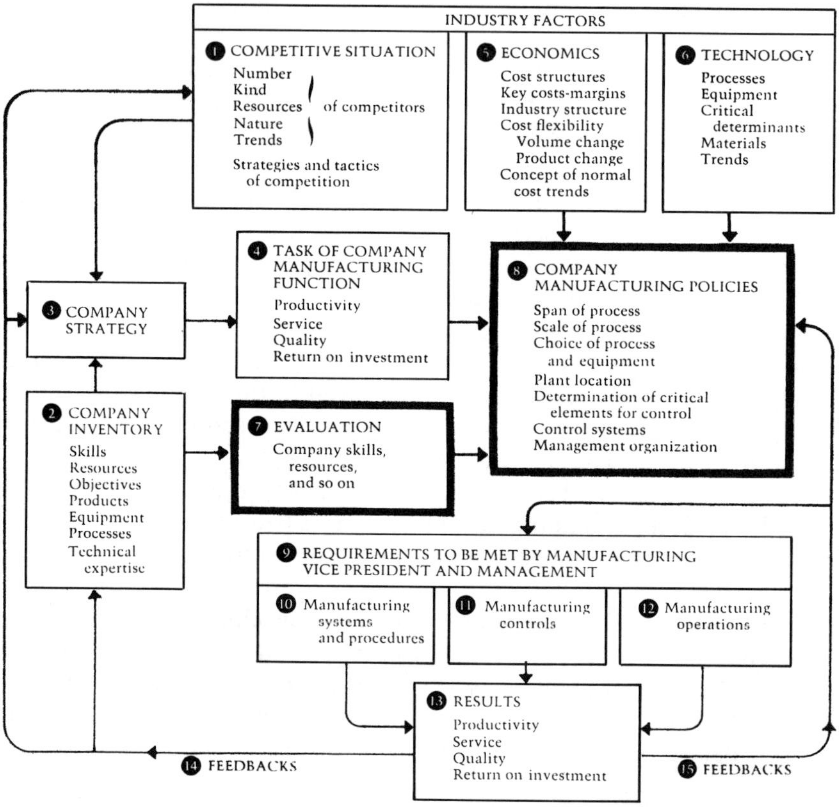

Key

1. What the others are doing
2. What we have got or can get to compete with
3. How we can compete
4. What we must accomplish in manufacturing in order to compete
5. Economic constraints and opportunities common to the industry
6. Constraints and opportunities common to the technology
7. Our resources evaluated
8. How we should set ourselves up to match resources, economics, and technology to meet the tasks required by our competitive strategy
9. The implementation requirements of our manufacturing policies
10. Basic systems in manufacturing (e.g., production planning, use of inventories, use of standards, and wage systems)
11. Controls of cost, quality, flows, inventory, and time
12. Selection of operations or ingredients critical to success (e.g., labor skills, equipment utilization, and yields)
13. How we are performing
14. Changes in what we have got, effects on competitive situation, and review of strategy
15. Analysis and review of manufacturing operations and policies

Figure 7.9

THE PROCESS OF MANUFACTURING PLANNING AND POLICY DEVELOPMENT

Facilities planning deals with the separate but interrelated costs of material, supplies, manpower, services and facilities, and has as its mission to find ways to minimize the aggregate of such costs in making and distributing the products at the proper time.[40]

The facilities plan covers both adjustments of present facilities and additions of new ones, and includes:

1. Location analysis and selection.
2. The design and specifications, including layouts, of equipment, plant, warehouses, and related services.
3. Maintainance requirements.
4. Provision for additional expansion.

Once it has been determined that a new plant location is desirable (and that other alternatives, such as buying from outside suppliers, are not more economical or efficient), a planner establishes the requirements for the new plant site. For example, a small manufacturer of automobile parts established these four objectives for a new plant location: reduce labor rates significantly, without reducing productivity; locate close to a dependable source of the types of steel required; provide overnight or next day service to customers; obtain ample space for present and future needs. Among its specific requirements was location next to a railroad siding. Obviously, no location will be perfect and some compromises will always be needed, but a detailed list of specifications will serve to direct the search and organize the evaluation of competing alternatives.

The actual investigation may be done by an outside consultant or by company personnel or by both. Any location should enable a company to deliver the product to the customer at a cost equal to or less than the competition, and at the time and in the quantities needed to meet the customer's requirements. In selecting the general area for the plant, significant factors affecting this objective are examined, including (depending on the industry): nearness of markets and sources of supply; availability and cost of raw materials; supply and cost of labor; state or local tax structure; legislation; weather; availability of financial assistance; relation to other company facilities; and exceptional requirements as to fuel, power, water supply, transportation and waste disposal. The selection of the community will depend on the above factors, as well as: community attitudes, appearance, and facilities; local government and taxation; availability and cost of utilities, satisfactory sites, and financing. The selection of the actual site is based on the same factors, plus such considerations as size and shape of the location, site and building costs, drainage, access, topography, soil conditions, zoning, fire and police protection, existing structures, and the like. Using these factors, the various available alternative sites are evaluated to determine which is the most efficient and economical.

[40]Henry DeVos and Paul A. Henschen, "Facilities Planning," *Journal of Accountancy*, August 1967, p. 81.

Machinery selection and layout will in a large measure dictate plant design. In selecting machinery a planner follows these steps:

1. Study specifications and prepare process charts of the jobs or operations to be performed, and based on these determine in general the kinds of machinery needed.
2. Study the projected volume of output to determine the extent to which mass production is economically feasible, and where special purpose equipment is needed.
3. Determine the operational facilities required in the machines (manual, semi-manual, automatic, automated).
4. Study probable changes in products to determine the amount of adaptability required.
5. Study the capacities of available machines and compute the number of machines required to achieve the desired rate of output and a uniform work flow.
6. Select the equipment best suited to achieving overall balanced capacity, minimum idle capacity, and ability to expand.

The layout of the machinery and production process in the plant is determined next, before finalizing the design of the building. Plant layout involves the arrangement and location of production machinery, work centers, and auxiliary facilities and activities (inspection, handling of material, storage and shipping) for the purpose of achieving efficiency in manufacturing products or supplying consumer services. Plant layout should coordinate use of material, men and machines, and achieve the following specific objectives: facilitate the manufacturing process, minimize materials handling, maintain flexibility of arrangement and of operation, maintain high turnover in the work process, hold down investment in equipment, make economical use of floor space, promote effective utilization of manpower, and provide for employee convenience, safety, and comfort in doing work.

The procedure followed in planning equipment and machinery layouts includes the following steps:

1. Acquire a statement of the manufacturing objectives and compile process and equipment data.
2. Develop an overall plan for the general arrangement of the process (covering key operations and other work areas supporting key operations, main and minor aisles, production departments, etc.), building and site.
3. Develop a template arrangement of production machinery.
4. Arrange plant service departments to facilitate the production process.
5. Prepare building specifications to fit the needs of the layout.
6. Prepare detailed layout drawings, flow process charts and flow diagrams, and test.

As can be seen from the above discussions, the design of the buildings and building services depends on the production layout requirements, since it must meet the requirements of the firm's operations at a minimum cost in land, construction, maintenance, and depreciation. Layout requirements, combined with costs, site selection factors, machinery characteristics, maintenance requirements, and manufacturing objectives, will thus determine to a great degree many aspects of building and building services design, including: whether a multi- or single-story building is used; the amount of floor space required; the carrying capacity of the floor; ceiling heights; mezzanine requirements; size and location of elevators and stairways; the lighting, ventilation, heating, noise control, service, and waste disposal facilities; and location of partitions, doors, skylights, offices, windows, etc. Techniques, such as PERT, CPM, and simulation, which are useful in plant design, layout, and construction are discussed in Chapters 10 and 11.

Maintenance of equipment is an important facility planning consideration and should cover four points: regularly scheduled replacement; back-up or substitute equipment; reserve safety stock inventory; and preventive maintenance. Plans for the maintenance of buildings would also be covered during this phase of manufacturing planning.

As a last part of facilities planning, consideration would be given to possible future expansion, and where possible present facilities would be laid out, land bought, and construction done with future plans in mind.

Most companies have developed a systematic procedure for estimating the costs of alternative facilities. Both the cost of the facilities and their impact on operating costs are calculated, usually with the help of the financial and accounting departments. Some of the techniques used in evaluating capital expenditures are discussed in the financial planning section of this chapter.

Production Scheduling.

The overall objective of production scheduling is to produce a company's products at the required time, and in the quantities needed, as efficiently and economically as possible. Specific sub-objectives of production scheduling include: completing and shipping all orders in compliance with promises that are made on customer orders; keeping worker, machine, and equipment idle time at a minimum; seeing that the materials and supplies are available for each order that is scheduled; seeing that the production loads are balanced, so that no departments become overloaded and cause disruptions in production; providing information on which to base reliable sales promises.

The complexity of production scheduling varies with the type of production process—from job shop and intermittent production to continuous flow production, or some combination of the two. In job shop production, the whole gamut of scheduling problems are usually encountered, from making up the production order to delivering the finished product. In other types of production processes, the production scheduling job will range from planning the entire flow of production to planning the production of small subassemblies. Whatever the type of production process, though, there are basic production scheduling functions and basic scheduling tools which can be used effectively.

The basis of all production scheduling is the sales forecast and inventory control, which directly or indirectly generate order requirements to be met by production scheduling. In all companies, orders are issued periodically from inventory control to replenish stocks in anticipation of sales. Depending on the type of operation, marketing may also issue sales orders directly to production which cannot be filled from stock.

A basic planning tool used in production scheduling is the master schedule or plan, which translates sales forecasts into production requirements. The purpose of the master schedule is to establish the overall production scheduling needs and to determine the elapsed time available for the various jobs to be performed. A master schedule covering a large order at Hughes Aircraft Company, for example, covers the following:

1. Proposal to management for approval.
2. Proposal to the customer for approval.
3. A contract—initially a letter contract followed by a firm contract.
4. Advance bills of materials—this is a listing of purchased items requiring a long lead time.
5. Schematic drawings and specifications.
6. Outline and mounting drawings.
7. Release of production drawings—engineering data received prior to this has been for information, for prototype construction, or for advance planning.
8. Manufacturing planning—this includes fabrication and assembly planning.
9. Procurement.
10. Tool design and fabrication.
11. Production fabrication—this includes the fabrication of detailed parts and sub-assemblies, such as sheet metal assemblies.
12. Assembly.
13. Completion of first production unit.[41]

The job of the production scheduler is to meet the requirements of the sales forecast and inventory control contained in the master schedule. His functions include: scheduling the purchase of the material needed for production based on the master schedule; preparing, distributing, and maintaining production department schedules; revising and updating schedules based on changes in forecast, parts shortages, material rejects, and the like; coordinating all activities required to maintain production

[41]Charles A. Rook, "Techniques of Scheduling and Follow Up at Hughes Aircraft," American Management Association Seminar, 1960 (manuscript copy in the Production Control file at the American Management Association library, New York).

schedules; and providing the sales department with expected shipping dates on individual orders as necessary. In carrying out these functions, he might perform the following jobs in a typical job shop situation:

1. Confirm sales forcasts or inventory control requirements.
2. Prepare work orders.
3. Clarify, amplify, and compile drawings, bills of material, and specifications.
4. Develop procedures for how the work is to be done.
5. Plan for the resources needed to do the work, including materials, tools, equipment, and manpower.
6. Prepare routing plans for where the work is to be done.
7. Develop time estimates and determine how long it will take to perform the work.
8. Plan when the work is to be done. This involves determining priorities, timing, and sequence of work.

Many tools are used in scheduling the actual production work. Four of these are discussed briefly here: methods for estimating time values; graphic techniques; operations research; and simulation.

In order to prepare his schedule, the production scheduling manager needs estimates of the time required for the various parts of the production operation. The scheduler may draw upon past experience with similar jobs and base his estimates on the time sheets of past jobs. Or, his estimates may be based on work sampling, that is, a series of random observations of the operation over a period of time. In more scientifically controlled operations, these estimates would be based on actual stop-watch studies or predetermined time and motion studies. Depending on the situation, the scheduler would use any one of the above techniques, or a combination of them, to develop his estimates.

Among the better-known graphic techniques used in production scheduling and control are Gantt charts, PERT/CPM, and Line of Balance.

A sample of a Gantt chart is given in Figure 7.10. A Gantt chart consists of a series of light horizontal bars, each of which represents a given amount of planned performance over a specified period of time. Below each bar is a second contrasting heavy bar representing actual accomplishment, as of a certain date. The chart in Figure 7.10 was last posted on Tuesday evening, as indicated by the small "V" mark at the top. Order number one, which was started on Monday noon and is to be completed on Wednesday night, is ahead of schedule, since the heavy line extends beyond the present time. Order number two is behind schedule, as indicated by the bar, and order number three has not been started. A Gantt chart thus shows at a glance whether a job is ahead of schedule, behind schedule or on schedule.

PERT/CPM, a graphic planning technique which is described in detail in Chapter 10, is used in production in single project planning. The

Figure 7.10

A SIMPLIFIED GANTT CHART

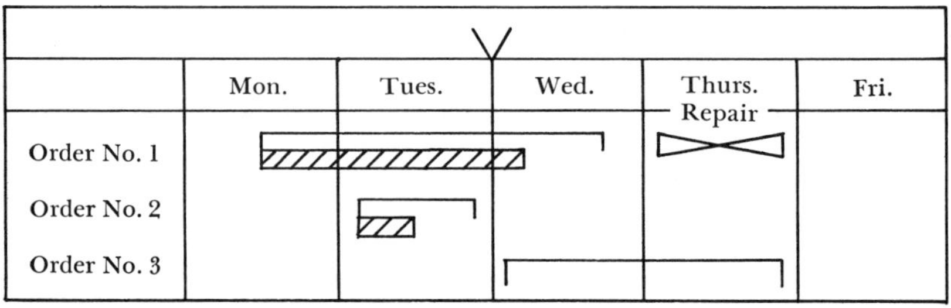

Note: Key to symbols

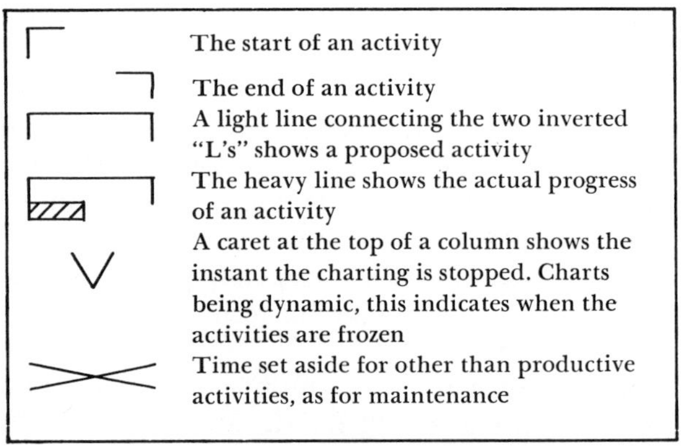

Line-of-Balance technique, which incorporates some of the Gantt charting techniques but which is considerably more complex, is used only in more sophisticated production scheduling operations.[42]

The use of operations research tools in production management has increased markedly over the last decade. Some of the more widely-used operations research tools, such as linear programming and decision theory, are discussed in Chapter 10, and a number of examples are given there of how these tools are used in scheduling and controlling production operations.

In many companies computer simulation is now being used extensively for production scheduling. For example, Hazeltine Corporation uses com-

[42]James H. Greene, *Production Control* (Homewood, Illinois: Richard D. Irwin, Inc., 1965), pp. 443-446.

puter simulation for its complex job-shop scheduling.[43] A "simulated" model of the job-shop is programmed. First, priority rules are established for dispatching order. A large number of different factors are taken into account in calculating priorities, including estimated processing time, order due date, amount of work remaining after current operation, and the value of the order. Once such a priority rule has been established, the scheduling of orders on hand and anticipated orders is simulated on the computer, using the priority rules. The simulated results are then examined: some orders have been completed on time, others have not; work-in-process inventory averaged some given level; and machine and labor capacity were utilized at a given rate. If the decisions made in the simulated model are satisfactory, the same simulated job sequence is used in the shop. If not, corrective steps can be taken, such as modifying the priority rules or adjusting overtime work, until a satisfactory schedule is developed. It would be foolish to say that the computer can handle all situations better than the human dispatcher, since unusual situation continually arise. The computer system, therefore, is designed to permit an experienced dispatcher to review and possible change computer decisions.

Materials.

The objective of materials planning is to create an efficient and economical materials control and handling operation for a company—which will furnish the company with the materials it wants, where it wants it, when it wants it, and at a reasonable cost.

Materials are defined as any compound, element, part, item, or consumable that is used to make either a finished product, or a part of a finished product, or another "item" that will be further manufactured. Materials also include items that do not become part of the manufactured product but are necessary to its production. Among these other items can be included lubricating oils and greases; chemicals needed for cleaning, stripping, coating or otherwise preparing raw stock and components for the manufacturing process; catalysts and inhibitors for any chemicals used; consumable machine parts such as drill bits, saw blades, cutting and threading dies, and sanding disks; materials needed for the upkeep of the production facilities and the machines; special materials needed for handling and packing both the raw materials and the finished products.

The first step in materials planning is to study the place of materials in the total system of production, storage, and distribution within a company, because materials planning is only one aspect of a company's total logistics planning system—that is the total system which moves materials

[43]M. J. Kantrowitz, *Dynamic Priorities* (Little Neck, N.J.: Hazeltine Corporation, September 1968).

and products from source to user.[44] Materials planning covers the first half of such a logistics system, the flow of materials from suppliers to storage areas to manufacturing areas and back again. Distribution planning, which is discussed in the next section, covers the movement of finished goods from warehouses to users after the manufacturing operations are completed.

The materials manager's job has been defined by Dean Ammer as:

> The materials manager's responsibilities for planning begin with the receipt of blue prints and specifications for materials, components, or services that are either incorporated directly into the product or used in operation of the business. His responsibility ends when the material is used in production.[45]

The areas covered in carrying out this job include: purchasing, receiving, receiving inspection, storage (warehousing), non-productive stores (office supplies, perishable tools, maintenance, repair, and operating supplies), and material control (inventory control).

The basis for material planning is the production schedule, since materials must be available to meet production needs. Once these needs have been established, inventory must be planned and controlled to meet those needs at all stages of the production process.

Automated computer systems are used widely for material inventory planning and control. Under a computer system, each item of material is coded (usually on a punched card) as it arrives, and is placed in its specific location in the warehouse. The coded card usually contains such data as the part number, color, size, unit of pack, etc., depending on the information that is required for the operation. Dispersal of all materials so coded is recorded by the computer and stored in its memory unit. The computer will automatically order replacement material when the supply in inventory reaches a predetermined level.

The most widely used inventory reorder control technique is the min-max technique in which supplies are stocked at a predetermined *maximum* level and reorder action is automatically initiated when the supply of a specific material drops below the set *minimum* supply level. Maximum and minimum levels of inventory are determined after a careful study of such planning factors as consumption rates, lead times, safety levels, and seasonal influences.

In many cases, due to irregular production schedules or variable lead times, the min-max approach cannot be used. In these cases it may be possible to employ operations research techniques. Some of these techniques, such as linear programming and decision theory (and their computer applications), are discussed in Chapter 10 and 11 and examples given of their use in inventory control.

[44]John F. Magee, *Industrial Logistics* (New York: McGraw-Hill, 1968), p. 2.

[45]Dean S. Ammer, *Materials Management* (Homewood, Illinois: Richard D. Irwin, Inc., 1968), p. 3.

In planning the warehouses for storing raw materials, consideration is given to its proximity to the manufacturing area, access to transportation, automation of operations, and layout of the storage areas to guarantee accessibility and protection of all items in the warehouse. It is essential in material planning to insure a timely flow of materials and supplies to the production operation to avoid interruption of the production operations. Warehouses should be clean, orderly, well-lighted, and specifically designed for the materials being handled. Each item of material should be given a specific location in the building and this position should remain fixed. Handling equipment should be compatible with the materials being handled, should be in good working order and should be the most economical for the job at hand.

Many companies lose millions of dollars each year because of outdated warehouses, worn out and old handling equipment, old techniques, and poor record keeping, inventory control, and ordering procedures. When we consider that U.S. Steel Corporation spends $33\frac{1}{3}\%$ of its sales dollar on materials, supplies and parts, that General Motors spends 50% of its sales dollar on material purchases, and that the average American firm spends about 50% of its sales dollar in this area, one can begin to grasp the magnitude of the planning problems in the materials area.

When it comes to planning for handling finished products, the problem is really no different from that involved in planning for raw materials. Sufficient, adequate warehouses, efficient control procedures, good handling equipment, and proper packing and shipping operations are all very important to efficient, economical handling of finished products.

The areas discussed so far are not the only ones to be considered, for each company has it own peculiar problems. The planner would look at the specific materials used in his operation and judge for himself what the important considerations are. For example, seasonal materials, long lead-time items, the perishable nature of the materials, the likelihood of strikes, and possible government defense priorities are all variables to be considered.

The following checklist will aid the planner in identifying areas where more information may be required.

1. *Materials.*
   a. What materials are currently used?
   b. What materials does the company anticipate using?
   c. Are these off-the-shelf items or do they require advance ordering (lead-time)?
   d. Are they raw materials, or semi-manufactured or finished components needed in producing the finished product or are they miscellaneous tools, oils, etc.?
   e. Will strikes, industry stockpiling, limited availability, government priorities or fluctuating costs require advance ordering?

f. Are the materials affected by age? Are they seasonal items?
g. Are they perishable items? Do they need special environmental storage?
h. Are there any special problems associated with any of the materials?

2. *Facilities.*
   a. Are the existing facilities adequate?
   b. Are the warehouses centrally located? Are they modern, efficient and economical in their operations?
   c. Are there storage areas close to the production facilities?
   d. Are the miscellaneous items kept close to the production areas?
   e. What improvements could and should be made?

3. *Manpower.*
   a. What are the qualifications of our employees?
   b. How is employee morale?

4. *Equipment.*
   a. How much do we own?
   b. How does it perform, and what is its condition?
   c. Is it the proper type for the job?

5. *Transportation.*
   a. What modes are we served by?
   b. Do our warehouses have spur tracks? How large?
   c. What kinds of truck loading and unloading areas do our warehouses have?

6. *Operations.*
   a. Are the inventory control and record-keeping procedures adequate?
   b. Are the warehousing and handling techniques modern, effective, economic, and safe?
   c. Would automated inventory control and ordering be an improvement? Is it practical?
   d. Are there any other operational difficulties that should be studied?

7. Are there any other areas that should be studied?

Distribution.

The distribution function covers all those activities involving the movement of finished goods to the customer.[46]

Planning for distribution begins with an examination of company marketing and manufacturing distribution requirements, as well as any particular strategic planning factors affecting distribution. This review would cover such factors as the nature and organization of the company's operations, the importance and function of distribution within that organization, product characteristics, location of the company in relation to its customers, customer requirements, distribution and delivery offered by competitors, production capacity and output plans, climate considerations,

[46]Donald J. Bowersox, "Physical Distribution Development: Current Status and Potential," *Journal of Marketing*, January 1969, p. 63.

sales fluctuations (size, timing, area, and volatility), and inventory fluctuations. Next, the present company distribution operation and present company facilities and resources are examined, covering such areas as production and warehousing facilities, materials handling and transportation equipment, manpower, and costs and finances. Available outside transportation and warehousing facilities, their costs and their use by the company are also studied.

Developing an overall strategy for distribution, based on these planning premises, requires reconciling many conflicting customer service and cost requirements. This reconciliation is not easy. For example, customer service wants large supplies kept on hand to service customers quickly, while cost considerations dictate keeping small quantities on hand to reduce inventory expenses. Or, customer service argues for many stock points located close to customers, while cost control argues for reducing the number of points in order to reduce warehousing expenses. The optimum distribution strategy strives to balance sales and customer service requirements with manufacturing and distribution cost requirements at the least possible cost.

Distribution plans are made for all aspects of transportation (including loading, shipping, receiving, and packaging for transport) and warehousing (including their location, number, size and design, as well as the handling and control of inventory within the warehouses). In making these plans, the existing facilities and distribution practices, which were outlined during the premising stage, are first evaluated in the light of how well they fulfill service and cost requirements. Avenues of improvement and change that will increase customer service or reduce manufacturing or distribution costs are then explored.

In developing distribution plans, "total" costs are what count. For example, the savings gained from reducing warehouse space must be weighed against the costs of shorter production runs; the savings gained from bulk shipping must be weighed against any increased handling costs; and the savings gained from using slow modes of transportation, such as rail, instead of fast modes, such as air freight, must be weighed against the "cost" of any reduced sales resulting from decreases in customer service efficiency. In other words, each cost saving in any area of distribution will usually lead to increased costs in other areas of distribution, manufacturing, or marketing. All these costs, not just the immediate distribution cost savings, must be considered in developing distribution plans.

Operations research and computer simulation provide the distribution planner with tools to determine scientifically the total cost of alternative plans and so the most economical way to satisfy the sometimes conflicting demands placed upon his distribution system. Such operations research tools as linear programming are used to quantify and measure the economics of alternative transportation methods and shipping schedules, the effect on total costs of reducing or increasing the number of warehouses or changing their locations, and the impact on distribution costs of changes in demand, production schedules, product line, or service requirements. Examples of such studies and of other uses of operations research and computer simulation in distribution planning are discussed in Chapters 10 and 11 and in the articles cited in the footnote.[47]

In coordinating the requirements of the many sales and manufacturing activities affected by distribution planning, the distribution planner will frequently meet resistance from operating managers when plans which are best from an overall company viewpoint in some ways hurt individual operations. Operations research and simulation tools are helpful in overcoming this resistance, because they are quantitative yardsticks, and so provide objective decision-making standards.

Though the ultimate goal of the distribution manager is to balance the requirements of manufacturing and marketing in an economical distribution system, his performance is also judged on his ability to reduce actual distribution costs and improve distribution efficiency. The following is a checklist of some of the specific cost-cutting areas which might be explored in planning the movement of finished goods:

1. *Rate Reduction.* Commodity rates, both regular and incentive, can be sought. Increased volume, lower prices from competitive modes of transportation, and the introduction of a bulk handling system are just a few ways in which a company may gain rate reductions.
2. *Rates at New Shipping Points.* Before setting up a new shipping point, it is extremely important to negotiate the most favorable rate before the freight from that point becomes captive.
3. *Local Delivery Costs.* Although line haul charges normally provide the greatest potential for rate reduction, local delivery costs should not be overlooked. Rates and services are subject to outside fluctuations, even in the same area.
4. *Technological Developments.* New developments in carrier equipment and methods will often have an effect on transportation costs. Jumbo tank cars and hoppers, double deck highway trailers and extra high "containerized" trailers offer opportunities for increasing shipment volume and lowering unit transportation costs.
5. *Consolidation Opportunities.* One of the most fruitful areas for trans-

[47]For a discussion of some of these tools and their uses see: H. J. Lane, "Simulation, Powerful Tool for Distribution," *Distribution Manager,* May 1968, pp. 59-64; Ronald J. Lewis, "Strengthening Control of Physical Distribution Costs," *Management Services,* January-February 1968, pp. 37-46; Charles D. Ledden, "Management Science: A Simulation Example of Railroad Management," *Systems and Procedures Journal,* March-April 1968, pp. 23-27; L. Gayle Rayburn, "Setting Standards for Distribution Costs," *Management Services,* March-April 1967, pp. 42-52; Ward A. Fredericks, "Introduction to Operations Research Techniques," *Distribution Age,* January 1967, pp 22-28; Charles J. Stokes, "Linear Programming and All That," *Business Economics,* Fall 1967, pp. 48-54.

portation cost reduction is in consolidation of shipments to and from common origins and destinations. Such opportunities are most readily found in multi-divisional corporations where each division controls its own traffic.

6. *Making Use of Transit Privileges.* Traffic may authorize stopping off at origin or destination, or both, of a shipment for partial loading and/or partial unloading, allowing less-volume shipments to move at volume rates. Some tariffs also provide for transloading, storage in transit and manufacturing in transit.
7. *Changes in Distribution Network.* It should never be taken for granted that existing distribution systems are inflexible. Changes can always be made.
8. *Accurate Classification.* All classifications of freight both inbound and outbound should be checked to insure the correct classification is being used.
9. *Loss and Damage Claims.* Using a frequency distribution technique or other approach, a study of claims should be made to determine whether a particular product, carrier, shipping or receiving point can be isolated as a causal or contributing factor.[48]

In many ways then distribution planning resembles other types of manufacturing planning. The planner starts by examining overall company and manufacturing planning, isolates planning premises related specifically to his operation, integrates a number of operational planning areas which affect the development of his strategy and plans, uses sophisticated analytical tools to improve his planning, and needs considerable ingenuity in creating alternative solutions to his operational problems.

Manpower.

The job of manpower planning for manufacturing is to assure that the right number of people with the required abilities are available at the right time, place, and price to fulfill the needs of the operation.[49]

The steps involved in carrying out manpower planning are similar to those in other manufacturing areas. First, manufacturing plans and overall company plans are studied to identify factors affecting manpower planning and to determine manpower needs. Second, manpower planning objectives are established based on the study of these planning premises. Third, specific plans are made in the major areas covered in manpower planning.

The major external factors affecting manpower planning for manufacturing include the size and nature of the labor market, the availability of labor with the skills needed, industry and local wage structures, industrial concentration and competition for labor, seasonal demands in the labor market, and technological trends within the industry. Internal factors affecting manpower planning include the nature and complexity of

[48]R. M. Sutton, "A Checklist for Reducing Transportation Costs," *Transportation and Distribution Management*, August 1968, pp. 28-33.

[49]Theodore M. Alfred, "Checkers or Choice in Manpower Management," *Harvard Business Review*, January-February 1967, p. 157.

the production process, output quotas, seasonal and cyclical fluctuations, working conditions, growth plans, new product and process plans, and the degree of unionization.

Manpower planning objectives are based on manufacturing planning requirements. Manufacturing plans will provide information on the number of people required to meet manufacturing objectives, and where and when they are needed. While the manufacturing plan will indicate the kind of people needed, detailed information on job specifications and standard wage rates for job categories is usually also needed to supplement the overall planning information—if manpower plans are to be made to get the right kind of people at the right price.

Working within the limits of the planning premises, specific manpower plans are developed to achieve these objectives. These plans would cover employee staffing, training, and administration.

The staffing plans break down into three areas: recruiting, selecting, and placing. Recruiting involves securing a sufficient number of qualified candidates to allow for selectivity in hiring. Plans for both external recruiting (advertising, employment agencies, bonuses for personal referrals, etc.) and internal recruiting (transfers, promotions, etc.) are developed. Plans for screening and selecting employees cover interviewing and testing, while placing plans cover processing employees and matching them with appropriate job needs.

Education and training plans will vary with the level of employees and the technical skills required. During the late 1960's, skilled labor shortages led to much greater emphasis on internal development programs designed to fill skilled labor gaps by upgrading present employees. In addition to helping fill manpower needs, education and training programs help increase productivity, reduce supervision, heighten morale, reduce accidents, and increase organization stability and flexibility.

Besides the above plans, plans and procedures are also developed in such areas as performance evaluation, wages, salaries and benefits, worker motivation, employee services and working conditions, salary adjustments, and termination of employment of those workers who do not meet performance standards. These and other manpower plans are needed to insure effective administration of personnel.

Basic to all manpower planning in the manufacturing area are employee record-keeping systems, wage and salary structures, and work measurement standards. Employee record-keeping systems, which are discussed in Chapter 11, provide the information needed for developing and carrying out the above plans. A wage and salary structure is needed in manpower planning and control and administration, if plans are to be made within overall company cost guidelines, if total labor costs are to be controlled, and if staffing and promotion plans are to be objective and equitable. Work measurement standards are needed both in planning (for example, in production scheduling and in establishing manning requirements), as well as in evaluating worker performance.

Where company employees are unionized, plans must be made for bargaining with unions, and specific policies and procedures developed for guiding that bargaining. The extent and kind of union influence on a given business depends not only on the amount of bargaining power held by the unions, but also on the importance of union labor in the industry, the range of occupational skills employed, and the pace of technological change.

Manpower planning for manufacturing is only one aspect of a company's total manpower planning job. All operating and staff areas need the right people—at the right place, time, and price—to fulfill their needs. Manpower planning receives special attention in the manufacturing area for two reasons: first, manpower costs usually represent a higher percentage of costs in this area; second, the contributions of individual manpower units to the operation are in general more precisely measurable than in other areas.

PLANNING FOR FINANCE

Since the efficient management of capital is a basic purpose of any business, the financial function has always been an important one, and is usually handled by a firm's president or an officer working closely with him. As one authority has put it: "The financial manager plays a key role in the guidance of the firm. He has a central responsibility in analysis, planning and control which guide the firm's resources into the most profitable lines. . . . The importance of the financial manager is recognized by his place at the top levels in the organization structure of the firm. Financial decisions are crucial for the well being of a firm, because they determine the ability of the company to obtain plant and equipment when needed, to carry the requisite amount of inventories and receivables, to avoid burdensome fixed charges when sales and profits fall, and to prevent loss of effective control of the company."[50]

The financial function can be viewed as two separate but equally important tasks. First, financial management must provide the funds which the business needs to achieve its objectives, at the most reasonable rates. Second, financial management is concerned with the effective use of funds within a business.[51] In the sense that all company resources represent past, present, and future investments of funds, the financial officer is concerned with the most basic of all management planning decisions—the efficient allocation of resources.

[50]J. Fred Weston and Eugene F. Brigham, *Managerial Finance* (2nd ed.; New York: Holt, Rinehart and Winston, 1962), p. 15.

[51]Pearson Hunt, Charles M. Williams, and Gordon Donaldson, *Basic Business Finance: Text and Cases* (3rd ed.; Homewood, Illinois: Richard D. Irwin, Inc., 1966), p. 4.

Planning for finance can be broken down into four steps:

1. Examining overall company plans to be certain they have realistically taken into account the company's financial limitations.
2. Developing overall financial objectives and determining the specific financial resources required to meet the company's objectives and operating requirements.
3. Forecasting how much of these requirements will be met by generation of funds within the company and how much will have to be obtained outside the company, and then developing plans to obtain the funds needed from external sources.
4. Establishing and maintaining a system of financial controls governing the allocation and use of funds within the company.[52]

Financial planning is an integral part of overall company strategic planning, since available financial resources set limits on what kinds of strategy a company can or cannot pursue. Financial planning thus begins with overall company planning and its overall directions formulated along with company objectives and strategies. An example of the close relationship between financial and overall company planning is found in the Indian Head Mills study discussed in Chapter 5, where acquisition policies were dictated by the company's objective to expand without diluting common stock.

Next, the financial planner determines specific financial requirements. The average business maintains a substantial investment in inventory, credits to customers (receivables), cash, plant and equipment, and research and development. The financial manager examines all these areas and determines what funds will be needed to operate the business profitably. In addition, he will participate in the evaluation of proposed capital projects to help determine which ones should be undertaken to achieve company long-term goals, if funds can be obtained for them.

The basic method of planning the amount and timing of future funds needs is through the preparation of a *cash flow forecast* or a *cash budget*. Basically, the cash flow forecast is a plan which predicts when and in what quantity cash receipts will come into the company and when and in what quantity cash payments will be made. Anticipated cash receipts would include such items as cash from the sale of securities and fixed assets, as well as cash from sales and the collection of accounts receivable. Cash disbursements would include such non-routine disbursements as outlays for equipment, as well as routine payment of wages, accounts payable, taxes, dividends, and so on. Table 7.2 gives a simplified statement of cash flow for the ABC Company for the six months from January to June 1971.

[52]Jerome B. Cohen and Sidney M. Robbins, *The Financial Manager: Basic Aspects of Financial Administration* (New York: Harper and Row, Publishers, 1966), p. 5.

Table 7.2

SCHEDULE OF ESTIMATED CASH FLOWS
ABC COMPANY—JANUARY TO JUNE 1971
(IN THOUSANDS)

	Jan.	*Feb.*	*March*	*April*	*May*	*June*	*Total*
Total Receipts	$75	$60	$65	$55	$80	$85	$420
Total Payments	70	60	62	65	75	78	410
Net Inflow or (Outflow)	$ 5	—	$ 3	($10)	$ 5	$ 7	$ 10
Cumulative Inflow or (Outflow)	5	5	8	(2)	3	10	10

This cash budget allows the management of the ABC Company to determine approximately how much cash will flow into and out of the company for the first six months of the year. For the months in which there will be a net outflow of cash, management can plan to secure needed funds from outside sources. In the months in which there will be a net inflow of cash, management can plan to use the excess funds for investment or to reduce borrowing. The cash budget also serves as a standard or yardstick of performance. Management can compare the budgeted cash inflow and outflow with the actual inflow and outflow. If actual cash flows have deviated significantly from budgeted flows, management can determine the reasons for this deviation and either make plans to eliminate the problems in order to bring actual flows more in line with budget, or revise the cash budget to make it more realistic.

Once a forecast of funds needed has been made, the financial manager determines where funds can be obtained. Internally generated funds—funds arising from profitable sales—will usually meet some of these requirements. External financing, both long-term and short-term, must be used to fill the remaining funds needs. Long-term financing can be done either through debt (principally the issuance of bonds) or through equity (principally the issuance of common or preferred stock), depending on the needs, financial condition, and objectives of the company. Some sources of short-term financing are trade credits, bank loans, commercial paper, factoring of accounts receivable, and leasing.

The general availability of funds in the economy, the cost at which they are available, inflationary pressures on the economy, and government spending policies all affect financial planning. During periods such as early 1970, for example, when interest rates on long-term debt securities were relatively high, many companies were forced to seek alternative means of financing.

The tax environment in which the business operates also has a major impact on funds management. Frequently, the success of a company rests on how it adjusts to its tax environment. Planning for finance thus requires the study of the federal, state and local tax environment, as well as the economic environment, to determine its impact on company operations.

The financial manager thus has both an internal and external job. He must review the financial status of the firm to determine what funds will be needed, how funds can best be used, and how efficiently existing resources are being used. He must also look outside the firm at the environmental factors which affect the availability of funds, and the price at which they can be obtained.

Since there is never an unlimited supply of funds, the typical company has a wide range of alternatives competing for the use of its funds. Financial management is responsible for guiding the selection of the uses to which available funds will be put, and for insuring that funds are used in the most efficient manner possible. There are two basic criteria used in controlling funds allocations: first, funds should be used to help the company attain its objectives; and second, the allocation of funds should be guided by the principle of the maximization of return on investment.

Capital budgeting is a major tool used in planning and controlling the allocation and expenditure of long-term investment funds. The capital budget specifies the projects selected by management which will require capital investment, together with the estimated cost of and return on each project. Since capital budgets forecast requirements for capital funds, they enable management to plan in advance to secure whatever additional funds may be needed to finance profitable projects.[53]

Capital budgeting may be viewed as a four step process:

1. Determining the amount of money available that can be used for capital investments.
2. Examining each possible capital project to determine its cost in relation to its potential return on investment.
3. Selecting those projects which appear to be the most profitable and determining the total amount of money that will be needed for capital expenditures during the time period covered by the plan.
4. Determining how much money will have to be raised externally for capital expenditures, and selecting methods of external financing.

The first step in the capital budgeting process is the determination of what internal company funds can be used to finance capital investments, as well as what funds are available from sources outside the Company. This step facilitates the appraisal of potential capital projects, for it gives management an approximate idea of the company's capacity to undertake capital projects, and sets very general limits on what can and cannot realistically be done.

The heart of the capital budgeting process is the examination of

[53]Cohen and Robbins, *The Financial Manager*, p. 665.

potential capital investments to determine their possible profitability to the company. The process is extremely complex, since capital expenditures involve the spending of sums of money in the present, and then waiting for a period of years to receive the benefits resulting from those expenditures.[54]

In general, a capital expenditure should not be made if the investment will return less than what the firm has to pay on the funds necessary to finance the project.[55] In other words, a project's return must be sufficient to pay the interest on the debt invested in the project and/or the cost of equity (stock) capital used to finance the project. It should not be assumed that this is an adequate basis on which a company should make an investment, for in most instances the company will plan to earn a profit on the investment. Nor does this imply that a company may not occasionally use other investment criteria. For example, if a firm's main plant burns down, it may be rebuilt immediately simply to stay in business.

The cost of debt (percentage of interest) and equity capital (earnings as a percentage of equity) used to finance a project is known as the *cost of capital*.[56] It is based on a weighted average of the different types of funds needed. The cost of capital is usually calculated on the basis of after-tax figures.

By adding together the cost of capital and minimum earnings management will accept, the financial planner can establish a minimum acceptable return on investment. In the case of the ABC Company that figure was 13.56%: a cost of capital of 8.56% added to a 5% required minimum return on investment.

Next, each proposed project is studied and its expected return on investment (ROI) is calculated.[57] For example, the ABC Company might consider introducing a new product line which requires new machinery. The company expects to make 17% on the investment, based on reasonably conservative assumptions about price and volume. This 17% is comfortably above the 13.56% minimum, and so the project would be acceptable, provided that capital could be obtained.

Once the total investment for all the capital projects considered worthwhile has been calculated and the timing of the money needs has been forecast, the company must determine where the funds will be obtained. The initial funds flow forecast would indicate the amount of money available from operations. Any capital requirement in excess of this amount would have to be obtained from outside sources.

[54]C. G. Edge, "Capital Budgeting: Principles and Projection," *Financial Executive*, September 1965, p. 50.

[55]Alexander A. Robichek and John G. McDonald, "The Cost of Capital Concept: Potential Use and Misuse," *Financial Executive*, June 1965, p. 21.

[56]Edge, "Capital Budgeting," p. 52.

[57]Richard F. Perdunn, "Capital Investment and Large Projects," *Financial Executive*, June 1965, p. 15.

If funds are needed from outside sources, the company must next select the methods of external financing it will use. Funds can be raised externally through debt financing or through equity financing, or through some combination or variation of the two. The exact solution will depend on the requirements of the particular company. In those instances where adequate funds cannot be obtained to undertake all profitable projects, the planner must review his capital expenditures and eliminate the least desirable projects.

Capital budgeting is a useful tool which management can use to plan and control the long-term use of company funds. It enables management to analyze potential capital investments more thoroughly, to select those investments which will maximize return on investment, and to finance these projects according to a well-thought-out plan. The capital budget also serves as a yardstick or guideline for judging whether these assets are being used efficiently after their acquisition. It should be remembered, however, that the effectiveness of capital budgeting depends in large measure on the reliability of the planning forecasts.

A major technique used to study the extent of a company's financial needs, the efficiency of its use of capital, and its general financial health, is financial analysis through financial ratios.

These ratios cover the major areas of a business which the financial manager must plan for. They are generally grouped in four categories:[58]

1. *Liquidity ratios,* which are designed to measure the ability of the firm to meet its maturing short-term obligations. Liquidity analysis involves such ratios as current assets to current liabilities, cash or equivalent to current liabilities, and inventory to working capital.
2. *Leverage ratios,* which measure the contribution of owners as compared with the financing provided by the firm's creditors. Leverage analysis involves such ratios as debt to total assets, times interest earned, fixed-charge coverage, current liabilities to net worth, and fixed assets to net worth.
3. *Activity ratios,* which measure how effectively the firm is employing its resources. Activity analysis involves such ratios as cash velocity, inventory turnover, fixed assets turnover, average collection period, and total asset turnover.
4. *Profitability ratios,* which measure management's effectiveness as shown by the returns generated on sales and investment. Profitability analysis involves such ratios as gross operating margin, net operating margin, sales margin, productivity of assets, and return on net worth.

In order to use financial ratios for planning and control, their behavior should be examined over a period of time. By examining the same ratios over a period of months or years, the planner can get a picture of whether or not the company's position is improving, for the trend can be determined and the effect of seasonal factors and extraordinary events can

[58]Weston and Brigham, *Managerial Finance,* Chapter Four.

be eliminated from the analysis. Ratios should also be compared with those of other companies and with industry averages. Through such comparisons it is possible to determine just how well a company is doing within its industry, and to better judge relative efficiency, profitability, and potential earning power.

Financial analysis through financial ratios leads the planner to examine almost every area of a company's operation, from tax, insurance, and pension management to sales and production. Through this analysis he can pinpoint areas which need more careful consideration and in general build a sound information base for all financial planning.

CONCLUSION

This chapter has explored implementation planning in marketing, new products, research and development, manufacturing, and finance. The approach to planning in each of these areas is based on the general implementation planning process, which is outlined in Chapter 6. In developing the planning approach in each area from the general process, considerable amplification and refinement was needed, for each area has its own peculiar requirements to which the process must be adapted. The approaches to planning in each area, therefore, differ somewhat from each other in detail, in spite of the fact that they all have a common basis.

The five areas discussed in this chapter are not the only areas of implementation planning. The managers of every operating and staff area within a company, including personnel, systems, office administration, and accounting, face important planning decisions. The general implementation planning process, outlined in Chapter 6 and developed in this chapter, can be used in developing approaches to planning in all company operating and staff areas, not just the five discussed here.

While it is useful to know the different approaches to planning in each operating and staff area, it is equally important to know how to put these approaches to work. The discussion, therefore, included illustrations of how planning is carried out in a variety of actual business situations. *The National Observer* study, for example, showed how the approach to marketing planning was used in a circulation marketing operation. Additional examples of how implementation planning is carried out in other situations, such as budgetary planning, systems planning and planning for small companies, are given in the later chapters of this book.

The planning done in individual operating and staff areas is interrelated, so that plans can never be made in any one functional area without reference to other planning areas. Coordinating and controlling implementation planning is a complex job, especially in a large corporation, where a wide range of activities are being planned for and where many layers of management may be involved in the planning. The problems encountered in coordinating and controlling planning, and ways to overcome these problems, are discussed in Chapter 9.

Before getting into the problems of coordinating and controlling implementation planning, however, another phase of implementation planning—establishing operating and staff policies, procedures and rules—is discussed in the following chapter.

DISCUSSION QUESTIONS

1. Why is marketing the first area in which implementation plans are usually developed? Under what circumstances would you consider dealing with some other area first?
2. Outline the approach to marketing planning. Describe how it is related to the implementation planning process given in Chapter 6.
3. Discuss the ways in which the approach to marketing planning was adapted in solving *The National Observer*'s circulation problems.
4. What are the steps followed in new product planning? In what ways do they differ from those followed in marketing planning? In what ways are they similar?
5. Discuss the ways in which new product planning and R & D planning are related. In what ways are they distinct?
6. Define the major types of research and development and the criteria used for selecting the type of R & D a company should engage in.
7. What considerations are important in organizing and administering an R & D operation?
8. Discuss the circumstances under which manufacturing would be a relatively insignificant part of company planning. Under what circumstances would it dominate all company planning?
9. While there is a general approach to implementation planning, there are many refinements and amplifications needed when applying it. Describe the adjustments made to the implementation planning process in applying it to the distribution operation? To production scheduling?
10. Of all the areas discussed in this chapter, only finance is not strictly an "operational" business area. Discuss the ways in which finance has its own "operating" requirements which must be planned for.
11. In what ways does financial planning affect the overall company strategic plan?
12. Discuss the reasons why it is so important to coordinate the planning done in all operating and staff areas. What are some of the difficulties which might be encountered in performing this coordination in different size companies?
13. Develop implementation plans for the Blakeston and Wilson Company and the Superb Biscuits Company, both of which are described in the Appendices of this book.

CHAPTER 8

DEVELOPING OPERATING AND STAFF POLICIES, PROCEDURES, AND RULES

Planning for each operating and staff area should include formulation of derivative policies, procedures, and rules which are consistent with overall corporate policies, and which guide achievement of operating and staff objectives. This chapter describes the nature of derivative policies, procedures and rules, and discusses examples of how they are developed and used in practice.

DERIVATIVE POLICIES, PROCEDURES, AND RULES: SOME BASIC DEFINITIONS

Since overall corporate policies present guidelines for action only in very general terms, more detailed guidelines are needed within the various staff and operating areas. Operating and staff areas, therefore, have their own derivative policies, as well as procedures and rules, which provide guidelines for carrying out its plans and which extend and amplify the overall corporate policies.

Specific operating and staff policies fulfill two functions: first, they provide guidelines designed to achieve the sub-objective of the staff or operating area for which they are written; second, since they extend and amplify the overall corporate policies, they help insure action will be consistent with overall company planning. These policies are called "derivative" policies because they are derived from and related to overall company policies.

There may be many levels of derivative objectives and policies, depending on the organization and size of the company. In a large company, each geographic or product division will have its own objectives and policies. Each area within each division will in turn have derivative objectives and policies. For example, there will be basic objectives and policies for marketing, manufacturing, and any other areas within a division. The various segments of each of these operating areas will in turn have additional levels of objectives and policies. For example, in marketing there will be sub-objectives and policies for sales, products, customer service, and the like. A large company will thus have a whole network of objectives and policies, all developed within the overall strategic planning framework.

A procedure is a step-by-step process involving a chronological sequence or pattern of action. It operates within the areas designated by a policy, but is more specific and narrower than a policy. A procedure describes when, where, how, and by whom specific tasks are to be done within policy guidelines. In this way, it implements policy and ultimately results in the attainment of the overall objective. A minimum amount of interpretation is needed for the use of a procedure.[1]

A rule designates specific action that should either be taken or not be taken under specified circumstances. Although a rule, like a policy, is a guideline for action, it is narrower and more specific, and, unlike a policy, it is mandatory and permits no discretion. A rule differs from a procedure in that it does not specify a time sequence, or specific steps to be taken. Although they are distinct, in some cases rules are contained within procedures.[2] Rules are established when the need for uniformity and dependability of action is greater than that for good judgment.[3]

Companies are more likely to define procedures and rules before doing any formal strategic planning, even though the reverse is the recommended approach. For example, in the Blakeston and Wilson study, the procedural manual for store operations was written and printed before any thought was given to creating an overall company plan. The reason that this happens is because procedures guide daily operations, and so are needed immediately. The average manager is inclined to solve his immediate problems first, and put off forming longer-term, more conceptual jobs, such as strategic planning.

Examples of procedures and rules are legion. Every company has credit and collection procedures, procedures for paying its employees, quality control procedures, and the like. But not every company has an overall strategic plan or a well-defined network of derivative policies from which its procedures are developed.

[1]George R. Terry, *Principles of Management* (4th ed.; Homewood, Illinois: Richard D. Irwin, Inc., 1964), pp. 288-289.

[2]Harold Koontz and Cyril O'Donnell, *Principles of Management* (3rd ed., New York: McGraw-Hill Book Company, 1964), pp. 74-76.

[3]William H. Newman and Charles E. Summer, Jr., *The Process of Management: Concepts, Behavior and Practice* (2nd ed.; Englewood Cliffs, New Jersey: Prentice Hall, Inc., 1967), pp. 499-500.

This chapter, therefore, is not intended to provide guidance in writing procedural manuals. Rather, it focuses on how derivative policies are developed within the overall strategic planning framework, and then how procedures and rules are developed to support these policies and guide operations towards the achievement of its objectives.

A COMPANY STUDY

The following is an example of how derivative policies, procedures and rules are developed and used at Sears, Roebuck and Company in their customer service area.[4]

Sears' Overall Policy Development

Policy development is an important management tool at Sears for a number of reasons. Policies are a means of making store managers aware of chain management's overall plans, and of giving guidance to managers in those decision-making areas that have been decentralized. At the same time, because policies allow freedom for local decision making, they enable store managers to respond to local conditions which cannot be foreseen by chain management.

Policies help a retail chain maintain its image with consumers and stabilize its customer relations. By bringing uniformity to operations, customer recognition of the chain's name and its services are increased. Customer confidence in the chain is also increased, as he comes to realize that he will receive similar services and products in all of the chain's outlets.

The organization of Sears' retail operation consists of a parent unit, five territories, and numerous groups and zones of stores within these territories.

The parent unit is the operation's "banker . . . landlord . . . supplier of professional and technical skills; and in its president and chairman, the final authority of company management."[5] The parent unit is divided into fifty departments and is staffed by almost 5,000 employees. Some of the more important departments include the comptroller's and treasurer's offices, factory management, law, property, personnel, public relations, parent operating and parent merchandising.

The parent merchandising and operating departments are of most concern to this study. The parent merchandising department supervises

[4]Material for this section is based in large part on Herbert T. Wolf, *Policy Development & Implementation in a Large Retail Chain,* Unpublished Master's Paper (New York: St. John's University, 1968).

[5]*Merchant of the Millions—A Brief History of the Origin and Development of Sears, Roebuck and Company* (Chicago: Sears, Roebuck and Company, National Public Relations Department, 1967), p. 16.

catalogue production and distribution, economic research, product testing, and store planning and display, as well as the centralized buying of all merchandise. The parent operating department supervises retail and catalogue operations, and customer service on Sears' products.

Each of the five territorial organizations is headed by a vice-president, who is assisted by a staff organization. The catalogue outlets and larger self-contained stores report directly to the territorial level, while the other stores are organized into "groups" or "zones" within the territory. The groups consist of city stores, for example the New York Group, while the zones are made up of non-city stores. The group and zone staffs provide specialized services, coordination and operational advice to the individual stores.

Sears' Board of Directors is directly responsible for the formulation of corporate policy. The Board consists of the five territorial vice-presidents, the chairman, the president, the merchandising and personnel vice-presidents, and the controller. These men can formulate corporate policy only at formal Board meetings, and cannot formulate corporate policy for their own specialized areas on an individual basis.[6]

Special staff committees are assigned the task of investigating specific situations and recommending policy statements, but the Board alone can make these statements into binding corporate policies. In this way policy is always developed within the context of overall corporate objectives and philosophy.

While not formally involved in final policy formulation, other division and store management, as well as store level personnel, can affect the development of corporate policy. The store and division managers have opportunities to make suggestions directly to territorial management, through meetings and personal contact, while store level personnel can affect policy development through a suggestion box system, which on the basis of interviews with store personnel appears to be widely and effectively used throughout Sears' retail store system.

Sears' Policy Development in the Service Area

Sears' service area provides a good illustration of effective derivative policy development and administration.

The basic objective of Sears' service is to take care of the customer's needs after a sale has been made. This objective is broken down into the following specific responsibilities in the *Customer Service Manual*:

1. Rigid maintenance of all delivery and service promises to customers. This includes current orders and orders for future delivery.
2. Installation of mechanical merchandise by service technicians or delivery in a workman-like manner to the customer's satisfaction.

[6]Interview with management.

3. Prompt handling of inquiries and complaints received by mail, telephone or in person.
4. Maintenance of an adequate repair and mechanical service.
5. Maintenance of an efficient Lay-away service.
6. Prompt entry of new items and corrections in Repair Parts Price Lists.
7. Maintenance of Service Manuals, Service Memos and Service Sales Promotion Handbook.
8. Maintenance of an up-to-date file on bulletins pertaining to customer service work.
9. Conduct of service-training meetings in accordance with standards set up in Paragraph 1210.[7]

These responsibilities for customer service are carried out by several organizations within the zones and groups. They include central service centers, customer service units within the stores, and the service functions carried out by store managers, sales personnel and service technicians.

Within the New York Group, for example, there are six separate central service centers. These centers handle appliance repairs and some of the installation work for the Sears stores in their geographic area. Each center is headed by a central service manager, who has center responsibility. His expenses must be less than the income from the sales of maintenance agreements, from the sale of "parts," such as Kenmore detergent and TV antennas, and from "paid" service calls. The central service manager is on the same management level as the store manager.

The customer service units within each store are run by the customer service manager. In the larger stores, he handles questionable complaints, accepts defective and damaged merchandise for shipment to service centers, and supervises the delivery of merchandise from the store to its customers. In smaller stores, there is a customer service desk, which is handled by a clerk who also acts as parts order-taker and accepts merchandise for shipment to repair facilities. The store manager handles complaints.

Store managers and assistant store managers are involved in the customer service area largely on an exception basis—that is only when the customer service desk or customer service manager cannot handle the situation. The sales personnel are frequently the ones who receive returned merchandise, and so they are usually the ones who handle the initial customer complaint. The service technicians deal directly with the customer, when they visit customers to repair major appliances.

Sears' basic adjustment and service policy is "Satisfaction Guaranteed or Your Money Back."[8] This policy is related to Sears' overall philosophy of increased sales volume and increased breadth of services. It is designed as a convenience "that will keep them [customers] returning to us [Sears]

[7] *Customer Service Manual* (Rev. ed.; Chicago: Sears, Roebuck and Company, 1965), p. 3.

[8] *Customer Service Manual*, p. 17.

for their needs."[9] It is especially important today, with the increasing technical and mechanical complexity of products.

Sears interprets this policy literally. It is subject only to the limitations of common sense, and here any "edge" always lies with the customer. This means that any customer who is dissatisfied with a Sears product or service can request and obtain a full refund, if he acts within a reasonable period of time after the sale. A reasonable period of time is defined as one that is long enough to provide the customer with an opportunity to use the product and become familiar with it, and its exact length varies with the type of merchandise involved—except where product guarantees list a specific time period. The emphasis is on customer satisfaction and not on a refund, so that considerable use is made of Sears' service departments to remedy the cause of the complaint.

There are a number of derivative policies which flow from the overall service policy and which illustrate how policies for a specific operating area are developed within the framework of overall corporate policy.[10] The first group of derivative policies covers customer service in general and includes the following:

1. Sears policy requires that all refunds be made promptly and in the same friendly manner the original sale was made.
2. As a general policy, customers should be required to produce evidence of purchase before merchandise is accepted for refund.
3. Sears general policy is to accept, without question, unused merchandise purchased at Sears for exchange or refund.
4. Sears policy is to replace defective merchandise, either worn or new, with new merchandise. Do not charge the customer for the proportionate service obtained from a defective item unless it is guaranteed on a time service basis.
5. Sears policy is to review with the customer any requests for adjustments on non-defective merchandise that has been subjected to nature wear, and adjust reasonable complaints with new merchandise.
6. Partial adjustments of such merchandise (type discussed in #5) are not according to the company policy.
7. It is company policy that we accept the customer's judgment on what it takes to satisfy him, including refunding his full purchase price or the service charges paid.
8. Where merchandise or a service has been used and retained by the customer beyond a reasonable period, the complaint will be handled on a basis that

[9]Fowler B. McConnell, "How a Great Giant Grew," *Industrial Development and Manufacturing Record*, December 1958, p. 21.

[10]The policies, procedures and rules quoted in the following sections of this chapter are found in: *Handbook for Sales People—Retail Basic Training* (Rev. ed.; Chicago: Sears, Roebuck and Company, 1964), G. M. Metcalf and Crowley Baker, "Customer Complaint and Handling," *Bulletin 0-277*, a bulletin prepared by the Chairman of the Board and President for distribution to all managers down to and including the Division Manager (Chicago: Sears, Roebuck and Company, 1967); *Selling System Handbook* (Chicago: Sears, Roebuck and Company, 1963); and *Customer Service Manual.*

is acceptable to the customer as an equitable adjustment and confirms to the customer the integrity and business principles of the company.

9. If the customer is not satisfied within the terms of a specific product guarantee or if the specific guarantee is expired or non-existent, handle the complaint as a policy adjustment.

Although the above statements are largely self-explanatory, it should be remembered that they are policies and so are subject to interpretation according to the situation. For example, while Sears requires evidence of purchase when accepting a return, a refund is not to be refused on this basis alone. If the customer can properly identify himself, or if a salesman remembers the sale, it can be approved. If the refund request is questionable, a bank check mailed to the customer's home address is used instead of cash. Similarly, although partial adjustments are not normal, complaints involving used but non-defective merchandise are adjusted according to the circumstances involved.

The second group of derivative policies covers adjustments of sales made on credit only.

1. If a customer returns an Easy Payment purchase within thirty days from date of sale for a bonafide reason, it is our policy to return the customer's deposit, if any.
2. When the merchandise is returned after thirty days from date of sale, it is not customary to make any refund of deposit or subsequent payments.
3. In instances where the merchandise has not given the performance the customer has a right to expect, and no satisfactory adjustment can be made, refund of what has been paid, even though the return was made after thirty days.

The third group of derivative policies covers the return of merchandise sold by other Sears stores or through the catalogue. They include:

1. The general policy to be followed is to make all adjustments precisely as if the merchandise had been sold in your store.
2. As a general policy, stores are to adjust locally on all returned merchandise.
3. Customer complaints on merchandise purchased from the catalogue sales desk of a retail store must be remedied by the customer service department of the retail store in the same manner as for a sale made by one of the selling units of the store.
4. Accept overseas claims of difficulty with any merchandise (other than major electrical and mechanical items which are handled differently) as valid and handle as if merchandise is actually available for inspection.

This group of derivative policies permits the customer to deal with the company as a whole. These policies prevent a store from refusing to take remedial action because it does not carry a particular product or product line. Through these policies, the customer is given the feeling that he is dealing with Sears Roebuck and Company, with each store acting as a representative of a reputable, national company.

The fourth and last group of derivative policies, which covers the repair of defective merchandise by Sears Roebuck and Company, includes the following:

1. Sears' guarantee policy to customers obligates the company to provide and maintain efficient repair and service facilities. The full provisions stated in the guarantee should be extended to customers, and occasionally it will be necessary to render service beyond Sears' written responsibilities.
2. Company policy requires stores to provide emergency repair service if failure of the appliance could affect the customer's health or safety.

This final group of derivative policies serves as a guide for Sears' repair operations. These policies enable Sears to meet a wide range of adjustment demands from customers. In this way, the company is not limited to the use of an exchange or refund to satisfy a customer complaint, but can also offer to repair defective merchandise.

These derivative policies are presented in various levels of policy manuals: the *Customer Service Manual,* the *Division Manager's Manual,* and the *Handbook for Salespeople—Retail Basic Training.* The policy manuals are kept in loose leaf binders, into which supplementary bulletins may be added. For ease of reference, the policies are grouped under various subject headings and subheadings and are carefully indexed, each paragraph of the manual being designated by a code number. A cover letter is sent out with each manual showing its source and the people to whom it is to be distributed. Supplementary bulletins containing policy additions or revisions are issued periodically and contain subject titles and source statements, as well as lists of personnel who are to receive it and the bulletins it supercedes, if any.

Sears' service policies are developed at the corporate level and are distributed to all involved personnel, down to the selling division manager level within each store. Although lower level managers do not all get personal copies, the material is made available to them. A second method of policy communication involves direct contact among the personnel affected by the policy, through meetings of various store and service center representatives at which common problems are discussed, through conferences with store and service center managers and their subordinate managers in which problems that may arise in daily operations are discussed, and through face-to-face meetings among store and service center personnel below the subordinate manager level with store and service center management.

Sears uses several methods to control the use of policies in the customer service area. The first method involves pressure from above the store level. The Sears' customer, if he does not get satisfaction from a store manager, can write to Sears' group, territorial, and parent management. This factor affects the store manager in two ways: it implicitly encourages him to satisfy the customer whenever possible, in order to keep the customer from writing; where a customer does write, it forces him to justify his action. His superiors, without abridging his right to make a decision on a complaint, expect a detailed explanation when they receive a complaint of this type.

Second, the reasons for returns, as stated on Retail Credit Checks and Records of Return, are analyzed. One analysis is made by company auditors on their annual or semi-annual visits to the individual stores. The stores themselves also analyze these reasons. In the large stores, this analysis is done monthly, while in the smaller ones, it is done only if a problem arises. However, in both large and small stores, the individual credit checks are always reviewed by authorized personnel at the time of approval.

The stores also receive monthly profit and loss statements in which the total amount of returns and allowances is separated from gross sales, in order to provide overall control of service expenses. In addition, the stores themselves send out follow-up questionnaires to a small number of customers who have returned merchandise in the past in order to provide performance control. The questionnaire seeks to determine if the customer was treated satisfactorily by store personnel.

Within the service centers, the technicians' service reports are reviewed daily by their immediate supervisors. Problems are discussed at service center meetings and in personal conversations between the technicians and their supervisors. Supervisors occasionally accompany technicians on house calls, in order to observe how carefully the technicians comply with company policies and procedures. Service center managers also spot check complaints and service reports. In the Brooklyn (New York) Service Center, for example, the service manager analyzes the reports of a different technician each day, in addition to receiving summary reports from the technicians' supervisors.

Policy development, the policies themselves, and policy implementation in Sears' service area seem to be very effective. The overall policies are formulated, as they should be, by higher management, working in conjunction with operating personnel; the overall service policy is related to overall company objectives; derivative policies amplify and are closely related to the overall service policy; the policies are consistent among themselves; the manual is reviewed and revised periodically through bulletins; and field interviews indicated that policies are understood and used by store managers and lower level store personnel.

In addition, the Sears' service area appears to be operating effectively, judging from the professional level of service that is maintained, the cost of operation, the time span between a request for service and a completed service call, and the low incidence of customer complaints.

Developing Procedures and Rules in the Sears' Service Area

A study of the procedures and rules in the service area at Sears illustrates the ways that procedures and rules are developed and used in practice.

Procedures and rules are given along with policies in the *Customer Service Manual* and in other publications which contain policy statements. They are organized under the same headings and subheadings as policy, and are combined into the same paragraphs which give policy statements. This form of presentation is used because it is easier for store personnel to use. The following discussion uses extracts from various sections of the manual.

The language used to express procedures and rules is generally simple and direct. Statements of rules have a mandatory tone, as expressed by such words and phrases as "must," "in no case," and "absolutely." Procedures are identified by their sequential nature, that is, by the fact that they give a series of steps or a procedure for handling a specific situation.

The first procedure deals with general complaint handling.

1. When the customer calls in person or by phone, let him present his problem fully—don't interrupt or argue.
2. If necessary go back over the complaint to establish all points of the problem and what the customer wants.
3. In discussing the complaint, proceed promptly and completely to the point where the customer says, "I am satisfied."

The rules that support this general procedure are as follows:

1. No adjustment or refund is to be refused a customer without the approval of the store manager.
2. Neither this function nor its responsibility can be delegated to another person.
3. Complaints involving an item or situation affecting the health or safety of the customer or his property must receive immediate and concentrated attention and handling until completed and satisfied.
4. All returned merchandise should be examined by the division manager or someone in authority on the selling floor.

The above procedures and rules are applied in a variety of situations. The merchandise in question may be perfect or defective and may have been sold on a cash or credit basis. If a non-defective item is exchanged for one of the same value or a larger value within the same sales division, the exchange is recorded on a sales receipt and the customer pays any difference in price. If a refund is required, the transaction is recorded on a Retail Credit Check, which has spaces for authorization and reason for the return. Most division managers and the management personnel above them are empowered to authorize refunds. In all cases, the person authorizing the credit check should be different from the one who issued it. The reason for the return should be stated specifically. "Does not want" is not a sufficient explanation. Both of these items, authorization and reason for return, have a control function. The former controls the actual outflow of money from the store, while the latter provides data for analyzing past complaints and correcting the factors that caused them.

In many instances, the complaint will be handled by the sales person who made the original sale, since the customer usually contacts the sales department with his complaint. In the following instances, according to company policy, complaints must be referred to the store's customer service department:

1. Cash sales involving $50.00 or more.
2. Returns or exchanges of heavy merchandise such as washing machines, refrigerators, television sets and furniture. Pick-up and exchange may be initiated on the sales floor, but they are to be made only on the authorization of the Division Manager or other authorized person.
3. Soiled or damaged merchandise (unless defective).
4. Refunds on pending C.O.D.'s or Lay-aways.
5. Questionable cases (adjustments involving differences of opinions).
6. Catalogue order returns.
7. Returns of merchandise without receipt or evidence of purchase and without positive personal identification, or when the transaction is not remembered by a sales-person.

Complaints may be made to the store's customer service department by the customer in person, by phone, or by letter. The complaint also may be directed to the department after initial reception at the parent, group or store levels. There are procedures and rules for handling each situation. For example, the following is the procedure followed by the customer service department in handling complaints that are received at the parent, territorial, or group and zone levels and are then referred to the store for follow-up action:

1. Complaints referred by Department 731A (a parent service department) to the territorial, zone or group offices must be acknowledged to the customer within 24 hours of receipt . . . and be definite in advising the customer the name of the individual store or service unit manager selected to contact him.
2. The letter of complaint and the referral letter must be read by the store manager, central service manager, or general manager (of a catalog order plant) personally.
3. After reading the complaint he must decide who should handle it and how it should be handled to regain the confidence of the customer in Sears' policies.
4. When the contact is made by letter, phone or in person, be sure it is over the name of the specific individual whose name and/or title has been given to the customer, which in every case is the store manager, central service manager, or catalog order plant manager.

To support this procedure, Sears has formulated the following rules:

1. This function (reading of letter of complaint) cannot be delegated to an

assistant except when the store manager, or general manager is absent for more than a day because of business, illness, or vacation.

2. It is extremely important that initial contact be made within 24 hours of its receipt.

Procedures and rules have also been drawn up to guide Sears' service center personnel. Sears' central service centers repair defective or otherwise inoperative merchandise sold by Sears. The repairs are made at the service centers, the customers' homes, or Sears retail outlets. The "in-store" repairs are limited primarily to minor television, radio and phonograph repairs and are handled by central service technicians, who visit for this purpose. Major repairs are handled at the service centers.

Service center procedures and rules cover a variety of activities: the processing of service requests, actual repair work, emergency service, guarantee coverage and service charges, and the collection of fees on charge repairs. For example, the general procedure for processing a request for service is as follows:

1. Each service order should be checked with the Service Record Card File at the time of the customer's request for service in cases where the guarantee (merchandise or repair) status is in doubt.
2. Upon the completion of all service calls, notate the Service Record Card with the date only that service was completed.
3. Cards pulled for verification of guarantee at the time of request for service should be notated then with date of request for service in lieu of later showing date service was completed. Indicate on service order that date of request for service has been entered on Service Record Card.
4. If it is found that a customer has no card in the file for item serviced, create Universal Tag T10222 and enter the customer's name, address, type of merchandise, model number, date service was rendered, and return to file.
5. When cards are received notate in space provided the period of guarantee and file alphabetically by customer's name.
6. Accurate service records of repair parts sales are to be kept for a period of one year on all repairs fully paid by the customer.

And the rules governing Sears repair guarantees and the determining of service charges are:

1. Parts furnished under the original guarantee are covered only for the remaining period of time the guarantee is in effect, or as stated therein.
2. Charge repairs involving mechanical adjustment (labor only) are guaranteed for ninety (90) days from date of repair.
3. Charge repairs involving parts replacement are guaranteed for one (1) year from date of repair (covering both parts and labor).
4. If, within ninety (90) days from date of original repair, another part of the same piece of merchandise fails, Sears will make this repair, charging only the amount they would have charged (foregoing any trip and diagnosis expense) had this failure occurred at the time of the original repair.

5. When Division 98 (parts division) guarantees the replacement part for less than one (1) year, then the guarantee on labor is simply the same as that on the part.

The statements of procedures and rules for the service area at Sears, and the material explaining them, are concise and complete, and logically organized by subject category. The *Customer Service Manual* contains examples of the forms mentioned in the text, and provides information on how to fill out and use them. Technical terms are fully explained. Field interviews indicated that subordinate managers and store personnel who use the procedures and rules were generally satisfied with their presentation and organization, understood their meaning, and were unable to point out any gaps or conflicts.

Sears' service procedures and rules provide clear guidelines for decision-making responsibility. They establish limits on subordinates' decision making and insure that decisions are made at a level commensurate with the associated job responsibility and the needs of the customer. The procedures and rules provide for the proper handling of a customer's service request at the various management levels and provide for the transfer of requests between levels. They also specify in very precise terms the types of complaints that can be solved at the various management levels. As a result, complaints move upward through the store's management hierarchy only on an exception basis, until they reach the store manager, who is responsible for the overall store profit and has the authority to make a final decision.

Because they are presented in the manual along with the policies, the procedures and rules reinforce and carry out those policies. Procedures and rules are reviewed at weekly or monthly meetings, and revised when necessary. They are consistent among themselves, and provide for consistent handling of customer complaints at the central service center, the store's customer service unit, or the sales floor.

CONCLUSION

Derivative policies, procedures and rules are necessary guidelines for action, and are developed as part of the business planning process. Every operating and staff area of a business needs policies, procedures and rules, although they need not always be spelled out in the detail found in Sears Roebuck and Company's customer service area.

As was seen in the Blakeston and Wilson Company study discussed in Chapter 5, what might be called derivative policies at a large company such as Sears and Roebuck are frequently combined in a small company with overall company policies in a single policy manual—except in those areas (such as store operations at Blakeston and Wilson) where detailed and specific guidance is required. The larger the company and the more complex the company's operation, the more likely there is to be a need for separate manuals for each area in which derivative policies are developed.

The Sears case was selected for this chapter because it provides a detailed and specific example, down to the lowest level of operations, of how derivative policies, procedures, and rules are developed and used. The Sears case illustrates how these policies are derived from overall corporate policies, how procedures and rules are developed from these policies, how these derivative policies, procedures, and rules must cover all situations encountered in the operation, and how they must spell out down to the last detail exactly how action must be taken, if they are to be in accordance with overall policies, corporate philosophy, and the overall corporate objective.

Although individual procedures and rules concern very minor aspects of a company's operation, they are nonetheless an important final link in providing guidelines for action, and must be developed with care, if a complete set of guidelines for action is to be created.

DISCUSSION QUESTIONS

1. What is the relation of overall policy development and derivative implementation policy development?
2. In what ways are these two levels of policies distinct? In what ways are these two levels related?
3. What is the place of procedure and rule development in the business planning process?
4. In what areas of a business' operations are procedures and rules relatively unimportant? Why?
5. In what areas of a business' operations are detailed procedures and rules very important? Why?
6. Why do you think so little is written about the development of procedures and rules?
7. Develop derivative implementation policies for the Superb Biscuits Company (see Appendix C). How did you distinguish these implementation policies from the overall policies you developed earlier?

CHAPTER 9

COORDINATION AND CONTROL IN BUSINESS PLANNING

Specific operating and staff plans are not made in a vacuum, but must be coordinated and integrated with planning in related areas. The individual planning at each level of management in a company should thus be reviewed by the next higher management level until all individual plans are ultimately coordinated and integrated within the overall comprehensive company plan. Effective planning depends on this process of integrating individual operating and staff plans, reviewing and revising them in the light of their effect on other plans and on company profits, and summarizing the highlights of these plans and their budgets in a single overall company plan. Management control, especially through the budgetary process, provides tools for performing this coordination, as well as for controlling and measuring the effectiveness of the planning effort.

This chapter discusses some of the problems encountered in coordinating and controlling planning. The discussion covers overall coordination of operating and staff plans, the role of management control and the budgetary process in coordinating and controlling implementation planning, measuring the effectiveness of the planning effort, and the importance of behavioral science tools in coordinating and controlling planning.

COORDINATING SPECIFIC OPERATING AND STAFF PLANS WITHIN THE OVERALL CORPORATE PLAN

Coordinating and integrating individual operating and staff plans begins with assigning someone—a planning group, a planning executive, or some other company executive—the responsibility for doing it. Second, a manager must communicate essential strategic planning information (overall objectives, policies, and planning premises) to those developing the operating and staff plans, along with instructions on what is required in their individual plans. Third, a manager must establish procedures for review and coordination which encourage active participation of lower-level managers in planning, and insure that the comprehensive plan developed will be both realistic and well integrated. Fourth, the planning effort must be actively managed by a strong administrator. Fifth, top management support of the planning effort is needed, and adequate rewards given to those who do planning well, if the planning effort is to be taken seriously by company managers.

While all levels and kinds of strategic and implementation planning are closely related, responsibility for performing the various types of planning can be separated: the actual job of developing final overall strategic plans is always done by a corporate planning group or excutive; the specific operating and staff plans are normally developed by lower level managers; lower level plans are reviewed, coordinated, and controlled by higher management levels. The interrelation of these planning levels and responsibilities is shown in Figure 9.1.

The job of coordination and integration does not stop with just issuing instructions and communicating strategic planning information, for all operating managers do not have the same background, training and perspective. In the planning systems studied, a considerable amount of additional formal and informal communication was needed to produce an integrated corporate plan. There seems to be no substitute for personal contact, first in explaining the planning framework and second in following up on the individual planning efforts.

In all the situations studied, it was necessary to institute a systematic approach to developing and reviewing preliminary plans. The planning coordinator needs a preliminary draft (no matter how rough) of the operating and staff managers' plans well before the final plan is due. In attempting to get these preliminary plans, a considerable amount of pressure is frequently needed to extract them from the operating divisions—for operating problems are uppermost in the middle manager's mind, and if anything has to be put off, it is usually the planning. It is in this phase that most planning efforts falter. It is here that top management must forcefully assert its belief in the planning effort, and insist on compliance with deadlines, or the effort will fail.

At one company where the author worked recently, this preliminary review is made prior to preparation of annual and long-term budgets, since the budget is fundamentally no more than the quantification of a plan and so cannot be prepared until the plan upon which it is based is formulated. Only after the preliminary plans are complete, therefore, do the operating managers translate these plans into rough sales, cost, and profit estimates—usually called preliminary operating budgets.

Figure 9.1

VARIOUS LEVELS AND KINDS OF BUSINESS PLANS

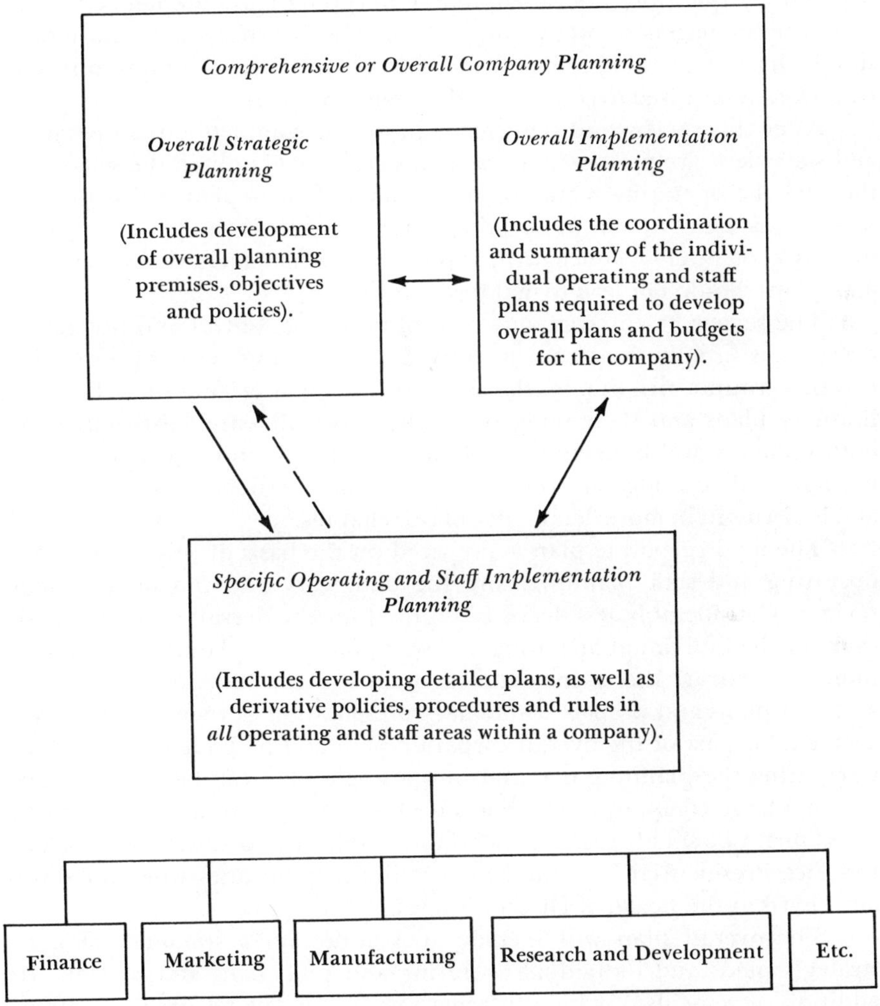

The preliminary plans are reviewed in detail by the planning coordinator. First, they are studied for compliance with corporate planning premises, the corporate objective and philosophy, and the overall policy guidelines. Second, they are studied in relation to each other. During this review differences and problems are noted.

At this point, the preliminary plans are discussed with the operating managers. Where one area's plans affects another area, the managers of each area are brought together, to insure that each has taken into account the plans of other related areas in developing final plans. Where refinements are needed, where plans appear unrealistic or incomplete, where inconsistencies with overall corporate directions are noted, where action programs are insufficient to provide adequate growth for the company, or where other questions are raised, individual conferences are held with the operating managers to work out problems. This process is by no means simple, for considerable conversation, tact, reconciliation, compromise and teamwork is required to come up with an effective plan.

After this review and refinement process is complete, final operating and staff plans are prepared. These plans are "final" only in the sense that they are the operating managers' final views of their plan. Subsequently, these plans are reviewed by corporate management. If the planning director has kept in close touch with top corporate managers their review of final plans should not lead to major revisions.

The review by the company control group or control and budgeting manager is usually done concurrently with the above review process, for it is this group which applies the acid test to plans—profitability. The preliminary plans and their budgets are thus normally studied together, by both planners and budgeters. This phase of the planning review process, normally called budgetary review, leads to many refinements in the plan and is discussed in more detail later in this chapter.

The final corporate plan is prepared on the basis of this preliminary operating and staff planning, and the budgetary and top management reviews. Considerably less detail is required for the overall corporate plan than for the individual operating and staff plans. The planner's job, therefore, is to extract the essence and highlights of the individual operating and staff plans and prepare a summary presentation of them for top management, as part of the overall corporate plan and its budget. The job of integrating the planning material into a single plan can be an enormous one in a large company, for as one Vice President put it, a comprehensive plan "might be six file cases of material in total, a two-or-three-inch book at the Vice Presidential level, and then only thirty minutes worth of slides and charts at the Board of Director's level."[1]

The overall plan will include at a minimum a summary of both strategic plans and individual operating and staff plans and budgets. In addition, it may also include information on current results for comparative purposes, as is seen from the outline of one company's plan given in Figure 9.2.[2]

Subsequent to the preparation of the company's comprehensive plan, the planner monitors results, develops ways to measure the effectiveness of

[1]Harold W. Henry, *Long-Range Planning Practices in 45 Industrial Companies* (Englewood Cliffs, New Jersey: Prentice-Hall, Inc., 1968), p. 70.

[2]Henry, *Long-Range Planning Practices*, p. 73.

Figure 9.2

OUTLINE OF A "FIVE-YEAR BUSINESS PLAN" PREPARED FOR ONE CORPORATION

Section	*Topic*
I	Business Results Summary
	Operations
	Business Indices
	Marketing
	Product
	Cost and Productivity
	Facilities
	Personnel
	Product Line Performance
II	Business Environment
III	Division Guidelines
IV	Most Important Problems and Opportunities
V	Business Strategy
VI	Major Business Plans and Programs
VII	Business Results
Appendix I	Line Analyses and Plans
Appendix II	Cost Analyses and Plans

the planning effort, reviews and refines plans, and institutes changes in plans where needed.

The above discussion is based on the study of a limited number of companies. The amount of formality in the review process, the points at which top management dictates planning directions and limitations, the degree to which top management dictates planning and limitations, the amount of control exercised by the budget group, and the like will naturally vary from company to company. The general pattern of interaction and review, however, remains the same in companies with formal planning efforts: strategic directions are determined by corporate management; individual operating and staff managers are involved in the planning in their areas; this individual planning is coordinated with planning in other areas and subjected to budgetary review; and a comprehensive overall company plan is prepared.

THE IMPORTANCE OF MANAGEMENT CONTROL IN PLANNING

Management control is a systematic effort to set performance standards consistent with planning objectives, to design information feedback systems, to compare actual performance with these predetermined standards, to determine whether there are any deviations and to measure their significance, and to take any action required to assure that all corporate resources are being used in the most effective and efficient way possible in achieving corporate objectives.[3]

Management control is basically an extension of the planning process—for control standards must accurately reflect the intent of the plan and exist for the sole purpose of enabling a manager to see whether performance is in line with plans. The budget is probably the best known control standard. It is also the control tool which most directly links planning and control, for the budget is both a plan (translated into numbers) and a control standard (the yardstick against which performance is measured).

There are a number of ways in which the budget and the budgetary process aid in controlling and coordinating the planning effort.

First, the budgetary process is a means of translating plans into specific numerical goals, and communicating these goals to operating managers through the operating budgets.

Second, the budgetary process helps test the validity of plans by translating them into profit projections.

Third, the budgetary process helps coordinate the planning process, for it shows the effect of individual operating and staff plans on total company profit and on the profitability of other company plans.

Fourth, the budgetary process can be used to measure or evaluate the effectiveness of plans and the planning effort, and through the information it generates enable a manager to review and revise plans where necessary.

THE BUDGET: A MAJOR PLANNING TOOL

The term "budget" has been the source of much confusion in business planning and control. A budget is a statement of expected results expressed in numerical terms. It is a quantification of a plan. As a result, a budget is only as good as the plans upon which it is based, and should not be mistaken for the entire plan.

The Budgetary Process

As was seen in the first section of this chapter, the place of a budget in the planning process comes after the development of the preliminary plan. When a plan is initially developed, it is quantified (usually in the form of a sales or profit projection) to test the ultimate profitability of the plan. The plan is then revised, based on this evaluation, and subsequently a revised budget is made. This process of quantification, evaluation, and revision continues until a satisfactory plan and budget are developed.

A budget must be prepared for each major operational and staff area of a company for a specified time period, usually one to five years. These budgets, which should be prepared along with plans under the direction of

[3]Robert J. Mockler, *The Management Control Process* (New York: Appleton-Century-Crofts, 1971) contains a complete discussion of the management control process.

the operating managers, are then usually reviewed by the budget director or his staff, which brings together the budgets of all the areas of the company—both operating and staff—and develops the overall corporate budget.

The sales plan and budget are generally considered to be the most important ones formulated, because other company planning is predicted to a large extent on the sales plan. Once the sales plan is fixed, plans and budgets can be prepared for other activities within a business.

There are overall income and expense budgets and balance sheet budgets, which are for the most part no more than extensions of standard accounting statements. There are capital outlay budgets, and budgets for cash receipts and expenditures for the financial area. In addition, there are a variety of budgets for individual operating and staff sections of a company. Marketing divisions, for example, have both unit and dollar sales budgets, as well as expense and manpower budgets. Manufacturing divisions have product output, manpower, and machine utilization budgets, as well as expense budgets based on cost accounting standards. There will also be budgets for all other business areas, including administration and overhead. Many budgets are expressed in physical terms, such as the budgets for direct-labor hours, machine hours, units of material, square feet allocated, and units produced—where the situation requires them. Most budgets, however, are expressed in monetary terms.

In developing budgets, it is necessary to have a clear definition of each manager's responsibility, accountability, and authority. An individual should not be accountable for achieving certain budget objectives unless he has the operational responsibility and authority to reach the goals.[4] The operating responsibility of each manager should, therefore, be stated in writing in unequivocal terms, and his authority for action should be clearly delineated.[5]

The human elements must be recognized in budgetary planning. As Chris Argyris has stated, budgets are tools designed to control performance through people.[6] As a result, the impact of budgets is felt by everyone in the organization. Those who will have the responsibility for the achievement of budget goals should, therefore, be involved in the setting of goals and the establishing of budgets.

In preparing the budget, there must be a balance between setting goals that are too easily attainable, and those that are too difficult to achieve. If budget standards are not reasonably attainable, there may be much inefficient and frustrating employee performance. On the other hand, budget standards that are too easily attainable are also inefficient,

[4]James L. Pierce, "Budgetary Accounting and Its Prospects," *Financial Executive*, February 1968, p. 68.

[5]Ernest I. Hanson, "The Budgetary Control Function," *Accounting Review*, April 1966, p. 242.

[6]Chris Argyris, "Human Problems with Budgets," *Harvard Business Review*, January-February 1953, p. 97.

since they can lead to lower performance than is possible. Both these extremes cause the budget to lose much of its effectiveness as a control tool. In order to obtain efficient and productive performance, budget goals should be attainable and yet challenging.[7]

One method for achieving this balance is the use of a flexible budget. Under a fixed budget, goals become meaningless as soon as the operating level varies from the one assumed. A flexible budget is intended to provide attainable goals regardless of the operating level, by setting different budget figures for different levels of operation. For example, a department might establish budget figures for operations at 100% of capacity, 95% of capacity, 90% of capacity and so on. Table 9.1 gives in summary form a flexible budget for manufacturing costs for the ABC Company under different levels of production.

Table 9.1

ABC COMPANY
MANUFACTURING COST BUDGET

Number of items produced	*100,000*	*150,000*	*175,000*	*200,000*
Manufacturing Costs:				
Materials	$ 50,000	$ 75,000	$ 87,500	$100,000
Direct Labor	25,000	37,500	43,750	50,000
Supervision	10,000	12,000	14,000	16,000
Maintenance	5,000	6,000	6,500	7,000
Depreciation	20,000	20,000	20,000	20,000
Other Overhead	10,000	10,000	12,000	13,000
Total Manufacturing Costs	$120,000	$160,000	$183,750	$206,000
Cost Per Item produced	$1.20	$1.07	$1.05	$1.03

Budgetary review practices vary from company to company. Budgets for individual operations may be reviewed quarterly, monthly, or even weekly, but whatever the time period, budget revision should be kept at a minimum, for frequent changes in standards undercut their validity and create the feeling that all company standards are poorly conceived and so valueless criteria for measuring performance. Budgets are not sacred, however, and budgetary practices should be reexamined constantly, for it is possible that continual variances from budget may be caused by poor budgeting rather than by below standard operating performance.

While there are these general ground rules for budget preparation, no two companies seem to develop their overall budgets in exactly the same way. In many large companies, major departments and divisions are asked to submit five-year budgets, with supporting plans, to a control section every year. These five year budgets and plans are broken down into yearly segments, except for the first year which is broken down into monthly or

[7]Hanson, "The Budgetary Control Function," p. 242.

quarterly segments. The control or planning section normally provides managers with the information needed for preparing these budgets, such as anticipated economic and market changes, overall sales forecasts, restrictions on spending, and overall corporate objectives and policies. There is usually considerable interaction between the control section, the various planning managers and the planning director concerning major factors affecting the plan and its budget, and many adjustments are made on the basis of this exchange of information.

This first developmental stage results in a plan and budget which the department or division manager believes are reasonable, and which he believes the managers above him will find reasonable. Then another round of development occurs, as pressures come from higher management to reach for higher sales goals, cut costs, or change the direction of a unit's efforts. A final plan and budget are agreed upon at this point.

There are many variations in this process. In some companies, the control section and higher management develop plans and their budget quantifications in more detail for sub-managers, and sub-managers are given less freedom to do their own planning. In general, this practice will hurt planning, but it may be justified by the particular corporation's circumstances. Many companies ask for one-year instead of five-year plans, others revise current plans quarterly and five-year plans annually, and still others vary the requirements by level of management.

Whatever budgetary process is followed, it is important that there be an interaction in the planning stage between the planning director and the managers who are developing and carrying out plans, and the control or financial executive or group who helps translate these plans into a realistic estimate of their profitability. Through this interaction, the profitability of plans can be tested, and greater reality can be given to the plans and the budgets based on them.

The following sections discuss the ways various companies handle budgetary planning.

Some Case Histories

Pennsalt Chemicals Corp. has a rigorous budget program (called the Program for Profit Control), which has been a very successful business planning tool.[8]

The budgetary process begins each fall when the company's profit analysis group prepares and provides all company departments with an economic forecast for the coming year. This forecast is tailored to the market served by each department. Plans are then developed and sales forecasts are prepared by each division sales manager working with his

[8] J. D. Baxter, "Budget Guides Profit Growth," *The Iron Age*, October 28, 1965, pp. 44-46.

salesmen and then assembled by the accounting and planning departments. A coordinated sales plan and forecast is in this way developed, which becomes the basis of all planning and budgeting. Manufacturing groups are given the sales plans and forecasts and they develop plans and cost estimates based on volume estimates. Staff groups also prepare budgets for their operations.

In December, top management planners review these plans and their budgets, and usually revise them to bring them into line with overall corporate plans. After this top-level review, the plans and their budgets go back to the departments and divisions for review and discussion. The final plan and its budget are set in January.

At Pennsalt, each manager is given responsibility, and is held accountable, for meeting the planned budget for the year. Once set, the budget is never changed during the year. Each month each department and division reports actual results, and these are reviewed against the budget by the president himself.

The key elements in the success of the Pennsalt budget, according to the president, are:

1. Full backing of the budget by top management.
2. Participation in planning and budget preparation by all managers and key employees who must live by the budget.
3. Coverage by the budget plan of every activity of the company on a coordinated and integrated basis.
4. No changing of the budget during the year once it is set.
5. Monthly review of performance by middle and top management.
6. Thorough checking of all deviations from the planned budget during the year.
7. Integration of a single-year budget with the longer-term plan.
8. Indoctrination of all employees in corporate objectives, as well as individual operating objectives.
9. Inclusion of top managers' accounts in the budget.

The National Observer study described in Chapter 7 provides another example of budget preparation and use. At *The Observer,* expense and sales plans and budgets were prepared by operating managers, working with corporate planners and the controller's department. These plans and budgets were presented in a format consistent with other reports used in the operation. *The National Observer's* circulation and subscription sales budget and the paper's monthly report comparing sales with budget standards are given below in Tables 9.2 and 9.3.[9] A similar set of reports

[9]Robert J. Mockler, *Circulation Planning and Development for the National Observer: A Research Study on Business Applications of Management Planning and Control Principles* ("Research Paper No. 39;" Atlanta, Georgia: Bureau of Business and Economic Research, School of Business Administration, Georgia State College, October, 1967), pp. 47-48.

Table 9.2

THE NATIONAL OBSERVER—Circulation Department

Estimated Subscription Sales and Circulation—1964 (1)

	Jan.	Feb.	March	First Quarter	April	May	June	Second Quarter	July	August	Sept.	Third Quarter	Oct.	Nov.	Dec.	Fourth Quarter	Year
Subscription Circulation (Paid) Beginning of Period:	100,000	100,000	109,600	100,000	127,600	150,200	148,800	127,600	146,400	114,000	86,400	146,400	95,600	115,000	131,600	95,600	100,000
I. Additions:																	
Subscription Sales:																	
Direct Mail	26,200	35,600	39,000	100,800	12,800	2,000	2,000	16,800	4,000	14,000	32,400	50,400	25,200	18,000	12,400	55,600	223,600
Advertising	10,000	17,000	15,000	42,000	8,400	1,200	1,200	10,800	2,000	4,000	12,800	18,800	6,000	2,000	400	8,400	80,000
House Ads in DJ Publications	800	800	800	2,400	600	600	600	1,800	600	600	600	1,800	400	400	400	1,200	7,200
Development and Testing	1,200	3,600	2,200	7,000	200	200	200	600	200	1,600	3,600	5,400	3,600	1,200	200	5,000	18,000
Community and Phone	1,000	1,200	1,200	3,400	2,000	2,000	2,000	6,000	2,000	2,000	2,000	6,000	2,000	2,000	2,000	6,000	21,400
Subscription Agency	200	200	200	600	200	200	200	600	200	200	200	600	200	200	200	600	2,400
Education and Clergy	1,600	1,200	600	3,400	-	-	-	-	-	-	1,000	1,000	6,000	3,000	1,000	10,000	14,400
Regular and Christmas Gift	200	200	200	600	200	200	200	600	200	200	200	600	200	200	5,800	6,200	8,000
Over the Counter, Employee and Institutional	1,800	1,800	1,800	5,400	1,200	1,200	1,200	3,600	1,400	1,400	1,400	4,200	1,400	1,200	200	2,800	16,000
Solicitation of Home Delivery Expires	2,000	-	-	2,000	-	-	-	-	-	-	-	-	-	-	-	-	2,000
Total Subscription Sales	45,000	61,600	61,000	167,600	25,600	7,600	7,600	40,800	10,600	24,000	54,200	88,800	45,000	28,200	22,600	95,800	393,000
Renewals: Long-term	8,000	10,000	4,000	22,000	4,000	10,000	14,000	28,000	8,000	6,000	6,000	20,000	8,000	6,000	6,000	20,000	90,000
Short-term	14,000	14,000	12,000	40,000	-	-	-	-	16,000	20,000	16,000	52,000	6,000	2,000	2,000	10,000	102,000
Total Additions	67,000	85,600	77,000	229,600	29,600	17,600	21,600	68,800	34,600	50,000	76,200	160,800	59,000	36,200	30,600	125,800	585,000
II. Losses: Long-term Expires	15,000	24,000	9,000	48,000	5,000	17,000	20,000	42,000	12,000	10,000	8,000	30,000	10,000	10,000	10,000	30,000	150,000
Short-term Expires	44,000	42,000	40,000	126,000	-	-	-	-	51,000	63,600	51,000	165,600	23,600	5,600	5,600	34,800	326,400
Education and Gift Expires	2,000	-	-	2,000	-	-	2,000	2,000	-	-	-	-	-	-	4,000	4,000	8,000
Credit Stops	6,000	10,000	10,000	26,000	2,000	2,000	2,000	6,000	4,000	4,000	8,000	16,000	6,000	4,000	2,000	12,000	60,000
Total Losses	67,000	76,000	59,000	202,000	7,000	19,000	24,000	50,000	67,000	77,600	67,000	211,600	39,600	19,600	21,600	80,800	544,400
Net Subscription Gain (or Loss) for Period	-	9,600	18,000	27,600	22,600	(1,400)	(2,400)	18,800	(32,400)	(27,600)	9,200	(50,800)	19,400	16,600	9,000	45,000	40,600
Subscription Circulation (Paid) End of Period	100,000	109,600	127,600	127,600	150,200	148,800	146,400	146,400	114,000	86,400	95,600	95,600	115,000	131,600	140,600	140,600	140,600
Unpaid Copies Delivered	12,000	10,000	6,000	6,000	6,000	6,000	4,000	4,000	6,000	6,000	6,000	6,000	6,000	6,000	6,000	6,000	6,000
Total ABC Subscription Circulation End of Period	112,000	129,600	133,600	133,600	156,200	154,800	150,400	150,400	120,000	92,400	101,600	101,600	121,000	137,600	146,600	146,600	146,600
Other ABC Circulation End of Period:																	
Newsstand and Home Delivery	16,000	16,000	16,000	16,000	16,000	16,000	16,000	16,000	16,000	17,000	17,000	17,000	17,000	18,000	18,000	18,000	18,000
Young Salesmen Program	3,600	3,800	4,000	4,000	4,200	4,400	4,700	4,700	4,800	5,000	5,200	5,200	5,600	5,800	6,000	6,000	6,000
Total ABC Circulation End of Period	131,600	149,400	153,600	153,600	176,400	175,200	171,100	171,100	140,800	114,400	123,800	123,800	143,600	161,400	170,600	170,600	170,600

(1) All figures have been disguised. However, the general relationships among the various components of the flow plan have been maintained to indicate the economics of circulation.

Table 9.3

THE NATIONAL OBSERVER—Circulation Department

Circulation and Subscription Sales Report—March 1964[1]

	First Quarter Jan - Mar 1964 Budget	First Quarter Jan - Mar 1964 Actual	March 1964 Budget	March 1964 Actual
Subscription Circulation (Paid) Beginning of Period:	100,000	100,000	109,600	142,800
I. Additions:				
Subscription Sales:				
Direct Mail: Regular	100,800	164,818	39,000	87,400
Testing				
Advertising: Regular	31,800	34,532	11,000	12,586
Reader's Digest (Oct.'63)[2]	2,000	2,240	600	618
Radio	8,200	8,418	3,400	5,178
House Ads in DJ Publications	2,400	3,250	800	1,512
Development: Dept. Store Envelopes	2,200	3,668	200	2,248
Adserts	1,400	1,456	200	842
Testing	3,400	-	1,800	-
Community and Phone	3,400	2,588	1,200	1,050
Subscription Agency	600	684	200	164
Education & Clergy: Individual	600	1,388	400	514
Bulk - Classroom	2,800	3,974	200	486
Gift	600	1,266	200	18
Over the Counter, Employee & Inst.	5,400	7,038	1,800	2,366
Solicitation of Home Delivery Expires[3]	2,000	3,480	-	46
Total Subscription Sales	167,600	238,800	61,000	115,028
Renewals: Long-term[4]	22,000	27,010	4,000	4,800
Short-term[4]	40,000	35,618	12,000	14,000
Total Additions[4]	229,600	301,428	77,000	133,828
II. Losses: Long-term Expires[4]	48,000	41,800	9,000	10,000
Short-term Expires[4]	126,000	118,000	40,000	48,000
Education and Gift Expires[4]	2,000	1,000	-	-
Credit Stops[4]	26,000	48,000	10,000	26,000
Total Losses[4]	202,000	208,800	59,000	84,000
Net Subscription Gain (or Loss) for Period[4]	27,600	92,628	18,000	49,828
Subscription Circulation (Paid) End of Period[4]	127,600	192,628	127,600	192,628
ABC Grace Carried[4]	6,000	14,000	6,000	14,000
Total ABC Subscription Circulation End of Period[4]	133,600	206,628	133,600	206,628
Other ABC Circulation End of Period:[4]				
Newsstand and Home Delivery	16,000	14,500	16,000	14,500
Young Salesmen Program	4,000	5,200	4,000	5,200
Total ABC Circulation End of Period[4]	153,600	226,328	153,600	226,328

(1) All figures have been disguised. However, the general relationships among the various components of the report have been maintained to indicate the economics of circulation.

(2) These returns are in addition to the 21,804 returns received in 1963.

(3) Net figure after deducting credit losses.

(4) Estimates.

covering circulation marketing expenses was also prepared. At *The Observer* operating management was given considerable leeway in developing budget standards, and there was a minimum of management pressure to adjust standards upward.

The budgetary procedure at the XYZ mail-order company discussed in Chapter 2 was somewhat different. Each year the company's president was required to make a formal planning presentation to the president of the parent company. The first part of the meeting was devoted to reviewing the prior year's results, and the second half to outlining plans and the budget for the coming year.

In preparing for this presentation in years past, the president had asked each operating manager to draw up a general budget plan for his department. The reference point for most of these budgets was the prior year's results. The department heads were provided with some sketchy economic forecasts, and the controller's staff was available to answer any questions the department heads might have. Once the preliminary department budgets were finished, the control section reviewed and refined them. Assumptions as to sales and costs were rechecked, and final figures were developed by the controller. Unfortunately, in this process figures were often distorted and arbitrary changes were made, since management was committed to satisfying certain profit goals of the parent company. Because of this, the budgets lost much of their impact. Operating managers devoted less and less time to preparing them, and felt little obligation to meet budget goals.

A few years ago the company created a long-range planning department, which assisted individual operating managers in preparing annual plans and their budgets, coordinated them with longer-range plans, and prepared consolidated five-year plans, with budgets. The final annual budgets continued to be prepared by the controller's department. Each operating department manager was asked to prepare a five-year plan at the same time he prepared his one-year plan, and only after these plans were completed to prepare his budgets. After three years, the company has had little success in long-range planning. Operating managers still are not convinced that management really takes planning seriously, for a relatively junior executive was put in charge of the planning department, and when deadlines were missed very little was said. As a result, planning was not done well, and managers continued to prepare budgets pretty much as they had in the past.

Unlike *The National Observer* and Pennsalt, this mail-order company did not have strong planning procedures, nor did it exercise tight control of operations. Emotion, instead of reason, dominated much of the decision making. And operating results reflected this lack of planning and control, for profits fell while those of competitors rose, unprofitable ventures were started, sales growth slowed, and a general lack of enthusiasm could be sensed among the staff.

Guidelines

The following are some useful guidelines for budget preparation and use:

1. A budget is both a planning tool and a control tool for it is both a quantification of a plan and a yardstick against which performance is measured.
2. All managers should be indoctrinated in overall corporate plans and their objectives, and have clearly defined individual department objectives. Preliminary plans should be developed before budgets are formulated.
3. Top management must give their full backing to planning and budgeting.
4. Plans and their budgets should be prepared for overall corporate operations, as well as for all divisions, departments and individual operations within the corporation.
5. The budgetary process should provide for thorough analysis of deviations from actual results, preferably on a monthly basis. A follow-up procedure for correction of undesirable conditions should be incorporated into the budget plan.
6. A budget plan that is built upon wishful thinking invites frustration and loss of confidence in the value of budgeting. If a budget's goals are designed to be surpassed with minimum effort on the part of the organization, a below-standard performance can be expected.
7. Operating responsibilities for achieving budgeted goals must be clearly defined. Those who are responsible for achieving budget goals should participate in the setting of these goals.
8. Individual managers must participate in the preparation of plans and budgets for their operations.
9. Individual plans and budgets should be integrated within an overall corporate budget and longer-term corporate plans.
10. Normal and abnormal expenditures should be segregated, in order that deviations from the norm can be accounted for.
11. Where operations warrant it, it is a good idea to set up a variable expense budget indicating precisely what the direct expense will be for each budget item at the various possible levels of activity.
12. Provision must be made for revising plans and budgets, but only at specific periods or when there are major changes in company operations or the company's market.

The budget is an important implementation planning tool. It provides the planning director with a means of testing the validity of plans, and reviewing and revising them. It is also a vehicle for more easily communicating plans to lower level operating managers, for the budgetary process translates plans into terms more readily understood by operating managers. In addition, the budget provides standards and goals against which actual performance can be measured. When information on actual results is fed back, it can be compared with budgeted results, thus enabling management to take corrective steps to bring operations more in line with planned performance.

BUDGETS AND PEOPLE

Behavioral science principles and methods seem to be most neglected in the budgetary planning area. In the 1950's Chris Argyris[10] conducted a pioneer study of budgetary planning, which pinpointed many of the problems that can arise from not making use of behavioral science tools in this phase of planning.

Argyris studied four plants of a large corporation. At each, top management used budgets to motivate, to "pressure," and to evaluate factory supervisors. In carrying out their jobs, the budget personnel placed emphasis on finding things that were "sour," and when they did, they reported errors immediately to top management—not to the factory supervisor involved. This was only natural, because it was the only way for budget personnel to look good, to stand out, to get raises.

To the factory personnel, budgets had become symbols which aroused fear, resentment, hostility and aggression. The factory personnel objected that the budgets showed only that something was wrong, that budgets would only be raised if met, and that the use of budgets implied a lack of motivation in factory personnel. They felt that the budget personnel were not flexible enough to understand the daily problems at the factory level, emphasized past history too much, and were generally too remote from the actual working situation. Factory personnel described the budget personnel as "sarcastic," with "over-exalted" opinions of their positions.

The executives interviewed by Argyris generally felt that accountants, controllers and budget supervisors needed more training in human relations. Some typical comments were: "They're technicians. They don't know how to handle people." "They have a narrow breadth of view." "The better the accountant, the poorer he is in human relations." "They are too figure conscious."

The study concluded that this kind of budget pressure tended to unite the employees against management and to place factory supervisors under tension that could lead to inefficiency, aggression, or even a complete breakdown on the part of the supervisor. Instead of focusing on the entire plant or company outlook, this kind of budget pressure tended to make each party defensive: the factory supervisor concentrated on his own department's problems, and the budget supervisor looked for more and more "errors" in order to increase his impact on the organization.

To make matters worse, there was very little supervisor participation in goal setting. While most controllers interviewed held review meetings and paid lip service to factory supervisors' participation in budgeting, the supervisors were in reality asked to accept, reject or modify the controller's

[10]Chris Argyris, *The Impact of Budgets on People* (New York: Controllership Foundation, Inc., 1952).

budget—not to help create their *own* budgets. In his study, Argyris applied human relations techniques in developing a method for obtaining truly active participation by supervisors in the budget planning process. The new method involved the following participative approach:

1. The executive in charge first determines if the factory supervisors really see the need for changes in the budget or for a new budget. He then determines how ready the supervisors are for a change.
2. The executive in charge encourages and supports the supervisors in building up a picture of what they can get out of the new budget. He has the supervisors list the advantages and disadvantages, while he makes contributions.
3. The executive in charge helps the group make a step-by-step plan of the best way to introduce the new budget plan or system.
4. The executive in charge then helps the group membership list the resources they feel they have or could obtain as individuals or as a group to meet the budget.
5. Finally, the executive in charge creates a feeling on the part of all the group members that they are responsible for active participation.

The participative approach does not necessarily diminish the manager's control of planning performance. As Arnold Tannenbaum points out in *Control in Organization*,[11] use of the participative approach, greater concern for the individual, and increased control of his own operation by the worker can lead to more efficient operations. Involving the individual in planning actually increases his commitment to goals and standards, and places greater obligations on him to achieve these goals and standards. The planning and control system can, of course, break down, if the leadership is weak, and the manager fails to maintain his final decision-making authority. But given strong leadership, the studies made under Tannenbaum's direction show that increased individual participation in the planning process can lead to increased effectiveness.

MEASURING THE EFFECTIVENESS OF PLANNING

The methods used for measuring the effectiveness of implementation planning and strategic planning differ considerably.

Implementation Planning

Implementation plans and the efforts of middle managers in creating these plans can be effectively measured through the budgetary process.

At first glance, measuring the effectiveness of the planning effort through the budgetary process seems to be an easy task. For example, where there is a systematically developed budget plan, the planning director can

[11]Arnold S. Tannenbaum, *Control in Organizations* (New York: McGraw-Hill Book Company, Inc., 1968).

tell very easily when sales goals are not being reached, costs are higher than anticipated, the desired return on investment will not be achieved, a facility will not be built on time, adequate funds will not be available, management reserves are not keeping up with plans, and the like.

This review is only a beginning, however, for these are merely symptoms. Isolating true causes of problems is often not a simple process. For example, in a credit mail-order retail operation with which the author recently worked, a higher-than-anticipated number of accounts were defaulting. The credit manager believed that credit clearing of accounts should be tightened, since he felt that too many orders had been taken from high risk customers in an effort to get higher initial sales. The marketing manager was convinced that the problem was caused by poor order servicing and by carrying too many products oriented towards teenagers, which attracted poor risk accounts.

In reality what was happening was that the nature of the company's business was changing. The market was becoming a younger market, mainly because of a major population shift and growing sophistication of the teenage market. More teenagers were opening charge accounts, and buying on credit. The company had failed to anticipate the extent of this marketing shift and develop plans to profit by it. New products, servicing, credit screening and advertising policies were needed.

In this case, the company's planning was poorly organized and executed. The planning was done after the fact, and only after two very poor years did the company correct its fundamental problem of lack of strategy for the market they were servicing. Many expedients were tried, people fired, money wasted, and personal aggravations encountered. Much of this could have been avoided by better planning.

Two pitfalls to be avoided in using budgets to measure and insure progress towards planning goals are, therefore: failure to probe far enough beneath the symptoms to isolate the real causes of problems; failure to develop comprehensive plans for solving these problems, and settling instead for piecemeal, short-term solutions to problems.

Another major pitfall in measuring and controlling planning performance through budgets, which is discussed at some length in Chapter 2 above, is the unreliability of many standards used by companies to judge performance. However wrong it may be, standards are frequently "adjusted" by management during the planning process. Sometimes this is done because of internal political pressures. Sometimes this is done because many managers wish to apply pressure to the organization and so set standards slightly beyond realistic expectations, as a device for getting maximum performance from people. Sound plans cannot be built on "incentive" criteria, however, nor can planning be effectively performed when criteria such as profit and sales goals, timing of expansion, and the like are distorted to accommodate the biases of higher management.

In spite of the problems associated with using budgetary review as a way to measure the effectiveness of implementation planning, the budget is nonetheless a very useful tool for measuring implementation planning, when used correctly.

Strategic Planning

Budgetary review can rarely be used to measure the effectiveness of strategic planning efforts, for the lead times between making strategic planning decisions and realizing sales and profits from these decisions are usually quite long, and so prevent measurement of progress towards planned long-term objectives on an interim basis by any traditional sales or profit yardstick.

Over the long-term, return on investment is one of the principal criteria of planning success. DuPont has developed such a measure of their planning efforts.[12] Success meeting return-on-investment goals in this area may, however, be caused by many factors; and cannot always be directly related to specific planning efforts. Other measures are, therefore, needed to supplement return-on-investment analysis.

Bruce Payne has outlined some other criteria which can be used in judging the effectiveness of strategic planning during its initial stages:

1. Has the planning team determined the key influences in the growth of the industry and evaluated the influence of each?
2. Have the strengths and weaknesses of the company been accurately evaluated?
3. Have the capacities of different company functions to support the plan been projected far enough ahead?
4. Is there a practical timetable?
5. Have alternatives been considered?
6. What provisions have been made for future reverses?[13]

In practice, it is not difficult to judge the effectiveness of a strategic planning effort after the first or second year. First, are the major objectives detailed in the plan being met, and if they are not is it because the initial strategic planning was unrealistic? Second, are the major environmental trends that were forecast actually occurring? Third, have major emergencies been anticipated, and have the plans to meet them proved adequate? Fourth, have new external developments been incorporated into the plan when they occurred, and have major company programs been continuously reviewed within the long-range planning perspective? Fifth, has return on investment fared better than industry competition? Sixth,

[12]William Travers Jerome III, *Executive Control—The Catalyst* (New York: John Wiley and Sons, Inc., 1961), Chapter 13.

[13]Bruce Payne, "Steps in Long-Range Planning," in *Long-Range Planning for Management*, ed. David Ewing (Rev. ed.; New York: Harper & Row, Publishers, 1964), pp. 235-237.

has the company led or followed the competition in product, market, and facility development? In other words, if the major things management planned to happen are happening, and if the company is successfully meeting unanticipated emergencies (without a continual crisis atmosphere), then the planning effort has been successful.

At one company, where division managers were responsible for making long-range strategic plans, with assistance from a corporate staff, semi-annual review meetings were held with top management to explore deviations from long-term plans. These meetings were used to judge the effectiveness of planning efforts on the basis of the criteria outlined above. Separate, more frequent meetings, similar to the review procedure set up by Pennsalt, were held for top management budget review of short-term plans. Since many of the criteria used for evaluating strategic planning are subjective, it is really only through personal involvement in such reviews that top management can form any judgment on the strategic planning effort.

CONCLUSION

This chapter has outlined the steps involved in coordinating and controlling planning activities at all levels within a company. The budgetary process, a management control tool, is important in performing this phase of the planning effort. It is not only a means for reviewing the effectiveness of the planning effort and for revising plans, but it is also a method of coordinating the planning effort, communicating plans, and judging whether performance is in line with plans.

The budget is the principal device through which management control and business planning work together. This chapter has given guidelines for carrying out the budgetary process and for integrating planning and budgeting. The budget is not, however, the only management control tool used in planning. The planner can also employ quantitative and graphic analysis, electronic data processing, and systems simulation to improve his planning effort.

DISCUSSION QUESTIONS

1. What steps are involved in coordinating the development of implementation plans? In what ways does the budgetary process help in this coordination?
2. Define management control. What is the distinction between business control and planning?
3. What are the principle ways in which control tools can be used in business planning?
4. How can the budget be used in business planning? What are the limitations in that use?

5. What are the steps in the budgetary process? Why is it so important that budgets be based on plans? How does budgeting help improve planning?
6. List and discuss the guidelines for carrying out the budgetary process.
7. In what ways do you think behavioral science tools can be used to plan and control more effectively?
8. What problems are encountered in measuring the effectiveness of both strategic and implementation planning? How can they be overcome?
9. Discuss the planning coordination and control aspects of the Superb Biscuit Company and Blakeston and Wilson Company cases given in the Appendices.

CHAPTER 10

SOME QUANTITATIVE AND GRAPHIC TECHNIQUES USED IN PLANNING

The purpose of this chapter is to discuss some more widely used quantitative and graphic techniques useful to the manager in short term operational planning. The first part of the chapter describes the basic approach underlying the use of these techniques, model building and simulation. Next, six techniques are described, and examples are given of how they are applied to specific business planning problems.

THE BASIC APPROACH: MODEL BUILDING AND SIMULATION

The six techniques described in the next section all make use of the basic model building and simulation approach. Each in essence requires that a model of the situation under study be developed, using the specific technique. This model is then manipulated in some way to simulate the situation variables, in order to give the planner outcome information upon which to base his decision. The following are brief definitions of model building and simulation.

Model Building

A model is a representation or abstraction of an actual object or situation, which attempts to explain the behavior of some aspect of that object or situation.[1] While a model is only a representation of reality and so is less complex than reality, it must be sufficiently complete to approximate those aspects of reality being investigated.

[1]David W. Miller and Martin K. Starr, *Executive Decisions and Operations Research* (Rev. ed.; Englewood Cliffs, N.J.: Prentice-Hall, Inc., 1969), p. 145.

The three most common types of models are:

Physical. A three-dimensional scale reproduction of the system. A model plane would be an example of a physical model. This type of model is used when studying the geometric or physical relationships of a system.

Diagrammatic. A schematic representation of activities. Examples of diagrammatic models are the flow charts shown below in the discussion of PERT/CPM.

Mathematical. Equations or formulas which describe the operations symbolically. Examples of mathematical models are given in the discussion of linear programming and decision theory below.

The basic steps in model building are:

1. Observe the situation, and define the problem and the objective.
2. Investigate controllable input factors.
3. Study the network of interconnections and observe changing inputs and outputs until a hypothesis (a model or statement of how changing inputs are expected to affect outputs) is reached.
4. Evaluate uncontrollable factors.
5. Test the model for validity.
6. Repeat steps 2-5 until a model is found that predicts as reliably as is necessary to solve the management problem.[2]

Simulation

Simulation is a method of approaching a problem first by constructing a model which abstracts elements of the real situation that are pertinent to the problem, and second by manipulating this model in such a way as to draw some conclusions about the real situation which will aid in planning.[3] Business managers use simulation to visualize the components of the situation, in order to plan an effective solution to the problem. Simulation takes many forms (for example, flying a plane in a wind tunnel, manipulating mathematical formulas in order to solve linear programming and queuing problems, and playing computerized executive business games)[4] and in business very often involves the use of a computer.

[2]Billy E. Goetz, *Quantitative Methods: A Survey and Guide for Managers* (New York: McGraw Hill Book Company, 1965), pp. 84-90.

[3]John Dearden and F. Warren McFarlan, *Management Information Systems: Text and Cases* (Homewood, Illinois: Richard D. Irwin, Inc., 1966), p. 92.

[4]For an explanation of the various types of simulation see Joel M. Kibbee, "Management Control Simulation," in *Management Control Systems*, eds. Donald G. Malcolm and Alan J. Rowe (New York: John Wiley and Sons, 1960), pp. 300-320; Thomas R. Prince, *Information Systems for Management Planning and Control* (Rev. ed.; Homewood, Illinois: Richard D. Irwin, Inc., 1970), Chapter 17; Jay W. Forrester, *Industrial Dynamics* (Cambridge, Mass.: The M.I.T. Press, 1961); Charles P. Bonini, *Simulation of Information and Decision Systems in the Firm* (Englewood Cliffs, N.J.: Prentice-Hall, Inc., 1963); and Paul S. Greenlaw, Lowell W. Herron, and Richard H. Rawdon, *Business Simulation in Industrial and University Education* (Englewood Cliffs, N.J.: Prentice-Hall, Inc., 1962).

A variety of examples of the use of model building and simulation in planning are given in the following sections of this chapter and in Chapter 11.

THE TECHNIQUES

The six techniques discussed in this section are: linear programming, dynamic programming, probability and decision theory, queuing or waiting line theory, game theory, and PERT/CPM.

Linear Programming

Linear programming is a mathematical technique employed in business for finding the best uses of the firm's limited resources, including money, raw materials, machines, space, transportation equipment, time and personnel, to accomplish specific goals.[5] The adjective "linear" is used to describe a directly proportional relationship between or among two or more variables. For example, if a 10 per cent increase in productive hours causes a 10 per cent rise in output, the relationship between productive hours and output is linear. "Programming" refers to the use of mathematical techniques to determine the best solution.[6]

The basic requirements for the use of linear programming are:[7]

1. There must be a specified objective. For example, a furniture company uses one facility to produce both tables and chairs and wants to find the most profitable product mix.
2. There must be alternative courses of action, each of which will achieve the objective. For example, should the furniture company allocate manufacturing capacity to tables and chairs in the ration of 50:50? 25:75? 70:30? Some other ratio?
3. Resources are in limited supply. A limited number of machine hours are available; consequently, the more hours scheduled for tables, the fewer chairs can be made.
4. The variables must be interrelated. For example, if profit is $8 per table and $6 per chair, the total profit will reflect the ratio of tables to chairs.
5. The company's objective and operational limitations must be expressible as

[5]Richard I. Levin and C. A. Kirkpatrick, *Quantitative Approaches to Management* (New York: McGraw-Hill Book Company, 1965), p. 198.

[6]Linear programming has sometimes been called mathematical programming, but this is incorrect. Linear programming is only one type of mathematical programming. There are also non-linear types of mathematical programming, such as dynamic programming, which is discussed below. See Alexander Henderson and Robert Schlaifer, "Mathematical Information of Better Decisions," in *Scientific Decision Making for Business: Readings in Operations Research for Non-Mathematicians*, ed. Abe Shuchman (New York: Holt, Rinehart and Winston, Inc., 1963), pp. 149-223, for a complete discussion of mathematical programming.

[7]Levin and Kirkpatrick, *Quantitative Approaches to Management*, p. 199.

(or approximated by) linear mathematical equations or inequalities. For example, the furniture company's objective, dollar profits, can be expressed in this simple equation:
p (profit) = \$8A (where A is the number of tables) + \$6B (where B is the number of chairs).

The following is an example of how linear programming can be used to plan a company's production mix. A company has two products in its line—Autoscopes and Flexibars.[8] Each Autoscope produces \$40 profit and each Flexibar yields \$50 profit.

The company wants the answers to the following question:

1. What combination of products uses plant facilities best and still maximizes profits?
2. Do we have enough testing capacity?
3. Can we change product mix and still maximize profits?

The three main operations in the plant are machining, assembling, and testing. Table 10.1 shows available production time and time used in each department by each product.

Table 10.1

PRODUCTION TIME

	Machining	*Assembling*	*Testing*
Each Autoscope requires	1 hour	5 hours	3 hours
Each Flexibar requires	2 hours	4 hours	1 hour
Total Production time available	720 hours	1800 hours	900 hours

As in the case of the furniture company described above, the total profit from the operation can be expressed in an equation: profit = \$40 times the number of Autoscopes + \$50 times the number of Flexibars. If we substitute X for the number of Autoscopes and Y for the number of Flexibars, the equation can be simplified to: $p = 40X + 50Y$.

First, the *machining* time available for each product is calculated. If only Autoscopes were made, 720 could be produced (1 hour divided into 720 available hours). If only Flexibars were made, 360 could be produced (2 hours divided into 720 available hours).

Next, the *assembling* time available for each product is calculated. If only Autoscopes were made, 360 could be produced (5 hours divided into

[8]General Electric, *G-E Linear Programming* (Phoenix, Arizona: Information Service Division, General Electric Company, 1966), pp. 3-8.

1800 available hours). If only Flexibars were made, 450 could be produced (4 hours divided into 1800 available hours).

Last, the *testing* time available for each product is calculated. If only Autoscopes were made, 300 could be produced (3 hours divided into 900 available hours). If only Flexibars were made, 900 could be produced (1 hour divided into 900 available hours).

These calculations give the maximum and minimum ranges for our solution. By plotting these ranges on a single chart, the entire range of possible solutions can be visualized (Figure 10.1). The shaded area represents the range of feasible solutions.

Figure 10.1

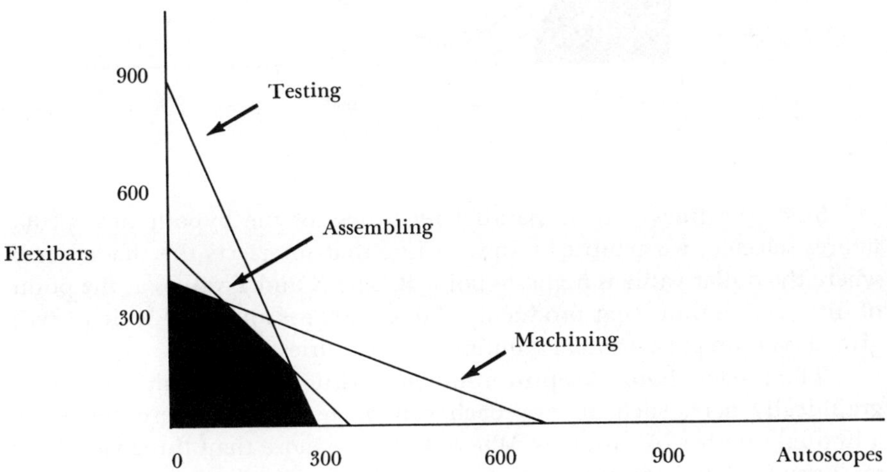

Once these limits have been established, profit calculations can be made. The formula given above is p = 40X + 50Y. We arbitrarily pick a profit which by inspection is close to what could be expected in the situation, $25,000. The formula then reads $25,000 = 40X + 50Y. If only Autoscopes were made, 625 would have to be made to produce this profit ($25,000 divided by 40). If only Flexibars were made, 500 would have to be made to produce this profit ($25,000 divided by 50). This hypothetical line is now plotted on the chart (Figure 10.2).

The same calculations are then made at a $15,000 profit level and plotted on the chart, since $25,000 profit does not intersect the feasible solution area. The $15,000 line does intersect the feasible solution area, but does not give maximum use of facilities.

Figure 10.2

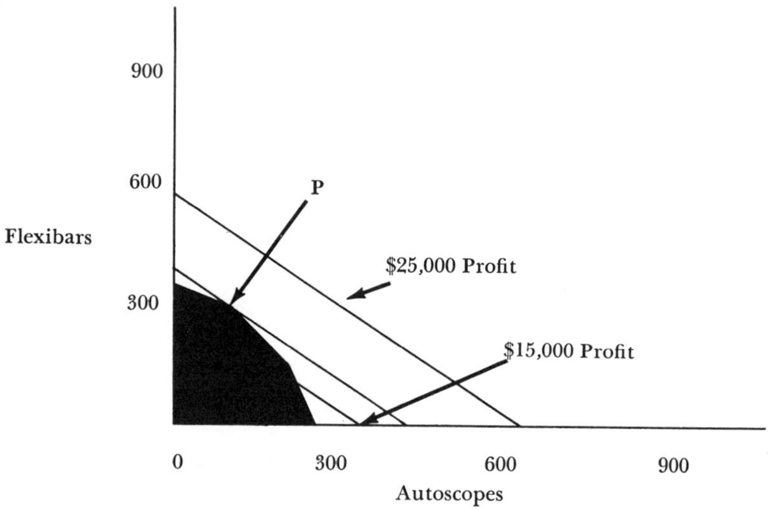

Since the lines will be parallel regardless of the hypothetical profit figures selected, we arbitrarily draw a line that intersects the shaded area where the dollar value is highest—point P. The X and Y values at the point of intersection show that producing 120 Autoscopes and 300 Flexibars will give maximum profits and maximum use of facilities.

The reader should keep in mind that while the problem was solved graphically here, such an approach can be used only where there are a limited number of variables. Where there are more than three variables, mathematical techniques are used. Because the mathematical computations for linear programming are often quite complex, the computer is frequently used in linear programming.

In addition to solving production, scheduling, or facilities allocation problems, linear programming can be used to solve a variety of business planning problems, such as:

1. Finding the best way to transport and warehouse products, taking into account customer demands at various locations around the country, and varying costs of transportation.
2. Finding the best method of allocating raw materials to several manufacturing plants.
3. Determining optimum inventory levels.
4. Scheduling assignment of personnel, such as airline stewardesses and pilots, in situations where there are complex routing and work assignment restrictions.

5. Reducing trim losses in cutting rolls of paper, textiles and other such materials.
6. Allocating limited amounts of electronic service equipment in manufacturing and testing operations.
7. Determining an optimum diet, and subsistence levels.
8. Assigning personnel to engineering project planning groups in accordance with project priority.
9. Finding the most economical blend of grain and wheat products and of oil and chemical products, taking current supplies and demands into consideration.

This list is by no means complete, but it gives some idea of the variety of business planning problems which linear programming can help solve.

Dynamic Programming

When the relationship between variables is not linear but continuously changing, linear programming cannot be used in solving resource allocation problems. In the furniture company example mentioned previously, suppose that the profit realized was not constant but varied between $0 and $8 per table and $0 and $6 per chair, depending upon such things as the timing of the run, market conditions, consumer acceptance, and economic fluctuations. In this instance the company's resources must be allocated by a technique that incorporates decisions made over a period of time.

Dynamic programming is one of the best known techniques for solving business problems in which resources are allocated in a sequence of interdependent decisions over a period of time, and the objective is to obtain the maximum return on the entire sequence of decisions.[9] In such instances, dynamic programming can show management how some gain from one decision can be sacrificed to make possible a greater gain from another decision.

Dynamic programming can be used for solving a variety of business problems, from marketing and production to financial planning. For example, a particular market has three advertising media: A, B, and C. The cost per advertisement in A is $2,500, in B, $5,000, and in C, $10,000. The advertising director of a manufacturing company with a total advertising budget of $20,000 can use dynamic programming to calculate the total cost involved under various combinations of advertising frequencies in media A, B, and C, and to predict probable sales from each of the combinations.[10]

[9]Abe Shuchman, "The Nature and Characteristics of Dynamic Programming Problems," in *Scientific Decision Making for Business*, ed. Shuchman, p. 207; A. Vazsonyi, *Scientific Programming in Business and Industry* (New York: John Wiley and Sons, Inc., 1958).

[10]Richard B. Maffei, "Planning Advertising Expenditures by Dynamic Programming Methods," in *Scientific Decision Making in Business*, ed. Shuchman, pp. 209-216.

Assuming that historical figures were available which showed the range of unit sales (optimistic to pessimistic) that might be produced from each ad, then Table 2 could be constructed.

Table 10.2

TOTAL COSTS AND TOTAL EXPECTED SALES FOR SEVEN KEY COMBINATIONS UNDER BOTH PESSIMISTIC AND OPTIMISTIC ASSUMPTIONS[11]

# of Ad Inserts	*Pessimistic Assumptions*		*Optimistic Assumptions*	
(A, B, C)	*Total Cost*	*Total Expected Sales*	*Total Cost*	*Total Expected Sales*
(0, 4, 0)	$20,000	350	$20,000	360
(2, 3, 0)	20,000	510	20,000	550
(4, 2, 0)	20,000	540	20,000	580
(0, 2, 1)	20,000	510	20,000	590
(2, 1, 1)	20,000	580	20,000	690
(4, 0, 1)	20,000	530	20,000	640
(0, 0, 2)	20,000	300	20,000	350

According to the Table, the best course of action under either optimistic or pessimistic assumptions would be two appearances in A, one in B and one in C.

Other business planning problems that can be solved through dynamic programming include allocating salesmen to marketing areas, allocating funds for dividends, planning capital requirements over a period of years, and determining shipping and warehouse arrangements.

Decision Theory and Probability Theory

Decision theory is a method used to select from several alternatives the best course of action to achieve a desired objective in a given situation under conditions of uncertainty.[12] It enables the decision maker to analyze a set of complex situations with many alternatives and many different possible consequences. Decision theory is sometimes referred to as decision making under uncertainty, or statistical decision theory.

Decision theory makes use of probability theory. Probability theory is a technique used for drawing inferences from statistical data. It deals with events of a special kind: random events, whose outcome is determined by chance.[13] The probability of an outcome can be most easily understood as a percentage of time a particular outcome will occur if an event is repeated a great many times. For example, in tossing a coin the probability

[11]Maffei, "Planning Advertising Expenditures," p. 212.

[12]Harold Bierman, Jr., *et al.*, *Quantitative Analysis for Business Decisions* (Rev. ed., Homewood, Illinois: Richard D. Irwin, Inc., 1965), p. 55.

[13]Miller and Starr, *Executive Decisions and Operations Research*, p. 58.

that heads will come up is one half, because an infinite number of tosses has to produce about 50 per cent heads and 50 per cent tails.

Through the use of probability theory the decision maker can judge which events are more probable than others, when faced with a decision under uncertainty. Combining this probability estimate with the expected consequences (potential profit or loss) of each possible event, he can weigh the potential profit against the probability of each alternative outcome, determine the risk, and decide which course of action is most *likely* to yield the greatest gain.

Decision theory has been used effectively in a wide range of business situations, such as capital budgeting and product pricing, as well as determining where to drill oil wells, how much inventory to carry, whether or not to buy a new machine or introduce a new product, and whether to make or buy an item.

The systematic approach to making a decision under uncertainty is given by Robert Schlaifer:[14]

1. Attach a definite numerical *value* to the consequence of every possible act given every possible event.
2. Attach a definite numerical *probability weight* to every possible event.
3. For each act separately, use these weights to compute a *weighted average* of all the values attached to the act.
4. Select the act whose weighted average value is highest.

The following problem and solution illustrates how these steps are carried out in practice.[15] Suppose we have a product to market at a price of $50 per unit. We have to invest $5000 in fixed costs and are uncertain whether sales will be 100 units, 250 units or 1000 units. The profit (or loss) at each level of sales has been calculated: $3000 loss at 100 units, $0 at 250 units, $15,000 profit at 1000 units. These figures are written in the first and third columns of our decision chart in Table 10.3.

Next the chances or probability of the event occurring (100 units, 250 units, and 1,000 units sale) are estimated by the decision maker, based on

Table 10.3

COMPUTATION OF EXPECTED PROFIT FROM NEW PRODUCT

Sales (Units)	*Probability (Weight)*	*Profit*	*Weight X Profit*
100	0.40	—$3,000	—$1,200
250	0.40	0	0
1,000	0.20	15,000	3,000
	1.00		$1,800

[14]Robert Schlaifer, *Probability and Statistics for Business Decisions* (New York: McGraw-Hill Book Company, 1959), p. 5.

[15]Bierman, *et al.*, *Quantitative Analysis*, pp. 6-8.

his experience or historical data, and written in the second column of the chart in Table 10.3.

Step three is to multiply the profit anticipated (outcome) by the probability of it occurring (probability weight) to arrive at a weighted average.

The last step is to make the decision. The expected profit or expected monetary value for marketing the product is $1,800, compared with zero for rejecting the project. Hence, using decision theory, we proceed to market the product (this conclusion assumes that the consequences measured in dollars also measure utility).

Another typical problem in decision theory, which illustrates more complex applications of probability theory in making decisions under uncertainty, has been described by Schlaifer.[16] This problem concerns a machine which is about to be used for the production of 500 units of one of a company's products. The number of reject units produced depends on the setting of the machine. If the setting is correct, only 1% will be defective. Since the manufacturer is not certain of the setting, he must decide whether to pay $6 to have it checked, or accept the present setting and the number of rejected items, each costing $.40, that might result.

The first step in applying decision theory to this situation is to construct a model, in this case a probabilistic model. No model is necessary for the choice of having the setting checked, for in this case the cost is known to be $6 and the expected result is known to be 1% defective.

The choice of not checking the setting is more complicated. Each setting on the machine will have a different defective production rate. Since the setting is unknown, the model for this situation must show the different possible defective rates, indicated by N, and the probability that this will be the actual rate once production starts, indicated by $P_{(N)}$. This data can be obtained from either past production records or experience. The model for this decision is represented in the table given in Table 10.4.

Table 10.4

THE ESTIMATED PROBABLE "COST" OF THE DECISION

Defective Production Level (N)	*Number of Defective Units*	*Cost for Defective Units @ 40¢ Each (C)*	*Executive's Estimates of the Probability of the Event Occurring P(N)*	*Expected Value of Cost C times P(N)*
1%	5	$ 2	.7	$ 1.40
5%	25	10	.1	1.00
15%	75	30	.1	3.00
25%	125	50	.1	5.00
				$10.40

[16]This example is an adaptation of one given in Schlaifer, *Probability and Statistics*, Chapter 22.

As shown in the decision table, each level of defective production has an associated cost for defective units, for example, $10 when the level is 5%. However, this $10 is the cost only if the defective rate is actually 5%. Since the actual defective rate is not known, a theoretical (or expected) cost is computed for each rate by estimating (based on experience) the probability of that defective rate occurring. For example, the manufacturing manager estimated that chances were 7 out of 10 that the defective rate would be 1% and only 1 out of 10 that it would be at each higher level. Knowing the expected cost for each defective production level and its probability of occurring allows the computation of the total theoretical (or expected) cost of the decision of $10.40. Comparing this with the cost of having the setting checked, $6.00, the manufacturer would decide to have the machine adjusted.

The manufacturer does, however, have another alternative which was not considered above. This alternative is to make a test production run. Suppose that the manufacturer made such a test run and that ten units are produced, of which none are defective. Based on this information, it is possible to revise the $10.40 estimate of the cost of not checking the setting.

The method is as follows: For the 1% defective level, the probability of getting a defective unit is .01. Therefore the probability of a non-defective unit is .99. Knowing the probabilistic process involved (in this case a Bernoulli process)[17] one knows that the probability of two *successive* non-defective units is .99 times .99 or .9801. Continuing, one determines that the probability of 10 successive nondefective units is .99 to the tenth power, or .904. Since the probability of having a 1% level was initially estimated to be .7 (this is called the "a priori" probability), the probability of *both* events occurring, that is getting 10 non-defective units *and* being at the 1% level, is the product of the two individual probabilities, or .904 x .7 = .6328. This is termed the "joint" probability. The data for all four levels of defective production is shown in Table 10.5.

Now one can revise the probabilities assigned the various defective levels, in light of the new information. First one notes the total of the joint probabilities, .7180. This is the total probability of getting 10 non-defective units, regardless of the setting. One of the theorems of probability theory, Baye's Theorem,[18] then provides that the probability of the machine being

[17]A Bernoulli process is a series of trials, each trial having two possible outcomes; success or failure. The probability of success is designated by P and the probability of failure is (1-P). In the Bernoulli process, each trial is independent of the results of preceding trials. An example of this process would be the flipping of a coin where, for instance, heads could be called a success and tails a failure. For a more detailed description of this process see any introductory text in probability theory, or Richard C. Dubes, *The Theory of Applied Probability* (Englewood Cliffs, N.J.: Prentice-Hall, Inc., 1968), or A. Papoulis, *Probability, Random Variables, and Stochastic Processes* (New York: McGraw-Hill Book Company, 1965).

[18]See R. Pratt, H. Raiffa and R. Schlaifer, *Introduction to Statistical Decision Theory* (New York: McGraw-Hill Book Company, 1965), Ch. 10, or the Dubes or Papoulis books cited in footnote 17 above.

Table 10.5

Level (N)	*Probability "a priori"*	*Probability of 10 non-defective units*	*Joint Probability*	*Probability "a posteriori"*	*Cost C*	*Expected Value of Cost*
1%	.7	.904	.6328	.881	$2	1.76
5%	.1	.599	.0599	.083	10	.83
10%	.1	.197	.0197	.028	30	.84
25%	.1	.056	.0056	.008	50	.40
	1.0		.7180	1.000		$3.83

set for a given level is the joint probability *for that level,* divided by the total joint probability of getting 10 non-defective units (for example, .6328 divided by .7180 equals .881, and so forth). This is termed the "a posteriori" probability, indicating that it is obtained after the introduction of new information. As shown, the "a posteriori" probabilities favor the occasion of the machine being set properly, as the test run would lead one to believe.

Now, the manufacturer can re-evaluate the expected cost of not having the machine setting checked. His new expectation, $3.83, is less than the $6.00 charge to check the machine, leading him to a different conclusion than was reached on the basic of the "a priori" probabilities in Table 10.5, providing the cost of making the test run did not exceed the saving.

Another application of probability in decision theory is found in the development of an anti-ballistic missile system. In developing such a system, for example, it may be determined that the probability of a missile hitting its target is .70. It is known that it takes 35 seconds to load and launch a missile. It is also known that at present the system's radar will detect a target at a distance that allows one minute warning. It is required that the ABM system have a .97 probability of success. The system designer must, therefore, determine if this requirement is met.

The designer assumes that a missile is always loaded and ready to launch. Therefore, in one minute it is possible to load and launch a second missile, but not a third.

The probability of success with two missiles is the probability of hitting the target with the first missile plus the probability of hitting it with the second. The first probability is given as .70. The second missile, though, contributes only if the first misses. Therefore, the probability of success on the second missile is the probability of the first missing times that of the second being successful. Since the missile has a .70 probability of success, it has a .30 probability of failure (the sum of the probabilities of success and failure must equal 1.0). Therefore, the probability of success with two missiles is .70 plus .21 (.70 times .30), or .91. Since this figure for hitting the target does not meet the requirement of .97, the systems designer must select a means of improving performance. He estimates that he can improve the design of the missile, thus increasing the likelihood of success, at a cost of $1 million per .01 improvement. Another alternative would be to improve radar performance at a cost of $1 million for each added second of warning.

Realizing that an added 10 seconds of warning will permit the launching of a third missile, the designer computes the probability of success with a third missile. The third missile will hit the target if the first two fail and the third is successful. The probability of the third being successful is .09 times .70, or .063. Thus the performance for three missiles is .7 plus .21 plus .063, or .973 which is satisfactory. The cost of this alternative is $10 million (each second of improvement times $1 million).

He next calculates the improvements needed to obtain satisfactory performance with only two missiles. The system designer finds that he must increase the performance of each missile to a value of .83 from .70, in order to reach the required standard of .97 probability of success (.83 plus .83 times .17, or .971). The cost of this alternative is thus $13 million (each .01 improvement times $1 million).

In this way, the designer determines that required performance can be obtained at a cost of $3 million less by improving the system's radar, than by improving missile performance.

It should be noted that probability theory does not replace executive knowledge and judgement. On the contrary, these are important ingredients, for example, in calculating "a priori" probabilities. Probability theory simply enables the organization of knowledge to permit its more effective use in reaching a decision.

Queuing or Waiting Line Theory

Bottlenecks, backlogs, and idle capacity are common problems in business. Each of these arises from a variable rate of arrival of some kind of unit requiring some kind of service, and by a variable rate of completing the service required.[19] Queuing, or waiting line, theory is a mathematical technique used in planning how to schedule and handle the arrival and service of these units, for through it the manager can determine the most economical balance between the cost of waiting for service and the cost of providing additional facilities.

A study conducted by Boeing Aircraft to determine the number of clerks that should man a factory tool crib counter illustrates how waiting

[19]Goetz, *Quantitative Methods*, p. 426; Bierman, *et al.*, *Quantitative Analysis*, p. 328.

line theory can be used to solve a business planning problem.[20] At the Boeing factory, the tools used by assembly line and shop mechanics are stored in special rooms or "tool cribs." Clerks hand out the tools when mechanics arrive at the crib counter and request tools. The mechanics return the tools to the clerks when no longer needed. In this situation, management wants the lowest possible overhead, or fewest clerks; the factory foremen want their mechanics to spend a minimum of time waiting on line and so argue for a greater number of clerks.

Study of the operation showed that the average time between arrivals of mechanics was 50 seconds and the average time required by a clerk to fill a mechanic's request was 60 seconds. If arrivals were evenly spaced, therefore, two clerks would be more than enough to man the tool crib. However, since service times varied and arrivals occurred at random, at certain times a long line of mechanics would build up, while at other times clerks would be idle. Queuing theory was, therefore, employed to predict the *average* length of time an arriving mechanic would have to wait before being served. Using the appropriate mathematical model or formula,[21] the average waiting time was calculated to be 33.8 seconds with two clerks, 4.7 seconds with three clerks, and 0.8 seconds with four clerks. Since there was an average of 540 requests during a 7½ hour working day, increasing the number of clerks from two to three would reduce the mechanics' waiting time by approximately 4½ hours. However, the amount of time clerks were idle would be increased by 7½ hours a day for each additional clerk. If the cost of idle time was $7 per hour for mechanics and $3 per hour for clerks, the average daily cost of idle time could be calculated as follows:[22] with two clerks, $53.50; with three clerks, $45.40; with four clerks, $63.80. Based on the study, three clerks should be assigned to this tool crib.

Queuing or waiting line theory can be applied to a variety of business planning situations, where questions are raised concerning numbers of services or service facilities or the method in which the service is offered. These include: checkout stands at grocery stores, loading and unloading docks, secretarial typing pools, toll booths at bridges and tunnels, airline maintenance shops, retail store service counters, repair facilities for factory machine maintenance, telephone order taking or answering operations, job shops or departments producing custom orders, hospital emergency rooms, and electronic computer centers.

Game Theory

Game theory is a mathematical technique helpful in planning in situations of conflict, where the success of one party tends to be at the

[20]George Brigham, "On a Congestion Problem in an Aircraft Factory," *Operations Research*, November 1955, pp. 412-428.

[21]Frederick S. Hillier and Gerald J. Lieberman, *Introduction to Operations Research* (San Francisco: Holden-Day, Inc., 1967), pp. 307-310.

[22]Hillier and Lieberman, *Introduction to Operations Research*, p. 347.

expense of others, and where the individual decision maker is not in complete control of the factors influencing the outcome.[23] For example, a general whose forces face the enemy, an industrialist whose products compete with others, a player in a poker game, and a politician fighting other candidates for an office are all involved in struggles that may be classified as game situations.

The simplest example of game theory is the two person zero-sum game: in a two person coin flipping match, when one person loses a coin the other person wins a coin, so that the sum of one person's loses and the other person's gain is zero (that is, loses equal gains). Decision making in such a game situation is more difficult than in the situations discussed in the programming sections above, for when one party wins, the other loses. The individual has to work out how to achieve as much as possible, taking into account the fact that there are others whose goals are different and whose actions have an effect on all his decisions.[24]

The following is a simple illustration (two person zero-sum game) of how game theory can help in planning marketing strategy.[25] Two competing companies, Jones and Smith, each prepare a display featuring one of its products in a supermarket at the beginning of each week. Once the display has been set up it cannot be changed for the remainder of the week.

The Jones Company has three products, A, B and C, which it may display in competition with the Smith Company's products, D, E and F. The Jones Company marketing manager constructs the chart shown in Table 10.6, and estimates the chances of the success of each of his products against each of Smith's products.

Table 10.6

		Smith Company Displays		
		D	*E*	*F*
Jones Company Displays	A	good	fair	fair
	B	fair	good	poor
	C	poor	fair	good

He then gives numerical values to each of his general value judgments—1 for poor, 2 for fair, and 3 for good—and inserts them in his chart (Table 10.7).

Table 10.7

		Smith Company Displays		
		D	*E*	*F*
Jones Company Displays	A	3	2	2
	B	2	3	1
	C	1	2	3

23Bierman, *et al.*, *Quantitative Analysis for Business Decisions*, p. 226; Martin Shubik, "The Uses of Game Theory in Management Sciences," in *Scientific Decision Making in Business*, ed. Shuchman, p. 332.

24Shubik, "The Uses of Game Theory," p. 333.

25Levin and Kirkpatrick, *Quantitative Approaches to Management*, pp. 304-305. Used with permission of McGraw-Hill Book Company.

Using game theory[26] it is possible to calculate the best strategy for the Jones Company: feature product A $\frac{1}{2}$ of the time, product B $\frac{1}{6}$ of the time, and product C $\frac{1}{3}$ of the time.

The theory of games provides a conceptual framework within which most competitive problems can be formulated.[27] It is especially useful in solving such problems as planning strategy for introducing new products or for meeting other forms of market competition.

PERT and CPM

PERT (Program Evaluation and Review Technique) and CPM (Critical Path Method) are two other model building techniques that can aid in the planning and scheduling of projects. PERT and CPM both use graphic network techniques to develop the maximum utilization of manpower, machines and time in the accomplishment of a project.[28] Through PERT and CPM techniques, a project is divided into its components in order to determine the sequence of activities needed to complete the project. Normally the entire project is then presented in flow chart form.

Through the use of the flow chart, PERT and CPM help the manager visualize the interrelationships of all aspects of a project. Both methods can be used to decide whether to undertake a project, to develop a reasonable plan for carrying out a project, and to control the progress of the project. These techniques are widely used in solving business problems, such as construction and new product programs, as well as in military missile programs.

PERT and CPM differ in some respects. PERT is mainly used to plan and schedule complicated jobs where previous experience is lacking. For this reason PERT uses three time estimates, the most optimistic, the most pessimistic, and the average or most likely. CPM, on the other hand, is used where there has been enough experience to determine with reasonable accuracy how much time is required to complete each activity in the project. CPM thus uses only one estimate of time for each job.[29]

When first used, PERT (sometimes called PERT/Time) was concerned only with the time needed to complete each component of a project and the total time for the project. PERT/Cost was subsequently developed. The technique, which is still in the developmental stage, is concerned with both the time and the cost of completing each component and the total project.[30]

[26]Levin and Kirkpatrick, *Quantitative Approaches to Management*, pp. 268-304.

[27]Russell L. Ackoff and Patrick Rivett, *A Manager's Guide to Operations Research* (New York: John Wiley and Sons, Inc., 1963), p. 51.

[28]Dearden and McFarlan, *Management Information Systems*, p. 63.

[29]Prince, *Information Systems*, p. 104.

[30]Richard I. Levin and Charles A. Kirkpatrick, *Planning and Control with PERT/CPM* (New York: McGraw-Hill Book Company, 1966), p. 153.

The following is an example of the use of PERT/Time scheduling in introducing a new product line.[31] The first phase is to outline the steps involved in completing the project, the relationships of each step to the others, and the expected time required to complete each step. In this case the expected time is arrived at by making three time estimates, optimistic (To), most likely (Tm) and pessimistic (Tp), and using the following equation:

$$\frac{\text{To} + 4\text{Tm} + \text{Tp}}{6} = \text{Expected time}$$

Based on this initial analysis, a flow chart is drawn up, as shown in Figure 10.3. In the figure the numbers in parentheses are the expected times in weeks for each step, the lines the steps to be taken, and the circles the start and finish of each step.

Figure 10.3

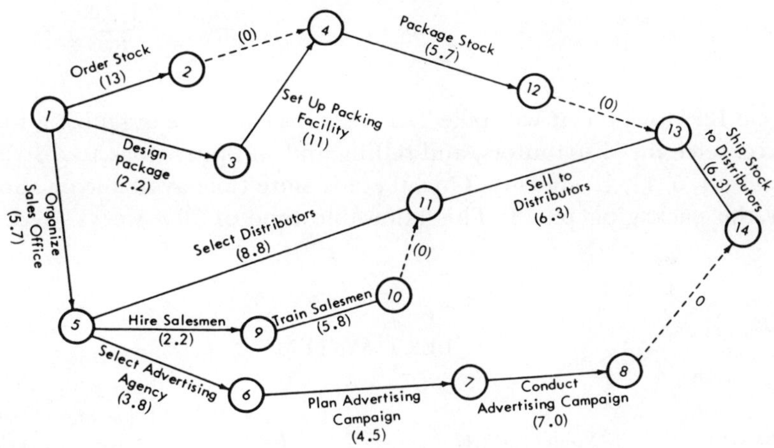

The next phase is to study the interrelationships of all the steps and calculate the earliest expected time and latest allowable time for each series of steps. The earliest expected time is calculated by adding up the expected times for each step. These figures are written in boxes on the chart shown in Figure 10.4.

The latest allowable time is calculated by starting from the end of the project (circle 14) and working backwards, subtracting the expected time of each preceding activity. For example, it is anticipated that it takes only 18.9 weeks to design the package (circles 1 to 3) and package the stock (circles 4 to 12), so this expected time figure was written in the box next to

[31]Dearden and McFarlan, *Management Information Systems*, pp. 80-83.

Figure 10.4

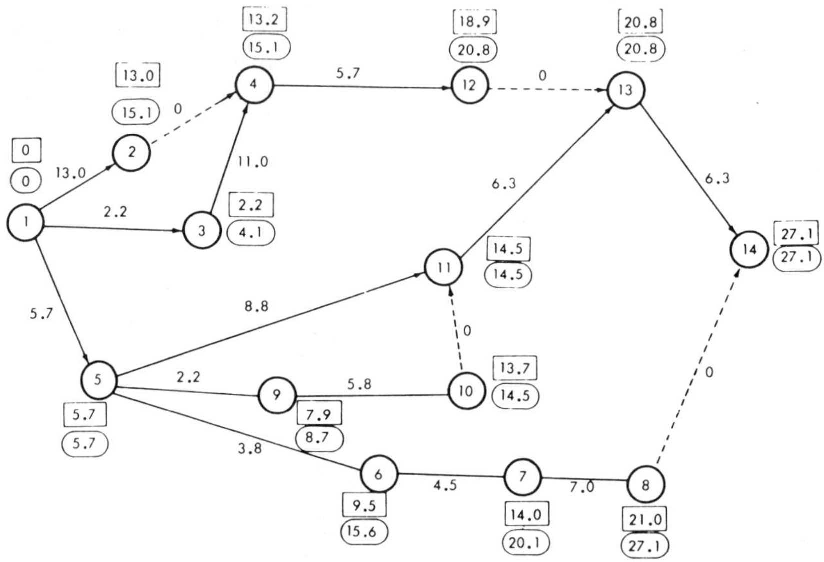

circle 12. However, it will take 27.1 weeks to complete organizing the sales force, selecting distributors, and selling and shipping stock to distributors (circles 1, 5, 11, 13 and 14). Thus there is more time available or allowable for the packaging phase. This allowable time of 20.8 weeks (27.1 weeks

Table 10.8

PERT SYSTEM

Event	*Nomenclature*	*Expected Date*	*Latest Allowable Date*	*Slack Time (in weeks)*
1	Start ordering stock & package design	5/ 7/63	5/ 7/63	0
2	Finish ordering stock	8/ 6/63	8/20/63	2.1
3	Start packaging facility	5/22/63	6/ 5/63	1.9
4	Start package stock	8/ 7/63	8/20/63	1.9
5	Start selecting distributors, hire salesmen, select ad agency	6/14/63	6/14/63	0
6	Start plans for ad campaign	7/11/63	8/22/63	6.1
7	Start conducting ad campaign	8/13/63	9/24/63	6.1
8	Finish conducting ad campaign	10/ 1/63	11/12/63	6.1
9	Start salesmen training	6/29/63	7/ 5/63	.8
10	Finish training salesmen	8/ 9/63	8/15/63	.8
11	Finish selecting distributors	8/15/76	8/15/63	0
12	Finish packaging stock	9/14/63	9/28/63	1.9
13	Finish selling to distributors	9/28/63	9/28/63	0
14	Finish shipping stock to distributors	11/12/63	11/12/63	0

minus 6.3 weeks) for the packaging steps is written in the oval next to step 12.

The final phase is to translate the network chart into a tabular format and to give actual dates for the expected and allowable times. Such a tabular summary is given in Table 10.8.

PERT/CPM can be applied to almost any type of project planning problem in business.

CONCLUSION

The problem the average manager faces in understanding all areas related to effective business planning is staggering. The preceding discussion has attempted to give an outline of some of the techniques that relate to more effective business planning, to define them, and to show how they may be used for more effective short-term operational planning. It was not intended to convey technical knowledge, but only to expand the reader's understanding of what business planning is, and to provide a framework for his further investigation.

For the most part, these techniques are used for short-term operational planning, although many of the situations discussed, such as new product planning and facility location, have long-term strategic planning implications. These techniques can, therefore, be important in any type of planning situation, and at all levels of planning.

DISCUSSION QUESTIONS

1. Describe the ways in which the techniques discussed in this chapter relate to business planning.
2. Discuss the relation of the process used for building a model and the problem-solving/decision-making process outline in Chapter 1.
3. In what sense is the planning process outline given in Chapter 1 a model?
4. In what ways can linear programming be used to plan production, and in what ways can dynamic programming be used to plan advertising expenditures?
5. Discuss the ways in which decision theory is helpful in planning.
6. How valid do you think the Jones Company's decision based on game theory was? In your opinion, did the application of game theory to the situation improve planning the allocation of display space?
7. PERT/CPM is a technique which helps in planning projects. This chapter described how a PERT system was developed and used in planning the intoduction of a new product. Describe how you would go about applying PERT to planning in another area of business with which you are familiar.
8. In what ways do you think the computer might be employed to increase the effectiveness of the techniques described in this chapter.

CHAPTER 11

INFORMATION SYSTEMS FOR PLANNING

Information systems have a major impact on coordination and control in business planning, and computer systems are used extensively in conjunction with the quantitative and graphic tools reviewed in the preceding chapter. The purpose of this chapter is three-fold: first, to discuss the basic theory of systems and its relation to business planning; second, to describe how business information systems work; and third, to explore the ways in which electronic data processing (EDP) systems can be used in business planning. The discussion is divided into six parts: the nature of business information systems and the systems approach; the systems approach and business planning; various kinds of business information systems; planning and developing an information system; business applications of EDP systems; and advanced computer models for planning.

THE NATURE OF BUSINESS INFORMATION SYSTEMS AND THE SYSTEMS APPROACH

Company managers require information of all sorts in order to plan, make decisions and operate a business. The company thus needs some sort of data processing system for collecting, screening, collating, rearranging, storing, and disseminating data required by company managers. Since these data processing systems are used to meet managers' information needs, they are usually called business or management information systems.

Information systems development has had a major impact on business operations. Many an operating executive has found the revolution chaotic, for it has come in the form of the intrusion of computer and systems personnel into his operations. He has felt his authority and control slowly stripped away by a movement he little understands, and because of this has resisted it.

The systems analyst and the computer are not, however, the villains. What normally happens is that the introduction of the computer sets in motion a systematic reevaluation of what the business is and how it can operate most efficiently, as the systems analyst charts the flow of information within the business and questions each decision maker about how he uses this information.

The systems analyst normally is not trying to create problems and expose sloppy decision-making practices. His job is to create an information system for planning, control, and operational decision-making. To perform this job, he needs to establish a logical basis for the information system. Since his system is designed to help managers make better business decisions, the systems analyst proceeds to chart the flow of the business, the decisions made at critical points, and the information needed to make these decisions, in order to create a logical basis for the system. Any exposure and correction of existing poor practices is a bi-product of this analysis, as existing information systems are modernized and as managers are forced to abandon outdated, inefficient practices in making use of the new system.

The reevaluation by the systems analysts exposes a common business problem—the gradual fragmentation of information and decision-making systems within a company over the years. The exposure of the problem in turn leads to an effort to reestablish smoothly working, fully coordinated decision-making systems for the business. Systems theory provides a conceptual basis, as well as principles and guidelines, for establishing a more efficient system within a business for planning, control, and operational decision making.

A system may be defined as an orderly grouping of separate but interdependent components for the purpose of attaining some predetermined objective.[1] Three important aspects of systems are implied by this definition. First, the arrangement of components must be orderly and hierarchical, no matter how complex it may be. Second, since the components of the system are interdependent, there must be communication among them. Third, since a system is oriented towards an objective, any interaction among the components must be designed to achieve that objective.

[1]There are a number of variations on this definition: For example, Warren Brown, "Systems, Boundaries, and Information Flow," *Academy of Management Journal*, Vol. 9, No. 4, December 1966, p. 318, defines a system as "a group or complex of parts (such as people, machines, etc.) interrelated in their actions towards some goals," and Richard A. Johnson, Fremont E. Kast and James E. Rosenzweig, *The Theory and Management of System* (Second edition, New York: McGraw-Hill Book Company, Inc., 1967), p. 4, defines a system as "an organized or complex whole; an assemblage or combination of things or parts forming a complex or unitary whole."

Systems theory, and the various aspects of it explored by scientists,[2] are important to business and business managers for several reasons.[3] First, since the systems approach is objective-oriented, systems organization automatically centers attention upon the objectives for which the firm has been established, and helps to generate concerted and coordinated activity towards attainment of these objectives. Second, the systems approach stresses the inter-dependence of elements, so that a manager is continually forced both to view his operation in relation to others within the business and to view the business firm as a component of the overall operating economy.

From a systems viewpoint, therefore, a business organization can be viewed on one level as a complete, integrated decision-making system designed to achieve some specific objective, such as producing automobiles or paper products. On another level, this internal business system can be viewed as a component or sub-system of a larger system—the economic, social, and competitive environment within which the business operates.

THE SYSTEMS APPROACH AND BUSINESS PLANNING

Looking upon the business firm as an integrated decision-making system, whose components are connected by a network of information flows, aids planning in a number of ways. First, it forces an individual operating or

[2]A number of authorities working in diverse fields of specialization, such as geology, communications theory, and business management, have contributed to the development of systems theory. Four of the better known of these authorities are Ludwig von Bertalanffy, Kenneth Boulding, Norbert Weiner, and Herbert Simon. Johnson, Kast and Rosenzweig, *Ibid.* (first edition, 1963) p. 6, n. 1, assert that von Bertalanffy was the first to use the term, "Systems Theory." For further information on von Bertalanffy's Systems Theory see his *Problems of Life: An Evaluation of Modern Biological and Scientific Thought* (London: C. A. Watts and Company, Ltd., 1952) and a series of papers by von Bertalanffy, Carl G. Hempel, Robert E. Bass, and Hans Jonas, published under the overall title "General Systems Theory: A New Approach to Unity of Science," in *Human Biology*, Vol. 23, No. 4, December 1951, pp. 302-361. For information on the works of the other see: Kenneth E. Boulding, "General Systems Theory—The Skeleton of Science," *Management Science*, Vol. 2, No. 3, April 1956, pp. 197-208; Norbert Wiener, *The Human Use of Human Beings: Cybernetics and Society* (Boston: Houghton Mifflin Company, 1950); Herbert A. Simon, *The New Science of Management Decision* (New York: Harper and Row, Publishers, 1960).

[3]Within the last few years a number of authors have studied the application of systems theory to business operations: Robert N. Anthony, John Dearden and Richard F. Vancil, *Management Control Systems: Cases and Readings* (Homewood, Illinois: Richard D. Irwin, Inc., 1965); John Dearden and F. Warren McFarlan, *Management Information Systems Engineering* (Homewood, Illinois: Richard D. Irwin Inc., 1966); David I. Cleland and William R. King, *Systems Analysis and Project Management* (New York: McGraw-Hill Book Company, 1968); John Dearden and F. Warren McFarlan, *Management Information Systems Engineering* (Homewood, Illinois: Richard D. Irwin, Inc., 1966); Thomas B. Glans, Burton Grad, David Holstein, William E. Meyers, and Richard N. Schmidt, *Management Systems* (New York: Holt, Rinehart and Winston, Inc., 1968); Thomas R. Prince, *Information Systems and Management Planning and Control* (Rev. Ed.; Homewood, Illinois: Richard D. Irwin, Inc., 1970); Peter P. Schoderbek, ed., *Management Systems* (Second ed.; New York: John Wiley & Sons, Inc., 1971).

staff manager to study the impact of his planning decisions on other activities within the business, and to take into account the impact of these other activities in his planning. Second, the systems approach provides an orderly approach to determining the influence of internal company factors on planning and uncovers new sources of information which can help improve planning at all levels. Third, it leads the planning manager to question the way he makes planning decisions and the use he makes of the information supplied him, and to look for ways to improve his planning practices.

Looking upon the social, economic and competitive environment as an integrated system, of which a particular business is a sub-system, also aids business planning. First, managers are led to give greater consideration to the political and social values of the environment and the potential impact that these values, and the legislation they produce, have on their business planning. Second, managers become more aware of the economic forces affecting their business. The company's long- and short-range planning is thus influenced to a greater degree by such economic factors as: supply and demand; population growth and labor force trends; gross national product and income estimates; technological developments; trends in governmental receipts and expenditures; fluctuations in industrial production, price levels, business, and the economy in general; and seasonal factors.[4] Third, a company's managers are made more aware of the specific influences of the competitive system on their operations. As a result, a company's sales forecasting is improved, for greater consideration is given to such market and industry factors as anticipated market standing and share, competitive strategy and action, and new product and market development. Projected profit levels, rates of return on investment, and specific production, marketing and financial plans are also developed with more precise estimates of competitive conditions in mind.

A business manager acquires such a systematic approach to planning by following the principles of scientific business planning described in the earlier chapters of this book. However, the systems approach supplements and reinforces the disciplines laid down in scientific planning, by impressing upon the manager the relationships among the various components of his business and between his internal business operation and its economic environment.

[4]A review of the kinds of environmental information needed for business planning, control and operational decision making can be found in the following books: Francis Joseph Aguilar, *Scanning the Business Environment* (New York: Macmillan, 1968); V. Lewis Bassie, *Economic Forecasting* (New York: McGraw-Hill Book Company, Inc., 1958); Elmer Clark Bratt, *Business Cycles and Forecasting* (5th ed.; Homewood, Illinois: Richard D. Irwin, Inc., 1961); John F. Due and Robert W. Clower, *Intermediate Economic Analysis: Resource Allocation, Factor Pricing and Welfare* (5th ed.; Homewood, Illinois: Richard D. Irwin, Inc., 1966); Milton H. Spencer, Colin G. Clark and Peter W. Hoguet, *Business and Economic Forecasting: An Econometric Approach* (Homewood: Illinois; Richard D. Irwin, Inc., 1961).

The systems approach also aids the planning manager indirectly through improving the flow of information to him, for the systems approach is the basis for developing improved business information systems. In companies with effective information systems, the planner has access to more timely information upon which to base his plans, and a more efficient system for communicating planning information to operating personnel for controlling performance.

VARIOUS KINDS OF BUSINESS INFORMATION SYSTEMS

Information processing may be performed manually, by electrical accounting machines (punched card systems), or by electronic data processing machines (computers).

Manual Systems[5]

A data processing system for a very small business would most likely be a manual system. In such a system, a business transaction is first recorded manually on some originating source document (such as a sales slip or shipping receipt). The transaction is then transferred to a journal (a chronological record of transactions) and then to the ledger, where the transactions are grouped together in accounts (for example, accounts receivable). Many action documents (such as monthly invoices, production and purchase orders, or shipping instructions) are issued on the basis of these records, as are many reports used for planning and control (such as sales and production reports, profit and loss statements, and balance sheets).

Electrical (or Electromechanical) Data Processing[6]

Electrical data processing systems offer significant advantages over manual systems, and many small and medium-sized companies find these systems useful and economical. Even though more firms will probably switch to computers as their cost continues to decline, a basic understanding of electrical accounting systems is important to understanding the concept of electronic (computer-based) data processing systems.

Both electrical and electronic data processing systems make use of the unit record principle. In a system using this principle, a transaction is recorded on one document—punched card, paper tape or magnetic tape, for example. This single record is then used over and over again, to pro-

[5]See Frederick P. Brooks, Jr. and Kenneth E. Iverson, *Automatic Data Processing* (New York: John Wiley and Sons, Inc., 1963), Chapter 2, for further discussion of manual systems.

[6]See E. Jerome McCarthy, J. A. McCarthy, and Durward Humes *Integrated Data Processing Systems* (New York. John Wiley and Sons, Inc., 1966), pp. 52-65, for further discussions of this topic.

duce such documents as the inventory, sales and accounts receivable records.

Electrical data processing involves the use of punched cards on which the data is recorded and of machines for interpreting, reproducing, sorting, selecting, merging, matching, tabulating and reporting the data contained on these cards. For this reason, electrical systems and machines are usually called punched card systems and machines. Since the different versions of these machines are neither strictly electrical nor strictly mechanical, the systems using them are sometimes called electromechanical system.

Electronic Data Processing (EDP) Systems

In business today the word computer has come to mean an *electronic* data processing machine. Strictly speaking, a computer is any calculating device, and the term could be correctly applied to an abacus or an adding machine, as well as to a modern computing machine. In recent years, however, the term has come to apply to a special type of modern calculating machine, the electronic computer.

Several characteristics typically found in digital computers (the type of computer in most common use today) differentiate them from electrical accounting machines. These characteristics are speed, internal memory, and storage capacity. The electric circuitry is what gives the electronic computer its great speed. While electromechanical devices, such as the electrical accounting machine, are characterized by speeds of hundreds of operations per second, electronic devices, such as the electronic computer, can perform millions of operations per second. Electronic computers can also hold data and instructions in an electronic representation in an internal memory unit, enabling use of a stored program and adding to processing speed.

The functions performed in an EDP system are similar to those performed in an electromechanical system: information is prepared, fed into the system through punched card readers, magnetic or paper tape readers, and optical scanners, or directly through keyboard-type machines; it is either processed or stored for processing at a later date; information is generated for use through a printer, typewriter, cathode (TV-like) tube, graphic display, sound machine, etc.

A company cannot, however, simply buy a computer and set it to work. Instructions for each job it is to do must be "programmed" for it in computer language. This translation process is a demanding one, for the "programmer" must have considerable knowledge and skill in the use of the computer in order to provide effective programs or instructions to complete an assigned task. Programming also can be a very time consuming task, depending upon the complexity of the system and the experience level of the programmer. However, once a program has been developed for a particular operation it can be recorded in the computer's memory or storage and used at will when the proper input is fed in.

Degree of Mastery Needed

The executive interested in performing business planning and control more effectively in today's business environment cannot avoid learning something about electrical and electronic data processing. While he does not necessarily need to learn how to program or how to operate a console, he does need to be familiar with how information systems are developed, the kinds and timing of reports they can produce, the calculations and other functions they can perform, and the costs of these information services, so that when participating in the designing of information systems for planning and control in his operation, he will not ask for the impossible or for information services whose costs exceed the benefits derived from their use. And he must know enough about EDP systems to be able to use available information systems effectively.[7]

PLANNING AND DEVELOPING AN INFORMATION SYSTEM: GUIDELINES FOR OVERCOMING SOME TYPICAL PROBLEMS

Electronic and electromechanical processing machines are only one part of a company's information system—the system which supplies information to the computer for processing and in turn feeds processed information back to managers to use for making decisions.

During the past few years the author has worked with a number of companies in developing information systems for planning, control and operating decision making.[8] All of the companies were of moderate size, under $70,000,000 in annual sales. In each case a large portion of the business was done through direct-response selling—that is, selling a product or service through an advertisement or mailing piece which asks the customer to write directly to the company to order the item advertised. The products these companies sold through direct-response advertising ranged from magazine subscriptions and book club memberships to phonographs and television sets.

As they grew, each of these companies saw the need to convert to a computer information system. This need was based on the fact that the companies required more data on a more timely basis in order to improve their planning, control, and operating decision making. For all of them

[7]Irving I. Solomon and Laurence O. Weingart, *Management Uses of the Computer* (New York: Harper and Row, Publishers, 1966).

[8]Robert J. Mockler, "Developing a New Information and Control System," *Michigan Business Review*, March 1968, pp. 13-19; Robert J. Mockler, ed., *Putting Computers to Work More Effectively in Business Publishing* (New York: American Business Press, 1969).

the conversion was a difficult task. Because there were many similarities in the problems encountered in developing the system, and in the ways these problems were overcome at each of these companies, it seemed that others might benefit from a review of the lessons learned about identifying and overcoming these problems.

The Decision to Develop a New System

In each company the development of the new system began the same way: management decided to install a new computer to process orders, to maintain the file of customer names for billing and repromotion, and to generate planning and control reports. In all instances the customer names were currently being maintained on punch cards, but the lists were growing so fast that the punched card systems were becoming inefficient and uneconomical.

In no case was there a formal feasibility or cost study which compared the old card electromechanical and new tape electronic systems and which determined how much time and expense would be involved in developing the new system. At first glance this may seem puzzling, since many authorities recommend such studies.[9] Most companies, however, are slow to adapt management theory to practice, and the situation encountered at the mail-order companies studied is probably more the rule than the exception.

Formal feasibility studies were not conducted because each company already seemed to have made an instinctive commitment to a new computerized system. As a result, the mission of the systems manager was to develop a new system and perform the conversion as economically as possible, not to determine whether or not the new system should be installed or what should be involved in the development and conversion phases.

The first problem common to all these companies, therefore, was the lack of a preparatory or feasibility study. Fortunately, in all instances the economy and efficiency of an updated, high-speed, computerized processing system proved beneficial to company operations.

Preparing for the Systems Study

The actual systems development study was begun in the traditional way. A group from the systems analysis section was appointed to develop a systems proposal and prepare program requirements for the new computer. Then all the operating managers affected by the new information system were notified that the study was to be undertaken.

[9]See, for example, James Greenwood, *EDP: The Feasibility Study—Analysis and Improvement of Data Processing*, Systems Education Monograph, No. 4 (Washington, D.C.: Systems and Procedures Association, 1962), and Thomas Hindelang, "EDP Feasibility Study—An Indispensible Prerequisite for EDP Success," *Computer Applications Service*, V, 1965, pp. 36-41.

Corporate management gave verbal support to the project, but did not appoint a corporate officer (or other responsible manager) to head the study group and, in fact, attended few of the group's meetings during the year or so spent developing the new information system.

The second problem, therefore, was the lack of top management guidance, support and, most important, participation in the systems development study.

The Changing Scope of the Initial Study

Because no feasibility study was done, the exact scope of the systems development study and the time and effort needed to develop a new information and control system were not clearly spelled out from the beginning. In retrospect it seemed that management thought of the project as writing a program for a new computer. Only as the systems development group delved deeper into their study did the scope of the undertaking expand into a true information systems study, which was what management finally determined they really needed and wanted.

Through the study group's efforts management came to realize that no judgment about where a computer can be used effectively and economically is possible until the decision-making processes within the company and the flow of information needed for decision making are studied and defined. A computer system can be a great aid in decision making, but only if it is structured to meet the specific decision-making needs of the company using it.

Because no one had expected the project to be so complex, it had to be significantly modified as it progressed. The confusion, resistance, and waste of time and money this caused could have been avoided by defining the mission broadly rather than narrowly at the beginning. Then management could have either provided the time, money, and manpower needed to do a complete job, or lowered their sights and settled for a system of more limited scope.

The third problem, therefore, was not understanding that a total information system was needed, not realizing what such a study entailed, and not providing the people, organization, time and money needed to complete the study.

The Initial Phase of the Study

Because at the outset the project was narrowly defined as a computer program writing project, the systems study group first examined each of the individual operations being computerized. As the work progressed, however, the group found they needed to do more background work before they could understand these operations, and they began exploring in more depth such areas as:

1. The general nature of the business and the markets within which the company operated.
2. The company's entire business process, from order receipt to customer payment.
3. The kind of information needed for decision making at the various critical points in the business process.
4. The timing and format of the information needs.

The businesses being studied were mail-order selling operations. Sales or inquiries were solicited by mailings, by magazine or newspaper coupon ads, or by radio and television commercials asking for customer orders. The products sold ranged from $500 television sets to $2 gift merchandise and magazine subscriptions. Sales were solicited from former customers, from the general consumer market, and from customers served by other divisions of the company. Most sales were on credit, but lower-priced merchandise was frequently sold on a cash-with-order basis. The companies were, therefore, retailers, and all of the functions normally handled in the retail store would have to be handled by the new system.

Once the general nature of the business was defined, the systems groups looked at the internal flow of business. Orders and payments were received in the mail room. Payments were sent to the collection section, which deposited the money and credited the payment to the customer's account. Orders were sent to the applications section. If the order was from a customer in good standing, it was processed; if not, it was sent to the credit department for clearance or rejection. Once the cleared orders were processed, the products were shipped and customer billing was begun. In all, five operating sections were involved:

1. Production or product procurement, including warehousing.
2. Marketing.
3. Accounting and financial analysis.
4. Fulfillment: order processing and file maintenance, including billing.
5. Credit.

As the systems group extended their study, they found how little they knew about the areas other than order processing, and how much they would need to know to develop a sophisticated information system to meet information requirements in all these sections.

The systems study group encountered some problems when they began the necessary detailed study of each of the five areas. Although they had been told to call upon all sections involved in the operation, no one person in each operating section was designated to help the study group and no executives from the operating departments were appointed members of the study group.[10] Since the systems group was part of the fulfillment (order

[10]The importance of involving operating executives *directly* in the systems study is emphasized by such authorities as Dearden and McFarlan, *Management Information Systems*, p. 49.

processing and file maintenance) section and since they could obtain little assistance from the other four sections, they naturally tended to create an information system designed principally for the fulfillment area, a system which would only secondarily serve the information needs of the other sections.

At each company it was necessary for a corporate executive to intervene to resolve the problem. At one of the companies, for example, the marketing manager met with the systems group, saw the inadequacies of the new system, discussed the problem with them, and recommended expanding the study group to include a representative from each operating section. Four operating managers were then appointed to the group, although most of the work was still done by the original study group of systems analysis. A timetable for completion was developed at the same time.

Only at this point, therefore, was the true breadth of the new system officially recognized. What had originally been basically an order processing and file maintenance system now became a total information system, and the group was given the manpower needed to complete the project successfully.

Prior to this step, the scope of the project had been limited, not because management wanted it to be limited, but because they had not provided the mechanism or organization to implement a broader study. The fourth problem, therefore, was that representatives of each operating section were not made part of the original study group and so did not participate in the work of the systems planning.

Defining Information Needs

The next step in developing the information system was to have each operating section define its functions, the kinds of decisions it made, the information needed to make these decisions, and the form in which that information was needed.

This was not a simple task. First, the operating managers were reluctant to spend the time required to do this. Each felt that he knew his job and that describing it in a report would be a waste of time. In addition, he felt that he would be reporting to the systems analysts, although he had been told that the system would be serving his needs and thought that the analysts would be reporting to him. Second, a systems analyst needs considerable skill in interviewing in order to draw out information about future or ideal operating needs, for the operating managers tends to speak of the information he now gets, instead of what is required to make good decisions.

Again the corporate officer closest to the study was forced to intervene. He explained that a periodic review of job objectives and functions was good business and normal, that the systems group was working for the operational managers, and that the new system was a wonderful opportunity to relieve operational managers of a considerable amount of detail work and to obtain better reports for them, in more readable form and on a more timely basis. However, the price to be paid over the short run was that each operating manager would be required to devote time and attention to the project. If the operational managers did not give such time, they could not justifiably complain later of lacking the information needed to make decisions or of not having it in the form needed to make decisions quickly.

The fifth problem, therefore, was getting a clear definition of the information needs of each of the decision makers within the system.

Balancing the Information Needs of Each Operating Section

Because of the lack of direction from management and support from the operational managers and because of the systems analysts' training in machine applications, it was difficult for the systems group to maintain a "total information system" perspective and to be objective in balancing the needs of each operational group in the new system.

This point escapes the systems theorist. Prince, for example, overlooks it when he describes the job of the systems analyst:

> The systems analyst, like the financial accountant, the financial manager, the sales manager, and the production manager, is concerned with designing observations of certain manifestations of a business organization. But unlike the other cited trained observers, the systems analyst does not respond to any traditional set of theories associated with a functional area of the business. . . .
>
> The systems analyst is concerned with the information dimension of decision-making activities throughout the business organization. . . .
>
> The systems analyst desires to establish the ideal set of information systems that is compatible with the major decision-making requirements in the existing unique environment of a particular business organization.[11]

While ideally the systems analyst is supposed to have the perspective to view an entire business system objectively and to pull together all aspects of an operation, there is no guarantee that he will. The systems analyst is usually a trained programmer. Because of his background and training he tends to be machine-oriented and to think in terms of the efficiency of machine applications instead of operational decision-making needs. Like the sales manager, production manager and financial manager, then, the systems analyst has a functional bias.

The ability to view an operation objectively and in its entirety is not an exclusive characteristic of any particular functional area in a corporation. It is a characteristic of effective management. Any good manager, in

[11]Prince, *Information Systems*, pp. 17 and 19.

any functional area, should be able to maintain a broad, comprehensive, objective viewpoint.

In the companies studied the problem of maintaining a balanced viewpoint was further compounded by the fact that the systems group in a mail-order operation is part of the fulfillment operation. Where compromises had to be made, therefore, the group tended to accommodate either machine efficiency or the efficiency of the processing system for the fulfillment area.

As a result, operational managers came to believe that the information needs of their areas—whether product procurement or marketing—were considered secondary to the needs of the fulfillment area. However, these managers were not willing to devote the time needed to help shape the new system to their own needs. The systems group wanted to be objective, but in the absence of sufficient guidance from top management and from the operating managers, they naturally concentrated on satisfying the needs of the areas they knew best: fulfillment and computer applications.

The situation at this point became very confused. For example, the marketing section wanted the fulfillment section to make daily manual tabulations of customer orders received by media and to report them daily to the marketing section. This would enable the marketing section to make quicker decisions on the profitability of promotions. The systems group immediately reacted negatively, for the request would require adjustments and delays in the order processing system. In other words, the systems group revealed an unconscious bias towards creating the most efficient fulfillment system possible, even at the expense of efficiency in other operating sections.

The same kind of problem arose when the credit manager asked that certain credit checks be built into the system, when the marketing manager asked that the billing envelopes be enlarged so that he could enclose promotional material in them, when the product procurement management asked for an on-line perpetual inventory sub-system, when the financial analysis group asked for a returned merchandise count by promotion, and so on.

The situation fortunately did not get out of hand, for in all these cases objectivity was supplied by the informal intervention of a corporate executive, who knew systems, understood all the operations affected by the system, and was well-liked by the persons working on the development of the system. It was this executive who prevented the systems group from fashioning the parts of the system to suit machine efficiency exclusively and arbitrated the compromises necessary to create a system that served the needs of all operational areas. It was he who filled the gap left when top management failed to become directly involved in the project.

The sixth problem, therefore, was maintaining objectivity and balance in the new system.

The Final Determination of the Costs and Performance Characteristics of the New System

Not only did management underestimate the costs and complications of developing the system, they also underestimated the costs and performance characteristics of the final system. Fortunately, even though the costs of the final system were higher than anticipated, the savings under the new system were sufficient to justify its installation.

But modifications in the design and size of the new system occasioned sizeable delays. In all cases the computer system originally ordered turned out to be too small. The order was changed, delays resulted, and management had to adjust to increased cost. The machine hardware configuration (that is, number of drives, printers, and computer specifications) also changed and its final form differed radically from that originally proposed to the manufacturer. Management also had to adjust to some basic changes in the system performance. It was found, for example, that the new system could not substantially decrease order processing time, and that it could provide only a modified on-line inventory control.

While some changes are inevitable, a more complete feasibility study would have reduced the number and size of these changes. The seventh problem, therefore, was making a commitment for the new computer before completing a detailed study of costs and the computer configuration needed for the new system.

The Organization Impact of the New System

The systems development program at the companies studied led to major changes in the organization structures of the companies. As a result of the project, attention was shifted from what each department had done in the past—that is, which department had handled what functions—to the operations and functions that were needed to run this type of business successfully.

Some personnel with narrow viewpoints saw the study as a threat to their positions. And they were right. For the study made it obvious that certain changes in the organization were needed. Other personnel, however, realized that a business is dynamic, and that internal changes are constantly needed to meet changing market conditions and improve operating efficiency. To these persons the new system represented an opportunity, not a threat.

While the adjustments came easily for some, the adjustments were painful for others who were not prepared for the changes and resisted them. Some pockets of bureaucratic resistance were wiped out, for a number of departments were eliminated and their remaining functions were put under existing departments. For the most part this was healthy, but in the process some good people were unfortunately lost. With proper forethought and planning, these people might have been retained.

The eighth problem, therefore, was in not anticipating the changes in organization structure, and the dislocations in personnel that would be occasioned by the new system, and not developing plans and educating personnel to meet these changes.

Other Benefits Derived from the New System

A number of other benefits resulted from the new systems in these companies. In addition to a thorough reevaluation of corporate goals and the interaction of the various functional operations needed to achieve these goals, a considerable amount of coordination and education occurred. A spirit of cooperation gradually developed as operating personnel found that their ideas were needed and used. In turn, the interchange helped to educate operating personnel in the problems of other operating departments, and in management objectives and policies, both for the coming year and for the longer term.

Such coordination and education benefits did not happen by chance. They came about because in administering the later stages of the system's development management took the time to listen to ideas and followed up on them, and to communicate the nuances of corporate policies and the rationale behind them. Where deviations from plans or operational deficiencies were found, they were not made a cause for reprimand. Rather, the problems were explored to find their causes and means were developed to prevent their recurrence.

As a result, a well-knit operating group emerged from the systems development program. Operating personnel had a common purpose. They knew what was expected of them and what the major problems of the business were. They knew that they had the freedom to innovate and make mistakes, and that their suggestions would be considered. Most important, they knew why they were doing their job and how it fit into the rest of the company's operations.

All of these side benefits of the systems development project could have been lost, if time and attention had not been devoted to cultivating them.

Summary Guidelines

Managers cannot expect everything to go smoothly in developing a new system, but they should not use this as a rationale for tolerating unnecessary inefficiency. Systems development is a new area, in which most managers lack experience. Clearly, performance in this area can be improved, and this discussion has attempted to establish some guidelines for improving systems development programs on the basis of the experience of the companies studied.

These guidelines may be summarized as follows:

1. Systems development should begin with a feasibility study.
2. A corporate executive (or other responsible company manager) should be appointed to head the systems development group (where the system being developed affects a major segment of a company's business), and he should participate actively in the work. Control points should be developed, where top corporate management can participate in and demonstrate their support of the project.
3. The scope of the project should be defined early, so that management will have realistic expectations as to what the systems development program will accomplish and will know how much work will have to be done to fulfill these expectations. Adequate time, money, and manpower must be allocated for the project.
4. The study should include someone from each operating section affected by the new system, to insure the direct involvement of these areas in the project. Deadlines for each stage of the project should be set, to insure the continuing involvement of all parties.
5. Time should be taken to develop an adequate definition of the major decision-making areas within the business system, and of the information needed for effective decision making in each of these areas.
6. Balance and an overall company perspective should be maintained in the new system. Extreme care should be taken to see that no one functional area dominates the structure and development of the system.
7. The final commitment for machinery should be withheld until a very precise idea of what is needed has been formed.
8. Major changes in organization structure and major dislocations in personnel will occur, and plans and programs should be developed for making these changes and dislocations as painless as possible. This includes educating everyone concerned in what is happening.
9. Time and effort should be taken to realize the education and coordination side benefits possible from a systems development program.
10. The study should result in the preparation of a formal report listing all findings, conclusions and recommendations.

The companies examined in this study had alert, bright, and realistic management. Although there were problems, once they were recognized management took the necessary steps to resolve them. These steps could, however, have been taken earlier in the systems development project, thus avoiding many of the problems. Instead of false starts, which made the normal activities required to develop a system seem like problems, each step could have been conceived of positively, as a necessary activity in the normal development of a new information system. In this way, there would have been less negative feeling about the project and fewer hours and dollars would have been lost in carrying out the project.

EDP SYSTEMS APPLICATIONS

One of the best ways to understand how EDP information systems can be used for business planning is to review some of their principal uses in business today.

Record-Keeping

Although the earliest computers were not developed for the record-keeping function, their potential in this area was soon recognized, and today the record-keeping application takes up considerably more computer time than any other application. For example, the processing and maintaining of customer account records and the keeping of employee payroll records are among the most common uses of computers today. Other applications of computerized systems are found in inventory accounting and in production planning and scheduling.[12] For example, the Thomas and Betts Company has cut the length of its inventory reporting cycle from one month to ten days by means of a one-pass computerized system for handling all inventory planning. All orders go directly to the computer, which maintains the inventory records for six warehouses across the country. The computer produces all the planning and control documents, invoices, and shipping papers. Compton and Knowles Company has developed a computerized system which combines inventory control with production scheduling. When an inventory item is out of stock, the computer generates a production order, including: department, work center, operation to be performed, job code and obtainment code, setup hours, standard hours required, description of the department, and scheduled due date.[13]

Advanced Information Systems

The more exciting applications of electronic data processing are outside the area of routine record-keeping.

While there is some disagreement as to whether a company can ever have a "total information system"[14]—that is, a completely integrated

[12]L. James Sasanecki, "Introduction to EDP—Controlled Inventory Control," *Management Services*, November-December 1967, p. 35. For a description of how other companies have used the computer for inventory control see: William S. Price and Edward J. Neppl, "Automated Inventory Control," *N.A.A.-Management Accounting*, October 1966, pp. 52-58; C. E. Viscione, "3 Automatic Warehouses . . . Luxurious? . . . 'Nó, They are Practical and Economical,' " *Factory*, October 1964, pp. 100-102; Anthony A. Vallario, "An Inventory Control System with Profitable By-Products," *Management Services*, January-February 1967, pp. 31-36; and William N. Smith and G. F. Reichenbach, "Maintenance Material Inventory Control," *N.A.A.—Management Accounting*, August 1967, p. 51.

[13]William J. McLaughlin, "EDP Contribution to a Manufacturing Operation," *Financial Executive*, April 1966, pp. 14-26.

[14]John Dearden, "Can Management Information be Automated?" *Harvard Business Review*, March-April 1964, pp. 128-135.

system—, considerable progress is being made towards greater integration of information systems. This is a natural outgrowth of the systems approach, which promotes the study of the entire decision-making process within the company. The systems approach inevitably leads to a broader based EDP system than might be achieved if only one operation was studied.

Within an integrated system for a mail-order sales operation, for example, a single entry would be made for a sale. This entry would then be input into the computer, which would perform the following functions:

1. Check whether present customer account is in arrears and whether customer's credit status justifies charging the present purchase.
2. Record sale in sales record.
3. Produce customer invoice.
4. Enter transaction in accounts receivable.
5. Check availability of item in inventory.
6. If available, withdraw item from inventory, update inventory balance, and schedule inventory replacement. If item is not available, notify customer there will be a delay and check inventory on order.
7. Issue shipping instructions.
8. Report sales by media for advertising planning and control.

Rollaway Bearing Company provides an example of an advanced computer system in the production area.[15] Rollaway used the computer to convert engineering designs automatically into precise manufacturing instructions, including: directions as to the operations that must be performed; the sequence in which the operations must be performed; the work methods that must be employed; the raw material form that must be used; the exact tools and fixtures that will be required, in-process dimensions and temperatures, if applicable; time standards; and detailed cost estimates.

Many advanced information systems are real-time systems—i.e., a system in which data is processed at such speed that output may be fed back to control current operations.[16] An airline reservation system is one of the most familiar real-time EDP systems. Each reservation ticket counter has an input-output electronic typewriter wired directly to a large centralized computer. This machine is used to determine whether seats are available and to reduce the "inventory" of seats available for that particular flight, if the customer reserves a seat. American Airlines' SABRE system is one of the many such systems used by airline companies.[17]

[15]"Automated Manufacturing Planning: Computer Solves a Big Production Problem," *Business Management,* January 1966, pp. 41-43.

[16]John Dearden, *Computers in Business Management* (Homewood, Illinois: Dow Jones-Irwin, Inc., 1966), p. 275.

[17]E. W. Martin, Jr., *Electronic Data Processing: An Introduction* (Rev. ed.; Homewood, Illinois: Richard D. Irwin, Inc., 1965), pp. 12-13.

Information Retrieval

One of the major problems of our technological civilization is the staggering volume of information the individual is expected to use. Approximately 60,000 books, 100,000 research treatises and 1,300,000 articles are published each year throughout the world.[18] As a result, people are finding it increasingly difficult to keep up with the literature on subjects of interest to them, and there is much needless duplication of research.

The computer can provide assistance in solving this information retrieval problem. One system being developed uses key words to identify subject matter.[19] An article or a subject, such as the Van Allen belt, is identified by metals, radiation, Van Allen belt and space. These key word identifiers and a brief abstract are stored on magnetic tape for reference use by researchers.

Guidance and Control

Guidance and control systems also make use of computers. The computer receives information, makes the necessary calculations instantaneously and continuously, and then adjusts the process being regulated. Missile guidance and manufacturing process planning and control are some of the uses of the computer in this area.

NIKE anti-aircraft missiles are controlled by computer. The guidance computer tracks the enemy plane by radar. When the plane changes course, the radar transmits instructions to the missile to adjust its speed and flight path to intercept the plane.

In the process industries, such as oil refining and chemical production, computers often form an integral part of the planning and control network that operates the process. In these situations the computer is applied to a continuously changing situation to control and maintain optimum performance of the system.[20] For example, the Western Division of Chevron Oil Company uses its computer facilities for product blending and refinery operation planning.[21] Among the questions answered by the computer are: how much more of Product A can be made without reducing the production of other products and how much would it cost to increase by a

[18]Martin, *Electronic Data Processing*, pp. 15-16.

[19]Gordon B. Davis, *An Introduction to Electronic Computers* (New York: McGraw-Hill Book Company, Inc., 1965), p. 35. Various governmental agencies and scientific organizations have established information retrieval systems. Each document is read and abstracted, and a list of key words which indicates the document's information content is prepared. For example, Chemical Abstracts Service (CAS), a government agency, periodically offers magnetic tapes containing references to printed reports of scientific and technical research (See "Speeding Up the Search," *Chemical Week*, February 18, 1967, p. 49).

[20]Solomon and Weingart, *Management Uses of the Computer*, p. 205.

[21]"Hands on Computer," *Chemical Week*, November 18, 1967, p. 156.

certain amount the output of Product A? The computer is also used to evaluate ways to get rid of production bottlenecks.

Heuristics

The term "heuristic" means serving to discover or to stimulate investigation. In its technical sense, heuristic is frequently associated with the simulation of human problem-solving techniques by means of computers.[22]

Heuristic programming attempts to simulate the thinking process of a manager by storing and analyzing past experience on a computer. The heuristic approach to problem solving is based on judgment, rather than on an exact, analytical solution. Heuristic programming searches for a satisfactory, rather than the optimal, solution to a problem.

The recent surge of interest in heuristic approaches to planning has led to the development of heuristic computer programs designed to:

1. Schedule construction activity.
2. Balance assembly lines in automotive and electronic plants.
3. Schedule job shop assignments.
4. Locate warehouses.
5. Schedule local truck delivery to many small customers.
6. Design electric motors and transformers.[23]

The problem of warehouse locations has been considerably simplified by the use of heuristic programming, which helps to determine the locations that will be most profitable to the company by equating the marginal costs of operating the warehouse with the cost savings and profit increments to be realized. The heuristic program considers plant-warehouse location with the relation to raw materials, the kind of warehouse needed, and even preferred shipping and inventory arrangements.

Computer decision simulation or management gaming[24]

Decision-making games are used to teach planning and decision making to business students and management trainees. Through the use of computers, it is possible to simulate years of business experience in a matter of hours. This compression of time makes it possible for the game player to see the long-run, as well as the immediate, results of his decision.

Several times each year groups of Proctor and Gamble employees, including new sales personnel and management trainees, are asked to spend

[22]Martin, *Electronic Data Processing*, p. 524.

[23]Charles L. Hinkle and Alfred A. Kuehn, "Heuristic Models: Mapping the Maze for Management," *California Management Review*, Fall 1967, pp. 61-62.

[24]John R. Carson, "Business Games: A Technique for Teaching Decision-Making," *N.A.A.—Management Accounting*, October 1967, p. 32.

six hours playing Venture, a company game.[25] The game puts Proctor and Gamble employees in the shoes of a simulated management team running a manufacturer of cake mix or detergents, and gives them the opportunity to see the total decision-making processes involved in running a business. An International Business Machines Corporation game carries computer involvement a step further than most business games.[26] Rather than relying on the computer as merely an umpire, players use the machine to analyze problems and alternatives before they decide what to do.

Systems Simulation

Once a system has been designed, the essence of it can be simulated in a way that permits the system developer to test and refine the system. Because of the computer's ability to do extensive, complex computations quickly, it is possible to develop very sophisticated systems models.

A business system is simulated by formulating a quantitative description or model of it. The model is then programmed for a computer, which can compress real-time and permit the effect of years of operations to be studied in a few minutes. Two interesting planning applications of systems simulation are weapons simulation and industrial dynamics.

Jay W. Forrester was a pioneer in developing the industrial dynamics approach to the study of the business organization and planning.[27] Using this approach, the business organization is viewed as interrelated flows of many variables: materials, money, information, manpower and capital equipment. Through the use of simulation management can study the effects of the interrelationships of these variables on organizational performance, allowing management to determine how a change in one variable will effect the other variables. For example, an optimum inventory system may cause serious difficulties in the production department, so that the inventory system is best understood in the context of a simulation model which includes production, inventory, sales, and so on.

Airlines use computerized simulation models extensively to solve facilities and flight schedule planning problems. For example, computer simulation of airline systems is used to plan flight schedules and terminal service facilities. The specific questions this simulation program is designed to answer are:

1. Determine the minimum number of gate positions required at a terminal facility.
2. Identify the best mix of gate types to service the fleet schedule. (Ideally, for maximum flexibility, all gate positions would serve all types of aircraft. But,

[25]Elliot Carlson, "The Versatile Business Game: Its Growing Use in Industry," *Management Review*, September 1966, p. 46.

[26]Carlson, "The Versatile Business Game," p. 47.

[27]Martin, *Electronic Data Processing*, p. 16.

this is not always economical, especially as more larger aircraft such as the 747 and DC10 are introduced into service).

3. Determine the number of backup gate positions needed to prevent excessive aircraft delays due to schedule "bunching" which may occur during bad weather or severe air or ground congestions.
4. Identify flights which might be particularly vulnerable to delays under unusual local conditions.

The systems simulation program has two functions, schedule processing and gate assignment; it is programmed to read raw schedule data (including type of aircraft and special factors affecting holding time), assign gates, and estimate delays and conflicts. With such a simulation program the planner can study both proposed schedules and terminal layouts, test a variety of alternatives in a relatively short time, and develop an improved plan. In using the program, the planner feeds into the computer a planned terminal facilities layout and a simulated arrival and departure schedule. He then examines the printout to determine:

1. Are there any gate delays?
2. Are there any flights in particular more subject to delays than others?
3. What delay times are typically encountered?
4. Are any types of aircraft more vulnerable to delay than others?
5. Do some gates show excessive utilization while others are being underutilized?

Based on the above examination, the planner can adjust the number of gates available, the mix of gate types and restrictions, and aircraft schedules. He then reruns the simulated daily arrival and departure pattern and restudies the results until he has developed a satisfactory solution.

The above solution covers only normal operating patterns, that is, it does not allow for delays or variations from the regular schedule. The program is also capable of simulating typical random variations in arrival and departure times, so that the planner can also determine the number of "back up" or reserve gates that will be needed when there are variations from the regular schedule.

COMPLEX COMPUTER MODELS FOR CORPORATE PLANNING

Work is being done on greater use of complex computerized models for planning. For example, a number of major oil companies are working on such planning models.

All the major oil companies have developed computer models for planning. In their simplest form, these models are basically no more than computerized versions of former financial planning procedures. Sun Oil Company, for example, developed such a system, which used some 2,500 equations (based on regression analysis) which related to return on investment calculations. More advanced models are being developed, however, which integrate all functional planning within a single computerized model. The following is a summary of how such a model was developed.[28]

Oil companies are faced with a complex planning problem, since there is a close relation among marketing, manufacturing and supply, and distribution—an investment in any one area often commits the company to compensating investments in other areas to avoid imbalances of supply and usage. Such imbalances have a major impact on profits. For example, too many gas stations in any one area might require the company to buy gas at a premium from an outside supplier, if the company does not have adequate available facilities; and excessive refinery production must be sold off at a discount, if expansion of the company's marketing operations has not kept pace with production expansion.

The purpose of a new model developed by one oil company is to provide management with an analytical decision-making tool, through which it could test out or "simulate" the effects of alternative plans, in order to project the effect of a decision in one area on other functional areas and eventually their ultimate effect on return on investment. The model is also able to pinpoint any potential supply and demand imbalances within the company and so minimize them by identifying additional investment requirements.

The model focuses on the timing, cost, geographical location, form, and profitability of new investments in each area of an oil company's operation. It can be used to analyze additions, as well as divestments, in the facilities area. To do this, the model stores information on all reasonable supply and distribution product movement patterns, manufacturing refinery capabilities, and marketing alternatives and intentions—both now and in the foreseeable future.

Some of the planning decisions which can be studied with the model are:

1. *Marketing decisions.*
   a) Construction of new service stations in established areas.
   b) Construction of new service stations in new areas.
   c) Purchase of existing service stations.
   d) Closing or disposing of existing service stations.
   e) Rehabilitation of existing stations.
   f) Significant departures from current product sales mixes.
2. *Manufacturing decisions.*
   a) Major expansion or revision of existing facilities.
   b) Closing existing refineries.
   c) Measuring the importance to the company of new technologies.
   d) Evaluating new crude oils.

[28]This discussion is based in part on George W. Gershefski, "Building a Corporate Financial Model," *Harvard Business Review*, July-August 1969, pp. 61-72, as well as on information given by companies who wish to remain anonymous.

e) Assessing the company's ability to meet continually changing product quality requirements.

3. *Supply and Distribution decisions.*
   a) Expansion of existing major pipelines.
   b) Withdrawal from participation in existing pipelines.
   c) Participation in new pipeline arrangements.
   d) Changing tanker loading facilities.

These are only some of the planning decisions the model can be used for. The model's major breakthrough is in being able to examine all the functional capabilities simultaneously, and determine how they interact. For example, when considering entering a new market area the model can simultaneously analyze crude supply, refining capabilities, product distribution, and marketing alternatives. The circular problem arising from the fact that the size and capability of a new refinery depends on the market it will serve, while at the same time the size and kind of marketing effort depends on the refinery capability, is thus solved by the computer model. The model is also able to project the changes in manufacturing facilities required by changes in current product mixes in the marketing area. The model's most important contribution thus is in the area of such interacting decisions.

The model is basically a large linear program, with four major sub-models: manufacturing; marketing; supply and distribution; and finance.

The manufacturing sub-model contains detail on all the company's refineries and major processing agreements. Since it is capable of studying interactions among manufacturing, marketing, and supply and distribution, it can estimate the costs associated with various levels of product demands, crude supplies, crude prices and refinery capacities. To do this, the model includes representations of the size and capabilities of major refinery processes in each refinery (present or proposed) and the significant quality variations which distinguish various crudes and products.

The marketing sub-model is principally a description of demands for each major product in each of the company's geographical areas. The demand description is broken down into four parts: base demand arising from existing marketing outlets; increments in demand arising from proposed and planned investments in new outlets; decreases in base demand resulting from outlet divestments; and large, foreseen, discretionary sales contracts.

The supply and distribution sub-model contains formulas representing processing agreements, product movements from source to market, and product exchange opportunities at either supply points or market areas.

The financial sub-model contains the financial criteria which management has established (objectives and restraints). This sub-model is the integrating aspect of the total model, for it is used to estimate the financial impact of any plan, that is, its impact on earnings and return on investment. Depending on data supplied, this model can also be used to generate any type of financial report in any proposed plan: funds flow statements, balance sheets, profit or loss statements, sources and applications of funds statements, etc.

The integrated planning model requires a considerable amount of data. For example, the manufacturing sub-model needs the following information on an annual basis: crude prices, availability and qualities; yields for each major crude representation; product quality specifications; unit configuration and capacities in each refinery; economics and extent of processing agreements; variable operating cost data for each refinery; yields and capacities of planned or considered new units in each refinery; unit expansion or modernization and their planned effects; foreseeable new techniques (new yields or processes); yield, capital and operating costs of refinery processing units of various sizes; and financial and economic data regarding refinery assets and fixed operating costs. A similar amount of information is needed for each sub-model.

It should be clear from the above discussion that such a model is expensive, and only within the scope of large companies. For example, development of a model like the oil company one described above might take four people three years (around $240,000 in salaries and supporting services), and require extensive computer time ($100,000) and information services from many operating departments ($100,000). The total cost, therefore, allowing for estimating errors could run close to $500,000. In addition, yearly operating costs for maintaining and using the model could run between $100,000 and $150,000.

CONCLUSION

EDP systems are being used more and more for planning in larger companies. An EDP system can store a huge amount of information useful during the premising stage of planning. For example, there are now computer models capable of storing economic and industry data which the long-term planner or economist can manipulate in making economic forecasts and evaluating alternative objectives.

The computer can be used for evaluating alternative plans. The IBM management simulation game and oil company computer planning model discussed in this chapter are examples of how this is being done. And in the areas of linear programming, PERT/CPM, decision theory, and the like where specific quantitative decision criteria can be established the computer is being used to both make complex calculations quickly and to compare alternative outcomes to established criteria and so choose the best alternative.

The computer's potential for long-term planning is still in the early stages of development, however, and it is here that its exciting potential needs to be unlocked. A study made in 1968 by McKinsey and Company points up the concern over the computer's applications to future planning:[29]

> Recently the president of a German chemical company was asked to examine and approve a proposal for an exciting new management information system. Featuring a desk-wide cathode-ray tube inquiry terminal that would display on demand any data in the computer files, the system would enable the president to compare current production figures, by product and/or by plant, against plan; it would break down current sales figures in half a dozen different ways; it would display inventory levels, current labor costs and trends, material costs—in short, just about any kind of operating data he might care to request. A few years earlier such a project would have looked like science fiction; in 1967 its technical feasibility was assured. Nevertheless, the president turned the proposal down. As he explained his decision . . . "I care more about what will happen five years from now than what happened yesterday."

Merely wanting information about the future will not produce it. The mutual efforts of planners, computer specialists, and management theorists will be needed to make this dream a reality.

DISCUSSION QUESTIONS

1. The idea of a system is not new, for we see natural systems at work all around us every day. What, then, is new about the systems theory and its application to business decision making?
2. How much of an effect do you feel the growth in business use of computers has had on acceptance of the systems approach by business managers?
3. Discuss the variety of ways in which the systems approach can affect business planning.
4. Why is it so important to define decision-making needs before developing an information system?
5. Why do you think the computer, instead of the information system, receives so much attention? Why is it a major mistake to focus on the computer, instead of the information system?
6. It has been said that when converting to computers the major economies come from the systems study and not from the introduction of the computer. Discuss.
7. List the mistakes made by the mail-order companies discussed in this chapter in introducing a new computer-based information and control system. Why was it natural to make each of these mistakes?

[29] *Unlocking the Computer's Potential,* a research report to management (New York: McKinsey and Company, 1968), p. 13.

8. Since it was natural to make these mistakes, do you think it is necessary and helpful to have a more scientific approach to information systems development? In what ways does systems theory provide such an approach?
9. Review the guidelines developed from the mail-order companies' experiences. Are they clear? Do they cover all situations? In what ways could they be amplified or modified?
10. What are some of the major present day uses of computers?
11. Computers and computer systems are just beginning to be used for planning. Discuss some of these uses. Can you think of additional future applications?
12. Define exactly what kinds of planning could be performed by the oil company's advanced computer model described in this chapter. Would it be possible to construct a model for doing even longer-term planning? Explain.

CHAPTER 12

ORGANIZATION PLANNING

One of the last steps in the planning process involves developing the organization needed to carry out a company's plans. Because it is designed to help "carry out" or implement plans, this type of planning is part of implementation planning, rather than strategic planning.

Organization planning is the process of logically grouping related business activities, delineating authority and responsibility within these groups, and establishing working relationships among groups that will enable both the company and its employees to realize their mutual objectives.[1] Organization planning thus involves answering four basic questions:

1. What are the jobs to be done and how can they most effectively be grouped?
2. How are the authority and responsibility for the jobs to be assigned?
3. In the light of human factors and management coordination needs, what can be done to facilitate the effective interworking of the organization segments?
4. How is the new organizaton or organization change to be introduced?

Answering the first question involves an examination of company plans, especially company objectives, strategies, policies and implementation plans, to determine generally what activities or tasks are required to

[1]For further discussions of organization see:
Rocco Carzo and John N. Yanouzas, *Formal Organization: A Systems Approach* (Homewood, Illinois: Richard D. Irwin, Inc., 1967); Fred J. Carvell, *Human Relation in Business* (New York: Macmillan, 1970); William W. Cooper, Harold J. Leavitt, and Maynard W. Skelly III, *New Perspectives in Organization Research* (New York: John Wiley and Sons, 1964); Paul R. Lawrence and Jay W. Lorsch, *Organization and Environment* (Homewood, Illinois: Richard D. Irwin, Inc., 1969); Albert H. Rubenstein and Chadwick J. Haberstroh, *Some Theories of Organization: Reedings* (Rev. ed.; Homewood, Illinois: Richard D. Irwin, 1966); William G. Scott, *Organization Theory: A Behavioral Analysis for Management* (Homewood, Illinois: Richard D. Irwin, 1967).

achieve company objectives. The tasks or jobs to be done can be divided into two categories: operating or operator tasks, and management tasks. The first involves the work required to make and sell a company's products; the second, the activities involved in supervising the work of others. Normally, unless the earlier planning is quite detailed, the plans themselves up to this point would not contain complete task definitions. As a result, a manager would have to go beyond the initial plans and study in detail the specific jobs which must be performed to carry out the plans and effectively run the business.

In answering the first question a manager would concentrate on the operating tasks, and how these tasks might most logically be grouped to meet operating requirements. For example, he might think in terms of breaking the manufacturing and marketing jobs into separate groups, and then in turn creating sub-divisions or groups within each category(selling, advertising, engineering, transportation, packing, machining, etc.).

A manager would also study the management tasks which must be performed in supervising the operating work. For example, the circulation job at *The National Observer* requires not only writing and designing promotions and mailing and placing them—all operating tasks needed to get and keep subscribers. It also requires management activities, such as planning and controlling circulation activities and coordinating circulation jobs with related jobs in other areas, such as order processing and subscriber record keeping. Any grouping of tasks would have to take into account these management activities, if the organization is to operate effectively.

Based on this examination of situation factors, some kind of organization structure is developed to accommodate both operating and management tasks requirements. Very often the structure will be an overlapping or hybrid one. For example, a marketing department may have a manager for each marketing operation (such as sales, advertising, customer service, forecasting and market research), who is responsible for seeing to it that each operation is performed effectively. In addition, there might also be a manager for each major product line, who handles the management of each product and so is responsible for planning, controlling and coordinating the various product activities performed by each operating manager. This organization is then usually charted, as shown in Figure 12.1, in such a way as to show both the grouping of tasks and their major interrelationships. This is only the first phase of organization development, however, the classification, structuring, and charting of operating and management tasks.

The answer to the second question involves defining how management responsibility and authority for performing these tasks are to be assigned. During this phase a manager determines to whom each organization position reports and the limits of power of each position.

Figure 12.1

A BRAND MANAGER ORGANIZATION

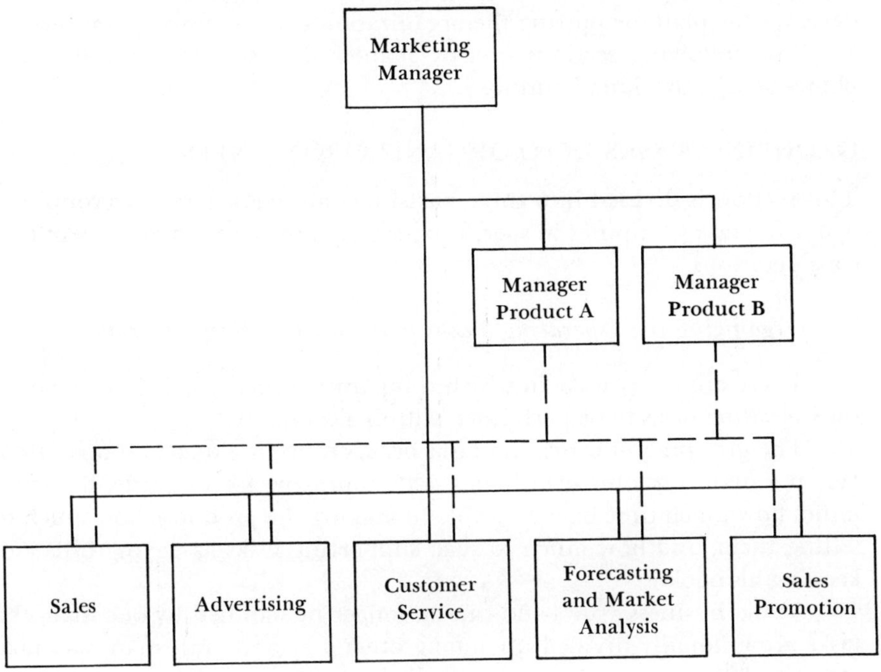

The answers to questions one and two are often put into the form of job definitions. These definitions supplement the organization structure. They not only spell out in detail the exact tasks assigned to each position; they also give the management responsibilities and authority limits, the interrelationships of organization segments, shared responsibilities and authority, and any other factors not shown in an organization chart.

Answering the third question involves a study of the human factors affecting organization development. This study invariably leads to adjustments in the organization structure and job definitions established earlier. For example, one might decide to reorganize segments of the operation around informal groupings which have developed over the years, or design specific job positions to exploit specialized talents of particular individuals. It is in answering this third question that a manager reconciles the behavioral and rational approaches to organization, for it is here that he decides what balance he will strike between the requirements of the job and the limitations imposed by individual and group behavior.

The answer to the fourth question involves determining how to introduce proposed organization changes. Since in most situations there will be an existing organization, a manager first examines the existing structure to determine where major changes will be needed and where resistance to change is likely to arise. Once the problems have been isolated, a manager develops his plan for putting the organization changes into operation.

The following sections of this chapter discuss these four different phases of organization planning.

GROUPING TASKS INTO ORGANIZATION UNITS

This section is divided into three parts: overall operating task groupings; operating task groupings in specific operating units; and management task considerations.

Organizing the Operating Tasks Performed Within a Company

There are many ways in which companies formally group or organize the operating tasks to be performed within a company.[2]

The grouping of operating tasks occurs even in a one-man operation. When a man starts his own hobby-craft company, for example, he determines how much time he will devote to making the products, how much to selling them, and how much to such supporting tasks as paying bills and keeping his books.

As the business grows and can no longer be handled by one man, the tasks are gradually divided up among others: a local craftsman may take over production, a salesman may call on customers, and an accountant may handle bookkeeping and finances. These three areas are in essence separate units or organization segments of the company. At first, the entrepreneur who started the business supervises the three men personally, and helps in doing some of the work in each area, as the need arises.

As the business continues to grow, the work is divided into additional sub-units and new levels of management are created. In addition, managerial positions may be established for directing the various levels of manufacturing operations.

This process of sub-dividing the manufacturing, marketing, and other operating tasks into more and more organizational units will continue as the company grows—as the company engages in more and more activities and as the work needs to be broken down into segments that can be per-

[2] Further discussions of this phase of organization development are found in: Rubinstein and Haberstroh, *Some Theories of Organization*, Part Two; Carzo and Yanouzas, *Formal Organization: A Systems Approach*, Part I; Bertram M. Gross, *Organizations and Their Managing* (New York: The Macmillan Company, 1968), Part 9; Louis A. Allen, *Management and Organization* (New York: McGraw-Hill Book Company, Inc., 1958), Part Two.

formed by individual workers and effectively directed by individual managers.

Thus far, the company has what is known as a *functional* organization, as shown in Figure 12.2. If growth continues, such an organization may eventually become inefficient—as the product line expands and as additional manufacturing facilities are built around the country.

Figure 12.2

FUNCTIONAL ORGANIZATION
HOBBY-CRAFT COMPANY

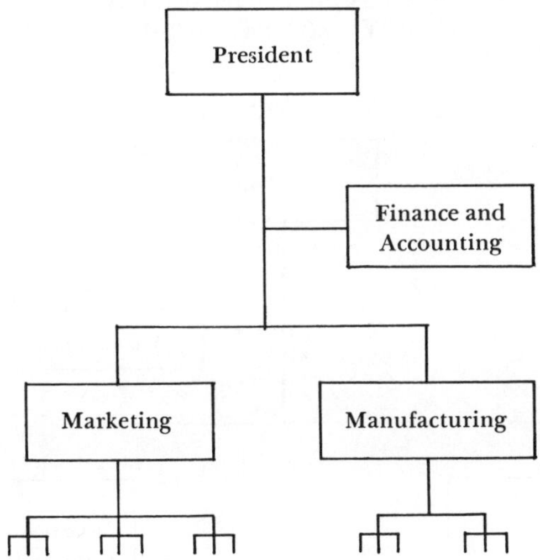

With expansion many problems can arise with a functional organization. As additional layers of management are created, communication and coordination become difficult. Individual organization segments become isolated and lose sight of basic business objectives. The problems arising from bigness can be overcome by reorganizing the units into divisions designed to meet the new management and operating requirements.

A company has several options at this point. It may *divisionalize* around geographic areas, products or services, type of customer, or any combination of these in conjunction with a functional organization. The divisionalized approach used is dictated by the situation requirements.

For example, the hobby-craft company's product line may have expanded to include both leather and cloth goods, as well as electronic hobby products, such as radio kits. The marketing department may find that certain new products are not receiving the attention they need, because each salesman sells a wide range of products; the company may, therefore, appoint sales or marketing managers for each product line, to insure adequate performance of the marketing job on each product. If the products are manufactured in different places, the company may find it convenient to go further and group the sales and manufacturing functions for each product into separate units, such as is shown in Figure 12.3. In this figure, the company has in essence split into two smaller companies, with the parent company providing financial services to each company. This organizational approach is called *product divisionalization.*

Figure 12.3

PRODUCT DIVISION ORGANIZATION
HOBBY-CRAFT COMPANY

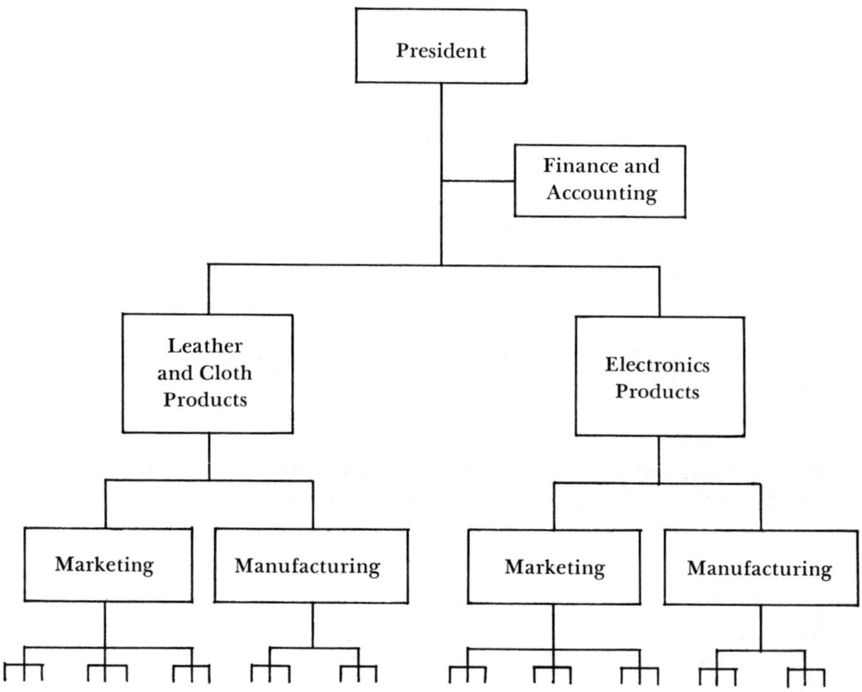

On the other hand, a company may have a homogeneous product line, for example, a milk products company, which as it grew built many manufacturing facilities around the country to meet local delivery requirements. In this situation, the company may find it best to organize around territorial units, such as is shown in Figure 12.4. This kind of organizational approach is called *geographic divisionalization.*

Figure 12.4

GEOGRAPHIC DIVISION ORGANIZATION
HOBBY-CRAFT COMPANY

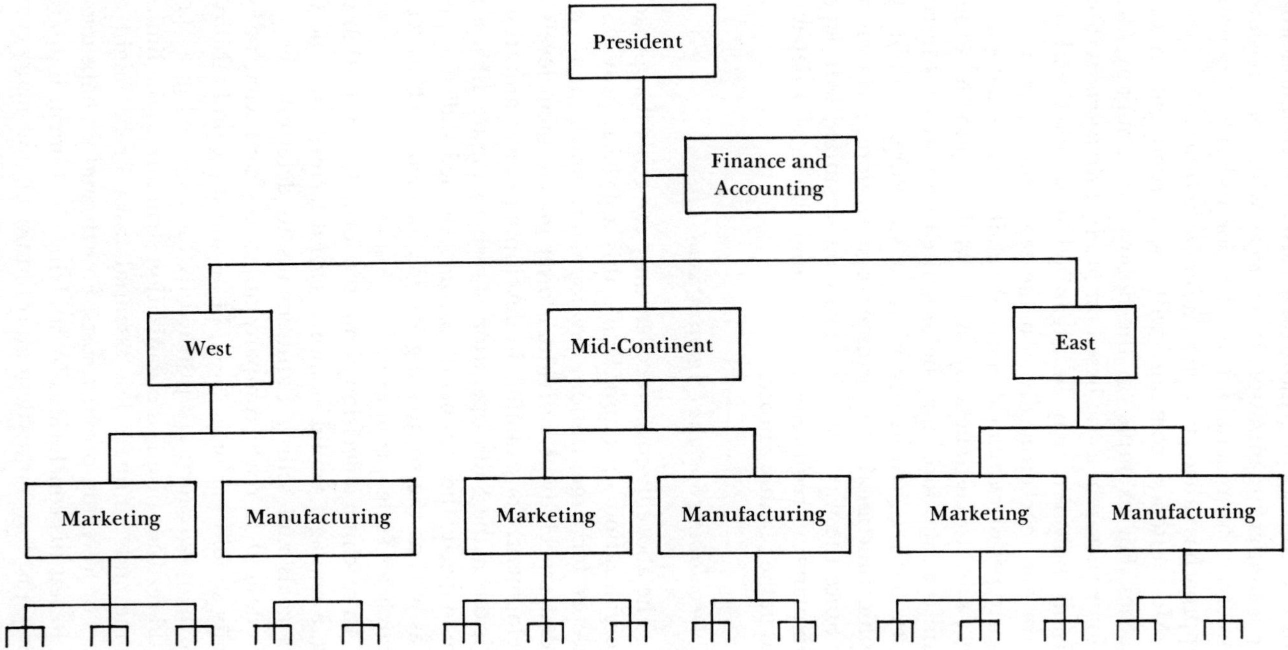

Many companies, such as banks and brokerage houses, find that the best way to sub-divide its operating tasks is by type of customer. For example, many brokerage houses have an institutional division, serving such customers as mutual funds, insurance companies and pension funds, and a retail division, serving individual buyers of common stock. A bank may have a similar organizational structure, with one division for business or commercial customers and another for individual depositors. This type of approach is called *customer divisionalization.*

Most often a company will use a combination of these four approaches. For example, in the hobby-craft company, the overall organization structure may be based on *product divisionalization*. Each product division, however, may be organized into *functional* departments, and within one marketing division the sales force may be organized around major types of *customers* (such as retail stores, catalogue companies, and direct sales to customers by mail), while within the other marketing division the sales force may be organized around sales territories (East and West). Such a hybrid organization structure, combining product, geographic, functional and customer organizations, is shown in Figure 12.5.

Since the way operating tasks are organized will depend on the strategic planning requirements, the final choice will depend on the earlier steps in the planning process.

Developing Specific Organization Units

The above discussion covers only the general approach to developing an organization structure. While this approach provides overall guiding concepts for organization development, much more detailed work is needed, especially at individual lower management levels, in organization development. For example, in developing the organization of the Western Division of the Sales operation shown in Figure 12.5, a manager would have to specify the number of salesmen needed and what their duties would be, as well as the supporting services needed, such as secretarial, market research, and sales promotion.

In reaching a decision about the formal organization structure in that area, a manager would examine several factors. First, he would study the sales goals and selling requirements to determine how many salesmen were desired to reach company objectives, and what tasks each salesman ideally should perform. Next, he would do a profitability analysis to see how many salesmen are justified by the expected gross profits. Third, he would readjust his ideal organization structure to the limits set by business income and eliminate less essential tasks, or he might consider raising prices or lowering product costs. Fourth, and perhaps most important, he would test his conclusions by studying the human limitations in the situation—just how far a salesman could travel, how many customers he could

Figure 12.5

HYBRID ORGANIZATION
HOBBY-CRAFT COMPANY

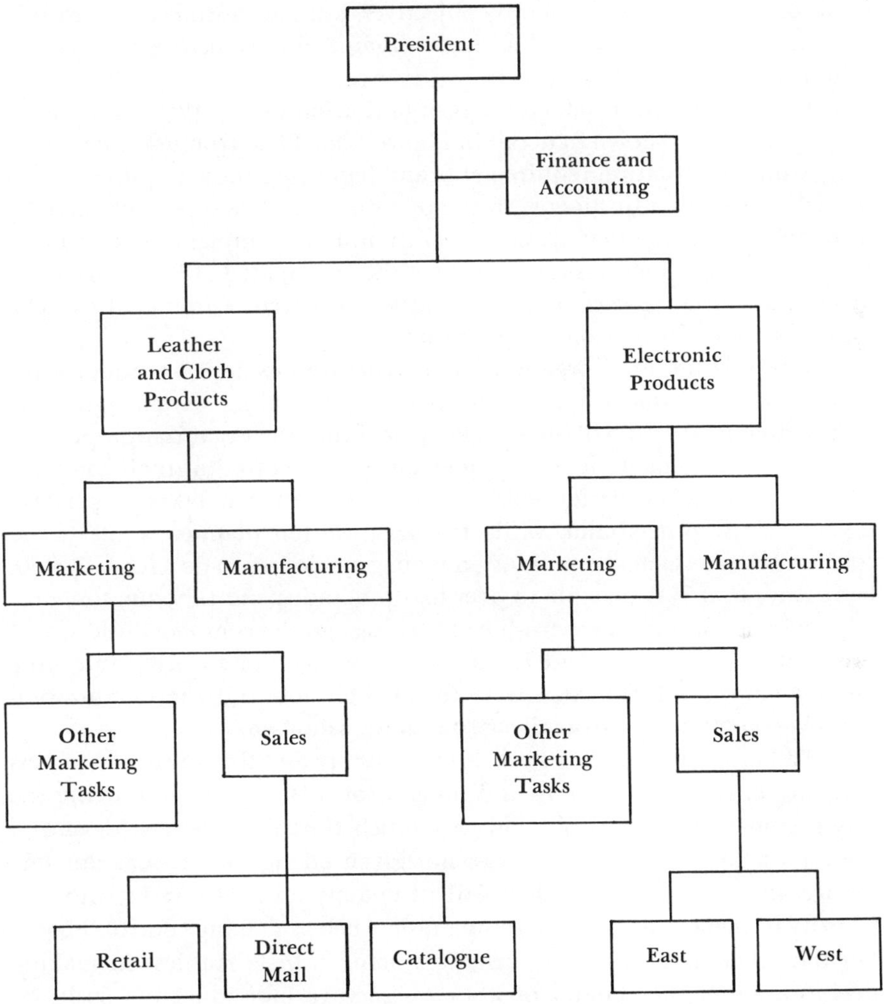

call on, how many sales he could make in a 35 or 40 hour week, and what kind of men would be available (or potentially available) to fill these positions. Next, a manager would make adjustments in the number of people and amount and kind of sales supporting services which can be provided within financial limitations.

As can be seen from this example, while a manager can determine the activities ideally desired to achieve company or department objectives, he is not always able to create the organization positions needed to perform all these activities as well as he would like, usually because of practical financial restraints. Many individual department managers instinctively think in terms of all the tasks they'd like to perform when developing their department organization structures. Higher level management, therefore, needs to clearly spell out not only objectives, but also restraints controlling organization development, if a viable organization structure is to be developed.

The Electronics Products Sales organization of the Western division (in Figure 12.5) is shown in detail in Figure 12.6. This structure was arrived at by studying situation requirements and balancing those requirements—partially through adjustments in the organization structure, and partially through changes in other areas of operation. For example, in one instance the price of a product was raised to meet the anticipated sales expenses and in another instance certain promotion services were eliminated to keep expenses in line with income expectations.

Rarely is the final organizational structure developed without some arguments and some friction. The person performing or managing the tasks being organized will almost always feel that the organization planner or higher management does not understand all the tasks (or their complexity) that have to be performed, nor how much time it takes to perform them. On the other hand, while the organization planner wants to encourage the salesmen's or promotion manager's desires to do each task well, he realizes that it is possible to overdo a job and spend time uneconomically, so he sets a limit on the value of each task to the company. Additional problems arise, because there is a tendency on each side to exaggerate—the salesmen want a little extra time to do their job and the organization planner wants a little extra mileage out of the salesmen.

If a fair balance is not struck, human nature and the course of business will correct it. Good training and supervision will help in improving the way salesmen use their time and how much time the salesmen devote to their jobs. But if the salesmen are not given enough time to adequately service and sell customers, they will ultimately eliminate tasks with low priority to them—usually non-selling tasks, such as making control reports. On the other hand, in many instances being a little ruthless in making decisions about the amount of work assigned to individual job positions can force people to be more efficient and to eliminate tasks which do not relate directly to profits.

Management Considerations

In developing a formal organization structure, a manager would also study the management tasks to be performed within a given organ-

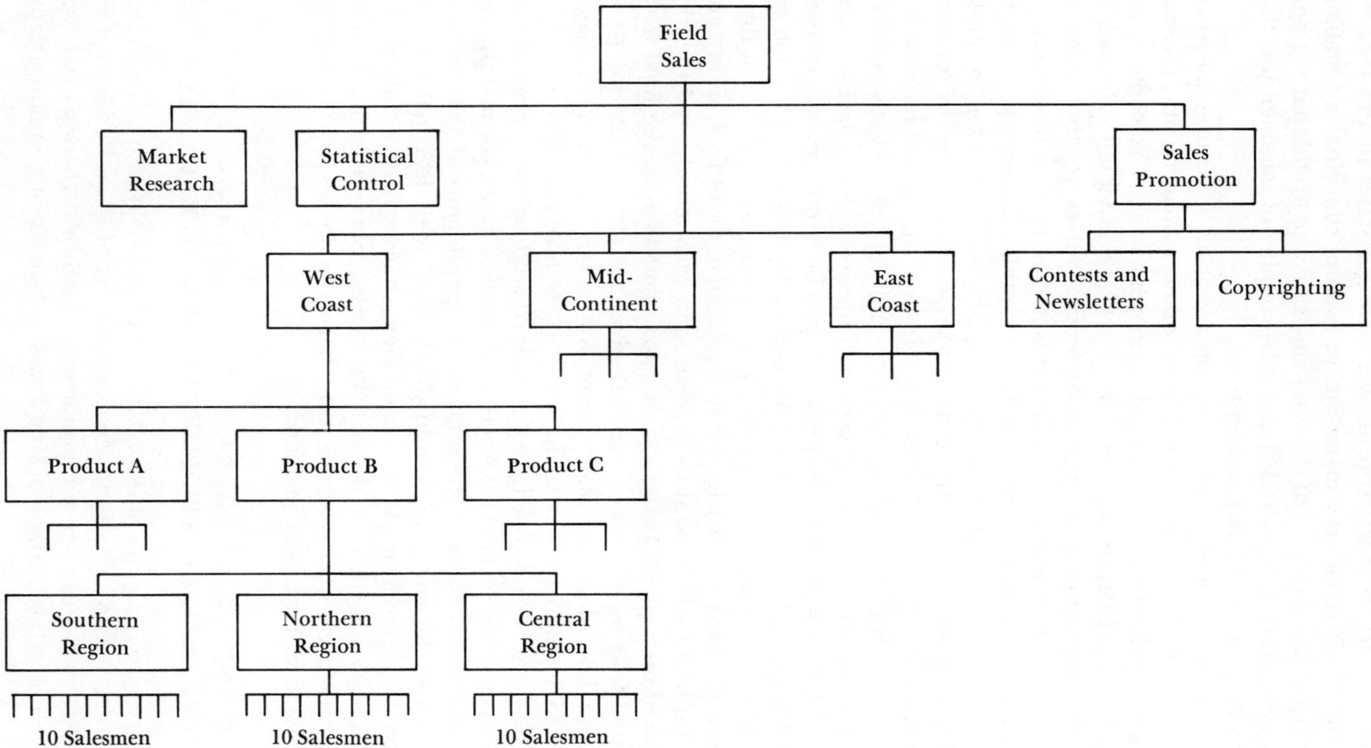

Figure 12.6

A FIELD SALES ORGANIZATION

ization segment. In the sales situation, for example, there were thirty salesmen for electronics products spread over fourteen states in the Western division. In this situation, the management tasks of coordinating, staffing, and supervising the activities of these salesmen were so broad that regional managers were needed. This additional sub-grouping of salesmen was thus based on management task requirements.

The process followed in adjusting organization structures based on management considerations is similar to other management processes. First, a manager determines the overall management requirements in the situation: for example, to supervise the work of individual salesmen in selling a specific number of correspondence courses in the home of customers who had answered advertisements and wanted to have more information about the course. Second, he determines the specific management activities involved in fulfilling company objectives; for example, establishing controls over twenty different salesmen working in fourteen states; planning their sales activities; interviewing, hiring and terminating salesmen; conducting individual salesmen training, as well as training meetings periodically; developing ways to improve selling efficiency, and the like. Third, a manager identifies the precise requirements in each task area: for example, salesmen will be personally trained on the job for one week by the manager; the manager will also spend one day each three months over the next year with each new salesman; monthly training and incentive bulletins will be sent to the sales staff each month; and the like. Fourth, based on a profit analysis, a decision is made as to the final management positions which will be established within the organization structure. This final decision is normally a compromise between what a manager would like to do and what he can do based on resource limitations.

The decision is thus based on a combined study of management task requirements and the level of sales activity or profits. If sales or margins are not large enough to support the salaries or commissions of two regional managers, then the company would "make do" with less management supervision and guidance. At the same time, however, expectations for how well the management tasks will be carried out would have to be lowered, or the company may drive its managers to the grave or to another company because of excessive pressures.

DEFINING AND ASSIGNING RESPONSIBILITY AND AUTHORITY, AND ESTABLISHING WORKING RELATIONSHIPS

In addition to grouping operating and management tasks into an organized structure, organization planning also involves defining and assigning the responsibility and authority for performance within each organizational unit, as well as establishing working relationships among organizational units.

Responsibility and Authority

Subsequent to (or concurrent with) developing the formal organization structure, a manager formalizes the list of tasks or duties designated for each organization segment into what is called a "job definition" or "job description." When a person is given a particular job he assumes a responsibility or an *obligation* for performing the duties or achieving the objectives designated for that organization position. He is also told at the same time *to whom* he is obligated or responsible. For example, in *The National Observer*'s circulation sales department a secretary is responsible to (that is, "reports to") the copy-writer, the copy-writer to the promotion manager, the promotion manager to the circulation manager, the circulation manager to the publisher, and the publisher to the president for performing the duties identified.

This thread of responsibility or obligation ties an organization together, and enables coordinated management by the company president of the various segments of the organization. Without such a network of responsibility a company president would have difficulty in insuring that work was managed and tasks performed in line with planned objectives.

At the same time that responsibility for performing operating and management tasks is assigned, authority is usually also given (either formally or informally) which enables performance of the tasks. Authority is the right to act. A machinist, for example, needs the authority to enter his work area, start and run his machine, requisition materials for machining, and the like. In the same way, a manager needs the authority to spend company money, make commitments to outsiders, command those working for him, and in general obtain and use the men, machines, money and material needed to get his job done. Without the authority to do a job, a worker or manager may be unable to fulfill his responsibilities.

A typical job definition or description covers these three areas: duties, responsibilities and authority. For example, *The National Observer*'s circulation manager was *responsible* to the publisher for the following *duties*: circulation planning and budgeting, control, organization, staffing, and directing performance of all circulation sales activities in such a way as to achieve circulation goals within agreed upon budgets. He was at the same time given *authority* to spend funds up to the limits specified in the annual budget and to hire the advertising agency and other suppliers he felt could perform the tasks designated for his area.

The Process of Delegation

The process by which tasks or duties, responsibility and authority are assigned is called *delegation*.

When the circulation manager took over his job at *The National Observer*, he first reviewed the list of tasks or duties to be performed in the circulation area and for which he was responsibile, and verified the limits of the authority he was given to fulfill these responsibilities and perform his job.

Next, he studied how the management and operating tasks could be divided into units, and he grouped them into such areas as newstand sales, direct mail, advertising, liaison with the order-processing group, planning and budgeting, coordination and the like. He then assigned the operating tasks (and some of the management tasks) to his subordinates and told them they were responsible to him for performing the tasks. He concurrently spelled out the authority each of his subordinates would have.

In essence, after developing his organization structure and job definitions, the circulation manager had delegated specific tasks, authority, and responsibility to his personnel for performing each task.

Centralization and Decentralization

Where a great deal of authority is delegated within an organization, the organization can be said to be highly decentralized. Conversely, where very little authority is delegated on an organization-wide basis, the organization is centralized.

A company never decentralizes fully, since corporate management will always exercise operational control and coordinate planning. The question to be answered then is "How decentralized should our operation be?" One way to approach decentralization is to determine how far down in the organization should authority be delegated. Another way is to determine how much authority should be delegated at each level.

At the highest level, a decision is first made as to who will be chief operating officer. Normally, it is the president or executive vice president. Next, one determines how much authority is delegated to the next management level—that is, divisional or functional managers. This process continues, as one examines the amount of authority delegated to each successively lower level of management.

One good index of the extent of decentralization is the amount of spending authority the various levels of management have. At one manufacturing company, for example, the president could approve capital expenditures up to $100,000 within general budget limitations, a department head up to $25,000, and division superintendents up to $10,000. At another company in the same industry, the president had to refer requests of over $50,000 to the Board of Directors, and department heads were limited to $15,000 and superintendents to $5,000. Decentralization of one important kind of authority was considerably greater in the first company.

Other concrete measures of the amount and level of decentralization are authority to do such things as: hire and fire employees; approve wage and salary increases, travel expenses, and promotions; employ outside consultants; lease property and equipment; set prices; and make contracts commiting the company. A subtler measure of the degree of decentralization is the amount of control management levels have over making their own budgets. Someone just entering the business would get a fairly good idea of the degree of decentralization (and so his chances of developing his management talents) at a prospective employer by judiciously questioning authority delegations in these and other areas critical to company operations.

Shared Responsibility and Authority: Modifying the Initial Structure

The expectations of those who have studied traditional organization theory is that authority and responsibility can be assigned to specific individuals, tasks broken down into unique, separate organization units, rigid formulas established for ideal spans of supervision, and reporting relationships delineated in precise terms. The traditional organization block diagram reinforces this belief.

Traditional organization theory is based on the concept of differentiation or departmentalization of tasks—that is, the study of the tasks to be done in order to achieve the corporate objective, and the grouping of these tasks into departments. The principal authorities who developed these theories were Taylor, Weber, Fayol, and Mooney and Reilly.[3]

Except in very rare instances, such an approach to organization development is only a starting point. In today's dynamic business corporations, neat divisions between organization segments aren't always possible —except at the lowest operating and supervisory levels. Authority and responsibility often have to be shared by several managers, and formal organizations (especially those in which there is a high degree of decentralization) must be adjusted to these integration requirements.

Under the concept of brand management described earlier (Figure 12-1), for example, a product manager is appointed to coordinate all activities going into the production and marketing of a product. A brand manager is needed in those companies where common production, warehousing, distribution, and sales facilities service a variety of products, in order to assure that each product is receiving the balanced attention it needs for success. The brand manager concept cuts across established lines of authority. In companies with brand managers, responsibility for a product's success is shared, for example, by the sales manager (who is responsible for selling budgeted quantities of the product), by the production manager (who is responsible for producing the product on time, in the

[3]Frederick W. Taylor, *Scientific Management* (New York: Harper and Row, 1947); Max Weber, *The Theory of Social and Economic Organization*, trans. A. M. Henderson and Talcott Parsons (New York: Oxford University Press, 1947); James D. Mooney and Alan C. Reiley, *Onward Industry!* (New York: Harper and Bros., 1931).

quantities desired and at a competitive cost) and by the product manager (who is responsible for the profitability and success of the total product line). Under these circumstances it is impossible to have a "clear line of authority running from top to bottom." Thus, the traditional approach to organization development must be adjusted to accommodate the brand management "crossways" organization.

The establishment of centralized information systems also cuts across and blurs traditional lines of authority and responsibility. As a result, information systems studies and systems development have an impact on organization planning.

In developing a company-wide information system, a manager views his business organization as an information network, with the flow of information providing the decision makers at varying management levels with the information needed to make decisions of all types. His attention is thus focused on the working relationships among organization segments, and on those areas where problems in integrating operations may arise.

The difference between the traditional and systems approach to organization is mainly one of viewpoint, for in using the systems approach emphasis is given to the flow of the business and to the interaction and integration of the various business operations, rather than to the departmentation or segmentation of the operations. The systems approach, therefore, is useful mainly at the point in organization development where a manager is studying ways to strengthen the working relationships within his organization and to adjust his formal organization structure to improve the integration of operations.

The widespread growth in computer usage has led to greater use of the systems approach to organization, for the introduction of a centralized EDP system, with its enormous expense and enormous capacity for storing and processing information, has literally forced many managers to give greater emphasis to integrating their operations with other operations in a company.

When changes are introduced within the traditional organization structure, new departments or units are added or new responsibilities are given to existing departments. Sometimes these additions or changes are made to meet new business needs, sometimes to take maximum advantage of an individual executive's particular combination of talents, and sometimes merely to adjust to the personalities of individual executives. Such a fragmented development process almost invariably leads to some decrease in the integration of decision-making processes with an organization.

When introducing a new computer, many companies at first make the mistake of approaching the changeover in the same piecemeal, department by department manner. Such a piecemeal approach only reinforces the fragmentation and segmentation of the organization.

Instead, as most companies sooner or later discover, before major decisions concerning computerization are made, management must step back and reevaluate the entire flow of business, not merely the individual operations begin computerized, in order to isolate the major decision-making areas, their interrelationships, and the information needed to make these decisions most effectively. In other words, the systems approach has proved in practice to be the best one when introducing computers.

For example, in a large merchandise mail-order business which has recently been changing to computerized order processing and information handling, the first inclination was to write programs in steps, first for marketing, then for order processing, billing, inventory control, and so on, for each of the components or departments currently operating in the company.

It soon became apparent that this was not the best approach. At this time management directed the systems group to study the nature of the business in which the company was then engaged, the business in which the company hoped to be engaged within the next five years, and the environment in which the company would operate in the future.

The group next constructed a chart of the flow of business operation, starting with the coupon advertisement offering the product and asking for the order, and following the customer's order through processing and billing until the product is shipped, the merchandise restocked, and the bill paid. A simplified version of this flow chart is given in Figure 12.7. For each phase in the flow chart a supplemental list was made of the significant planning, control and operational decisions necessary to perform that phase well. The information needed to make these decisions and the form in which this information was needed was then determined.

Only after the above planning studies were completed was a decision made as to which aspects of the business process could most economically be computerized, which could best be done clerically, and which were of sufficiently minor importance to the overall functioning of the business that they could be done in a less than ideal way or eliminated altogether.

Since the systems study covered many factors which were relevant to the company's organization, as a final step the actual organization of the operation was restructured around the picture of the business which had been developed in the systems studies. The diagram of the restructured organization may have looked to the casual observer like the traditional organization chart of the former organization, for there were departments for marketing, order processing, billing and credit, product procurement and inventory, and liaison among all these operations. But the changes made to bring the organization into line with the known decision-making needs of the business were enormous.

On closer examination it was clear that the new organization had little relation to the old organization. Pockets of personal strength had been wiped out, and antiquated reporting relationships and responsibility and

Figure 12.7

A SIMPLIFIED FLOW CHART

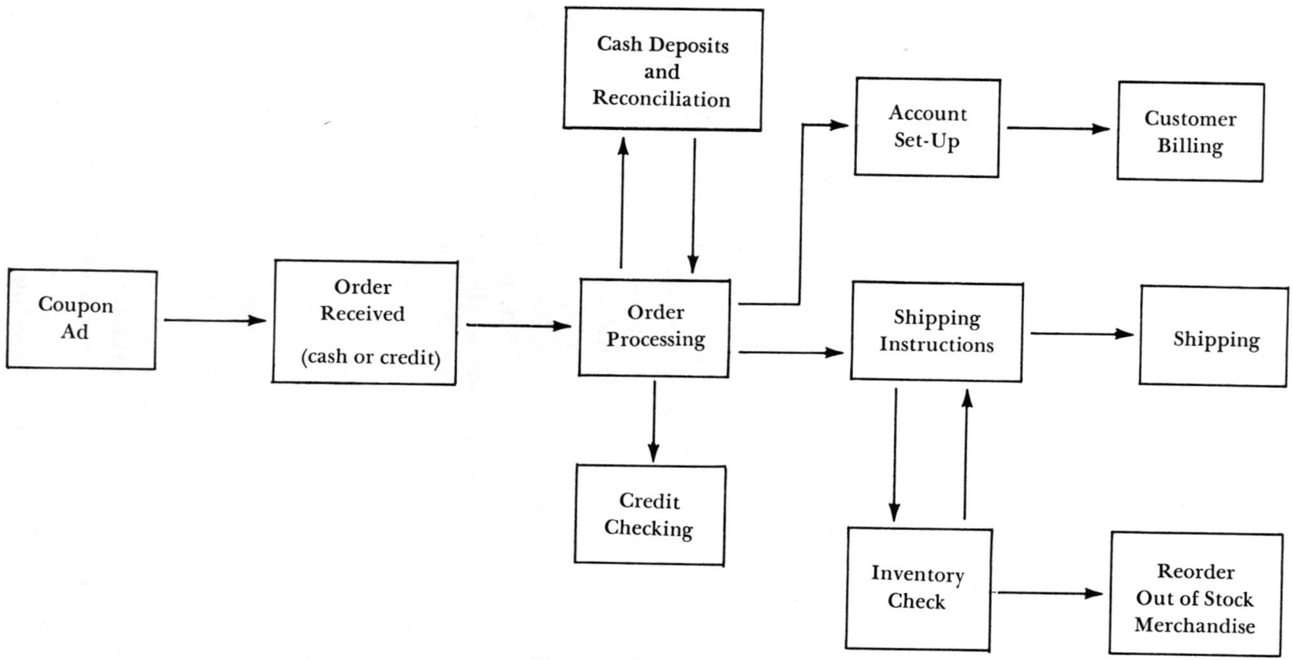

authority definitions had been changed drastically. Major adjustments had been made in the daily interworkings between departments and in the groupings of tasks within each department. For example, the old advertising department had become a broader marketing department, order processing included customer service, and product procurement and warehousing were combined. In general, the old "authority" organizational structure had given way to an organization in which the formal divisions of authority and responsibility had become blurred—as greater emphasis was placed on integration of operations.

Such changes occur because systems development emphasizes integration of organization units, rather than their differentiation. It leads very often to increased attention to shared responsibility and authority—as managers are forced to view their decisions more in relation to the decision-making needs of other managers. In redefining authority and responsibility, managers find that they no longer have "sole" authority for decisions and are required to do more "consulting" with other managers. While this does not make for neat and simple dividing lines between management jobs and takes away some of a manager's authority, some compromises are needed in this direction to insure effective integration of operations.

Systems studies and the systems approach are useful tools in organization development, for they can provide information needed for adjusting and modifying organization structures and definitions of responsibility and authority, as a manager searches for ways to improve working relationships and integration of operations within his organization structure.

Other Areas of Shared Responsibility and Authority: Staff or Advisory Relationships

The terms "line" and "staff" are used to designate relationships within an organization. "Line" refers to the line of authority relationships between superiors and subordinates down through an organization, and "staff" refers to advisory and service relationships within an organization.

When a department's relationships to other organization segments is mainly advisory or service, it is commonly referred to as a "staff" department. This is misleading, however, since many so-called "staff" departments are also assigned operating tasks, responsibility, and authority.

The term staff is confusing, because there are different degrees of authority and responsibility associated with different staff functions. Some staff departments merely advise operating managers. For example, economic analysis personnel sometimes act as in-company consultants, providing company management with information, financial evaluations and recommendations.

Other staff departments provide assistance so specialized that operating managers are in fact obligated to take staff advice. Legal departments, as well as operations research departments, often make operating decisions in this way. It is possible, therefore, on occasion for operating and staff managers to share decision-making authority.

Other so-called staff departments assist corporate management in integrating company operations. For example, a planning department may have the responsibility for coordinating division implementation planning and for preparing a comprehensive plan. While division managers report to the executive vice president, they are still responsible to the planning department for preparing implementation plans for their division and submitting them by a certain date. At the same time that division managers are obligated to provide information to the planning department, the planning department is obligated to provide advisory services to division managers. For example, the planning department would develop overall strategic planning guidelines for division managers and advise them on how to prepare their implementation plans.

It is easy in practice to accidentally overstep authority and responsibility limits in a staffing situation. For example, a company president may ask his controller to find out why a deviation occurred, simply because the controller was in the president's office at the time the report was read. If authority and responsibility limits are not clearly defined and adhered to, an over-zealous controller might take it upon himself to start investigating the cause, asking questions of operating personnel, and preparing a report on the causes of the deviation for the president—instead of calling the division manager and saying "the president would like a report next week on the cause of the deviation", thus recognizing the division manager's responsibility to the president and executive vice president for performance.

Advisory positions are necessary to assist operating managers and corporate executives in carrying out management tasks, and in providing technical expertise in such areas as market research, economic analysis, engineering, and the like. But advisory jobs are often difficult to perform. Advisory positions by definition limit a manager's ability to put ideas or recommendations into practice, for the authority to implement the idea or recommendation rests largely with the operating manager, not the advisory manager. Persuasion, not authority, then is the principle management tool of the advisor, and he bears the burden of convincing (often a time-consuming job) rather than giving orders to those carrying out the idea.

No two staff relationships seem to operate in the same way in business. And they probably should not, since each business situation will have its own requirements, the personal relationships between managers will differ with the personalities involved, and the degree of expertise of each staff manager will vary.

Use of Committees and Special Task-Teams

It is frequently useful to establish special groups within the formal organization to perform specific management and operating tasks.

Committees may be formed for integrating and coordinating operations. For example, the Board of Directors is itself a committee responsible for managing the entire company. A single chief executive may be assigned responsibility for running the company, but he still acts as the representative of the Board.

Managers make use of many types of committees in performing their jobs. Many companies have permanent planning committees, policy development committees, grievance committees, new product review and coordination committees, personnel committees, budget committees, and the like, which are part of the formal organization structure. These committees can be useful extensions of the executive providing they are not established for the wrong reasons (for example, to avoid making decisions) and providing they are not a substitute for individual management.

Special groups can also be effective in handling special projects, such as developing a new computerized information system, getting a new product off the ground, developing and building a new manufacturing plant, and establishing a new pension fund. In these cases a task-team may be formed, which will exist only until the project is complete.

There are many advantages to establishing such special groups. It facilitates group study, and use of diverse skills in dealing with a specific problem. Judgment can also be improved by exposing ideas to different viewpoints. A committee may also serve as an information link, and as a means of coordination and motivation. Special groups are also a means of insuring that tasks which cut across organization lines and which otherwise might not get the attention they deserve are performed.

On occasion, however, special committees are formed because of the unwillingness of some executives to exercise authority and take action. Unless a committee is assigned a specific and meaningful objective, this can lead to wasted time and money, inaction, indecision, and compromises which lower performance levels.

Balancing Differentiation and Integration Requirements

Differentiation or departmentation is needed in every business organization. Operating tasks have to be segregated, for example, so that they can be performed and managed by individuals. And assigning profit and performance responsibility to individual managers and workers, and decentralizing authority, can increase performance and enable better control of an operation. Task differentiation is normally the basis upon which formal organization charts are built. Differentiation does not stop with just the structure of the organization, however, for there will also be differences in the attitudes, orientation, and values of individuals within each formal organization segment.

On the other hand, it is equally important to provide for integration of operations at the different levels within a company. To some degree integration requirements can be shown by dotted lines on a formal organization chart, by decision-making and business-flow charts, and by job definitions which indicate the interrelationships among different organization segments and the areas of shared responsibility and authority. Integration is not, however, necessarily achieved by using these formal organization tools and the formal chain of command represented by them.

The methods used for integrating operations vary with situation requirements. As an example of the varying balance between integration and differentiation needed in business organizations and the different integration techniques which might be used, Lawrence and Lorsch studied high performing companies in a stable industry and in a dynamic industry:[4]

> The plastics organization, which functioned in the most dynamic and diverse of the environments studied, was consequently the most highly differentiated of the three high-performing organizations. Since this condition could create major problems in maintaining the required state of integration, this organization, as we have seen, had developed an elaborate set of formal devices (both an integrating unit and cross-functional teams) to facilitate the resolution of conflict and the achievement of integration. Because market and scientific factors were uncertain and complex, the lower and middle echelons of management had to be involved in reaching joint departmental decisions; these managers were centrally involved in the resolution of conflict. This organization also met all the determinants of effective conflict resolution. The integrators had balanced orientations and felt that they were being rewarded for the total performance of their product group. Relative to the functional managers they had high influence, which was based on their competence and knowledge. In resolving conflict all the managers relied heavily on open confrontation.
>
> In contrast to the plastics organization, the container organization was in a relatively stable and homogeneous environment. Thus its functional units were not highly differentiated, which meant that the only formal integrating device required was the managerial hierarchy. But in using this device this organization also met the determinants of effective conflict resolution. The sales and production units, which were centrally involved in the crucial decisions related to scheduling and delivery, both felt that they had much influence over decisions. Around these issues influence was concentrated at the top of the organization, where top managers could centrally collect the relevant information to reach decisions. Middle managers, particularly those dealing with technical matters, did have some influence. The great influence of the top managers stemmed not only from their position, but also from their competence and knowledge. Finally, conflicts be-

[4]Paul R. Lawrence and Jay W. Lorsch, *Organization and Environment* (Homewood, Illinois: Richard D. Irwin, Inc., 1969), pp. 151-152.

tween departments were resolved and decisions reached through problem-solving behavior.

Some of the integrating techniques used by these companies have been discussed in this section: for example, committees, task teams, and integrating staff units. As is indicated by the above quotes, integration also involves the use of behavioral techniques, such as participative management. The behavioral techniques used in integrating operations and resolving organization conflicts are discussed in the following section.

In their studies, Lawrence and Lorsch describe two entirely different kinds of organizations, each of which seems well equipped to deal with its own external environment. Each had different degrees of differentiation in their organization and each used different integrating tools. Each was successful not because they used any "best" techniques, but because the balance of integration and differentiation, and the techniques used were appropriate to the situation.

The reader will have observed that the discussion in this chapter has gradually shifted from a highly structured approach to organization planning to a highly flexible one. This is consistent with how a manager might perform organization planning. First, a manager tends to analyze the different operating tasks to be done and to develop a general framework or chart of these tasks. As he goes deeper into the problem, he develops the details of the operational organization and begins to adjust his original chart to meet management requirements. Where the organization is large and decentralized, he begins to focus on how to strengthen the interrelationships of the differentiated groups—to better perform the management tasks, and insure the organization will respond to market needs in a unified way.

At this point, he attempts to build into his organization plans ways of establishing working relationships—either through coordinating managers (such as a brand manager) or organization units (such as staff, service, task teams or committees) to perform this integration. He will also spell out in as much detail as possible the nature of these interrelationships in the job definitions, in order to encourage and direct individual managers to act as integrators where necessary. The tools he used, the exact balance he strikes, will during this phase be dictated by the varying situation requirements.

HUMAN FACTORS AND ORGANIZATION PLANNING

While a formal organization structure and formal job definitions are important in organization planning, human behavior does not always conform to formal organization patterns. Nor are working relationships always established by responsibility definitions, lines on an organization chart, or integrating organization positions. Human beings often form their own organization groups and establish their own working relationships—both for personal and business reasons.

This section considers the behavioral factors which affect organization, and ways in which these factors can be taken into account both formally and informally in organization planning.

Behavioral Science and Organization Planning

Both the traditional departmentation approach and the newer systems approach to organization development are important organization tools. Both approaches, however, view people somewhat mechanistically, and so are incomplete guides to structuring organizations to meet behavioral requirements.

A complex change is taking place in our society in general, and it is having a profound effect on business organization. The individual now has greater mobility and affluence, and so has a less compelling attraction to the stability a bureaucracy can offer. He demands, and can get, more from a company. For this reason, in developing its organization a company must allow for this greater individual freedom, and for other social changes which affect the way individuals and groups of human beings react to the business environment. Today, business is being forced more and more to reconcile its purely business objectives with the personal needs and desires of the individual.[5]

Behavioral science tools help meet these new organization planning needs and to fill the gap left by the traditional and systems approaches to organization development. The term "Behavioral Science" has been defined as:

> A combined endeavor of many fields investigating all aspects of behavior, leading to understanding of human beings as individuals and in social relations. Behavioral science, therefore, includes many studies in the field of anthropology, bio-chemistry, ecology, economics, genetics, geography, history, linguistics, mathematics, neurology, pharmacology, physiology, political science, psychiatry, psychology, sociology, statistics, and zoology.[6]

Behavioral science, through studying the causes and patterns of human behavior, opens up an entirely new way to look at organization development. Behavioral scientists, such as Chris Argyris, Rensis Likert and Mason Haire, believe that a business organization today is too complex to rely solely on formal organization approaches.[7] These men feel that it is im-

[5]Warren G. Bennis, *Changing Organizations: Essays on the Development and Evolution of Human Organization* (New York: McGraw-Hill Book Company, 1966).

[6]Maneck S. Wadia, *Management and the Behavioral Sciences: Text and Readings* (Boston: Allyn and Bacon, Inc., 1968), p. 22.

[7]Chris Argyris, *Integrating the Individual and the Organization* (New York: John Wiley and Sons, Inc., 1964) and *Understanding Organization Behavior* (Homewood, Illinois: The Dorsey Press, Inc., 1960); Rensis Likert, *New Patterns of Management* (New York: McGraw-Hill Book Company, Inc., 1961); Mason Haire, ed., *Organization Theory in Industrial Practice: A Symposium* (New York: John Wiley and Sons, Inc., 1962).

possible to plan an organization structure today in business without at least an implicit concept of the nature of man and of human behavior.

What Motivates Individuals in Their Work Environment?

Before a manager can organize and administer people's efforts, he must first understand what motivates them to work. Each individual's behavior can be viewed as an action designed to satisfy his own needs. Every person has needs that are never fully satisfied, and the presence of unsatisfied needs motivates an individual to act. If the action arising from a need is directed to some goal or objective that results in the elimination of the need, then there can be said to be a motive for the action.[8]

A person is motivated to work in order to satisfy some need. In its simplest form, a worker's need, motivation or goal setting occurs as follows: first, a need, such as hunger or self-realization, arises in a person; second, the person recognizes that he must satisfy this need and so is motivated to action; third, he takes action to satisfy the need, either by getting a job or deciding to keep working at his job.

Douglas McGregor, drawing on the work of Abraham Maslow, has arranged needs into a five-level hierarchy:[9]

1. *Physiological needs.* Man's most basic needs are his physiological needs, that is, those needs he must satisfy to function as a normal human being, such as the needs for food and shelter.
2. *Safety needs.* Man has an instinctive need to protect himself and his family and to make himself as safe as he can from danger, threat and deprivation.
3. *Social needs.* Man is basically a social animal, who does not want to be alone, and so has a great need for belonging, for association, for acceptance, and for giving and receiving friendship and love.
4. *Ego needs.* Ego needs can be divided into two classes: those that are related to one's self-esteem, such as self-confidence, independence, achievement, competence and knowledge, and those that related to one's reputation, such as status, recognition, appreciation, and respect.
5. *Self-fulfillment needs.* Most men feel that they must fulfill a role in life. Self-fulfillment needs include the realization of one's own potentialities, continued self-development, and continued creativity.

Man's basic physiological needs are normally satisfied when he obtains employment, for he is able to buy food and obtain shelter with the money he earns. Safety needs are partially satisfied by job security, so long as arbitrary management actions do not create uncertainty about continued employment or reflect favoritism or discrimination.[10] In the business en-

[8]John F. Hall, *Psychology of Motivation* (Chicago: J. B. Lippincott Company, 1961), p. 30.

[9]Douglas McGregor, "The Human Side of Enterprise," in *Management of Human Resources*, eds. Paul Pigors, Charles A. Meyers and F. T. Malm (New York: McGraw-Hill Book Company, Inc., 1964), pp. 57-58.

[10]James V. Clark, "Motivation in Work Groups: A Tentative View," in *Psychology in Administration*, eds. Timothy W. Costello and Sheldon S. Zalkind (Englewood Cliffs, N.J.: Prentice-Hall, Inc., 1963), p. 62.

vironment, the worker satisfies his social needs by belonging to work groups. The typical worker in mass-production industries has little opportunity to satisfy his ego and self-fulfillment needs through his job; these needs, therefore, can stimulate workers to seek supervisory jobs, since these jobs have decision-making responsibility and so allow a man to satisfy ego and self-fulfillment needs.

Both McGregor and Maslow discuss these five needs in terms of a hierarchy of importance, with higher needs (social, ego and self-fulfillment) being acted upon only after lower needs (physiological and safety) are satisfied.[11] While it is possible to speak *theoretically* of needs in a five-level hierarchy, in practice this is not the case. Man tries to satisfy a diversity of needs at the same time. Higher needs emerge and are acted upon before lower needs have been completely satisfied. Thus a worker, in performing his job, is trying to satisfy many needs at the same time.

The study of human needs provides only a partial explanation of human behavior, however, for the same needs may lead to different responses or satisfiers (for example, two hungry people may choose different foods to satisfy their hunger) and the same action may be motivated by different needs (for example, one person may work to earn money and another to gain prestige or power). Need, therefore, is only one of the many factors which influences how a person will react to a specific situation. Other factors affecting an individual's response to his environment are previous experience, expectancy, level of aspiration, group relationships, ethical values and religious beliefs, cultural influences, an individual's emotional make-up, and the like.[12]

Organizational Behavior

While human needs and motivation are of concern in specific situations involving management direction, behavior in groups or organizations is of greatest concern in organization planning.[13]

Although the field is relatively new, a considerable amount of systematic research has been done in organization behavior. The research has concentrated on finding out how organizations behave and why they behave the way they do. For example, the research has attempted to answer such questions as why operating groups persistently get into so many costly feuds, or why some groups deliberately restrict their output. Based on the insights gained from this research, it has become possible to predict

[11]McGregor, "The Human Side of Enterprise," p. 57; Abraham H. Maslow, *Motivation and Personality* (New York: Harper and Row, Publishers, 1954), Chapter Five.

[12]Costellow and Zalkind, *Psychology in Administration*, pp. 64-66.

[13]The discussion in this section is based on: Fred J. Carvell, *Human Relations in Business*; Blair J. Kolosa, *Introduction to Behavioral Science for Business* (New York: John Wiley and Sons, Inc., 1969); Bertram M. Gross, *Organizations and Their Managing*; and Paul R. Lawrence, *et. al.*, *Organization Behavior and Administration* (Homewood, Illinois: Richard D. Irwin, 1961).

(within certain limits) the behavior of people in organizations, and so provide a basis for more effective organization planning.

When studying a formal business organization, it has been possible to distinguish several different but interrelated aspects of organization behavior. Three of these are discussed here: the informal activities within a formal organization (its informal organization); the behavior of small work groups; and intergroup behavior.

Formal versus Informal Organization

The formal organization, as discussed and charted in the preceding sections, is a hierarchal arrangement of authority and responsibility. The existence of this formal arrangement or chart, however, does not mean that all the activities and interactions of the organization members conform to this formal structure.

Informal social structures arise in every formal organization, as the groups in the formal organization develop their practices, values, norms, and social relations while the members work together. As a result, complex networks of social relations and informal status structures emerge within groups and between them. The informal organization develops in response to the opportunities and problems posed by the environment. The formal organization structure is only the immediate environment of the work groups.

The informal organization may lend its support to the objectives of the enterprise. For instance, the formation of informal groups might lead to increased cohesion of work groups which in turn raises worker satisfaction and productivity and lowers turnover and absenteeism. On the other hand, the existence of a certain type of informal organization may also seriously restrict a company's ability to achieve its goals.

In organization planning, therefore, one must consider how to gain the cooperation of the informal organization, as well as develop the formal organization and job definitions.

Work Group Behavior

Members of a complex business organization generally do not behave as isolated individuals, but as members of small groups. Most behavior in organizations, of managers and workers alike, can thus best be understood and predicted through analyzing relationships among people who share group memberships at work. Work group behavior refers to the various ways in which members of small groups of people at work behave and can be expected to behave at every organizational level.

Based on the research done on organization behavior, several useful conclusions or generalizations about work group behavior can be developed, which can be helpful in organization planning.

First, a distinction can be drawn between the work group behavior which is required by external forces and conditions in performing the tasks assigned to the group, and the behavior which develops internally in the group beyond that which is required or given. There is a close relationship between the behavior required by the job and the behavior which *emerges* above and beyond the required behavior. For example, if management sees that a group is restricting output (emergent behavior), it will take action to change the formal job requirements (the required or given job). This action will in turn modify or reinforce the original output-restricting behavior of the work group.

The interrelationships of the many aspects of work group behavior are shown in Figure 12.8.[14] The first column of figures shows the factors which influence the required activities, interactions, sentiments, and values of the work group. All the required or given behavior is in theory determined by these influencing factors, over which group members have little or no control.

The emergent or actual behavior of a work group (shown in the third column of Figure 12.8) is far more complex than the given or required behavior from which the actual behavior emerges. The consequences of emergent behavior in a group is that an informal structure emerges which generally functions to preserve group norms and protect the group from outside pressure. The informal group will have a leader (or leaders) and the social standing of group members will depend on faithfulness to group norms.

Work group behavior patterns produce several different kinds of results (the fourth column in Figure 12.8):

1. A certain output (productivity).
2. Various degrees of satisfaction which group members derive from their work experience and the accomplishment of the formal task.
3. A certain individual development.

The results of work group behavior, which are determined by external and internal group factors, in turn provide a feedback and become partial determinants of behavior in succeeding periods of time. For example, a certain level of productivity may lead management to modify the technology or, recognizing a low work satisfaction, to improve satisfaction through a program of job enlargement.

Intergroup Behavior

In addition to the behavior of groups of employees, intergroup behavior plays an important role in organization behavior. Each group in an organization is typified by behavior patterns which differentiate it from

[14]Adapted from Lawrence, *Organization Behavior and Administration*, p. 217.

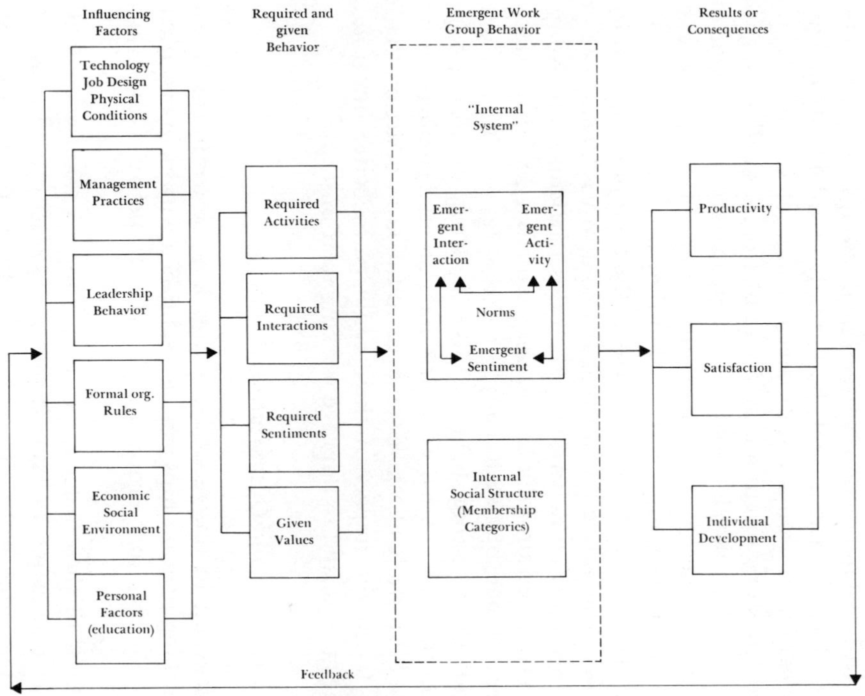

Figure 12.8
WORK GROUP BEHAVIOR

other groups. These behavior patterns are governed by rules or norms which the groups adopt for regulating and evaluating their group behavior. Yet, the successful functioning of the enterprise requires a high degree of coordination and cooperation among these groups.

The analysis of the intergroup behavior deals with problems of collaboration and conflict between groups, and among supervisors and managers. It also deals with relationships at least one step above the small group work, with the interaction between small groups, as well as between departments, plants, divisions, and the formally or informally designated representatives of those groups at the management level.

Every complex organization is an accumulation of small work groups, each of which tends to develop some persistent patterns of behavior in its relations with the other groups. These intergroup relations may take on various forms in different organizations, but they will always have a strong impact upon the achievement of the goals of the total organization. If, for example, the sales department of a particular company is having a running feud with the production department, then this particular intergroup behavior will have a certain influence upon productivity, work satisfaction, and the general climate of the company.

The study of intergroup behavior, like the study of work group behavior, reveals the causes of many conflicts and potential conflicts within an organization. Such study also gives clues as to the kind of action that can be taken to lessen the impact of these conflicts, to better integrate the actions of the groups, and to improve working relationships.

Behavior Patterns and Organization Planning

The discussion in this section explores how better integration and improved working relationships can be established within an organization —in the light of the work group and intergroup behavior patterns discussed above.

In the light of these behavior considerations, a manager would examine the specific existing and anticipated human factors that might affect organization planning in the situation under study. Based on this situation analysis, he would study ways to adjust the organization plan to meet critical behavioral requirements.

Emergent group behavior can affect organizational development in many ways. Where emergent behavior conflicts with formal organizational patterns, conflicts will often arise. For example, at a computer manufacturing company, where salesmen were supposed to develop systems proposals for new customers and programmers were supposed to develop computer programs based on these proposals, some programmers were in fact doing systems development work and falling behind on their programming work. The first step when conflicts are identified is to examine the reasons for the emergent behavior, since this behavior may have arisen for sound business reasons.

At the computer company, for example, the salesmen were not doing systems development work because their main job was to sell computers. The programmers tended to fill the gap because they were trained to do the work and because the gap was there. The company solved the problem by creating a new organization position, systems development managers, who worked with salesmen in developing systems to meet customer requirements and with the programmers in seeing that the systems were programmed. In other words, an integrating position was established to provide coordination of operations and to enable the salesmen to concentrate on their specialized jobs (differentiation or departmentation).

It is often possible to anticipate and take advantage of expected emergent group behavior patterns. For example, in some situations involving either temporary or permanent tasks which cut across organizational lines, it may be best to recognize and encourage special group formations by formally establishing task-teams. If these teams are given specific objectives, and have the necessary skills and information needed to get the job done, then they can be effective. By formally establishing such teams, as in the systems development study described in Chapter 11, management recognized that such a group would eventually form anyway informally, gave better direction to its formation, and helped overcome any resentment which might arise from conflicts among the informal group and existing formal organization units. Before management took this step, the informal group of systems developers that formed in the situation under study lacked the required manpower, and was unable to accomplish organization objectives.

Lawrence and Lorsch's study mentioned in the last section has several examples of how cross functional teams were created in a successful plastics company to fill the communication gaps created by decentralization. Their study also cites examples of emergent behavior (job dissatisfaction, informal cliches, poor performance) arising in the less successful companies, which did not develop such integrating units. In the less successful companies the emergent behavior was a clue to basic organization problems, which management did not act upon.[15]

Not only are many organization changes made to support and exploit emergent work group behavior. They are also often made to counteract emergent group behavior, where it decreases efficiency. For example, in an industrial engineering staff group at a large company informal social groups had formed (because of the formal organization structure) around engineering specialities (methods, standards and incentives). Difficulties

[15]Paul R. Lawrence and Jay W. Lorsch, *Organization and Environment* (Homewood, Illinois: Richard D. Irwin, Inc., 1969), Chapter VI.

were encountered in coordinating the work of these specialist groups on project assignments for production sections, as the men used their formal ties with specialty managers as constant excuses for missed deadlines (ostensibly because of conflicting work pressures, but really because of a reluctance to help out other competing social groups). In this situation, the groupings of the industrial engineering staff were formally changed (project teams were formed consisting of specialists in methods, standards and incentives), in order to overcome the coordination problems.

Many kinds of organizational adjustments can also be made to reduce intergroup conflicts. For example, in one situation where a design unit (a high status group) was required to deal frequently with a production unit on the shop floor (a low status group which shared few values with the higher status group), conflict was avoided by assigning a small production unit permanently to the design group to produce designs. In this case an integrating unit was not established, but integration was achieved by greater departmentation of the production function.

In another intergroup-conflict situation, an advertising agency, the art department was run by one of the agency's owners and so consistently was able to overrule objections from the copy-writing department when artists cut down copy to make room for larger pictures or other design changes in advertisements. Only after the agency's best copy-writer resigned was the organization changed, so that both the art and copy departments reported to an executive who gave equal importance to the functions of each group. Conflict is almost inevitable when one organization unit gives orders to another of equal status, as in this situation. Here, conflict was avoided only when equality was restored through an organization change which established an integrating executive position, which still left the specialized units in tact—so that they could continue to concentrate on their specialities. At the same time it provided for a balanced integration of the two operations.

A common instance of intergroup conflict is in the relationships between staff budgeting groups and operating divisions. In defining job responsibilities for the budget manager, a company should avoid making him just a watchdog, who prepares budgets, collects and analyzes result information on division manager performance, and reports deviations to the senior company executive. Such an arrangement almost always produces resentment and conflict, since from the operating managers viewpoint the budgeting group is probably a lower status group—for example, "bookkeepers". In order to reduce the potential for conflict in this type of situation, the budget manager should be required to *assist* division managers in preparing their budgets and to report deviations to both division managers and senior company executives. In addition, the division managers should be required to present explanations for deviations to senior company executives, and not to the budget manager. By making these formal job definition changes in the light of known intergroup behavior factors, a better working relationship will be allowed to develop between the budgeting and operating groups.

Individual needs are not as easy to satisfy through organization adjustments, because a business is, by definition, a group; and group involvement is only one of the many ways in which individual needs are satisfied. There are, none the less, some steps which can be taken in organizational development which can help satisfy individual needs.

First, wherever possible large groups should be broken down into smaller units—for example, a typing pool of 45 girls might be broken down into 5, 6 or 7 smaller groups, in order to allow informal social groups (which are usually small) to form around work groups and so reinforce work goals.

Second, wherever possible one should avoid isolating individuals from the rest of the organization, in order to permit on-the-job social contacts among individuals.

Third, specialization should not be carried too far. If an assembly line is segmented to a degree that each station becomes so routine and monotonous a job that the individual becomes bored, he may fail to perform it well. For example, the American Management Association reports on how one company, which had been using assembly-line production for a complex electronics product, reorganized production to allow workers (who were relatively skilled) to work on assembling the entire product and through this reorganization increased productivity—because worker interest and satisfaction was increased.

Fourth, reciprocal exchanges should be encouraged within the organization. Someone who is always taking orders, and who is exposed to very few situations in which his knowledge and experience dominates, will find very few ego satisfactions on the job. The problem is particularly severe among management trainees, who have good educational backgrounds and strong achievement aspirations, but who are treated as learners and not doers. One Harvard Business School graduate who was working for a midwest oil company quit after six months of training, when he met another "trainee" who had been working for the company for three years. Many large companies have developed organizational positions where relatively new managers can be given authority and responsibility within the limits of their training and experience.

Fifth, steps can also be taken to increase the status of a job and so the individual's feeling of pride about the job. While position titles should be a true reflection of the jobs to be performed, a little imagination in writing a title can exchange its prestige. For example, Bigelow Carpet Company has for years conducted a major advertising campaign based on this human need for recognition, "A title on the door and a Bigelow on the floor. . . ." While a title can never be a substitute for real authority and responsibility, or for significant salary increases, it can be used selectively to increase worker and manager satisfaction.

In the same vein, one should consider the prestige attached to where in the corporate hierarchy a position is placed when making organization changes—the higher in the executive ladder a man reports to, the higher the prestige of his job. Some thought should, therefore, be given to the affect on prestige of the addition of new supervisory positions. For example, if an executive vice president creates a new subordinate manager position, to which two executives would report who had formerly reported to the executive vice president, these two executives will in all likelihood feel they have been "demoted," even though their pay and duties remained the same. As a result, their effectiveness may be reduced, or in some situations they may even quit.

As is seen from the discussion in this section, while there are limitations to just how far one can go in adjusting organization structures and job definitions to meet behavior requirements, many steps can be taken to improve the working relationships and integration within an organization. These steps can be taken more intelligently if a manager has a good working knowledge of individual, work group and intergroup behavior patterns.

PLANNING FOR ORGANIZATION CHANGE

The last step in organization planning discussed in this chapter is the planning involved in introducing organization changes.

Since most organization planning situations involve going businesses with existing organizations, this step begins with a review of the existing organization structure, job definitions, and personnel. A planner would then compare the existing proposed organizations to determine where specific changes will be required. The purpose of this phase of organization planning is to provide a detailed list of the specific structural and personnel changes required to convert the existing organization to the proposed organization. In addition, during this phase of his study, a planner would also draw up an inventory of available manpower resources for staffing the new organization.

Unless an entirely new staff is to be hired, a planner also identifies the attitudes and feelings of the personnel involved which might affect the change significantly or the effective functioning of the organization after the change is made. As Warren Bennis points out,[16] if the proposed change threatens an individual (psychological implications) or his social relations (sociological implications), then any benefits from the proposed change may be nullified by the behavior of the people working within the organization. A planner would then identify the degree to which attitude or

[16]Warren G. Bennis, *Changing Organizations*, p. 175.

behavior changes would be needed and also plan steps to induce the attitude and behavioral changes required to make the new organization work.

Next, a plan is developed for introducing the change. Where company-wide organization changes are being proposed, if possible it is best to plan to make the change in phases. For example, when Carrier Corporation was planning to switch from a functional to a divisional organization, it started by breaking off its Allied Products Division. This was done both to avoid major disruptions in operations by trying to do too much at once, and to give management an opportunity to test the new plan out and refine it, since it is an unusual major organization plan which does not need some refinement.[17]

In developing phase plans, a manager would consider both business requirements and the personnel involved in the change. Where possible, the organization change should be designed to take advantage of existing human resources. In line with this, some temporary adjustments may have to be made to accommodate individuals: for example, creating temporary advisory positions to make use of existing personnel who are not qualified to handle equivalent jobs in the new organization.

A survey of how large companies manage overall organization change showed that a participative (as well as phased) approach was used in all the successful changes studied.[18] Unlike the authoritative approach (where higher management dictates the solution) or the delegated approach (where lower level managers develop piecemeal solutions), the participative or shared approach allows both direction from higher management and some measure of decision making by those affected by the change.

A phased, participative approach overcomes many of the problems encountered in introducing major organization changes.[19] It allows communication both of objectives from above and needs from below, thus enabling a better reconciliation of both kinds of requirements in the new organization, and the gradual education of the personnel involved concerning major requirements in the situation. It also provides for the gradual redistribution of authority along new organization lines and verifies to those involved in the change the usefulness of the new organization by the success of each phase. And it is a vehicle for uncovering resistance to

[17]Another example of a successful phased organization change is described by William F. Glueck in "Organization Change in Business and Government," *Academy of Management Journal*, December 1969, pp. 439-449.

[18]Larry E. Greiner, "Patterns of Organization Change," *Harvard Business Review*, May-June 1967, pp. 119-130.

[19]Examples of the successful use of the participative approach in introducing organizational change are described in Richard Hoffman and R. W. Archibald's "Introducing Technological Change in a Bureaucratic Structure" and Raghu Nath's "Dynamics of Organizational Change: Some Effects of a Change Program in a Client System" (*Academy of Management Proceedings*, December 26-28, 1968, pp. 25-36 and 51-66) and in Ben Miller's *Managing Innovation For Growth and Profit* (Homewood, Illinois: Richard D. Irwin, 1970), pp. 243-257.

the change and for changing human attitudes towards, and behavior within, the new organization.[20]

The participative approach can create problems, however, if too many people are involved and if considerable time and effort are devoted to solving minor problems. Care must be taken, therefore, to limit use of the participative approach to those situations where the complexities warrant it.

Not all organization change situations require the use of participative approach. For example, in the industrial engineering staff study discussed earlier, the staff members realized that changes were needed (they were aware of the problems the production department was having in getting engineering services), so that after the changes were made they appeared fairly reasonable to those involved. The transition may have been made smoother if before the change was made, the nature of the change being studied, and the reasons behind it, were communicated to the staff involved; and a better balance may have been attained in the new organization if those involved had participated in developing the proposed changes. But these benefits were judged by management to be relatively minor and not sufficient to justify the costs of using the participative approach in this situation.

The need for participation also depends on the individuals involved. Behavioral studies indicate that individuals who are highly dependent and are authoritarian-oriented are affected less by the opportunity to participate in decision making and show no relationship between felt participation and job performance. As research studies indicate then, while in general participation in management decision making is related to performance and is important to group functioning, a manager should also examine variations in individuals in terms of their need for participation.[21]

As with any popular management technique, participative management can be overused and misused. As pointed out by George Berkwitt,[22] many companies have gone overboard in their use of participative management and only when problems arose (for example, during the recession during the early 1970's) come to realize that in many instances it was ineffective and a waste of money.

As in other areas of management, therefore, there are no panaceas or cure-alls for planning organization change. Each situation will require a unique approach and there is no "one best approach." In fact, as Denis Pym shows,[23] a manager who believes there is a "one best approach" to

[20]Tom Lupton, "The Practical Analysis of Change in Organizations," *The Journal of Management Studies,* May 1965, pp. 218-227.

[21]Blair Kolasa, *Introduction to Behavioral Sciences,* p. 465.

[22]George J. Berkwitt, *Dun's Review,* September 1970, p. 25.

[23]Denis Pym, "Effective Managerial Performance in Organizational Change," *The Journal of Management Studies,* February 1966, p. 81.

introducing organization changes is likely to be an ineffective manager of change or change-agent.

Resistance to change is inevitable, for change means extra work, disruption of routine, shifts in individual power and status, and uncertain new social relationships. Time and effort are needed to adjust to one's environment, so normally only the young in spirit and the creative actively seek out new challenges.

People realize in general, however, that in business change is as inevitable as resistance to change. So, while they may resist change, they also will accept it—providing change is handled in a way that considers and allows for its impact on individuals wthin a company.

Bennis has outlined some general guidelines for handling change in such a way as to minimize resistance to change:[24]

1. The *client-system* (organization involved in the change) should have as much understanding of the change and its consequences, as much influence in developing and controlling the fate of the change, and as much trust in the initiator of the change, as possible.
2. The *change effort* should be perceived as being as self-motivated and voluntary as possible. This can be done through the legitimization and reinforcement of the change by the top management group as well as by the significant reference groups adjacent to the client-system. This can also be done by providing as much true volition as possible.
3. The *change program* must include emotional and value as well as cognitive (informational) elements for successful implementation. It is doubtful that relying solely on rational persuasion (expert power) is sufficient. Too often, rational elements are denied or rendered impotent because they conflict with a strongly ingrained belief, consciously or unconsciously held. Intellectual commitment is a first step, but not a guarantee to action. Most organizations know what ails them or what could help them; the problem is utilization.
4. The *change-agent* can be crucial in reducing the resistance to change by providing consultation and psychological support during the transitional phase of the change. As I have stressed over and over again, the quality of the relationship is pivotal to the success of the change program. As long as the change-agent acts congruently with the principles of the program and as long as the client-system has a chance to test his competence and motives (his own and the change-agent's), he should be able to provide the support so necessary during the risky phases of change.

Where resistance does arise (and some always will in spite of how careful the planning), on occasion it is best to ignore it. At times, such resistance is for bargaining purposes—a manager *says* he will quit if the change is made, but really won't after he examines his alternatives and finds no other company will offer him a better deal. For example, when Chrysler decided to lay off a thousand white collar workers in early 1970,

[24]Bennis, *Changing Organizations*, p. 176.

some of them chose to take lower paying jobs within the company when faced with the alternative of having to look for another job.

At other times adjustments in the organization plan may be needed. If one is using a phased approach to organization change, one has the flexibility to make these adjustments and refinements—for example, by adjusting job definitions in such a way as to overcome individual managers' objections to the new organization. In many situations, tools from the staffing area can be helpful—for example, by providing ways to place men in positions best suited to their needs and capabilities, by retraining them, by objectively appraising their performance, and the like.

When taking steps to respond to resistance to change, reference should always be made to the total requirements affecting the change. All too often, where particularly strong resistance is met, there is a tendancy to compromise the entire organization structure—for example, by bending the structure to meet the desires of a major vice president. Individual decisions about how to handle resistance to change should thus be made as much as possible within the perspective of total organization plan.

CONCLUSION

This chapter has discussed four basic aspects of organization planning: grouping tasks into organization units; defining and assigning responsibility and authority, and establishing working relationships; human factors and organization planning; and planning for organization change.

There are two basic forms of overall company organization structure: the functional, in which all work of the same kind is put into one organization unit; and the divisionalized, in which all the different kinds of work necessary to accomplish a specific end result are put into one organizational unit. Small companies generally use a functional form, while larger companies use some combination of the two forms. Three kinds of divisionalization were discussed: product, geographic, and customer.

While these two basic approaches are useful in explaining how companies organize overall, many problems are encountered in developing organization structures at individual department or division levels. This chapter has explored some of these problems, and attempted to show how their final resolution will vary with each situation. The discussion also covered ways in which management task requirements can affect formal organization development.

Through assignment of tasks, responsibility, and authority, the corporate president is enabled to distribute the work throughout the many levels and organization segments of the company and provided a means for insuring performance of operating and management tasks. Delegation is the moving force in the effective distribution of work and responsibility for performance of that work. Delegation is thus an indispensible organization and management tool.

In developing formal organization structures and job definitions, proper emphasis should be given to the interrelation of organization segments and the steps which can be taken to establish and strengthen the working relationships among the various organization segments. It is only natural to try to simplify organization planning by drawing firm lines between organization segments on a chart, and categorizing and limiting hierarchal relationships among segments in job definitions.

Such a rigid approach has limited application in today's businesses, however, where the dynamic interaction and intercommunication among organization segments is important to success. Traditional organization structures and job definitions, therefore, need to have considerable flexibility built into them. In any formal organization scheme, allowance must be made for the interrelations of segments and the necessity for managers to share responsibility and authority for task completion.

The success of such a flexible organization approach depends first on the careful delineation and definition of tasks, authority and responsibility for each organization position. This is only a start, however, for success also depends on how well the formal organization has taken into account human needs and behavioral patterns.

Individual, work group, and intergroup behavior factors are important situation factors which affect organization planning. These factors should, therefore, be given equal weight with other operating and management task requirements when planning organizations.

As was seen from the discussion, there are obvious limitations to just how far one can go in making organization adjustments to satisfy individual, work group and intergroup behavior requirements. Business requirements will usually ultimately dominate, and where compromises in organization have to be made they more often favor business, rather than human, factor requirements.

Organization adjustments can none the less be made in many instances. And this chapter has outlined some of the organization tools which can be used to satisfy behavioral requirements.

The last section of this chapter discussed the different phases which may be involved in planning organization change:

1. Identifying the scope and nature of the change and the attitudes and feelings of the personnel involved.
2. Developing a plan for introducing the change. There is evidence that where major changes are involved a phased, participative approach will be most successful.
3. Planning steps to reduce resistance to change, if possible without compromising the integrity and major objectives of the new proposal.

The participative approach is a major tool of change. Combining direction from both those in authority and those affected by the change, this approach enables all participants to share in the structuring and activating of organization plans, while still maintaining direction and control over the change.

But this approach provides only a bare framework for action in organization. There is no tidy bundle of theories in introducing organization change, as there are for example in operations research, but only general directions. People have a way of not fitting into theoretical pigeon holes—either subordinates or leaders.

As in other areas of planning, a manager is involved in a balancing act in planning for organization change, for rarely can every business and human requirement be completely satisfied. What is important is to satisfy major requirements, within the constraints of the situation, and to make maximum use of the people involved both during and after the transition to a new organization.

DISCUSSION QUESTIONS

1. What are the basic differences between functional and divisional organizations? What are the advantages and disadvantages of each? What are the different kinds of divisionalized organization structures found in businesses? Describe the types of situations in which each approach can best be used.
2. What is a hybrid organization structure, and why are hybrid structures so common in medium-size and large businesses?
3. What are some of the operating factors which might affect developing the details of organization structures? What are some of the management tasks which may affect the development of organization structures? Describe the ways in which these considerations can affect organization development.
4. Define and distinguish among task, responsibility, and authority. In what ways are responsibility and authority the life lines linking a corporate enterprise's operations together?
5. What is delegation and why is it so important to effective management of a business enterprise?
6. Describe the ways in which information systems development might lead to changes in organization structures and job definitions.
7. Describe staff and line relationships, and the ways in which staff groups can help improve company operations. What are some of the problems which may arise in staff operations?
8. Discuss the different tools used for integrating operations in the container and plastics companies described by Lawrence and Lorsch. In what ways was each appropriate to the company organization and industry involved?
9. Define behavioral science, and its relation to the organization planning.
10. Describe the ways in which behavioral approaches are necessary to supplement the traditional departmentation and newer systems approaches to organization planning.

11. Describe the various aspects of individual, work group and intergroup behavior discussed in this chapter which have relevance to organization planning.
12. Describe some of the organization adjustments which can be made to meet individual behavior requirements. To meet work group behavior requirements. To meet intergroup behavior requirements.
13. Describe the way a manager might go about identifying the scope and nature of the changes involved in introducing a major company-wide organization change.
14. What is the phased, participative approach to organization change, and in what kinds of situations is it effective? Discuss the limitations of the use of this approach.
15. Why is a study of available human resources important in preparing for organization change? What kinds of personnel adjustments may be required in an organization change?
16. Describe the steps a manager can take to identify and overcome resistance to organization change.

CHAPTER 13

PLANNING FOR A SMALL COMPANY

The planning problems faced by small companies have been touched upon throughout this book, but not to the same degree as those problems faced by large companies and by lower level managers in larger companies.

The general approach to planning is the same no matter what size a company is. And almost everything said about business planning thus far in the book can be applied equally well to a small company as to a large company. A small company does have special problems, however, which are not encountered in planning for a large company. The management resources a small company can devote to planning are limited, immediate survival is often the most pressing problem, capital is always limited, its business is more sensitive to minor changes in the market, it cannot sustain major reverses, and the like. Because of these unique problems encountered in planning for a small business, the subject is treated separately in this last chapter.

A small company can be defined as one with less than 500 employees or less than $500,000 in profits before taxes. A number of studies of the problems faced by small companies have been made, and each study came to the conclusion that the classic weakness in most small businesses is an almost total lack of planning. Each of these studies attempted to develop guidelines for planning in small companies. The following discussion gives the highlights to these studies, as well as the author's experiences in the area.[1]

[1]For example, see George A. Steiner, "Approaches to Long-Range Planning for Small Business," *California Management Review*, Fall 1967, pp. 3-16; Roger A. Golde, "Practical Planning for Small Business," *Harvard Business Review*, Sept.-Oct. 1964, pp. 147-161; *Planning for Future Growth: A Small Company Must*, "Research Institute Staff Recommendations, File 32" (New York: The Research Institute of America, 1967).

AN APPROACH TO PLANNING FOR SMALL COMPANIES

Almost every top executive in a small company agrees in principle that he should spend more time planning the future of his company. In practice, however, the pressures of immediate problems tend to push planning into the area of wishful thinking. Looking ahead is too often considered a luxury rather than a necessity. Actually the reverse is true.

If it is to be done at all, planning for the small company must be scaled down to the limitations of time, energy and data available. It must be simple and graphic. Above all, it must be easy to start, since getting started seems to be the hardest part of planning in small companies.[2]

The small business planner should begin with some basic, concrete questions in starting the first phase of his planning—developing overall planning premises, objectives, strategies, and policies:

1. What business am I in?
2. What is my place in the industry?
3. What customers am I serving? Where is my market?
4. What is my company image to my customers?
5. What business do I want to be in five years from now?
6. What are my specific goals for profit improvement?
7. What plans do I need for product improvement?
8. What is my greatest strength? Am I using it?
9. What is my greatest problem? How am I to solve it?
10. What share of the market do I want? Next month? Next year?
11. Are my personnel policies acceptable to employees?
12. How can I finance growth?[3]

This list is essentially designed to guide the planner into thinking strategically. It is not enough, however, for this general thinking needs to be crystalized in a more systematic way. One business consultant has developed a form for small business planning. This form, which is given in Table 13.1,[4] helps the manager begin to list the specific planning premises affecting his business. Because it helps him visualize all factors on a single sheet, he can see factors in relation to each other and so begin to think strategically.

In using this form in conjunction with the above list of questions, the manager can quickly get into the "strategic" stage of small business planning, for through this exercise he will establish an overall direction, guidelines and planning premises for his company's plan. The next stage is to develop the detailed action steps he must take to implement his overall strategy.

[2]Delbert C. Hastings, *The Place of Forecasting in Basic Planning for Small Business* (Minneapolis: University of Minnesota Press, 1961), p. 23.

[3]Steiner, "Approaches to Long-Range Planning for Small Business," p. 7.

[4]Golde, "Practical Planning for Small Business," p. 152.

Table 13.1

HYPOTHETICAL COMPLETED MASTER PLANNING FORM

Item	Change		Comment
	NY	*YAN*	
RESEARCH & DEVELOPMENT	Mm	S	Start development of new altimeter for executive planes.
PRODUCTS		Ss	First sales of new altimeter.
PRODUCT MIX			
SERVICE		s	Slightly different for private planes.
SUPPLIES		s	Needed for new altimeter.
SUPPLIERS			
INVENTORY			
SUBCONTRACTS		S	Most of subassemblies will be subcontracted.
STORAGE & HANDLING			
QUALITY CONTROL			
SPACE		S	Little bit of production space for new altimeter.
LEASEHOLD IMPROVEMENTS	M		Need for dust-free area.
EQUIPMENT	S		New test equipment.
EMPLOYEES	S		Couple of technicians for development work.
FRINGE BENEFITS			
CUSTOMERS		sS	Plan to hit owners of executive planes.
SALES OUTLETS		Mm	Will need more sales representatives rather than own sales force.
TERMS OF SALE			
PRICING			
TRANSPORTATION			
ADVERTISING		M	Not so effective to private owners.
PROMOTION		m	Will switch to more demonstrations and trade shows.
PACKAGING			
MARKET RESEARCH	S		Informal poll of private owners known by company.

FINANCING	S		Additional working capital for production.
INSURANCE			
INVESTMENTS			
MANAGEMENT REPORTS		l	Need for simple product costing system.
MANAGEMENT PROCEDURES			
MANAGEMENT ORGANIZATION		m	Will have to reorganize production department.
GOVERNMENTAL ENVIRONMENT		s	CAB regulations more favorable to our device.
ECONOMIC ENVIRONMENT			
INDUSTRIAL ENVIRONMENT	Mm	Mm	Tremendous growth in private executive plane field.
COMPETITION			
COMMUNITY ENVIRONMENT			

INSTRUCTIONS:

NY = next year; YAN = year after next. All changes are estimated in relation to the preceding year.

If a quantitative change is anticipated—i.e., change in size or amount—use the following symbols: L = large, M = medium, and S = small. Quantitative changes are assumed to be increases unless preceded by a minus sign.

If a qualitative change is anticipated, use the following symbols: l = large, m = medium, s = small.

Note that the notions of small, medium, and large changes are obviously subjective and will vary with the person using the form.

In general, a small change denotes some sort of minimum level of change which is thought important enough to make note of. Most of the expected changes will probably fall in the medium category, indicating significant change of some magnitude. The large category will usually be reserved for unusual changes of striking impact.

The notion of qualitative changes may need some clarification. This category of change would cover such items as a change in customer mix (which might or might not result in an increased number of customers). Using a new source of supply for raw materials and changing the media allocation of the advertising budget would also be examples of qualitative changes.

BUILDING AN ACTION PLAN

The Research Institute of America has developed the following four-step approach to implementation planning for a small business:[5]

1. Project probable, or desired, *sales growth,* by years, for the next five years—or for a similar meaningful period and convert these sales dollars into *units,* for each year, based on the present product mix, allowing for expected changes. Whether the company sells goods or services, the process is the same.
2. Calculate the amount of *equipment* that will be needed to produce this volume each year. Allow for retiring old units, and figure how much new capacity would have to be brought on stream. Then compute the annual cost of adding to this new capacity.
3. Using present ratios of *receivables, inventories, etc.* to sales, calculate the added costs of maintaining these ratios as sales grow. This gives a rough estimate of capital tie-up, Added to (2), this shows how much new money will be needed. Few companies realize the amount involved before making the calculations. A typical manufacturer with $2.5 million in sales, for example, will need almost half a million dollars to back up a 42% growth.
4. List the company's total *manpower*—supervisors, skilled people, unskilled workers. Figure the rate of annual turnover for each, and the number of new people that will be needed to meet unit output growth goals. The combination tells how many will have to be hired every year.

Step One

Step One is to answer the question "How fast will the company grow?" The natural starting point for any measure of the future is the sales forecast. All other company activities must eventually be geared to support this function.

The planner will undoubtedly already have some well-conceived ideas of the desired growth rate for his firm in mind, if not on paper. If so, this is a good place to start planning. The planner can then check out his own ideas by using the simple method of projecting sales given in Table 13.2. Keep in mind that the purpose of these procedures is to uncover the major growth-limiting factors so that pinpoint accuracy is unnecessary. Also, it is suggested that the sales forecast cover the next five years, but it can be limited to two or three years if updated periodically. One caution: extend the forecast far enough ahead so that there will be adequate time to take action to overcome the obstacles spotlighted. For example, planning for, funding, and bringing new production capacity on-stream may require at least two years advance notice.

A sample worksheet for projecting sales is shown in Table 13.2. The procedure given there is as follows:

[5]This section is based entirely on *Planning for Future Company Growth,* published by The Research Institute of America. Reprinted with the permission of the Institute.

1. Project current year sales and sales for the next five years.
2. Adjustments to these figures should then be made based on factors such as new product developments, unusual events, and the like.
3. A final sales forecast is then developed.
4. Total dollar sales are then broken down by product.
5. Dollar sales by product are then converted into unit sales by product.

Detailed instructions for carrying out this procedure are given in the notes to Table 13.2.

Table 13.2
SMALL BUSINESS PLANNING
SALES PROJECTIONS IN DOLLARS AND UNITS

	Current Year	Next Year	2 Years Ahead	3 Years Ahead	4 Years Ahead	5 Years Ahead
(1) Sales—dollars						
(2) Adjustments						
(3) Adjusted sales						
(4) Product Sales —dollars						
Product A						
Product B						
(5) Product Sales —units						
Product A						
Product B						

Directions for performing each step:

(1) For current years sales, the planner may wish to use either the actual figures for the last full year of year-to-date sales for the current year converted to an annual rate. Either should be satisfactory. To convert current year-to-year figures to an annual basis, first determine what part of the company's annual business, based on past performance, is normally secured in the period to date. If it is 60%, for example, divide year-to-date sales by 60, and multiply by 100.

To complete line 1, extend the growth curve achieved during the past five years for the next five. To do this, merely determine the percentage increase in annual sales, 1970 compared to 1965. Divide by five to obtain the average annual increase. For example, if sales in 1970 were $6,500,000 and in 1965 $4,575,000, the increase is 42% or 8.4% per year. *One caution*: if 1970 sales were abnormal for some reason (a strike at a competitor's plant, for example), adjust the figures before calculating the percentage increase.

To obtain the sales figure for the "next year," simply multiply $6,500,000 by 108.4 to arrive at $7,046,000. Similarly, for "two years ahead" the planner would multiply $6,500,000 by 116.8 to get $7,592,000 . . . and so on.

(2) Line 1, of course, is simply a mathematical projection of past performance. Line 2, provides for anticipated changes, either up or down, from the past growth curve. The anticipated changes may be the result of fixed plans: new products to be introduced, sustained higher level of advertising or sales promotion, a larger sales force or expansion into new markets. In other cases, the adjustments might stem from objectives that the top-executive wishes to establish: match or exceed estimated industry growth, reach a certain sales level by 1970. The adjustments, of course, could be downward as well as upward. The company, for example, might have introduced new or improved products

two or three years ago with a resulting sharp increase in sales. Looking ahead, sales will show a more gradual rise so a reduction is in order. Whatever the reason, the top executive's best estimate of the dollar effect on sales should be entered on Line 2.

(3) Lines 1 and 2 should be combined and the result entered on line 3. For advance planning purposes, the sales forecasts should be on the optimistic side. The reason, of course, is that it is always possible to *delay* the expansion or addition of capacity for example, but suddenly boosting output on short notice might be impossible.

(4) The objective, on line 4, is to convert total sales dollars into dollar sales of *each product* that will be sold in the years ahead. A good starting point is the present product sales mix. If the company currently sells 60% of Product A, and 40% of Product B, these same percentages can be applied to the sales forecast. The next step would be to adjust these figures for any changes in the mix that can be foreseen.

(5) Line 5 provides for the conversion of sales dollars into unit sales of each product for each year. If the planner has standard prices for each product, these can be used. If there are different prices for different models, the planner may want to use an average price. This can be obtained by dividing current sales dollars by the number of units sold. If changes in prices are expected, the estimate of these changes should be taken into account in determining the number of unit sales.

Step Two

Step two is to answer the question: "How much new machinery and equipment will be needed?" Once a growth goal is established for the future, the next logical question is, "Can the units required be produced by present machinery and equipment?" In most firms, one or two sections, departments, operations, or processes are the bottlenecks that must be broken if production capacity is to be expanded significantly. The planner undoubtedly knows which ones these are in his own company. The limiting factor might be a product or product component with critical tolerances, one where complex machinery operations are necessary, or even a cleaning process or an assembly section. Whatever the reason, whenever production capacity is mentioned, the planner and the company's production manager both know that something will have to be done about particular areas.

This knowledge is vital, of course, but planning should not be limited entirely to these bottlenecks, important as they are. The suggested form given in Table 13.3 is designed to assist in making a more complete review by identifying not only all the major items that will have to be added dur-

Table 13.3

SMALL BUSINESS PLANNING
MACHINERY AND EQUIPMENT REQUIREMENTS

Item	Next Year	2 Years Ahead	3 Years Ahead	4 Years Ahead	5 Years Ahead

ing the next five years, but also those key pieces of machinery or equipment now in use that will have to be replaced because of age, inefficiency, or obsolescence. In addition, by indicating the estimated installed cost in the columns to the right the planner will be able to roughly determine the timing and amount of funds that will be needed for this purpose.

A two-phase procedure is suggested. First, have someone list present key machines or other equipment in the left-hand column. Attention should be given to special-purpose machines, relatively high-cost items and those with a long lead-time based on past purchasing experience. Working with the company's production and purchasing people, the planner should indicate in the columns to the right the estimated installed cost of the new replacement machines.

Next, add the new machines and equipment, if any, that will have to be added each year to increase production capacity to the level required by projected sales. Hopefully, the new machinery and equipment required will fit into the company's present buildings. If, however, the company is now operating at the capacity of present floor space, plans will have to be made to schedule the additional buying, renting, or building of plant space.

Totaling the installed cost in each column will tell the planner how much of added funds will be required each year.

Step Three

Step three is to answer the question "Will the company need additional outside funds?" Finding the added capital necessary for sustained growth is a familiar problem for the top executives of most smaller concerns. That is why it is especially important to have as much advance notice of capital needs as possible.

Machines and other equipment can quite often be financed fairly easily through short-term loans, installment buying, or by leasing instead of outright purchase. But moving to a significantly higher level of sales typically involves a boost in long-term funds to carry the higher levels of receivables and inventories necessary, plus, in some cases, an increased investment in land and buildings. Cash and other miscellaneous accounts may be slightly higher, too, but major factors are our concern here.

The worksheet given in Table 13.4 is designed to assist the planner in determining the approximate timing and the total amount of additional funds that will be required during the next five years. It is the basic data that the planner will need to strike the proper balance between financing through cash generated by the business (profits plus depreciation), short-term loans, leasing, and long-term funds. The procedure involved in carrying out this phase of the planning process is given in the footnotes to Table 13.4.

Table 13.4

SMALL BUSINESS PLANNING
ADDITIONAL FUNDS REQUIRED

	Next Year	2 Years Ahead	3 Years Ahead	4 Years Ahead	5 Years Ahead
(1) Sales Increase $					
Additional Funds for:					
(2) Receivables					
(3) Inventories					
(4) Machinery & Equipment					
TOTAL					

Directions for performing each step:

(1) Enter on Line 1, the increase in sales for each of the next five years from Line 3 of the worksheet given in Figure Two.

(2) To determine the additional tie-up in receivables, it is suggested that the planner use his present ratio of receivables to sales unless some major changes are anticipated. For example, if present sales are $6,500,000 and average receivables $715,000, the ratio is 11%. Applying this to the sales increase mentioned in the example in Figure Two, $546,000, receivables would climb $60,060 in 1971. This would be entered in the column "Next Year" and similar calculations would be made for succeeding years.

(3) A similar procedure can be used to estimate the added tie-up in inventories. If sales are $6,500,000 and present average inventories are $910,000, the ratio is 14%. Applying this to the sales increase in (2) above, the planner would enter a figure of $76,440 as the additional inventory for "Next Year" . . . and so on.

(4) Enter on line 4 the approximate figures for additional and replacement machinery or equipment from previous calculations.

(5) Totaling the columns will give the planner a good idea of the additional funds required each year to support his planned growth.

Step Four

Step Four is to answer the question "Is the company properly staffed for growth?" If the company is already feeling the pinch of shortages in skilled manpower and managers, the planner had better expect increasing difficulty in the future. High employment during the late 1960's and the well-publicized "hollow generation" make it clear that new entries into the labor force or the ranks of managers will probably not meet the expanding needs of business.

Knowing his own firm's manpower requirements now will enable the planner to take appropriate action. Projecting manpower needs on a form such as the one given in Table 13.5 can help determine personnel needs, either to replace present key people or to handle expanded business. The procedure given in the footnotes to Table 13.5 provides the basic round numbers, so that the planner can determine how urgent a problem manpower represents.

Table 13.5

SMALL BUSINESS PLANNING
PERSONNEL REQUIREMENTS

Job Category	Next Year	2 Years Ahead	3 Years Ahead	4 Years Ahead	5 Years Ahead

Directions for completing this form:

(1) In the left-hand column, list the individuals or job titles of present key people: managers, supervisors, or skilled workmen. In the latter case, these might be listed by type of work. For example, the planner might list "Tool and Die Makers" or "Welders," and the number the company has of each.

(2) In the columns to the right, indicate the retirements and normal attrition based on past experience, plus the additions, if any, required to support higher sales volume.

Once this data is assembled, the planner should look back over all the figures and test the implications. Will the company be able to add that much new plant, raise the cash, and find the required number of capable key people who will be needed? If not, the obvious answer is a more practical sales goal.

This four step approach (and its forms) developed by The Research Institute enables the small company planner to assemble the data needed to project his company's needs in the three key areas of capacity, capital and manpower. It is an indispensable preliminary step to developing a plan of action. For the typical smaller company, a study of capacity, capital, and manpower, in terms of a projected sales goal, will uncover most of the potential internal obstacles to growth. Once the planner has reduced the implications of his sales objectives into numerical terms in these key areas, he will be in a good position to reevaluate his overall strategy.

When the planner has completed the information-gathering stage, he may want to get together with the company's key people to raise questions such as these:

. . . Are expectations realistic? Too optimistic? Too conservative?

. . . Can the company start paving the way by moving some items further up on the "do-it-now" agenda?

. . . Can the company begin to firm up the "next year" plans and agree on a tentative 5-year program, to be reviewed periodically?

. . . Should responsibility be assigned to someone to develop and spell out specific segments of the overall plan in greater depth?

The best single tool for achieving maximum control of operations—and, coincidentally, planning for growth—is the annual budget. Once long-range objectives are clarified, the budget can become an important planning tool, as is pointed out in some detail in Chapter 8.

Using the figures developed for planning and the budget, the planner is now also able to calculate a return on investment. Through return-on-investment analysis, plans are subjected to the acid test: how much money will they earn on the money invested in the company? George Steiner has prepared the diagram given in Figure 13.1 which shows how to calculate a return on investment.[6] In the diagram, the top half is a calculation of how much money will be invested in the company and the relation of the investment to sales, while the bottom half is a calculation of profits on sales. By combining the two at the end of the diagram, the planner can determine his percentage return on invested capital.

Where possible, the planner should also develop a break-even point, that is, the sales or production level at which the company neither makes money nor loses money. This gives the manager a bench mark for answering many day-to-day questions about the true profitability of incremental sales and the dangers in adding to fixed costs.

Obviously, even the best of plans will not guarantee success. But it is equally clear that, in an increasingly competitive climate, sound business judgments cannot be based on hunches or guesses. At the very minimum, the prudent businessman will want to do everything within his power to review those factors which are within his control.

When the planner is confident that his initial plans are sound, he may want to review his planning premises and reexamine the potential external threats to expanded sales and profits. In the following paragraphs, three of the most common of these outside influences are briefly discussed. A quick run-through will tell the planner whether any or all of these should be made a part of his look ahead.

1. *Markets*: Once upon a time, the smaller firm did not spend much time worrying about market potentials, saturation levels, and the like. Today, the fast pace of technological change in materials, processes, and products suggests the need for a somewhat closer watch, to avoid being caught completely off base if important customers suddenly discontinue their orders. The planner will probably be familiar with any major changes affecting industry through trade association or trade periodicals. But, in addition, he may want to maintain closer contact with major customers.

   There is one practical step that any company can take—and is undertaken by quite a few—to minimize the risk of being caught completely off base. A senior executive, most preferably the president, along with the marketing

[6]Steiner, "Approaches to Long-Range Planning for Small Business," p. 10.

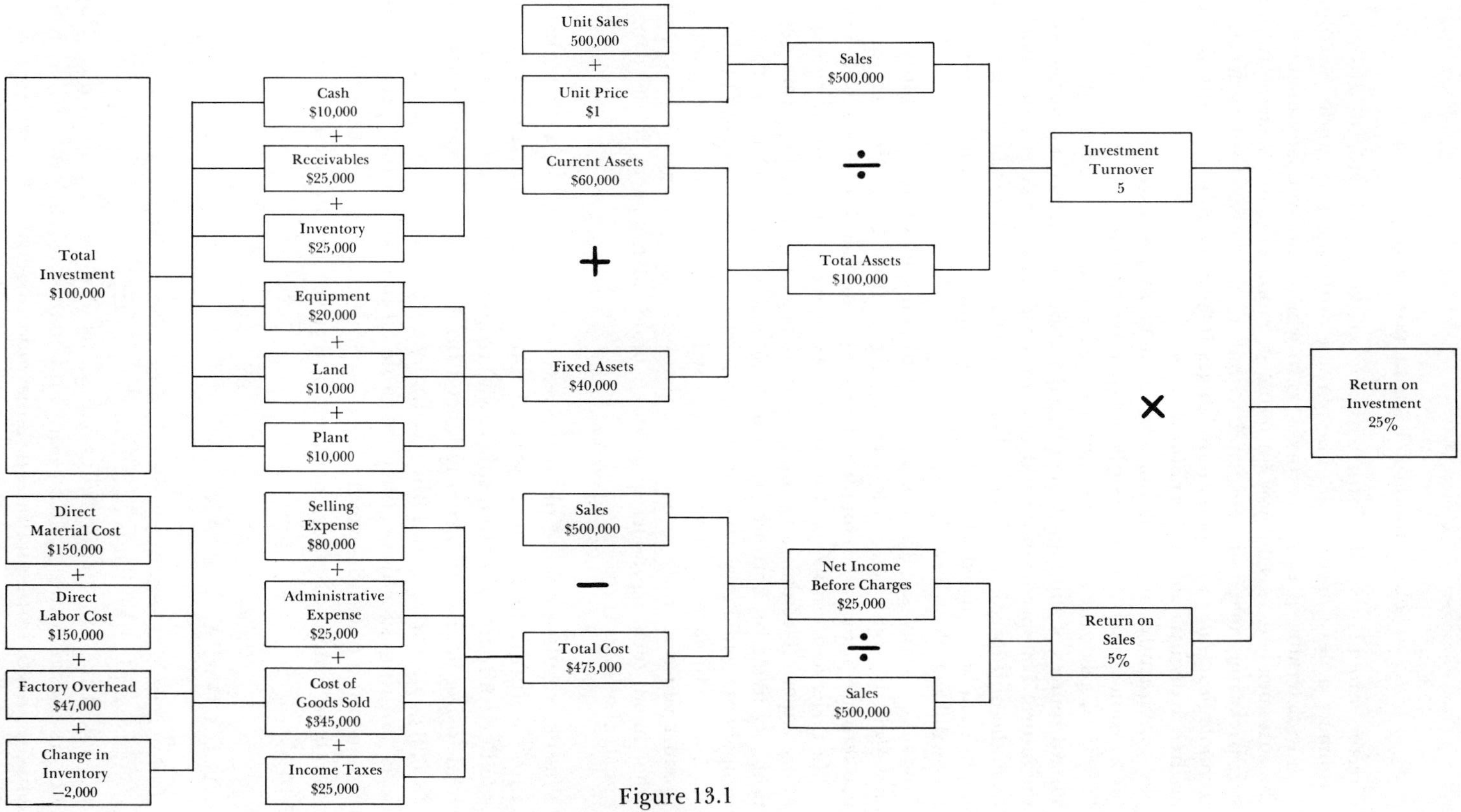

Figure 13.1

RETURN ON INVESTMENT

director, can plan to sit down with the marketing director of all major customers, at least once a year. The purpose of the meeting can be two-fold: first, to determine if there are any ways in which your company might serve the customer better, right now, in terms of improved delivery methods, timing, packaging, materials, etc.; and second, to determine likely marketing, technological and other potential changes in your customer's plans, if they are free to discuss them at this point in time.

Not infrequently, customers can assist a company project its own plans and on occasion can stave off a potentially expensive mistake.

2. *Suppliers*: For the same reason, it may be important to look ahead to make sure of sources of supplies if the company anticipates larger requirements in the future. The specific items and amounts needed can be determined quickly from the unit forecasts and the bill of materials for each product. Discussions might then be arranged with some current suppliers of vital items to be sure they will have adequate capacity.
3. *Products*: Many smaller companies bank on the strong possibility that there will be some detectable warning signal from their customers or the marketplace prior to the complete demise of a product. But products do have a life cycle, and, unlike people, the life cycle has been shortening rapidly. Many experts feel that any consumer product more than five years old is probably living on borrowed time, at least without major changes. Parts or components, while they generally have a longer life than consumer products, are more subject to sudden death. A heavily tooled, expensively engineered product which is costly to market tends to discourage competition. On the other hand, such a product quite often blinds management to the danger signals of obsolescence.

The net results of these planning activities will be to give a realistic look into the future and some degree of control over a company's growth. The smaller company too often shies away from advance planning because of fear of losing flexibility or being fenced in. Actually, an examination of long-range goals can expand the company's options and opportunities. There is nothing sacred or unchangeable about an initial projection. Planning is not a one-shot exercise. It is a continuous process that calls for periodic reassessment of goals, methods, objectives and future needs of the company.

A SMALL COMPANY PLAN

The following is a summary description of an actual small company comprehensive plan, which is based on the principles of planning outlined in this book. Like other comprehensive plans discussed in this study, this plan covers overall strategic directions and planning assumptions, as well as the highlights of implementation plans and budgets.[7]

[7]Steiner, "Approaches to Long-Range Planning for Small Business," pp. 12-15.

CORPORATE LONG-RANGE COMPREHENSIVE PLAN FOR MAGNETIC DESIGN, INC.

I. *Corporate Purposes.* The first section of the plan gave basic MDI corporate directions in three parts.

A. Two prime objectives of MDI are:
–To improve earnings through productive effort primarily applied (but not limited) to the manufacture of magnetic devices and power supply equipment.
–To conduct the business in a manner that is constructive honorable, and mutually profitable for stockholders, employees, customers, suppliers, and the general community.

B. These objectives are amplified further:
–To earn a reasonable return on investment with due regard to the interests of customers, employees, vendors.
–To expand sales while increasing profits.
–To support the military effort of the United States by producing top quality products.
–To grow at a steady rate.

C. Departmental purposes: This part gave departmental objectives for administration, marketing, production and engineering, and finance. The following are the objectives of the production and engineering department:
–Manufacture and design quality products with cost and delivery schedules which will be attractive to prospective customers.
–Stay alert to developments that promise new and improved company products.

II. *Basic Corporate Five- and Ten-Year Sales Profit Objectives.*

A. The five-year annual sales and profit objectives are:

	Sales	*Pre-tax Profits* $	%	*After-Tax Profits* $	%
First year					
Second year					
Third year		[Specified in dollars			
Fourth year		and percentages.]			
Fifth year					

B. The ten-year sales and profit objectives are:
–After taxes, sales will be $5,000,000 and earnings will be $750,000.

III. *Basic Premises.* This section gave forecasts of future markets, technology, competition, and evaluations of internal strengths and weaknesses. The following are some selections from the MDI plan.

A. External projections and forecasts:
–Projections of general business conditions, including Gross National Product forecast.

—Projections of markets for company products, based on agreed upon general economic conditions for industrial products and estimates of government spending for company products.

—Forecast of company sales based on the above two forecasts. (MDI made forecasts for each of the next five years. Since the company is in the Midwest, government spending for its products in the Midwest was estimated. Included were the Department of Defense, the National Aeronautics and Space Administration, and Federal Aviation Agency.)

B. Competition. This section not only looked at what the competition was, but also examined MDI's relation to the competition. For example:

—Several advantages have placed MDI a number of years in advance of competition in the magnetic devices equipment field. These are cryogenic magnets for commercial applications and high reliability power supplies for long-endurance military applications.

—However, in order to realize fully the growth commensurate with the above advantages, several weaknesses must be overcome by developing an ability to construct crystals, as well as developing more sophisticated test procedures.

C. Internal examination of the past and projections: This section contained analyses of various parts of the enterprise. For example:

—Product line analysis:

a. Product(s) performance (i.e., sales volume, profit margin, etc.).
b. Customer classes served.
c. Comparison with major competitors' product(s).
d. Comparison with substitutes and complementary performance.
e. Possibilities for product improvement.
f. Suggestions with regard to new products.

—Market analysis:

a. Important factors affecting projected sales changes: product success; marketing organization; advertising; and competitive pressures.
b. New markets to be penetrated (i.e., geographical areas and customer classes).

—Financial analysis:

a. Profit position.
b. Working capital.
c. Cash position.
d. Impact of financial policy on market price per share.
e. Prospects for future financing.

—Production analysis:

a. Plant and equipment (maintenance and depreciation).
b. Productive capacity and productivity.
c. Percent of capacity utilized.
d. Suggestions for: productivity improvements; cost reductions; excess capacity; and plant expansion.

—Technical analysis:

a. Research and development performance.
b. Suggestions for improving research and development effectiveness.

—Employees:
  a. Employment and future needs.
  b. Technical manpower deficiencies.
  c. Appraisal of employee attitudes.

—Facilities:
  a. Evaluation of current facilities to meet new business.
  b. Machine replacement policy and needs.

IV. *Departmental Objectives, Policies, and Strategies.* This section covered every important area of the business: marketing and sales; production, research; engineering; personnel; finance; capital expenditures; acquisitions; and organization. For example, MDI marketing objectives were set forth as follows:

—Increase sales of magnetic devices 100 per cent in the next five years. Increase sales of power supply equipment 200 per cent during the next five years.

—Increase the total volume of industrial sales from today's 25 per cent to 50 per cent of total sales at the end of five years.

—Penetrate the western market to the point where the company will control 10 per cent of it at the end of five years.

—Enter the foreign market within five years by a licensing agreement, a joint venture, or manufacturing facility.

For each of these objectives, the company prepared a detailed series of strategies and policies ranging from a strategy to "sell custom designs directly to prime contractors in geographic regions where their main plants are located" to details such as special services to selected specified customers, training programs for employees, and top management meetings with customers. These strategies and policies covered all major operating areas. For example, marketing strategies and policies covered organization, use of dealers, possibility of distributing products manufactured by others, salesmen's compensation plans, and pricing policy.

V. *Detailed Operating Plans.* More detailed plans growing out of the above were given in this section. These plans were developed for each of the succeeding five years and were summarized in the following schedules:

A. *Pro forma* balance sheet, yearly.
B. Sales projections and income statement, yearly.
C. Capital expenditure schedule, yearly.
D. Unit production schedule for major products, yearly.
E. Employment schedule, yearly.
F. Schedule on how to acquire within three years a company with design capability in solid state devices.

VI. *One-Year Plans.* The next year's budgets were given in this section. These budgets were, in the aggregate, the same as those given in the first year of the five-year plan, and were coordinated with the operating schedules and plans given in Section V, but were broken down into quarterly time periods. In addition, MDI had other budgets, principally purchasing schedules for major components and raw materials and typical detailed administrative budgets covering such things as travel and telephone.

The following is a brief analysis of the MDI comprehensive corporate long-range plan. The outline of the MDI plan is:

I. Basic Company Directions
II. Basic Five and Ten Year Sales and Profit Objectives
III. Planning Premises
IV. Departmental Objectives, Policies, and Strategies
V. Detailed Medium-Range Plans
VI. Detailed one-year plans.

As in all types of comprehensive planning, the first part of MDI's plan covers overall company strategic directions—both for the company as a whole, and for each major area of the company's business.

Next, five-year sales and profit goals are given in Part II. In some company plans these are given at the end and combined with one-year budgets. Most companies the author has worked with, however, prefer placing these figures early in the plan (as at MDI), since company managers are used to looking at figures first and since the figures give perspective to the specific plans which follow.

Planning premises are given in Part III. This section covers external premises such as trends in the economy, industry and market, as well as internal premises in all major company operating areas. As is often the case, this section contains forecasts of the potential or possible market. These estimates are adjusted later in the light of available company resources.

Part IV gives departmental objectives, strategies and policies. This section extends the overall company strategies and departmental objectives given in Part I, and provides a basis for the development of operating plans.

Part V gives the highlights of specific operating plans and translates them into five-year financial and quantitative schedules. These schedules were the basis for the profit objectives in Part II. Since the MDI plan is a comprehensive plan, just the highlights and financial results of the implementation plans were given in this plan. Each area manager maintained detailed action plans for each planning area.

Part VI, the last part of the plan, gives a detailed quarterly breakdown of the first year of the projections given in the earlier parts of the plan.

With certain modifications, MDI's comprehensive plan was developed following the planning principles outlined in this book. It should, therefore, serve as a model for other small company planners.

A COMPARISON BETWEEN LARGE AND SMALL COMPANY COMPREHENSIVE PLANNING

In order to give perspective not only to the above discussion of small company planning, but also to the planning process outlined in this book, this section discusses the approach to overall planning at a very large oil company and compares it to the MDI approach.

Instead of the simple steps followed by a small company (such as MDI or Blakeston and Wilson), the formal planning steps followed by a large company (such as a billion dollar oil company) are extensive and complex, as is seen in Figure 13.2. Recognizing that planning is a continuing process, the oil company's planning starts with a review of past planning assumptions and objectives (boxes 1 through 4 in the figure). The focus in box 1 is on identifying where changes in past assumptions are likely to occur—which would create both problems and opportunities. Box 2 represents a review of past objectives in the light of recent performance, and box 3 involves the special studies needed to develop new forecasts and assumptions—such as competitive developments in pipe line or gas station construction. Box 4 involves evaluating these factors and translating them into a context more useful for planning decision making. In this phase, the staff analysis covers such relationships as:

1. Company's past performance (including competitive performance) as compared to forecast.
2. Company's expected performance, as indicated by prevailing objectives, in the context of the forecasted environment.
3. Company's expected competitive position in view of the forecasted environment.
4. A comparison of the company's assumptions to actual events.

The planning phase covered by boxes 5 through 10 in the figure represents the more detailed study of the background factors upon which company objectives will be based: Box 5—actual results; box 6—company strengths and weaknesses; box 7—summary of material in boxes 1 through 4; box 8—a review of last year's objectives (and problems encountered in achieving them) with major department heads; box 9—special studies which generally fall outside the formal planning process, such as L. P. Gas studies and supersonic jet fuel studies; box 10—field recommendations, which opens up new sources of information, uncovers hidden opportunities, and increases lower management participation in planning.

The planning steps thus far are familiar ones, as all relevant background factors are examined prior to revising old objectives and developing new objectives. It was the process followed by MDI, Blakeston and Wilson, and Indian Head Mills. And it is a necessary step for any company in establishing objectives.

In the oil company's planning process, as at MDI and Blakeston and Wilson, the next phase (box 11) is to identify the areas that are critical to the development of an objective. A review is then made of existing objectives: some are revised, some are eliminated, and some new ones developed (boxes 12 through 15). A summary of the company's overall and

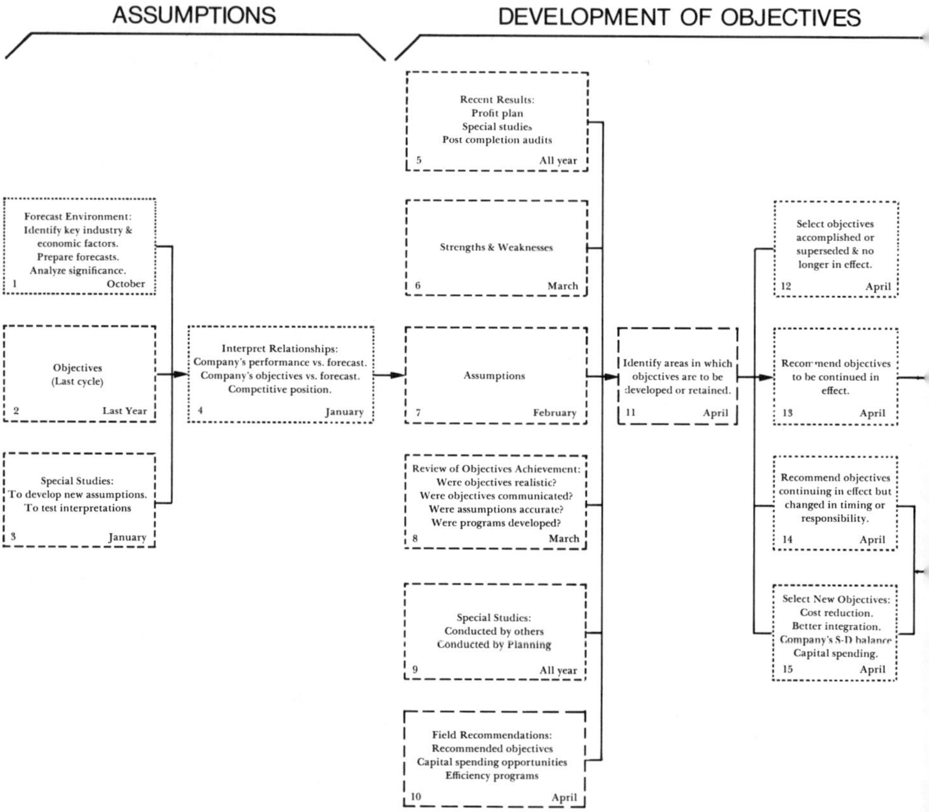

major divisional objectives is then made for the company's overall comprehensive plan (box 17).

As at MDI and Blakeston and Wilson, the overall comprehensive plan (box 17) also contains a summary of the highlights of long-range operating plans and programs. Boxes 18, 19 and 20 represent the steps taken to draw up more detailed action plans and to put the plans into operation.

In comparing the oil company planning process and the MDI plan, a question is sometimes raised as to the order of the steps. For example, why is it that in some company planning studies premising seems to come before objective development, while in others it seems to come after objective development? The order varies with the planning situation:

1. Where a formal plan is being presented, such as at Indian Head Mills or MDI, normally objectives are presented first, followed by statements of the assumptions upon which the objectives are based. This is done because the

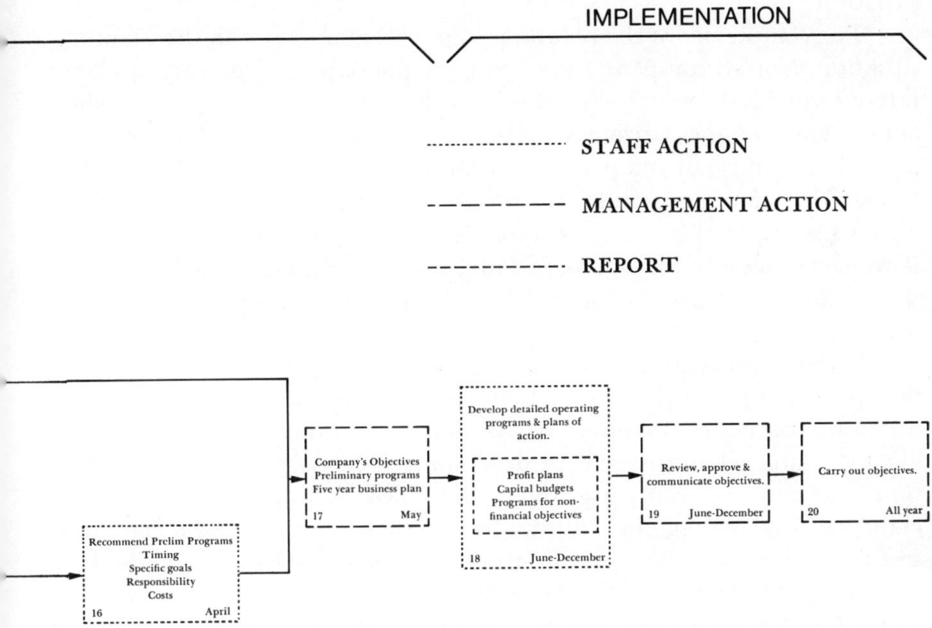

Figure 13.2

PLANNING STEPS AT A MAJOR OIL COMPANY

reader usually wants to first see the conclusion, and then the reasoning behind it.

2. Where one is preparing plans and doing the actual planning job, as in the oil company example and at other companies studied in this book, the whole range of premises (including past company objectives) must be examined before any final new objectives can be developed.

It is important that the planner understand the differences between these two aspects of planning—the preparation of plans and the presentation of plans—in using the planning process. Preparing and using plans is a dynamic activity, which goes on continually at all levels within a company. The plan presented is static, as though one had taken a photograph of the planning activity at a given point in time, and more formal procedures guide its development. While the planning process given in Chapter 1 applies to both types of situations, the order in which the planner carries out these steps will vary with the requirements of each situation.

The complexity of the planning steps will also vary with the planning situation. Not all companies need to have the steps in planning as elaborately formalized and structured as was done at the oil company studied above. For example, such formalization of the planning steps was not needed at such small companies as MDI and Blakeston and Wilson—even though the planning steps followed there were basically the same as at the oil company. At these small companies the process was telescoped into fewer steps, because the number of divisions being planned for was fewer, the product line narrower, and the total volume of business considerably less.

Both the procedures followed in developing comprehensive plans and the method of presenting these plans can thus vary considerably—from the elaborate procedures followed by a billion dollar oil company and carried out by a large planning staff in developing a 500-page plan, to a rather simple fifteen- to twenty-page plan developed by four or five company managers working together informally in a small company. The basic process in all size companies (and at all management levels) is, none the less, essentially the same. It is the process outlined in the first chapter of this book. To understand that process, however, one must understand how to deal with the problems encountered in applying the process in diverse situations and in maintaining the balance between the rigid discipline of planning and its flexible application.

CONCLUSION

The purpose of this chapter was to show how the planning process described earlier in this book can be applied in small companies, as well as in large companies.

When working with a small company situation, such as at MDI, the planning steps are the same as those for a large company. First, the planner organizes his time and decides on the procedures he will be using for planning. Second, he answers some very basic questions about his overall directions and the factors affecting major planning decisions. Third, using forms like those prepared by the Research Institute of America, he assembles the detailed information he needs to make specific implementation plans, makes (or coordinates the making of) these plans, reviews them in the light of key planning premises, and creates budgets. Fourth, he tests his plans for their return-on-investment potential and revises them where necessary. Last, he creates a formal comprehensive plan, into which he incorporates his strategic directions and the highlights of his implementation plans and budgets.

In this process the small company planner may bypass many of the steps the planner at a large corporation would go through. He may not have staffed a planning group, he may not have developed an elaborate policy framework, his plans may not cover as many functional areas, much less coordination is usually required, and the final document will be much less complex. In terms of complexity, therefore, the small company planner's job is closer to that of a middle manager in a large company. In terms of breadth, however, like the large company planning director, he looks at the company's entire operation, plans for every major area of operations, and covers all the steps in the overall business planning process.

In the discussion of how small business planning is carried out, this chapter has attempted to show the interrelation of each of the separate planning steps in an actual planning situation and how each step helps build a total company plan in both large and small companies. Because the small company planning executive, like all other planners, makes use of the same basic business planning process and techniques, this discussion serves as an integrating review of the business planning concepts presented throughout this book, for it has shown how all the various aspects of the planning process work together in creating effective business plans.

DISCUSSION QUESTIONS

1. Outline and discuss the approach to small business planning.
2. Compare how the basic business planning process is applied to a small company (such as MDI) and a large company (such as the oil company described in this chapter). What are the similarities in the two types of planning situations? What are the differences?
3. How would you see the forms given by the Research Institute of America in planning for Blakeston and Wilson Company (Appendix A)? For Superb Biscuits Company (Appendix B)?
4. Evaluate the model plan given for Magnetics Design, Inc. In what ways would you change it to improve it?
5. Develop a similar plan for the Blakeston and Wilson Company (Appendix A).
6. Develop a similar plan for the Superb Biscuits Company (Appendix B).
7. Can you think of any types of small companies to which the guidelines given in this chapter might not be applicable? How would the guidelines have to be modified or amplified to suit these situations?
8. How would these guidelines be modified and used by the manager of a small retail store?
9. Discuss the ways in which the guidelines given in this chapter could be made more realistic, practical and complete.
10. Why do you think that sales are not used as the sole criterion for judging the relative size of a company?
11. How "long" should long-term planning for a small company be? How "comprehensive" should it be?

CHAPTER 14

CONCLUSION

This chapter presents a summary of the business planning concepts discussed in this book, a brief review of other studies of business planning, and some comments on the continuing need for improved business planning practices in the future.

BUSINESS PLANNING: A SUMMARY

Business planning situations are diverse in nature. They vary according to the size and kind of company being planned for, the level of management doing the planning, and the kind of plans being developed.

The basic approach to business planning of all types is the same:

1. Plan and organize the planning effort.
2. Define planning premises.
3. Determine objectives and overall directions.
4. Develop policies and other overall guidelines for action.
5. Develop implementation plans and their budgets, including the sub-objectives, strategies, derivative policies, controls, systems and administrative guidelines needed to implement the plans, as well as plans for a suitable organization and staff.
6. Review and refine the plans periodically.

Because of the diversity of planning situations, putting the process to work is not a simple job—either at the corporate level or the middle management level.

In setting the stage for planning, it is necessary to determine the purpose of planning effort, the kind of plans being developed, the use to which the plans will be put, and how the planning effort is to be organized. At the corporate level in a large company, these questions are not easy to answer. Finding the right kind of man to head the planning effort, staffing the planning group, eliciting the cooperation of the operating managers, coordinating their efforts, and shaping the final comprehensive plan, are all challenging and difficult tasks which must be competently performed if the major roadblocks to planning are to be overcome and the planning effort is to succeed.

A plan must be based upon sound assumptions about the future. Before any parts of the plan are created, therefore, the key factors affecting the plan are studied and planning premises developed. The planner examines both the environment within which his business operates, and the resources he can marshall to operate successfully within the environment. In scanning the environment, the planner searches for factors pertinent to his company and his operation, isolates opportunities as well as potential problems, and wherever possible quantifies significant trends. In examining his company, he probes for both its strengths and weaknesses, and determines the resources of all types available to him and how these resources might best be put to work. He also studies the values of the owners and their personal objectives.

Within the framework of this background information, the planner evolves overall strategic directions for the operation being planned. These directions always include an objective. At the corporate level, the objective defines the kind of business the company wants to be in; at the lower levels of management, the objectives set more specific goals for the operation, which are designed to help the company reach its overall objective. The statement of overall directions should also include the company's philosophy, guiding principles of action, and strategy.

In the next phase of the planning process, the planner develops more specific guidelines for action, consistent with the overall directions spelled out in the prior phase. These guidelines are usually in the form of policies.

The most complex phase of the planning process is developing implementation plans. Each phase of a company's operation must be planned for. Each has its own specific planning premises. Each must have its own derivative objectives, strategies, policies, procedures, and rules. Each must spell out in detail the exact steps that must be taken to achieve department and overall corporate objectives. Each must be designed to overcome the special problems faced in the area being planned for. And each individual plan must be integrated within the overall company plan.

As part of the planning effort, the planner should prepare a budget—a quantification of his plan. The budget serves as a test of the plan's validity, a means of coordinating the planning effort, and a tool for measuring the success of the planning effort, and for reviewing and revising plans.

There are a number of tools useful in planning and control. These include systems theory, EDP, and numerous quantitative and graphic analysis techniques. The systems approach enables the manager to view the corporation as a unified business structure, which is linked very closely with its environment. The systems approach also provides him with a way of examining the firm as an interlocking network of decision makers, through whose interaction corporate plans are developed and action taken. EDP is a mechanism for speeding the transfer of information among the decision makers and for performing many of the laborious calculations needed in advanced planning. Quantitative tools include decision theory and probability statistics, linear programming, dynamic programming, queuing or waiting line theory, and game theory—all usually classified under the heading operations research. Graphic tools include PERT and CPM. All these tools are used to build models, which are in turn used to simulate future action and through this simulation help build better plans.

A number of approaches are used in organization planning: the traditional or classical, the systems and the behavioral. The final organizational plan will ultimately be a hybrid one, combining all three approaches.

The last part of the study dealt with the special problems encountered in planning for a small business.

The science of business planning will continue to grow, as new tools and techniques are developed and as practitioners and researchers refine the concepts and principles of business planning. None the less, a working science of business planning does exist now to guide the manager in his daily work. This book has attempted to introduce the reader to that science.

THE HISTORY OF THE STUDY OF BUSINESS PLANNING

The study of business planning has had a long history. For example, in 1916 in one of the earliest efforts to develop a science of management, Henri Fayol discussed the importance of planning to successful management and described the development of one-year and five-year budget plans. In his book he gives the following definition of business planning:

> The maxim "managing means looking ahead" gives some idea of the importance attached to planning in the business world, and it is true that if foresight is not the whole of management, at least it is an essential part of it. To foresee, in this context, means both to assess the future and make provision for it. . . . The plan of action is, at one and the same time, the result envisaged, the line of action to be followed, the stages to go through, and methods to use.[1]

Subsequent studies of general management written over the next 40 years echo Fayol's thinking, and reveal both a continuing interest in the subject and an ever-increasing awareness of the importance of planning

[1]Henri Fayol, *General and Industrial Management,* trans. Constance Storrs (New York: Pitman Publishing Corporation, 1949), p. 43.

to successful business management.[2] In their definitions of the planning process, the authors of these studies continue to stress two important aspects of planning: assessing the future and making plans to deal with that future. And like Fayol, they concentrate on operating planning for a corporation as a whole.

Although useful, these studies of business planning leave much to be desired. First, because they are brief, they do not cover the wide range of problems encountered by both individual managers and corporate planning departments in doing overall strategic planning, as well as day-to-day operating planning. Second, because they are part of books on general management, they fail to develop planning as a separate discipline, with its own set of guiding concepts and principles of action.

Prior to the publication of David Ewing's *Long-Range Planning for Management*[3] in 1958 very little effort had been made to study business planning as a separate discipline. Ewing thus broke new ground when he assembled the major articles written on planning up to that time. The articles in his book cover such areas as the nature and principles of planning, planning strategy, and the steps followed in making an overall corporate plan. The book was a milestone in the study of business planning, for it provided a single reference source for important articles on business planning that had been published in diverse periodicals, interrelated these articles, and gave focus and direction to subsequent studies on planning.

Early Studies of Planning Theory and Concept

Since 1960 the study of business planning has expanded rapidly. The earliest studies concentrated on exploring planning theory and developing a conceptual framework upon which a science of planning could be built. For example, in *Planning Theory*[4] (1961) Preston LeBreton and Dale Henning outline and discuss the theories underlying business planning and the planning process. The authors cover such topics as the importance of planning, the dimensions of a good plan, and the role of company per-

[2]The following are some of the better known studies to appear (or reappear) during the 1960's which contain extended discussions of business planning:

George R. Terry, *Principles of Management* (4th ed.; Homewood, Illinois: Richard D. Irwin, Inc., 1964), Chapter 10-14.

Harold Koontz and Cyril O'Donnell, *Principles of Management* (Fourth edition, New York: McGraw-Hill Book Company, Inc., 1968), Chapter 5-10.

William H. Newman, Charles E. Summer, and E. Kirby Warren, *The Process of Management: Concepts, Behaviour, and Practice* (2nd ed.,: Englewood Cliffs, New Jersey: Prentice-Hall, Inc., 1967), Chapters 13-22.

[3]David W. Ewing, ed., *Long-Range Planning for Management* (New York: Harper and Row, Publishers, 1958). A revised edition of this book was published in 1964.

[4]Preston R. LeBreton and Dale A. Henning, *Planning Theory* (Englewood Cliffs, New Jersey: Prentice-Hall, Inc., 1961).

sonnel in planning. In general, their stated purpose was to "build a superstructure for a theory of planning." In the closing chapters they discuss some practical aspects of planning, such as how all operating areas are a part of a company's planning network and how plans in each of these areas must be integrated in developing overall company plans. For the most part, however, because the book concerns the theoretical aspects of planning, the discussion is somewhat abstract. This work seems to be the earliest book-length study to attempt to develop a comprehensive outline of the science of business planning.

In *The Corporate Planning Process*[5] (1962) Melville Branch extends the study of business planning theory by exploring in more detail the complex activities involved in doing planning. For example, he goes more deeply than LeBreton and Henning into the problems involved in effectively setting objectives and goals, one of the main steps in strategic planning. In strategic corporate planning, objectives are not simple statements of targets the company wants to achieve. Rather, before final objectives can be established, the many factors affecting a company's future, as well as the available alternative directions, must be carefully analyzed.

Branch also goes more deeply into the problems encountered in administering a corporate planning department. For example, he devotes an entire chapter to the human factors affecting the coordination, integration and administration of the various planning activities within a company. He also discusses some of the new mathematical tools useful in planning and probes the difficult question "How do we measure the effectiveness of planning?" His book concludes with a discussion of the possible effects of EDP systems on corporate planning and the management characteristics and attitudes necessary for successful planning.[6]

Brian Scott's *Long-Range Planning in American Industry*[7] (1965) concentrates on strategic planning theory as applied to large companies. His discussion explores with even greater precision than Branch's the mental process involved in developing corporate objectives. In this regard his book is much like the current works on decision making, which go beyond giving a simple process outline and explore the dynamic nature of the process in action. Scott also examines more thoroughly than earlier writers the effect of company strengths and weaknesses and market and industry factors on the choice of corporate strategy. While the scope of his discussion

[5]Melville C. Branch, *The Corporate Planning Process* (New York: American Management Association, 1962).

[6]Ignacio Garcia Moreno's *Top Management Long-Range Planning* (New York: Vantage Press), which appeared in 1963, gives a general summary of corporate planning theory, but does not go deeply into the knotty problems involved in actually creating overall strategic company plans or coordinating the operating planning needed to implement them.

[7]Brian W. Scott, *Long-Range Planning in American Industry* (New York: American Management Association, 1965).

is more limited than Branch's, Scott's book is important because it presents an easy-to-read, comprehensive outline of strategic planning theory.[8]

Two other books written about the same time also contributed to the development of planning theory. In *Corporate Strategy*[9] (1965) H. Igor Ansoff studies management decision making at the highest corporate level. He views the development of overall company strategy as a key function of a company's top executives and discusses many important aspects of corporate strategy: what strategy is, the various kinds of strategy: what strategy is, the various kinds of strategy, how strategy is developed, the role of objectives in developing strategy, appraising alternative strategies, and uses to which strategies are put. Since corporate objectives and strategies are the foundations upon which all plans are built, Ansoff's book has a significant place in the history of planning studies. In the following year, in *Administrative Strategy and Decision Making*[10] (1966) C. T. Hardwick and B.F. Landuyt also treated this key area of business planning. In their discussion the authors explain what strategy is, how it is developed, and how diverse corporate objectives are reconciled.

The relationships between planning for business and planning in other areas of human activity were also studied during this period. Melville Branch's *Planning: Aspects and Applications*[11] (1966), for example, interrelates four types of planning: planning of physical projects, city planning, corporate planning, and military planning. Branch's book concludes with a summary of general theories and principles applicable to all types of planning.[12]

Studies of Company Planning Practices

At the same time that some writers were attempting to establish a conceptual basis for a science of planning, others were studying company plan-

[8]Franklyn H. Sweet, in *Strategic Planning . . . A Conceptual Study*, Research Monograph No. 26 (Austin, Texas: Bureau of Business Research, The University of Texas, 1964), develops a strategic planning model, which he tested in two case studies, one at a large company and one at a small company. Like most models, his is simply an outline of the process (or steps) followed. It is useful in that it attempts to go beyond generalities and graphically portray the nuances of the actual intellectual activity involved in strategic planning. In general, however, the book's coverage is much more limited than Branch's LeBreton and Henning's or Scott's.

[9]H. Igor Ansoff, *Corporate Strategy: An Analytic Approach to Business Policy for Growth and Expansion* (New York: McGraw-Hill Book Company, 1965).

[10]C. T. Hardwick and B. F. Landuyt, *Administrative Strategy and Decision Making* (2nd ed.; Cincinnati: Southwestern Publishing Company, 1966).

[11]Melville C. Branch, *Planning: Aspects and Applications* (New York: John Wiley and Sons, Inc., 1966). Neil W. Chamberlain's *Private and Public Planning* (New York: McGraw-Hill Book Company, 1965) also explores the relationship between government planning and short- and long-range corporate planning.

[12]In the same year, Branch also published a useful bibliography on planning. See: Melville C. Branch, *Selected References for Corporate Planning* (New York: American Management Association, 1966).

ning practices and the ways in which companies could more effectively apply planning theory in specific working situations—both at the operating level and at the overall corporate strategic planning level.

For example, in *Planning for Company Growth* (1963) Bruce Payne devotes most of his attention to the planning done in the major operating areas of a business, such as marketing, research and development, and manufacturing. This book is a brief, practical guide for business managers, which attempts to show how operating factors are explored in developing strategic plans and how operating plans are subsequently developed. The book is important because it explores the relation between overall strategic planning and the specific operating planning needed to implement overall strategic directions.

A number of studies have been done of planning at large, well-known United States and foreign companies. William T. Newell's *Long-Range Planning Policies and Practices: Selected Companies Operating in Texas*[14] (1963), for example, studies long-range planning at four companies: Aluminum Company of America, Texas Power and Light Company, Continental Oil Company and Texas Instruments Incorporated. His study covers the organization of the planning department, how a long-range plan is constructed, what it contains, and who develops it.[15] And in *Multinational Corporate Planning*[16] (1966) George Steiner and Warren Cannon bring together a collection of articles on the planning practices at various worldwide corporate enterprises. The articles show how these companies went about planning, compare the planning efforts of these companies, and describe the unique environmental factors affecting international planning.[17]

In *Customer-Oriented Planning*[18] (1964) Robert Ferrell studies the impact of marketing factors on corporate planning and the importance of a marketing orientation in doing strategic corporate planning. Like Fer-

[13]Bruce Payne, *Planning for Company Growth* (New York: McGraw-Hill Book Company, 1963).

[14]William T. Newell, *Long-Range Planning Policies and Practices: Selected Companies Operating in Texas* (Austin, Texas: Bureau of Business Research, The University of Texas, 1963).

[15]Stewart Thompson's *How Companies Plan*, AMA Research Study No. 54 (New York: American Management Association, 1963 also surveys the experiences of a number of companies in planning. His work concentrates on strategic planning for a company as a whole, including organizing a planning department, gathering and evaluating data for planning, and establishing overall strategy and objectives.

[16]George A. Steiner and Warren M. Cannon, eds., *Multinational Corporate Planning* (New York: The Macmillan Company, 1966).

[17]A series of papers on the actual experiences of such companies as Ford, Continental Oil Company and IBM in carrying out overall company strategic planning are given in George A. Steiner, ed., *Managerial Long-Range Planning* (New York: McGraw-Hill Book Company, 1963).

[18]Robert W. Ferrell, *Customer-Oriented Planning* (New York: American Management Association, 1964).

rell, Charles St. Thomas concentrates on the marketing aspects of business planning in his short "how to" book, *Practical Business Planning*[19] (1965). St. Thomas' book is clearly designed for busy executives, but in being brief it can deal only superficially with overall company strategic planning. And in its effort to be practical by focusing on marketing plans, it omits consideration of many other operating planning problems. Ferrell's and St. Thomas' books, however, make an important point: successful strategic and operating plans cannot be made without constant and careful consideration of the needs of the market and the customer.

In *Long-Range Planning Practices in 45 Industrial Companies* [20] (1967) Harold W. Henry gives the results of a survey of the formal long-range planning organizations and administrative procedures in 45 industrial companies. His book covers the different ways in which large companies organize their planning departments, how they formulate overall strategic directions, what is contained in their long-range plans, and how planning executives carry out their functions. Henry's study indicates that during the 1960's large companies were growing more interested in developing stronger planning organizations, and his book provides guidelines, based on actual experience, for organizing and carrying out planning functions in a large company.

As useful as these studies of company planning practices are, however, the reader should not always take them at face value. Since companies frequently are reluctant to talk about failures, these studies do not always give a realistic picture of what is involved in the struggle to create a planning operation. E. Kirby Warren's short book, *Long-Range Planning: The Executive Viewpoint*[21] (1966), for example, exposes the shortcomings of many of these case histories on planning by showing how few companies—even those whose advanced planning efforts have been written about—actually have adequate planning efforts and how enormously difficult it really is for a corporation to do planning effectively.

In *The Practice of Planning*[22] (1968) and *The Human Side of Planning*[23] (1969) David Ewing analyzes the various ways in which corporate managers develop strategic directions and explores an important, but often neglected, aspect of planning—the affect of human factors on the success of planning efforts. These books present specific, practical guidelines

[19]Charles E. St. Thomas, *Practical Business Planning* (New York: American Management Association, 1965).

[20]Harold W. Henry, *Long-Range Planning Practices in 45 Industrial Companies* (Englewood Cliffs, New Jersey: Prentice-Hall, Inc., 1967).

[21]E. Kirby Warren, *Long-Range Planning: The Executive Viewpoint* (Englewood Cliffs, New Jersey: Prentice-Hall, Inc., 1966).

[22]David W. Ewing, *The Practice of Planning* (New York: Harper and Row, Publishers, Inc., 1968).

[23]David W. Ewing, *The Human Side of Planning* (New York: The Macmillan Company, 1969).

for developing corporate strategy and for building human considerations into plans, thus enabling better implementation of plans.[24]

Recent Integrating Studies

Most of the books cited above are exploratory and developmental. While they are important to understanding the growth of planning theory and practice, they do not meet the needs of the business executive seeking a comprehensive, mature handbook of business planning.

In the late 1960's, a number of such handbooks appeared. These studies both integrated the previous work done on planning and added new dimensions to the study of business planning. They are indicative that planning was entering into a more mature phase during this period.

For example, in *Effective Long-Range Planning*[25] (1968) James R. Collier presents a comprehensive discussion of how a corporate planning director goes about his job. The book covers the strategic planning upon which all other company planning is based, the action plans designed to implement company strategy, the impact of financial considerations on strategic plans, and the problems encountered in administering a planning department. The author clearly distinguishes between the strategic phase of the job (establishing overall company planning premises, objectives, strategies and policies) and the implementation phase (developing and coordinating one- to five-year operating plans), and shows how both types of planning are integrated and carried out. Collier points out that strategic planning is a relatively new concept in business, and that business managers often have difficulty understanding and performing strategic planning, since they are accustomed to working only with one- to five-year action or implementation plans.

In 1968 Thomas Cannon analyzed strategic planning practices at major U.S. corporations in his *Business Strategy and Policy*.[26] Like other working corporate planners, such as Ferrell and St. Thomas, Cannon in essence equates strategic corporate planning with overall marketing planning, since in practice a corporate objective always contains a statement of the kind of products or services a company intends to offer. His discussion covers in detail the various kinds of marketing-related corporate strategies, such as product, market, geographic, and distribution-channel strategies, as well as the various phases of strategic planning.

[24]John Argenti's *Corporate Planning: A Practical Guide* (Homewood, Illinois: Dow Jones-Irwin, Inc.), which appeared in England in 1968 and was first published in this country in 1969, concentrates on the importance of strategic planning factors in constructing overall company financial plans. While the book covers corporate planning theory in general, its major focus is on how this theory is applied to financial planning in British companies and so is of limited value to American executives.

[25]James R. Collier, *Effective Long-Range Business Planning* (Englewood Cliffs, New Jersey: Prentice-Hall, Inc., 1968).

[26]J. Thomas Cannon, *Business Strategy and Policy* (New York: Harcourt, Brace and World., 1968).

George Steiner's *Top Management Planning*[27] (1969) is probably the the most complete study of corporate planning published to date. The book's 800 pages cover every aspect of planning—from overall long-term strategic planning, to short-term operational planning with such tools as PERT, to the coordination of operating plans and the development of corporate budgets. His book not only synthesizes previous planning studies by presenting a comprehensive outline of all facets of business planning. It also shows how modern mathematical, graphic, and systems tools are used in planning and summarizes the experiences of various companies who have successfully resolved the problems encountered in doing both strategic and implementation planning. Steiner's book gives an indication of the enormous complexities of business planning in action, and shows how far both planning theory and practice have progressed since 1961. While the book is very long and so not easy reading, it is indispensible to managers involved in company planning, for it is the most complete single source of information on business planning available today.

Russell Ackoff's *A Concept of Corporate Planning* (1970)[28] provides a stimulating introduction to corporate strategic planning. It is an easy-to-read, short review designed for more experienced managers who are familiar with planning practices. This book, while not a complete planning guide, is a good supplementary planning study.

Studies of Specialized Planning Areas

Overall policy development is one major aspect of strategic planning which has been studied extensively. In 1965, for example, in *Business Policies and Central Management*, William Newman and James Logan studied policy development within the context of overall corporate planning,[29] and in 1967 Alfred and Walter Gross put together a collection of readings[30] which attempts to show the development of corporate policies as part of the corporate planning process.[31]

[27]George A. Steiner, *Top Management Planning* (New York: The Macmillan Company, 1969).

[28]Russell L. Ackoff, *A Concept of Corporate Planning* (New York: John Wiley & Sons, Inc., 1970).

[29]William H. Newman and James P. Logan, *Business Policies and Central Management* (5th ed.; Cincinnati: Southwestern Publishing Company, 1965).

[30]Alfred Gross and Walter Gross, eds., *Business Policy: Selected Readings and Editorial Commentaries* (New York: The Ronald Press, 1967).

[31]The following four collections of case studies in policy development with editorial comments also appeared during this period:

Edmund P. Learned. *et al.*, *Business Policy: Text and Cases* (Homewood, Illinois: Richard D. Irwin, Inc., 1965).

Merwin M. Hargrove, Ike H. Harrison and Eugene L. Swearingen, eds., *Business Policy Cases with Behavioral Science Implications* (Rev. ed.; Homewood, Illinois: Richard D. Irwin, Inc., 1966).

Raymond J. Ziegler, *Business Policies and Decision Making* (New York: Appleton-Century-Crofts, 1966).

Thomas J. McNichols, *Policy Making and Executive Action: Cases on Business Policy* (3rd ed.; New York, McGraw-Hill Book Company, 1967).

M. Valliant Higginson's two volume study, *Management Policies*[32] (1966), is the most comprehensive study yet completed on the actual work done by corporations in developing policies. While the book concentrates on the steps followed in developing company policies, it also gives some consideration to the overall corporate planning framework within which policies are developed. The close links between policy development and planning are also emphasized in Edmund Gray's *Readings in Business Policy* (1969).[33] Although the book ostensibly concerns business policy, the majority of the articles are on planning, and the first third of the book covers material on the strategic planning base upon which policies are built.

These books on policy development are important because they pinpoint the precise place of policies in the planning process, and clear up some widespread misconceptions about policy development. For example, many executives think overall policies are the same as strategic objectives, while others think of policies as departmental guidelines only loosely integrated with overall company strategic planning. Neither of these two viewpoints is correct, for policies are extensions and amplifications of strategic objectives, which provide both overall corporate and departmental guidelines for action.

In addition to policy development, a number of other areas related to planning have been studied. These areas include the environmental factors affecting planning,[34] the relation of planning to control and organization development,[35] the strategic factors considered important in planning,[36] the use of systems analysis in planning,[37] and the special problems faced by small companies in doing planning.[38] This brief review does not cover all

[32]M. Valliant Higginson, *Management Policies, Vol. I: Their Development as Corporate Guides* and *Vol. II: Sourcebook of Statements*, AMA Research Studies Nos. 76 and 78 (New York: American Management Association, 1966).

[33]Edmund Gray, ed., *Readings in Business Policy* (New York: Appleton-Century-Crofts, 1969).

[34]Francis Joseph Aguilar, *Scanning the Business Environment* (New York: The Macmillan Company, 1967).

[35]Robert N. Anthony, *Planning and Control Systems: A Framework for Analysis* (Boston: Division of Research, Graduate School of Business Administration, Harvard University, 1965); and John C. Hutchinson, *Organizations: Theory and Classical Concepts* (New York: Holt, Rinehart and Winston, 1967).

[36]George A. Steiner, *Strategic Factors in Business Success* (New York: Financial Executives Research Foundation, 1969).

[37]Bernard H. Rudwick, *Systems Analysis for Effective Planning* (New York: John Wiley & Sons, Inc., 1969).

[38]George A. Steiner, "Approaches to Long-Range Planning for Small Business," *California Management Review*, Fall 1967, pp. 3-16; Roger A. Golde, "Practical Planning for Small business," *Harvard Business Review*, Sept.-Oct. 1964, pp. 147-161; *Planning for Future Company Growth: A Small Company Must*, Research Institute Staff Recommendations, File 32 (New York: The Research Institute of America, 1967); Delbert C. Hastings, *The Place of Forecasting in Basic Planning for Small Business* (Minneapolis: University of Minnesota Press, 1961).

the areas related to planning that have been studied, but it gives some idea of the ever-expanding scope of the study of planning in the late 1960's.

Other Areas of Study.

In addition to the books discussed above, there are a number of other sources of information on business planning. The American Management Association conducts an annual week-long seminar on long-range planning. The first day of the seminar covers basic planning principles. The remainder of the week is devoted to practical applications of planning theory in such areas as financial and marketing planning. The Institute of Management Sciences conducts similar seminars on long-range business planning.

In 1968 in England, the Society for Long-Range Planning introduced a new quarterly journal, *Long Range Planning,*[39] which contains articles on the planning experiences of both United States and foreign companies. A number of monographs and articles published during the 1960's also describe specific company planning experiences.[40] And Harvard Business School has begun a new program of research and instruction in formal planning systems, designed to develop new knowledge in the field and to show business executives how to put this knowledge to work promptly and effectively.[41]

The studies reviewed in this section are by no means the only work being done in developing the science of business planning. In businesses around the country (and the world) executives are daily working out practical approaches to planning which meet the particular needs of their companies. Much of this work, like similar work in the past, will be the basis of future studies on business planning. It is here that the dynamic development of business planning will occur, for it is only through the constant struggle of applying theory to practice and developing new theories from practice that a truly useful scientific discipline for business planning can be evolved.

THE FUTURE

The work done in the early 1960's in developing a science of planning was tentative and exploratory. On the one hand, men like LeBreton, Henning,

[39]Bernard Taylor, ed., *Long Range Planning,* quarterly Journal of the Society for Long Range Planning (Headington Hill Hall, Oxford, England: Permagon Press).

[40]For example: John T. Hickey, "Guidelines to Successful Future Planning," *Financial Executive,* November 1966, pp. 32-40; and Robert J. Mockler, *Circulation Planning and Development for The National Observer: A Research Study on Business Applications of Management Planning and Control Principles* (Atlanta, Georgia: Georgia State College, 1967).

[41]New Program on Formal Planning Systems," *Harvard Business School Bulletin,* July-August 1969, pp. 26-27.

Branch and Scott attempted to develop for the first time a systematic body of planning concepts and principles. On the other hand, many more authors and business executives focused on planning practices, testing the validity of planning theories in working situations and exploring what could be learned from studying how successful executives actually planned.

Out of this two-pronged effort, which covered both theory and practice, emerged the more mature, comprehensive studies of the late 1960's. In these later works by Steiner, Collier, and Cannon the business executive can find fairly comprehensive reviews of business planning theory and practice.

While much of the early work on planning now seems rudimentary and unsophisticated, this work was a necessary preliminary step if a science of business planning was to be developed. Gradually, as the decade progressed, the basic elements of the planning process were identified, distinctions and interrelationships were drawn among the various levels and kinds of planning done within a company, and guidelines were developed for organizing and carrying out the planning job.

In spite of the advances made in developing a science of planning, relatively few companies have developed effective planning operations—although many have tried. During the next decade attention will focus more and more on solving this problem. The solution will not necessarily be more planners and planning departments, or more expensive planning efforts, although this could help. Rather, it will come as management learns how to use present planning personnel and facilities more effectively.

A more precise definition of the role of planning departments and executives is needed and these departments and executives need to be given greater control over all major planning activities. For example, a planning department's primary function is to create a strategic plan and to coordinate operating plans within this strategic planning framework. George Steiner speculates that in the 1970's these two roles will be split into two separate planning departments, each with their own planning coordinator. Such a division is already taking place in several large companies, according to Steiner.[42] In addition the future corporate planning executive will do less actual planning & concentrate more on helping operating executives do better planning. As such, their role will be more one of staff advisor or coordinator.

Not only does the role of planning organizations need to be more clearly defined, but more and better-trained planning executives will be needed during the 1970's. Many schools, such as Harvard, are expanding their planning programs and many executives are gaining experience in planning, as more companies set up and maintain planning departments.

[42]George A. Steiner, "Rise of the Corporate Planner," *Harvard Business Review*, September-October 1970, pp. 133-139.

This growth in training facilities should help expand the available pool of planning managers and so provide the management resources needed to develop improved planning administration.

Another trend in the 1970's will be the greater use of computer systems in planning. For example, a large oil company has designed a computerized strategic planning model, which would enable testing and evaluating many more alternatives than is possible with manual methods. The major roadblock holding up the development and implementation of the system is money, for the cost of the manpower and computer time needed to create such a system using present programming techniques runs into hundreds of thousands of dollars. As more economical methods for using computers are developed in the 1970's, computer applications in planning will expand.

Much is known about planning, but not enough corporate managers understand how to carry out the specific planning steps and use sophisticated mathematical and computer tools in planning. As a result, they are not equipped to direct the money spent on planning into the most effective channels. At the same time, corporate managers frequently are unwilling to change existing organization structures and to give newly created planning areas the tools they need to get the job done. As a result, the planner often works in a vacuum, as a sounding board for corporate management's futuristic thinking, but isolated from the operating realities of the existing organization. Bolder and better-directed experiments with planning organization, administration, and use of new techniques are thus needed, if business planning is to become a truly useful management science. Because these are major problems and because business leaders are aware of them and anxious to solve them, these are the planning problems that are likely to receive the greatest attention in the 1970's.

APPENDIX A

BLAKESTON & WILSON COMPANY[1]

Blakeston & Wilson of Chicago, Illinois, was a manufacturer of medium-price, high-quality chocolate candy. Its chocolates, sold under the brand name Perfection, were distributed through company-controlled stores and by candy wholesalers (usually called jobbers in the candy trade).

The company was organized in 1938 when it purchased the assets of the brankrupt Sidwell Wilson Company. Mr. Wilson, who had been president of the defunct company, was instrumental in securing necessary capital and in organizing the new firm, of which he also became president. Whereas the original company had had an unsuccessful profit record, Blakeston & Wilson achieved immediate financial success. Profits were earned each year from 1938 through 1946. Mr. Wilson believed that the failure of his first company resulted from excessive sales costs; in turn, he believed that the success of the new company resulted from the fact that lower sales costs had been achieved. Profits for the first quarter of 1947 were the highest in the firm's history.

During 1947, Blakeston & Wilson planned to double the number of Perfection Chocolate Shops which marketed its candy. This expansion in retail store operations was the outgrowth of a policy adopted in 1943. Prior to that time, the company had sold its chocolates solely to wholesalers and large chain buyers. Mr. Wilson stated that his company had entered the retail sales field in 1943 to assure a stable, profitable postwar market for a part of his factory's manufacturing capacity. The opening of these Perfection Chocolate Shops was a real innovation in the company's distribution procedures; Blakeston & Wilson executive personnel had

[1]This case was prepared as the basis for discussion rather than to illustrate either effective or ineffective administration. Copyright 1947 © by the President and Fellows of Harvard College. Published in *Policy Formulation and Administration* by Smith, Christensen, and Berg (Homewood, Illinois: Richard D. Irwin, Inc., 1968). Used with permission.

The way in which this case is used in this text does not necessarily represent the way in which the case might be used by the Harvard Graduate School of Business Administration.

not had previous experience in retail store operation. Operating results from 1943 through April of 1947, however, had convinced Mr. Wilson of the success of the policy as well as of the wisdom of further retail store operation. Operating results from 1943 through April of 1947, however, had convinced Mr. Wilson of the success of the policy as well as of the wisdom of further retail sales expansion.

Predecessor Company

The Sidwell Wilson Company, incorporated in 1923, had sold packaged and bulk chocolates under several brand names. Sales volume had averaged $700,000 annually with selling expenses of approximately $100,000 (see Exhibit 1). The company had employed eight salesmen who, under the direction of Mr. Wilson, served wholesalers and buying syndicates in the Middle West and the East.

Stock ownership had been originally divided between Mr. Wilson (25%) and the majority stockholders (75%). By borrowing money from a company supplier, Mr. Wilson had purchased complete ownership of the company in 1926. Serious losses during the early 'thirties made repayment of the loan impossible and, in 1937 company assets were sold to satisfy creditor claims.

"The company failed," Mr. Wilson stated, "primarily because our selling expenses were too high. Moreover, we were selling to wholesalers who played one manufacturer against another to force prices down. We worked and sweated to make a few dollars manufacturing candy while the wholesalers and retailers took large margins for distributing and selling our products. Consequently, the consumer paid a high price for candy on which we did not make profits." The company had also been troubled by shortages in working capital. "We had just $3,000 plus equipment when we started in 1923, and when we did occasionally make money, the stockholders took it all out in dividends."

Formation of Blakeston & Wilson

After analyzing the difficulties which he had encountered in his first business, Mr. Wilson concluded that by reducing sales expense he could successfully compete in the candy business. To secure capital for his new enterprise, Mr. Wilson approached Mr. Blakeston, a director and operating executive of a large midwestern variety chain. Mr. Blakeston and three of his associates furnished the minimum amount required, $30,000. They received 500 shares of preferred stock; in addition, when all preferred stock had been retired from earnings, they were to be issued 48% of the company's authorized common stock. For services rendered, Mr. Wilson was then to receive 52% of the common stock.

By March of 1938, necessary machinery had been installed and production was initiated. Company offices, located in the factory building, were furnished simply; all administrative and overhead expense was kept to a minimum. The executive organization of the new company consisted of two men: Mr. Wilson, president and general manager, who was in charge of sales and promotion work, financial administration, and supervision of administrative personnel, and Mr. Herman Smith, production manager, who directed manufacturing, purchasing, and cost accounting work, in addition to performing some other miscellaneous duties.

Product

Blakeston & Wilson in 1947, manufactured quality boxed and bulk chocolates. The company's boxed chocolates were packed in attractive, but inexpensively designed, paper boxes. All Blakeston & Wilson candy was hand-dipped, a process normally used only for expensive packaged chocolates; medium-price and some expensive chocolates were usually dipped by machine. Hand-dipping was reputed to create thicker, creamier chocolate coatings over the candy center—qualities which the company believed were recognized and appreciated by consumers. Mr. Wilson stated that his chocolates (75 cents per pound) were equal in quality to those sold in the high-price range ($1.00–$2.50) and superior in quality to other medium-priced chocolates ($0.75–$1.00). "The difference in price between medium- and high-price chocolates lies primarily in expensive boxes and decorations and in large promotional expenditures, not in the quality of the candy," he stated.

Prior to World War II, the company had manufactured some standard hand-dipped chocolates for variety chains and grocery chains. Shortages of raw materials had forced the company to reduce sharply production for these outlets during the war years.

Original Sales Plan of Blakeston & Wilson

Blakeston & Wilson, until 1943, sold chocolate candy under a variety of brand names only to wholesalers and to two large chains. The company sold to 121 wholesalers in an area bounded by Madison, Wisconsin, Rock Island, Illinois, Louisville, Kentucky, and New York City. Wholesalers were given usual trade discounts (wholesale, 20%; retail, 33⅓%) and exclusive sales rights for a specificed area. A typical wholesaler's sales varied in volume from $4,000 to $25,000, with an average of $8,000. He, in turn, sold to outlets such as drug and department stores, clubs, and grocery stores. Wholesalers did not carry other brands of chocolates in a competitive price range. They did, however, carry both lower-price and higher-price chocolates.

"My theory was that there were more people who would buy our product because of its quality value than there were people who would have to be coaxed into buying it by expensive sales efforts," said Mr. Wilson. In carrying out his policy to cut sales expenses, Mr. Wilson personally handled all sales work; he had no salesmen or sales representatives. Mr. Wilson periodically visited wholesalers and syndicate buyers, determined credit policies, supervised sales accounting work, selected candy items, and designed candy packages. "My selling costs for the wholesale and syndicate trade vary between 1.5% to 2% of gross sales," Mr. Wilson stated, "whereas usually costs in the industry for selling to that trade amount to 6%." He attributed the industry's high selling costs to its use of numerous salesmen, expensive missionary sales work, and high promotional expense. "We do very little promotional work for our wholesalers, and the wholesalers do not do any promotional work on our candy. They have recognized our effort to shave expenses and therefore place the best box of candy in the consumer's hands at the lowest price." Company sales promotional material initially consisted of circulars describing candy manufacturing processes and counter display cards. "The quality of our candy will sell these chocolates without sales promotion," Mr. Wilson emphasized.

Mr. Wilson had personally selected his wholesalers when the new company was first organized. Thereafter, he visited each distributor approximately three times a year. These visits were informal and frequently amounted to a game of golf with the executives of the concern. Mr. Wilson knew each executive personally, and all business relations were on a first name basis. During World War II, his visits to company wholesalers became more infrequent, since selling at that time consisted of allocating scarce supplies of candy among these firms.

In 1947, commenting on the excellence of his original wholesaler selection, Mr. Wilson noted, "We haven't gained or lost a new account in over nine years." Shortages of candy as well as a heavy personal workload had prevented Mr. Wilson from returning to his prewar schedule of visits to wholesalers.

Entrance into Retail Sales Operations

During the depression years of the early 'thirties, the candy industry had been described as "sick"; its chief symptom was overcapacity with its attendant pains of price cutting, secret rebates, and overextension of credit. Since the incorporation of Blakeston & Wilson in 1938, however, candy production—as well as the price per pound received by the manufacturer—had increased substantially (see Exhibit 2). Company sales, following the general industry pattern, increased from $286,000 in 1938 to $909,000 in 1942. Though wartime sugar rationing had hampered production, this difficulty had been partially eliminated through the increased use of nonrationed substitute materials. Moreover, manufacturers of medium- and high-priced packaged chocolates had benefited greatly from the sharply increased national income. Consumers were willing to buy these more expensive candies, on which the manufacturer realized excellent margins, instead of cheaper bulk candy formerly purchased in variety stores.

Mr. Wilson, despite his firm's prosperity, was apprehensive over future prospects for sales to the wholesaler trade. On the basis of the experience with his former company, he believed that competition would first appear and be most severe on sales made to wholesaler organizations. Manufacturers selling through wholesalers, Mr. Wilson stated, could never be certain how much they could sell, and they had little control over prices received for their products. Mr. Wilson believed that a market for at least a part of his productive output could be secured at a controlled price by opening company-operated candy stores. He was not sure of making profits in these stores. "If we could just break even on store operations, our profits would come from manufacturing the candy."

Mr. Wilson, although he had worked in the candy industry since 1909, had not had any experience in retail sales work or in retail store management. He therefore discussed his idea for retail candy stores with his board, company bankers, and associates in the industry; they were unanimous in their disapproval of his plan. Despite these objections, Mr. Wilson announced that he planned to open a retail store, if necessary by supplying funds from his personal resources. The board of directors, after this statement, reluctantly approved the new policy.

Perfection Candy Stores, Inc., was organized to finance operations of the new retail store; the necessary capital was subscribed by Mr. Blakeston and his associates. They received the preferred stock of the new corporation plus 48% of its common stock. Mr. Wilson received the remaining 52% of the common stock for "services rendered." The 6% cumulative preferred stock did not have voting power unless three consecutive annual dividend payments were passed. The new corporation had the same management and board of directors as did Blakeston & Wilson; it was a separate corporate entity only for tax purposes and as a method of limiting the financial liability of Blakeston & Wilson.

The first Perfection Chocolate Shop was opened in Chicago in the fall of 1943. At that time all former brand names of the company, with the exception of those used for the syndicate trade, were abandoned, and the name "Perfection" was adopted for chocolates sold to the company store and to the wholesale trade.

Operation of Retail Stores

Success in the operation of the first Perfection shop led to further expansion during 1946. Between January and August of that year, five additional Perfection shops were opened in the business section of Chicago. Each new shop was organized, financed, and individually incorporated as was done in the case of the original store.

Perfection Chocolate Shops were located in sections of Chicago where pedestrian traffic passing each store was heavy, as well as where the possibilities that passers-by would purchase candy were high, i.e., near hotels, department store shopping areas, and financial districts. Shops featured Perfection packaged chocolates in ½-pound, 1-pound, and 2-pound boxes in addition to Perfection bulk chocolates; they sold only Blakeston & Wilson products and did not handle accessory lines such as nuts and noveleties. Most chocolates were 75 cents a pound or $1.45 for a two-pound box. A few specially packed boxes of chocolates retailed at higher prices—$1.25 to $1.50 a pound.

Each shop had a manager and, usually, four clerks. These were all girls and they were selected with regard to their appearance, character, and education. Starting weekly wages were $30, which were advanced to $35 after three months' service; competing firms started their sales girls at $22 a week. Managers were paid between $40 and $50 a week. In addition, both clerks and managers were paid a bonus if each girl sold over $480 of candy per week; clerks averaged between $2 and $14 per week in bonuses. Managers were eligible for an additional supervisors' bonus.

Mr. Wilson believed that any Perfection Chocolate Shop was in a strong competitive position because (1) it sold high-quality, reasonably priced candy, (2) all stores were efficiently operated, and (3) each store had a large sales volume.

Perfection chocolates were superior in quality to other medium-price chocolates. They were five cents less per pound, however, than chocolates sold by the leading competitor of Perfection Candy Shops—a seminational chain of retail candy stores. Savings resulting from reduced retail selling costs and efficient manufacturing operations were passed on to the customer through the use of highest quality candy ingredients, Mr. Wilson stated.

Perfection Candy Shops were operated more efficiently than competitive shops, Mr. Wilson said, because of several unique operating features which he had developed. He had designed all Perfection shops with a small display window in which several boxes of candy were high-lighted. Traditionally, retail candy stores had large display windows which, he believed, took several hundred dollars of display stock as well as many hours of time for decoration. Furthermore, Perfection bulk chocolates were packed in specially designed five-pound boxes at the factory; these boxes fit into display cases in the retail stores without rehandling. Competitive stores, said Mr. Wilson, packed their candies in stock boxes at the factory and the candy had to be repacked for store display. Moreover, he continued, through the operation of the bonus payment plan for store clerks, there was an incentive upon their part to keep store personnel at a minimum—the fewer clerks in a store, the higher the individual bonus payments to each girl.

He believed that Perfection sales volume per store (1947) was substantially higher than the sales volume of competitive candy outlets.

Mr. Wilson originally (1943 through August of 1946) personally directed all retail store operations. He visited each store daily to check on operations and to assure himself that everything was being handled satisfactorily. He hired all store personnel, supervised advertising and promotion campaigns, and determined details of operating procedures. Daily reports of cash and sales as well as a weekly report of inventory constituted his formal check on store operations. "It worked out beautifully," said Mr. Wilson. The primary management difficulty during this period was to find sufficient supplies of candy to meet the accelerated wartime demand for quality products.

To secure critically short materials, such as butter, sugar, and chocolate, which were necessary for the manufacture of Perfection chocolates for his retail trade,[2] Mr. Wilson reduced production of all low-margin chocolates sold to chain buyers; this sharply diminished sales to those two customers. Sales to wholesalers were maintained at varying percentages of their 1941 purchases. These material sources were not sufficient, however, to fill the retail store demand for Perfection chocolates, and a wartime customer ration of one pound per day was instituted. In April, 1947, the improved materials situation permitted the removal of this wartime customer ration in all shops.

Retail Management Corporation

To relieve a heavy personal workload, as well as to prepare for intensive postwar competition, Mr. Wilson organized the Retail Management Corporation; that company was to supervise the operations of all Perfection Chocolate Shops. "My usual business day was 15 hours long," he stated. "With conditions in the industry returning to normal I knew that more intensive management efforts were going to be required. I did not have the time to supervise retail store operations in addition to my regular work." Retail Management Corporation was incorporated on August 1, 1946; it was organized and financed in the same manner employed in the incorporation of Perfection shops. Mr. Wilson, as president of Retail Management Corporation, made all major decisions for the new concern.

[2]Sugar rationing for candy manufacturers was first set at 70% of the 1941 base use period; this quota was increased to 80% in July, 1942. The highest level of ration was reached from August, 1943, to December, 1944, when the sugar ration was 80% of the 1941 base, plus a 10% bonus. The lowest ration level was 50% for the last six months of 1945. In 1947 the ration was 75%, but was expected to end in October.

Exhibit 3 shows the intercorporate relationships among Blakeston & Wilson, Retail Management Corporation, and the several Perfection Chocolate Shop companies.

Mr. Wilson appointed his son Kenneth as manager of the new company. Kenneth upon graduation from college in 1937, had been employed by the Sidwell Wilson Company as a salesman. He was assigned to develop wholesale business in the Michigan area. After a six months' trial period, this attempt had been abandoned as unprofitable. Kenneth later worked in the leather industry until his induction into the army. He returned to work for his father in November of 1945. At that time Mr. Wilson planned to have his son handle sales to wholesalers in the Middle Atlantic states. "Sugar rationing continued during 1946, however, and selling to wholesalers was still primarily a matter of ordertaking," said Mr. Wilson, "so we placed Kenneth in charge of the Retail Management Corporation." Kenneth's experience with retail sales and with the candy industry was limited to his earlier work with his father. "I wanted to give my son a chance at the business. He doesn't know much about it, but the way I look at it, I would have to teach either a stranger or my son. I might as well gamble on my son."

The staff of Retail Management Corporation consisted of four persons in addition to Kenneth Wilson. A supervisor of stores inspected (weekly) the appearance of store property, displays, and personnel and filled out an inspection report which noted the results of his investigation; this report was given to the store manager with a duplicate copy forwarded to Kenneth Wilson. To correct any inadequacies noted on the inspection report, each manager checked her Perfection Operating Manual. This manual, written by Sidwell Wilson, outlined in detail approved operating procedures to be used in his retail stores. He believed that, through the use of this manual, store operations and activities were so systematized that necessary supervision was limited to an occasional check by the supervisor of stores, Kenneth Wilson, or himself. Sidwell Wilson's daughter, Thelma, was director of merchandising and purchasing. She determined inventory requirements for the shops and purchased supplies of chocolates from Blakeston & Wilson. A commercial artist developed display and counter card promotional material; radio and newspaper advertisements were prepared by a Chicago advertising agency. A bookkeeper kept necessary accounting records. Neither of the Wilson children had had previous experience in retail sales work.

Retail Management Corporation, in supervising the management of all Perfection Chocolate Shops, hired personnel, inspected the appearance of stores and store personnel, kept necessary accounting records, purchased candy and supplies, and furnished necessary financial service and advice. It received 10% of the gross sales of all Perfection shops as a management fee. Retail Management agreed to spend at least one-half of this sum for advertising purposes, the exact amount to be determined by Blakeston & Wilson.

The number of Perfection Chocolate Shops supervised by Retail Management increased from 6 to 17 between August, 1946, and April, 1947. Store sales averaged $90,000 per unit. Store rentals ranged from $5,000 to $20,000 a year, with an average payment of $8,000. Overhead costs were approximately 3% of gross store sales. Invested capital, per store, varied from $10,000 to $15,000. All shops were successful financially.

Eight of the eleven new shops had been established in towns within a 200-mile radius of Chicago, e.g., Gary, Indiana, and Peoria, Illinois. Perfection shops in all eight non-Chicago cities, came into competition with retail outlets such as drug and department stores which also sold Perfection packaged chocolates distributed by company wholesalers. This created a great deal of resentment on the part of the wholesalers who felt their market was being usurped.

Price

Perfection chocolates had originally retailed at 65 cents a pound; by 1946, as had been previously stated, the retail price had been increased to 75 cents a pound or $1.45 for the two-pound box. Retail prices were the same at both Perfection Chocolate Shops and retail stores supplied by company wholesalers. In 1947, Blakeston & Wilson sold Perfection chocolates to its wholesalers at 40 cents a pound and to Perfection shops at 42 cents a pound.

Manufacturing costs had increased 17 cents per pound between 1943 and 1946. Furthermore, prices of chocolate and other raw materials had continued to increase during the first quarter of 1947, and the possible removal of sugar rationing in October of 1947 was expected to raise the price of that important commodity.

Despite rising material costs, retail price reductions were already appearing among some brands of packaged chocolates. One leading chain competitor of Perfection had reduced the price of its two-pound box of candy from $1.55 to $1.50 in March of 1947. Mr. Sidwell Wilson did not plan to reduce the retail price of his candy to meet this competitive development. Any price reduction, he believed, would first have to be made to the wholesaler trade since he was well acquainted with the extremely competitive aspects of wholesaling.

When material prices returned to normal, Blakeston & Wilson planned to use any savings resulting from lowered costs to improve the quality of Perfection chocolates. "Our chocolates, which we sold for 65 cents a pound in 1943, were of better quality than chocolates which we now sell for 75 cents a pound," Mr. Wilson stated. The company had been forced to reduce product quality, as had its competitors, to take care of increased raw material prices.

Advertising

"We spent over $100,000 in 1946 advertising Perfection chocolates, said Mr. Wilson. Two-thirds of this money was expended for radio advertisements, the remaining one-third for newspaper advertisements. Blakeston & Wilson financed but a small part of the Perfection advertising fund; most of the money had been supplied by the Retail Management Corporation with assistance from individual Perfection stores. Radio and newspaper advertisements were concentrated in the Chicago area and in cities where Perfection shops were located. These advertisements stressed the quality of Perfection chocolates but did not mention that Perfection candies were hand-dipped; this was in conformity with industry advertising practices. By mutual agreement candy manufacturers did not advertise whether their chocolates were hand-dipped or machine-dipped.

Advertising expenditures for Perfection chocolates, among packaged and bulk chocolate manufacturers, were second only to those of the Stephen F. Whitman & Son Company in Philadelphia. That company manufactured nationally advertised and distributed Sampler chocolates which retailed at $1.75 for a 20-ounce package. Mr. Sidwell Wilson said that expenditures for advertising in 1947 would be substantially higher than 1946 totals.

Manufacturing

The Blakeston & Wilson factory originally occupied the first three floors of a warehouse; the company had recently expanded into two floors of an adjoining building. Manufacturing operations and storage facilities were located on each floor so that raw materials would be in close proximity to the production activities in which they were used. All manufacturing departments were air conditioned, and the plant was equipped with cold storage facilities capable of holding 300,000 pounds of finished candy. Candy-making machinery was old but in good repair. In 1947 the plant was producing approximately 22,000 pounds of candy per day, five days a week. Capacity plant production was 30,000 pounds per day.

Mr. Sidwell Wilson believed that company manufacturing operations were efficient because: (1) he personally owned and operated his business, which gave him a close check on all operations; (2) he had invented a continuous process production line which enabled him to hand-dip chocolates at a lower cost than other competitve hand-dip chocolate manufacturers; and (3) his labor force was more efficient and effective than employee groups in other companies.

Mr. Wilson did not believe that any company could secure a significant advantage over its competitors as far as raw materials purchasing was concerned. Sugar and chocolate prices, he said, were normally set by the New York City and foreign exchanges, and the price for a specified type of product was identical to all large-scale purchasers. Sugar, the primary ingredient of candy, was purchased by most companies on a day-to-day basis. "The only way normally to secure bargain sugar prices would be to gamble on futures—we tried that once and lost." Manufacturers of medium-priced candies, however, could and did make some savings on minor items by using substitute or average quality fruit centers, cream, and butter. Perfection chocolates, contrary to this practice, were always made from the highest grade ingredients obtainable.

Mr. Smith, production manager, was assisted in factory supervision by four foremen and two floor ladies. He believed this number was the minimum staff required. In fact, when one of these assistants was ill, Mr. Smith had to take over temporarily his or her duties. He received two weekly production reports, which were also available for Mr. Wilson's use. They listed production by department, the number of manufacturing employees and total hours worked, and indirect factory expenses. He believed, however, that his most effective control technique was close personal supervision over factory operations. Mr. Smith was completely responsible for all manufacturing activities; Mr. Wilson did not concern himself with production problems unless some major change in policy was contemplated.

Hand-dipped chocolates were more expensive to produce than machine-dipped candies primarily because of substantially increased labor costs. Mr. Smith estimated that machine-dipping resulted in savings of from four to five cents a pound in labor and material costs over Blakeston & Wilson's hand-dipping process. "We can afford to hand-dip our chocolates only because of the savings effected by our low sales cost."

Mr. Sidwell Wilson, in 1937, had developed and patented his continuous production line process for dipping, cooling, and packing varied selections of chocolates. This process, he believed, enabled Blakeston & Wilson to hand-dip chocolates for three cents less per pound than competing hand-dip chocolate manufacturers. He had installed four of these units in his factory in 1938 at a cost of $4,000 per unit. In 1947 two units were operating at capacity (7,500 pounds per unit a day); the other two units because of material shortages, were operating at partial capacity. Mr. Wilson had attempted to sell the process to other manufacturers for $100,000 per unit, but only one sale had been made to a small Evanston, Illinois, chocolate manufacturer.

The company's labor force was composed of 200 employees, most of whom were women engaged in dipping and packing chocolates. Labor and management relations were excellent; the company had never been organized. Wages equalled those of competing firms in the Chicago area; in addition to their base pay, all employees who had been with the company more than five years (96) participated in a profit-sharing plan which company officials believed stimulated employee interest and productive efficiency.

Wages of employees had risen steadily since 1938. At that time dippers were paid 30 cents an hour; in 1947 they started at 87 cents on hour. In addition to base pay, dippers were eligible for a bonus of from one to nine cents an hour if they approached or reached the maximum production rate (24 pieces a minute); in 1947 most dippers were earning the maximum bonus. Mr. Smith awarded the bonus to dippers by occasionally checking production operations. "The bonus is based on my judgment as to how well they are doing," he said, "not on time or motion studies." The bonus system, which had been in effect for four years, had not been extended to other employees.

Mr. Smith personally handled the limited amount of cost accounting work done on all manufacturing operations. He had established standard costs on materials and direct labor for producing one hundred pound lots of each type of candy included in the Perfection selection. Standards for burden had not been established, he said, since these charges were fairly constant from year to year. Standard costs were occasionally checked against actual costs when Mr. Smith believed this necessary. Though many of the company's standard cost sheets were obsolete because of changes in materials prices, Mr. Smith did not believe revisions were necessary so long as the company secured a 28% gross manufacturing operating profit (exclusive of burden charges). Exhibit 4 lists standard cost information on a typical chocolate item manufactured both for bulk and package sale.

Chain Store Customers

By April, 1947, increased sales of bulk and packaged chocolates were again being made to the variety chain with which Mr. Blakeston was associated. Mr. Wilson had not re-established sales relations with the retail grocery chain to which he had sold chocolates prior to World War II. That company was building its own large candy factory and was installing candy departments in all its retail outlets. "We don't want to sell to any customer who is in competition with us in the manufacture of candy," Mr. Wilson declared. He had not yet attempted to secure another large grocery chain outlet since a shortage of raw materials still hampered production. Such an outlet would be necessary during normal times, he felt, to insure his plant of capacity operations during the entire year.

Control

In conformity with Mr. Wilson's desire to keep administrative expenses to a minimum, only a few reports were prepared for his use. He received a monthly balance sheet and profit and loss statement from all corporations as well as daily reports on Blakeston & Wilson production and sales made by individual Perfection Chocolate Shops.

Mr. Sidwell Wilson, in addition to the investigations made by Retail Management Corporation, inspected several Perfection shops on one day each week. "As far as store operations are concerned, our best indicator of trouble is when customers begin to complain—then we start action," he said.

Mr. Sidwell Wilson personally checked wholesaler relations on his visits to those concerns. "That gives me all the control I need over those operations. I believe this system will be effective as long as I am personally running the business; it may not prove effective under other operating conditions." He further believed that the widespread advertising campaign for Perfection chocolates would provide an incentive both for his wholesalers to continue to carry the line and for the retailers supplied by these firms to hold to the advertised price.

Executive Organization

The executive organization of Blakeston & Wilson in April, 1947, was substantially the same as in 1938. An assistant treasurer had been engaged in 1946 to take charge of all detailed accounting work with the exception of cost accounting records. Mr. Sidwell Wilson, 56 years of age, was still actively engaged in all company operations. "I can do anything from firing a boiler to selling packaged chocolates," he stated. He personally approved all major policy and operating decisions made for Blakeston & Wilson, Retail Management Corporation, or any of the 17 Perfection Chocolate Shop corporations.

At quarterly meetings of the board of directors, Mr. Wilson discussed general company problems with the board. All Perfection Chocolate Shops were operating at a profit, and Mr. Blakeston and his associates were convinced that the decision to enter the retail sales field had been a wise one. All Blakeston & Wilson preferred stock had been retired by this time, and Mr. Wilson owned 52% of the outstanding common stock.

Mr. Smith, 45 years of age, had been an accounting instructor before becoming associated with the company. The office staff of the company, excluding secretarial help, consisted of three women who handled all sales and production records as well as payroll accounts. "Other companies of comparable size have large administrative organizations—up to 25 persons. By keeping a small stable customer list and using a minimum of expensive records, our administrative section can be kept to a minimum size," said Mr. Smith.

Expansion

Mr. Wilson was planning to expand his chain of retail shops. Four additional store leases had been signed, and before the end of 1947 the company planned to operate between 25 and 30 shops. "If I were a younger man, we would open 500." He believed that Perfection shops should expand immediately: (1) to get as many consumers as possible familiar with Perfection chocolates and (2) to become established in the retail candy business during 1947, a time when raw material shortages prevented other companies from entering this field. In 1947 about one-third of Blakeston & Wilson production was being sold through company-controlled stores, and Mr. Wilson wanted to increase substantially that amount.

Among the potential sites for new Perfection shops were Cleveland and Detroit. Retail candy shops, both locally owned and chain stores, were already in operation in these towns. Previous expansion had placed Perfection shops in direct competition with a seminational chain of retail candy stores. That company, incorporated in 1919, operated several hundred stores in the Middle West and along the East Coast which sold medium-price hand-dipped chocolates and salted nuts. Mr. Wilson believed that that company's sales volume averaged only $50,000 per store. "We know how to sell in volume at low costs."

Competition for Perfection chocolates sold by company wholesalers came from hundreds of locally and regionally promoted packaged chocolates as well as from several brands of nationally distributed candies.

Mr. Wilson estimated that the productive capacity of the candy industry had expanded by 30% since 1939. Industry sales in 1939 were approximately $308 million; in 1944 they were $658 million and in 1945 they were $620 million. During this period plain candies had increased 30% in volume whereas packaged candies, primarily boxed chocolates, had risen 310%. As of 1947, numerous companies were planning or were already in the process of plant expansion; for example, the Kraft Cheese Company, which had entered the caramel business before the war, planned erection of a $750,000 candy plant in Kendallville, Indiana. An interesting development was the rapid rise in chain grocery store candy sales. As one writer put it (in 1946) "Grocery stores now sell a larger volume of candy than of coffee or butter."

In Exhibits 5 and 6 are shown the income and balance sheet data of Blakeston & Wilson for the years 1938–1946 inclusive. In Exhibit 7 are shown the combined balance sheet data of the Perfection Chocolate Shops for the year 1946.

Exhibit 1

PREDECESSOR COMPANY—SIDWELL WILSON COMPANY

Profit and Loss Statement for the Year Ending December 31, 1935

		Percentage of Net Sales
Net sales	$623,069.97	
Less: Cost of Sales	520,616.71	83.56%
Gross profit	$102,453.26	16.44
Less: Selling, general, and administrative expenses		
Freight and cartage outward	$ 22,618.72	3.63
Shipping wages and supplies	10,505.42	1.69
Advertising	4,373.97	0.70
Selling expenses	40,536.91	6.50
Administrative expenses	19,740.40	3.17
Miscellaneous expenses	9,015.74	1.45
Total expenses	$106,791.16	17.14
Net loss for period	$ 4,337.90	0.70

Source: Company Records

Exhibit 2

AVERAGE WHOLESALE VALUE PER POUND OF CONFECTIONERY SOLD BY MANUFACTURER-WHOLESALERS AND MANUFACTURER-RETAILERS, 1925-1945

	Manufacturer-Wholesalers		Manufacturer-Retailers	
Year	Number of Firms	Average Value Per Pound	Number of Firms	Average Value Per Pound
1925	386	$0.229	96	$0.392
1926	386	0.226	96	0.396
1927	369	0.222	113	0.348
1928	381	0.224	118	0.319
1929	394	0.210	123	0.335
1930	405	0.196	113	0.386
1931	404	0.174	114	0.366
1932	337	0.136	81	0.340
1933	301	0.131	44	0.376
1934	354	0.137	44	0.387
1935	308	0.142	48	0.385
1936	308	0.143	40	0.420
1937	265	0.153	33	0.451
1938	265	0.144	33	0.453
1939	244	0.143	29	0.449
1940	244	0.144	29	0.436
1941	224	0.153	24	0.468
1942	235	0.188	29	0.489
1943	258	0.218	26	0.414
1944	258	0.232	40	0.490
1945	353	0.244	51	

*In 1945 total sales of candy were candy bars 55%, package candy (primarily boxed chocolates) 20%, bulk candy 15%, and specialty candies 10%.

Source: Department of Commerce, 19th Annual Report on Confectionery Sales and Distributions, 1946, p. 23.

Exhibit 3

BLAKESTON & WILSON

Intercorporation Relationships

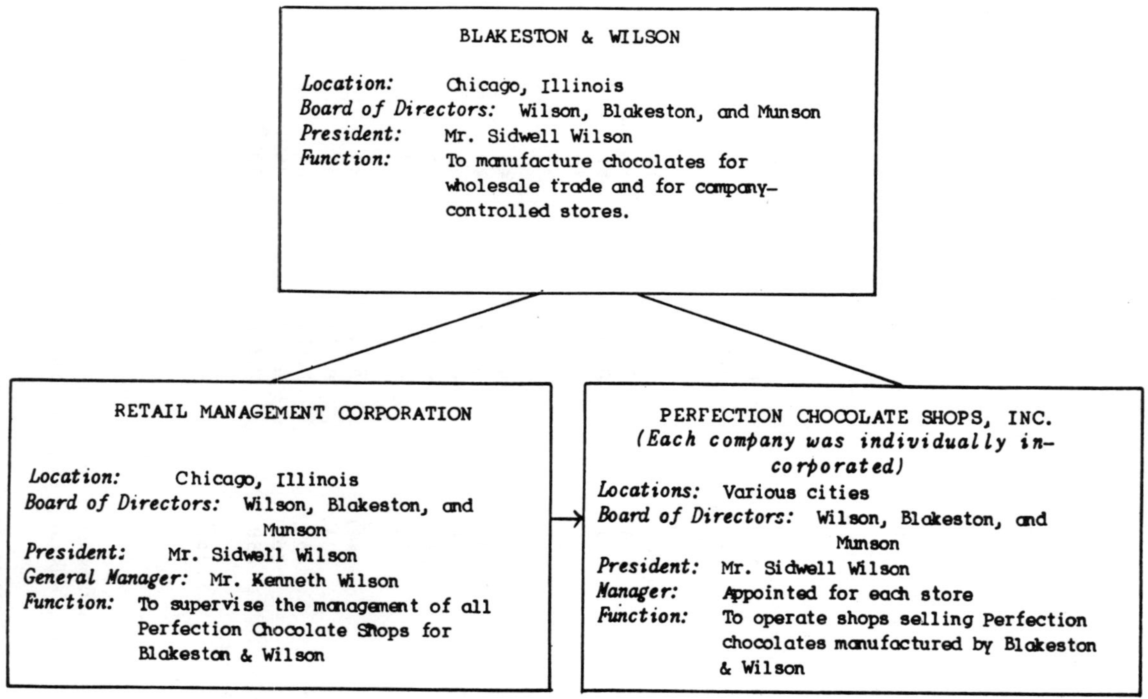

Note: Stock ownership of all companies was held by Mr. Wilson, Mr. Blakeston, and Mr. Blakeston's associates. Over-all management of all companies was handled by Mr. Sidwell Wilson.

Exhibit 4

BLAKESTON & WILSON

Standard Costs for 100-Pound Mix of Chocolate-Covered Cream Candy

Materials	$26.97
Direct Labor	7.65
	$34.62

Source: Company records.

Exhibit 5
BLAKESTON & WILSON
Income Statements—1938 through 1946
(in thousands)

	1938	1939	1940	1941	1942	1943	1944	1945	1946
Net sales	$286	$562	$668	$799	$909	$1,160	$1,239	$1,110	$1,349
% of sales	100.0%	100.0%	100.0%	100.0%	100.0%	100.0%	100.0%	100.0%	100.0%
Cost of sales	231	470	561	663	762	877	906	867	1,041
% of sales	80.8%	83.6%	84.0%	83.0%	83.8%	75.6%	73.1%	78.1%	77.2%
Gross profit on sales	$ 55	$ 92	$107	$136	$147	$ 283	$ 333	$ 243	$ 308
% of sales	19.2%	16.4%	16.0%	17.0%	16.2%	24.4%	26.9%	21.9%	22.8%
Selling, general and administrative expenses:									
Shipping	$ 13	$ 33	$ 44	$ 45	$ 37	$ 40	$ 44	$ 40	$ 44
% of sales	4.6%	5.9%	6.7%	5.6%	4.1%	3.5%	3.5%	3.7%	3.3%
Advertising, travel, entertainment, commissions, and other selling expenses	6	11	13	20	11	17	21	34	23
% of sales	2.1%	2.0%	1.9%	2.5%	1.2%	1.5%	1.7%	3.0%	1.7%
Executive and office salaries	12	18	19	26	40	40	40	45	50
% of sales	4.2%	3.2%	2.8%	3.2%	4.5%	3.3%	3.3%	4.0%	3.7%
Contributions to profit-sharing plan							19	21	27
% of sales							1.5%	1.9%	2.0%
Miscellaneous	6	5	11	16	16	23	25	25	30
% of sales	2.0%	0.9%	1.6%	2.1%	1.7%	2.0%	2.0%	2.3%	2.2%
Total expenses	$ 37	$ 67	$ 87	$107	$104	$ 120	$ 149	$ 165	$ 174
% of sales	12.9%	12.0%	13.0%	13.4%	11.5%	10.3%	12.0%	14.9%	12.9%
Net profit before federal taxes on income	$ 18	$ 25	$ 20	$ 29	$ 43	$ 163	$ 184	$ 78	$ 134
% of sales	6.3%	4.4%	3.0%	3.6%	4.7%	14.1%	14.9%	7.0%	9.9%
Provision for estimated federal taxes on income and excess profits	$ 3	$ 4	$ 3	$ 8	$ 18	$ 131	$ 150	$ 50	$ 60
% of sales	1.0%	0.7%	0.4%	1.0%	2.0%	11.3%	12.1%	4.5%	4.4%
Net profit carried to surplus	$ 15	$ 21	$ 17	$ 21	$ 25	$ 32	$ 34	$ 28	$ 74
% of sales	5.3%	3.7%	2.6%	2.6%	2.7%	2.8%	2.8%	2.5%	5.5%

Note: Totals, from 1943 through 1946, include sales made by Blakeston & Wilson to company-controlled Perfection shops.

Source: Company records

Exhibit 6

BLAKESTON & WILSON

Balance Sheets—1938 through 1946

(in thousands)

ASSETS	*1938*	*1939*	*1940*	*1941*	*1942*	*1943*	*1944*	*1945*	*1946*
Current Assets:									
Cash in Bank and on Hand	$ 11	$ 10	$ 13	$ 8	$ 32	$161	$202	$134	$227
Accounts Receivable	21	24	33	26	54	73	60	61	26
Inventories at Cost or Market, Whichever is Lower	9	21	24	90	44	36	56	62	118
Total Current Assets	$ 41	$ 55	$ 70	$124	$130	$270	$318	$257	$371
Cash Surrender Value of Life Insurance Policy	1	2	8	9	9	10	11	16	17
Together	$ 42	$ 57	$ 78	$133	$139	$280	$329	$273	$388
Postwar Refundable Portion of Estimated Excess Profits Tax						12	26		
Fixed Assets	13	39	45	45	38	34	38	33	39
Deferred Charges	8	13	19	11	10	9	17	17	14
TOTAL ASSETS	$ 63	$109	$142	$189	$187	$335	$410	$323	$441
LIABILITIES AND CAPITAL									
Current Liabilities:									
Note Payable at Bank			$ 7	$ 37	$ 7	$ 7	$ 6		
Accounts Payable and Accrued Expenses	$ 15	$ 19	31	25	20	29	67	$ 41	$58
Reserve for Federal and State Taxes	3	5	5	10	21	139	200	133	160
Total Current Liabilities	$ 18	$ 24	$ 43	$ 72	$ 48	$175	$273	$174	$218
Postwar Refund of Estimated Federal Excess Profits Tax						$ 12	$ 26		
Capital Stock:									
Preferred Stock:									
Authorized and Issued – 500 Shares of $6 Cumulative Without Par Value	$ 30*	$ 50	$ 50	$ 50	$ 50	$ 50	$ 50	$ 50	$ 50
Less: Held in Treasury						18	50	50	50
Common Stock:									
Authorized, Issued, and Outstanding 1,040 Shares Without Par Value							104**	104	104
Total Capital Stock	$ 30	$ 50	$ 50	$ 50	$ 50	$ 32	$104	$104	$104
Earned Surplus:									
Balance, January 1		$ 15	$ 35	$ 49	$ 67	$ 89	$116	$ 7	$ 45
Add: Net Profit	$ 15	21	17	21	25	32	34	28	74
Postwar Refund of Excess Profits Taxes								26#	
Less: Dividends Paid		1	2	3	3	3	39	16	
Amount Transferred to Capital Stock Account							104#		
Under Accrual of Prior Years' Taxes, etc.			1						
Balance, December 31	$ 15	$ 35	$ 49	$ 67	$ 89	$116	$ 7	$ 45	$119
TOTAL LIABILITIES AND CAPITAL	$ 63	$ 109	$142	$189	$187	$335	$410	$323	$441

*300 shares of preferred issued and outstanding December 31, 1938

**Stated value of $100 per share of common voted by board of directors

#Treated as deferred income in prior years, transferred to earned surplus December 31, 1945

Source: Company records

Exhibit 7

BLAKESTON & WILSON

Balance Sheet as of December 31, 1946
Perfection Chocolate Shops (Combined)
(in thousands)

ASSETS		
Current Assets:		
Cash		$130
Inventories (at cost)		18
Total Current Assets		$148
Fixed Assets		41
Deferred Charges:		
Improvement to Leased Premises	$56	
Unexpired Insurance Premiums	7	
Total Deferred Charges		63
TOTAL ASSETS		$252
LIABILITIES AND CAPITAL		
Current Liabilities:		
Accounts Payable		$ 32
Reserve for State and Federal Taxes		52
Total Current Liabilities		$ 84
Capital Stock and Surplus		
Capital Stock:		
Preferred	$47	
Common	19	66
Earned Surplus:		
Balance, December 31, 1945	$20	
Net Profit, 1946	113	
	$133	
Less: Dividends Paid	31	
Balance, December 31, 1946		102
TOTAL LIABILITIES AND CAPITAL		$252

Source: Company records

APPENDIX B

SUPERB BISCUITS COMPANY[1]

Crackers and cookies bearing the Superb name appeared on the shelves of about 80% of all retail food stores in the four-state area of Illinois, Michigan, Indiana, and Ohio. Superb Biscuits, Inc., of Chicago produced and distributed a wide line ranging from simple, square salt crackers to filled chocolate-coated cookies sold in foil-wrapped assortments. More than 80 different items and package sizes were available, and company sales reached $7.6 million in 1956. (For financial statements, see Exhibits 1 and 2.)

Competitive Situation

Superb encountered competition of two types. Most important were the "Big Three"—National Biscuit Company, Sunshine Biscuits, Inc., and United Biscuit Company, with combined sales of almost $700 million in 1956 (see Exhibits 3 and 4). According to Superb's estimates, National Biscuit reached 90% of all outlets and had about 40% of the market, while Sunshine sold to about 70% of the outlets and held about 25% of the market. Superb was believed to run a good third in its own territory, with about 22% of total sales.

Competition also came from about six medium-size or small companies, either local or regional in character, operating in part or all of Superb's territory. Several dozen such firms were scattered throughout the United States.

Product lines of the big companies were essentially the same as Superb's, although they put more emphasis on crackers and on offering a wider variety of items. The smaller companies generally specialized in high-priced fancy cookies, custom recipes, or accessories like ice cream cones.

In contrast to Superb and most other smaller companies, the three large firms were to some extent both horizontally and vertically integrated. Together

[1]This case was prepared as the basis for discussion rather than to illustrate either effective or ineffective administration. Copyright 1957 by the President and Fellows of Harvard College. Published in *Problems of General Management* by Learned, Christensen, and Andrews (Homewood, Illinois: Richard D. Irwin, Inc., 1961). Used with permission.

they had acquired almost 50 small baking or supply companies during the last 30 years, which were either operated as divisions, or supplied large portions of the parent companies' flour and packaging requirements. Furthermore, two of the large firms had divisions making bread, fresh cakes, cake mixes, dried fruits, potato chips, or similar foods.

Most crackers and a few sheet cookies were standardized high-volume products that carried a low margin and required large-scale automatic production to return a profit to the producer. Most sweet cookies, on the other hand, were specialized products or assortments commanding better prices at lower volumes. Their manufacture called for special machinery or hand operations, while shorter runs necessitated frequent changeovers, especially in single-plant companies. An industry spokesman indicated that the large companies favored the high-volume items that were better suited to their automatic production lines.

There was little differentiation among the high-volume products offered by various makers, except for package design. Significant price differences appeared only during special promotions. Specialties, on the other hand, were claimed to be new and different. Superb officials said new products had to be introduced periodically in order to "show new faces in the market." The large companies were active in this respect, and one of them was reported to have introduced about 10 new items over a six-month period. If a new product proved highly successful, however, competitors would probably develop similar items, and it would eventually become standard for the industry. Round cocktail crackers and fig bars, for example, had started out as specialties of two companies. On the other hand, according to Superb officials, many specialties showed a tendency to be "fads" that "went flat" after 90 days or so.

It was customary among the large- and medium-size companies, including Superb, to employ a sales force charged with order-taking in the food stores, and with arranging fresh stock on the shelves or in special displays featuring price reductions or new products. In most stores the salesmen checked stocks and replenished merchandise entirely on their own responsibility. In these cases they had developed a relationship with the store managers, who trusted them to keep the right amounts of saleable products on hand. The men also exchanged stale, unsalable packages, and rotated the stocks according to age-dates on the cartons.

These services were considered important to keep the good will of the store and its customers. Industry spokesmen indicated that volume in a given store depended a great deal on the personality and aggressiveness of the biscuit salesman, and they considered it unlikely that independent brokers or jobbers would give similar attention to service. Supermarkets and larger stores generally assigned fixed shelf space to each of the important firms in the area, and rotated special promotion privileges among them. Nevertheless, the relationship of the salesman to the store personnel influenced any preferential treatment the company might receive.

Two of the Big Three carried on national advertising programs, using magazines, radio and television. Smaller companies had to rely more heavily on advertising allowances to retailers, store promotions, and limited local radio, television, and billboard displays. Expenditures proportional to those of the large competitors were considered by Superb officials to be less than proportionately effective.

History and Organization

Superb Biscuits, Inc., was founded at the turn of the century; it thrived for 25 years, expanding its product line through new items. The depression, however, hit the company hard, and after experiencing severe losses Superb changed hands in 1936. The new majority stockholder was Earl T. Kingsbury, father of the current president, Richard F. Kingsbury. Although the plant was equipped with modern machinery, the previous management had allowed the quality of the product to slide when reverses set in, and Earl Kingsbury was faced with the task of upgrading standards and recovering the acceptance of Superb biscuits in the trade. He believed that poor sales service and lack of freshness-control had created considerable ill will.

Bringing with him a number of new executives, Earl Kingsbury attempted to reorient the company to his philosophy of giving high quality for the lowest possible price. Working against heavy financial odds, he effected changes in the production and sales departments, and sales and profits increased. Mr. Kingsbury was characterized by company officials as a shrewd financial operator whose frugality and determination were the main driving forces behind Superb's recovery. They said he had assumed close personal direction of the business and continually made decisions on both details and policy. His door was always open to subordinates, with whom his contacts were many and varied. Many who had worked under Mr. Kingsbury spoke of him as "wonderful" and "smart." When his health deteriorated seriously in 1954, Mr. Kingsbury was forced to resign all duties, and his son Richard, then 26, was elected president. Richard Kingsbury had served under his father for two years in production and traffic.

The company was organized into four departments—sales, production, finance, and legal and personnel. Each was headed by a vice president (see Exhibit 5). The president met monthly with this group of officers. The board of directors consisted of the president and four members representing some 300 stockholders; the Kingsbury family held a majority of the shares. These board members were the company's banker, an investment broker, and vice presidents of two suppliers. Meetings were held regularly every month, usually after the officers' meeting, and the board maintained a close interest in operating results and major capital expenditures.

Sales and Promotion

The company's sales organization, under James V. Cannon, vice president, aimed at three different markets. The first was composed of food stores in the company's four-state home territory. These were called on by 110 salesmen supervised by 10 district managers. Deliveries were made by company trucks, either from the plant or from eight scattered warehouses. William R. Stewart, territorial sales manager, personally administered the large chain store accounts where formal authorization by central buying offices was required for sale of products in the stores. This market accounted for about 60% of sales.

The second market, accounting for about 15% to 20% of Superb's volume, was outside the home territory in scattered centers of population like Milwaukee,

Kansas City, and even Washington, D.C. Five company salesmen, working directly under Mr. Cannon, called on the 10 independent distributors who served these areas.

The third market consisted of various private and governmental institutions to which several types of biscuits were supplied on a contract basis. Competition was keen in this field, and bids were negotiated individually. While the first two markets showed only moderate seasonal fluctuations, the third required its heaviest volume during the first four months of the year. Institutional sales were managed by Robert Decker, who had 21 years of service with Superb.

Mr. Cannon had joined the company in 1936 after spending 14 years in the sales department of Scott Paper Company. A relative of Earl Kingsbury, he started as a Superb route salesman and rose to his present position after serving as district manager and territorial sales manager for a number of years.

Mr. Cannon commented that he believed one of the company's bigger problems was the high cost of distribution for the home territory. "Bill Stewart and I wonder about the merits of the present system, which is the most expensive form of selling," he said. He indicated that costs in the home territory totalled about 35% of sales in 1956. This figure included sales salaries and commissions, trade discounts, advertising, delivery, and sales administration expenses, all allocated on the basis of dollar volume. In the large cities outside the territory, where limited advertising was carried on, total costs averaged about 31.5% of sales, while sales costs on institutional business averaged about 20% of net sales. Mr. Cannon said that while institutional accounts were the most desirable in terms of selling costs, their seasonal character and competitive nature prevented the company from taking on a higher volume. In general, Mr. Cannon foresaw even higher selling costs for all types of accounts. He mentioned, for example, that drivers' wages were bounding upward along with rail rates.

In the home territory, company salesmen averaged about 175 accounts each, on which they called weekly. It was estimated that one-fourth of these stores purchased as little as $5 to $10 per month. On an average, it required at least one hour per month to service even the smallest account. Salesmen received a base salary of about $300 per month, plus graduated percentage bonuses for sales in excess of the quotas set with their cooperation by Mr. Stewart. Salesmen generally exceeded their base quotas, and yearly contests were held for the best salesman. The men kept detailed records of calls made, new accounts opened, and sales volume by accounts. From this information, weekly summaries were prepared for the district managers and the home office. All salesmen worked from route books and timetables prepared by the district managers. Turnover among salesmen was low, according to Mr. Stewart.

The president commented that he felt the need for increased volume on present routes. He believed that his big competitors had an advantage in terms of selling costs. He estimated that their volume per salesman was from one and one-half to two times that of Superb, owing to larger territories or wider product lines. Furthermore, he estimated that Superb's delivery costs per sales dollar ran about 20% higher than competitors' costs, and sales administration about 10% higher. Advertising and promotional costs he considered about equal precentage-wise (see Table 1 below).

Table 1

SUPERB BISCUITS, INC.

Comparative Breakdown of Sales Dollar
Superb vs. Large Companies (Estimates)

	Superb	Estimate for Biscuit Operations of Large Competitors
Gross sales	110.0%	110.0%
Trade commissions	8.0	8.0
Returned merchandise	2.0	2.0
	10.0	10.0
Net sales	100.0%	100.0%
Raw materials and supplies	52.8	50.0*
Direct labor	9.3	9.5
Manufacturing overhead	6.5	7.5
	68.6	67.0
Gross margin	31.4	33.0
Selling expense:		
Advertising and promotion	2.8	3.0
Sales salaries and commissions	5.8	4.6
Other	1.1	.8
	9.7	8.4
Delivery, warehousing	3.3	2.3
Freight	5.1	4.5
General and administrative	10.7	11.2
Interest	.1	..1
	19.2	18.1
Total expenses	28.9	26.5
Net income (before taxes)	2.5	6.5
Federal income taxes	1.2	3.2
Net income	1.3%	3.3%

*Lower because of vertical integration.

Source: Company records and estimates of company officers.

Mr. Cannon was weighing the pros and cons of changing from direct selling in the home territory to independent distributors, as used in the extra-territorial market. These middlemen, located in the large cities, generally received a flat 25% discount off list price. Mr. Cannon stated that they had been very successful in selling Superb products and he was considering adding several more to the present 10 to enlarge the field. He stated that selling through these channels was "hard selling" but "good selling," explaining that distributors generally asked for "special deals" in terms of price concessions or free goods (e.g., one carton free for every dozen), but at the same time they assumed all risks and the company was not forced to stand behind them with a guarantee to take back unsalable stock. "Selling direct through salesmen is almost like selling on consignment," he said, "while distributors have no recourse. But then, distributors take on only 'good sellers'—which in a way is an advantage. Why clutter a store with slow-selling items?" Mr. Cannon stated that the company's rate of returned goods was not quite 2% of net sales. He added that selling through distributors required strong men "able to say no" to the many demands for special favors. Furthermore, he said, the company would be subject to greater price pressures, since distributors generally carried more than one brand of biscuits and would tend to push the brand most profitable to them.

Another change weighed by Mr. Cannon was modification of salesmen's compensation. He said, "We are considering the possibility of putting our men on straight commission, which would also cover their expenses. At the moment we have two or three of our district managers stewing over the problem. If they think it is a good idea, we shall tell the other managers, and in turn have them sell it to the salesmen."

Mr. Kingsbury thought the company might well be forced to change its distribution system in the long run. He stated that National Biscuit and some small firms had experimented with a split arrangement, putting salaried men in charge of large chain accounts, while paying the salesmen who covered independent stores on straight commission. "Under such a system," he said, "We would be better set for the eventual transition in food marketing to complete predominance of the large supermarket."

Mr. Kingsbury visualized, as a long-term possibility, the institution of direct delivery of biscuits to chain warehouses, elminating the individual store deliveries made at present. The few remaining small independent stores would be served by driver-salesmen carrying the necessary stocks in their trucks. This would reduce the number of men required to one-third or less, he said.

Mr. Cannon indicated that the company's resources were insufficient for the extensive market research carried on by its large competitors. The company used an outside firm to supply monthly reports on relative market shares. "Everyone is in research," he said, "but when you are small you must sell hard instead, get more outlets, and keep them well stocked." He said that Superb had to rely on its sales force to bring back information about competitive developments. The district managers held regular monthly meetings with their men, and occasionally all salesmen and sales personnel were brought together to discuss advertising or promotional problems. During 1956 there had been four such meetings, a considerable increase over the previous years.

New product and promotional ideas at times greatly stimulated sales according to Mr. Cannon. For example, during 1955 Superb had introduced three products aimed at different nationality groups, using authentic recipes; sales had jumped as much as 35% to 50% in outlying centers of population where these groups were heavily represented. Mr. Cannon believed that such specialties helped to promote regular sales by making the Superb name better known. Promotional ideas of the present year included handing out sample cookies, with an advertising message attached, in the elementary schools of Kansas City. The expense of the samples was borne by the distributor. "We must make little things pay," commented Mr. Cannon, and stated that he was glad the company had begun moving toward such new product ideas and promotions.

Advertising had undergone changes and was still being modified. Before 1936 the company had spent up to 10% of net sales on advertising, especially when sales began to slip. Earl Kingsbury had drastically cut expenditures to an average of $100,000 to $115,000 per year, including cooperative advertising for the home territory which amounted to about 40% of the total. In the recent past, most of the budget was spent on billboards (35%) and on some radio spots (25%). Magazine advertising was negligible. In 1956 the company initiated spots on local television and signed up for another billboard campaign (30% of budget) during the summer. Furthermore, the advertising agency was asked to come up with a suitable slogan tying the product line to reasons for consumer preference for Superb biscuits. The 1957 advertising budget was set at almost $250,000, an increase of about 24% over past years.

Richard Kingsbury believed that during his father's management the lines of authority in the sales department had become blurred because district managers were allowed to carry their problems directly to the president. "This custom resulted in nobody knowing who was to tell what to whom," he said, adding that it was not until five years ago that the sales vice president had begun to spend most of his time in the central office. Prior to that time he had been mainly occupied with extraterritorial sales. Mr. Kingsbury commented that, except for approving the size of the advertising budget, he made it a point not to interfere in the sales department. He wanted to foster the rebuilding of authority for the department head. He believed that morale and turn-over among sales personnel had improved greatly in the last five years, especially because there were no longer numerous hirings and firings.

Production

Increased efficiency and better mechanization were the main problems that concerned the vice president of production, Alfred Kingsbury, an uncle of Richard Kingsbury. He believed that it was vital for the company to increase production without increasing labor costs. "We have not been able to pass on increased costs to the consumer—competitors have not been able to do this either. Automation is the ultimate answer, and we are compelled to go into it, but in the intermediate period we must buy better and produce better. If I could schedule longer runs, for instance, I could double our tonnage output, but our sales force needs variety," he said.

Alfred Kingsbury was made a vice president when Earl Kingsbury took over the company. He had been a sales representative with another biscuit company and had run food stores before that. Reporting to him were Stephen R. Miller, plant superintendent, and William T. Pugh, head of scheduling. Mr. Miller, a chemist and former head of the laboratory, was placed in his present position early in 1956 by Richard Kingsbury, who explained that he had fired two men formerly serving as joint superintendents because they were unwilling to delegate authority and accept new ideas. Mr. Miller, aged 30, was in charge of production, efficiency control, the laboratory, and maintenance. Mr. Pugh, a man of 18 years' experience in the biscuit industry, was in charge of scheduling, hiring of production workers, and related personnel services.

The plant, together with the offices, was located in a four-story building in a suburban area and was served by a spur track of the Rock Island Railroad. The ground floor was used for warehousing and shipping, while the second and third floors contained offices and manufacturing area. The fourth floor was rented to another firm. Major items of equipment were four 200-foot continuous band ovens, a battery of dough mixers that handled about 400,000 pounds of flour and shortening per week, several kneading machines, packaging lines serving the ovens, and three icing, sandwiching, and coating lines. Most of the equipment had been of very advanced design at the time of installation and had been kept in good condition, according to Mr. Kingsbury. Several conveyor arrangements allowed continuous product-flow.

Production operations were divided into four sections, mixing, baking, icing, and packing. The plant worked in two shifts and the work force totalled close to 400 men and women. Labor relations were peaceful and all workers were unionized. Both Mr. Kingsbury and Mr. Miller indicated that they made sure to consult with union representatives before making any change in operations that affected the workers, and they thought this policy was one of the foundations of labor peace. "We have to build the strength of the union for our own good," said Mr. Miller, who indicated that union stewards attended the montly meetings of foremen and production management.

Mr. Miller was considered by Alfred Kingsbury to be aggressive, smart, and progressing well in his new job. Mr. Miller said he made it a point to rebuild authority of his foremen who had been undermined by his predecessors. He indicated that he allowed them more freedom to make operating decisions and required workers to see their foremen first before bringing complaints to him. At the same time he was concerned with quality and efficiency. "Every Friday I get together with my foremen and discuss what we mean by quality—I prefer to call it constancy—and analyze systematically how to do better in it. I also look for savings; just recently we cut expenses $400 per month by using paper towels instead of cloth to clean machinery." To avoid costly stoppages of the continuous production lines, Mr. Miller insisted on extensive preventive maintenance.

Mr. Miller shared the president's concern about introducing better machinery, and kept a file of new developments. He had joined Richard Kingsbury on an extended trip to machinery suppliers in the United States and Europe, and had assisted in selecting several new packaging machines.

Scheduling was described as complicated owing to the large variety of products offered. Both Alfred Kingsbury and Mr. Pugh spent most of their time working out the daily and weekly programs for the four sections. A minimum run of two hours was required for any one product, and the problem was to dove-tail inventories and current requirements of the eight warehouses and the extra-territorial markets.

New product development had historically been concentrated in the production area, where one specialist was spending his full time on trying out new recipes. Several years ago a committee had been formed which consisted of Messrs. Alfred Kingsbury, Cannon, Perry (vice president and treasurer), Stewart, as well as the new products specialist, and the company's part-time art director. According to the president, the committee produced little and met very infrequently until about a year ago when it was realized that more new products were needed. Since that time six new items had been developed and approved, and the committee now met three times per month. Of the six items which had been introduced through in-store promotions, only two showed continued success, two were "slowly dying," after a three-month life, while two never "went off the ground," he said. One of the successful items was a medium-priced assortment, while the other was a new form of cookie. Mr. Kingsbury believed that there were "too many thumbs" in the new product field and said that he was still looking for the best possible method of "hatching ideas" and accelerating their utilization. He said the majority of new ideas actually came from jobbers and distributors, while a few original ideas had emerged from production personnel. "There are not too many ideas that are completely new in this field," he said, and told of an instance where a new cookie had been developed by mistake when a worker used the "wrong" spices.

Alfred Kingsbury stated that new products had to meet high turnover requirements in addition to being different. "In the recent past all biscuit companies have lost five to ten items each due to stores wanting products with faster turnover. More and more items are competing for the available shelf space in a market." He believed that the industry would have to stimulate the basic demand for biscuits if it wanted to grow further.

Finance and Control

Donald T. Perry, vice president and treasurer, had spent his entire career in varying positions in the biscuit industry. Previously plant manager for a medium-size biscuit manufacturer, he had joined Superb as assistant to the president in 1936, and was appointed vice president soon thereafter.

Mr. Perry was in charge of finance and purchasing. The general office manager, Mr. Banister, supervised the office and accounting staffs. The company employed a product-cost system that traced labor and materials costs for each product, based on the daily runs through the four production departments. At least four times per year the average costs for each product were compiled and compared to current sales prices, and the gross margin was determined to see whether the product was profitable. Costs, except labor costs, were not recorded by department, but were allocated on the basis of weight of the finished product. Other data collected included average weight of output, barrels produced per hour, percentage yield from raw materials, and cost of finishes. Small variations in coatings, for instance, could prove very costly, according to Mr. Perry. Richard Kingsbury indicated that he favored several changes in the accounting area, particularly an attempt to establish basic standards of out-put on which to base a "more realistic" allocation of burden. He also wanted a more detailed breakdown of departmental expenses and reorganization of the company's monthly financial reports.

Inventories were taken weekly in each warehouse, and the central office maintained close control over the ordering procedures which were based on four-week moving averages. Owing to the semiperishable nature of the products, no more than one week's inventory of finished goods was kept on hand. Similarly, raw materials were kept down to four weeks' supply at the most. The company's spoilage experience was less than 1/4 of 1% of sales, according to Mr. Perry.

The treasurer considered his most serious problem to be "how to balance the budget." He worried over increased costs due to a rise from wage negotiations which were to start in the spring of 1957. Costs of raw materials and freight showed an upward trend. "There is no end to increases," he said, "and the Middle East troubles have sent commodities way up." He said that the biscuit industry had made general price advances in early 1957, but that this had been just enough to offset some of the cost increases in 1956, leaving no room for the expected 1957 rise. "Price advances are generally made uniformly by the whole industry with the large companies taking the lead," he said, "and only occasional reductions on single products are made individually."

Mr. Perry believed that the company was too small to do any hedging in the commodity markets, which he considered a special field in itself, not even tackled by the large companies. Superb generally bought flour requirements for about 120 days ahead, under standard millers' contracts, and once in a while ventured to buy six months' supplies. The latter action involved a risk of paying storage charges to millers should the company be unable to take delivery within the stated period; thus the advantage of lower prices might be eliminated. The purchasing agent, Mr. Sanders, who had 35 years' experience in procurement, believed that Superb paid essentially the same prices for its raw materials as the large competitors, owing to the fact that the large companies generally bought on the plant level rather than centrally.

Quarterly budgets were tentatively prepared, focused mainly on the cash flow required to meet seasonal swings. The president commented that since about one year formal budgeting procedures had "all but gone out the window," because of the difficulties of forecasting demand and costs.

Every year, to meet seasonal needs, Mr. Perry borrowed several hundred thousand dollars in short-term funds on a line of credit. Superb was still saddled with arrears of $71,000 on its preferred stock, but the president hoped to be able to pay this off within the next year and then start paying dividends on the common.

Proposals made by the production department or the president for expenditures on new machinery were analyzed by Mr. Perry. On the basis of his calculations, Mr. Richard Kingsbury decided on the merits of the purchase and defended it before the board, which passed on every expenditure over $2,000. The board gave its approval on almost all projects presented by him, he said. Richard Kingsbury spent most of his time on finding new ways to mechanize the processes of manufacture.

In the past, many special machines had been developed and built by Superb, but this had become increasingly difficult in recent years, said Mr. Perry. In the early years, Earl Kingsbury had economized greatly and held back on capital expenditures where possible. Up to 1956 Superb had relied solely on internally generated funds for capital outlays and had not considered outside money. The president now felt it was high time the company started looking for long-term loans to finance more machinery.

Mr. Perry also assisted in setting product prices based on cost data, but he said the company had little leeway in pricing standard products where prices tended to be industry-wide. "We must find more specialties on which we can put a price tag of our own," said Mr. Perry, "but still most of the volume is done with a limited number of standard varieties that you must have in order to be competitive. If we withdrew these low-margin products, the customer in the store might not pick up the specialty items either, and our display space would be cut. Moreover, our factory would have greatly reduced volume which would shift burden costs onto other products."

Personnel and Legal

Frank J. Newman, vice president and secretary, was in charge of the legal affairs of the company and also directed personnel policies. He hired all personnel except production workers. A lawyer by training, Mr. Newman left private practice in 1936 to join Earl Kingsbury first as counsel, later as secretary and clerk; he was made vice president in 1954. Mr. Newman obtained leases for district warehouses, appraised distributors' contracts, and gave advice on provisions of the Pure Food and Drug Act. Furthermore, he negotiated union contracts with the teamster and bakery worker locals.

Mr. Newman also prepared the agenda for officers', directors' and stockholders' meetings. He said that about a year ago the officers' meetings had "petered out" and Richard Kingsbury had temporarily stopped them altogether. About six months later they were resumed and had been kept up regularly to date. Mr. Newman said that in these meetings the officers considered "matters of overall policy," which included items like group insurance coverage, the problems of uniform package design, and the volume of institutional sales desirable.

Traffic

Superb maintained a shipping and receiving department under Mr. Thomas McNamara, who had spent 20 years with the Great Northern Railroad before joining the company in 1936. Mr. McNamara supervised the compilation of truck and rail loads of finished products and determined the best possible routing. He worked closely with the sales department.

Organizational Developments

Before becoming president, Richard Kingsbury had worked in two functional departments looking for improvements. His interest in efficiency had led to substantial labor savings in shipping. He said it had been easier to convince the teamsters' union of the need for changes than some of the foremen, and he believed that resistance to new ideas had been fostered by the centralized control of his father. Mr. Kingsbury described the two plant superintendents he had fired as uncooperative, hard-headed, anti-labor, and as standing in the way of improvements. He said he had eliminated three additional foremen showing similar attitudes. Mr. Kingsbury felt he now had the right man in the superintendent's position, one who could lead the foremen and look for better manufacturing methods.

Soon after becoming president, Richard Kingsbury had issued a directive that prohibited on-the-spot firing by foremen. He said his father had never agreed to this change while he was in control, but Richard Kingsbury believed the exercise of firing authority was inconsistent with good supervision. The directive stated that written requests for the release of a worker should be sent by the foreman to Mr. Newman and be approved by Alfred Kingsbury and Mr. Miller.

Mr. Kingsbury stated that his own youthful age had been a "small powder-keg" at the time of his father's resignation. "There was not much doubt in the minds of the directors about the succession," he said, "but the other executives did not share that certainty as they had little contact with the board. It became a question of whether I was taking over in name or in fact, and at least two of the officers had aspirations. Many lingering animosities came into the open at that time, and I finally had to stop the officers' meetings in early 1956 because nothing could be accomplished in them."

"Coordination was lacking between the departments," he continued, "and I stuck my neck out to cut bottlenecks. But the people involved had to cool down first, and I did not resume the meetings for about half a year."

Richard Kingsbury commented on the current meetings as follows: "We are now operating with the vice presidents as heads of functional line departments. Actually we never act as a management group. The only real cooperative efforts occur if two department heads have an overlapping problem like priority schedules of production. But other matters are treated separately and will likely continue to be treated as such. For instance, advertising policy is handled solely as a sales problem. Actually, the vice presidents have been used to operating this way since my father's time. There was even terrific interdepartmental animosity; each department tried to push the other around," he said. Mr. Kingsbury explained that there had been so-called "policy meetings" under Earl Kingsbury, but although ideas were debated collectively, Earl Kingsbury personally set policies.

"It is my prerogative to set policies which are self-governing, as contrasted with day-to-day affairs. I mainly concern myself with interdepartmental matters, or with weaknesses in any one department. For instance, I felt I had to take action in the production area—but I take action only if initial suggestions do not bring results," he explained.

In speaking of interdepartmental cooperation, Mr. Cannon said that until recently coordination between his department and the factory had not always been the best. During 1956, however, William Stewart had the idea of forming a production planning group to consist of Mr. Cannon, Alfred Kingsbury, the heads of scheduling and sales service, and himself. The group began by working on the problem of slack periods caused by seasonal demand for certain high-volume products, especially institutional biscuits. An attempt was made to forecast such fluctuations and schedule appropriate substitute products to keep the factory operating at capacity. Similarly, the group helped to schedule production on products for which demand was especially heavy. Mr. Cannon stated he felt this group had helped both his department and the production area.

Richard Kingsbury also thought the group was a good idea, as it taught certain sales personnel "the physical facts of life about the factory." He said that salesmen tended to push certain items too hard, thinking they could have more supplies immediately. This resulted in temporary but embarrassing shortages, during which the home territory was generally neglected in favor of outside areas. "This was quite contrary to the natural emphasis required—I still believe that our home territory is our mainstay," he said. "On the other hand," he added, "the factory was tempted to produce items that best fitted its production schedules."

The older executives commented that Richard Kingsbury showed great insight and capabilities, especially for his age. They said his interest in new machinery foreshadowed promising developments. Mr. Perry remarked: "Richard can do a lot of things with people who of themselves would not think of changing their old ways. By being in a position of authority he can spark new thought and urge its acceptance." Alfred Kingsbury said that no major steps were taken either by the president or by the officers without mutual consultation. "Dick is naturally more dependent on the department heads because his experience is shorter. He would not think of doing something without bringing it up with one or all of us. Likewise, we talk to him about our problems and listen to his views."

The Future

Mr. Kingsbury visualized a need for stricter cost control and a more unified sales promotion. "I consider our present product line a hodge-podge in terms of appearance," he said, and indicated that, as one step toward improving package design and uniformity, Superb had asked its paper and cardboard suppliers to analyze current packages and suggest changes. This practice was common among small biscuit companies that were unable to afford large sums for professional designers.

The question of product diversification had arisen several times during the past three years. The idea of going into cereals and cake mixes had been discarded owing to the difficulties envisioned in competing with nationally advertised brands. Mr. Kingsbury stated that he and some of his officers felt the company should expand its line "if and when the right opportunity comes." New products might be added either through subcontracting of production or through utilizing the present plant. Mr. Kingsbury felt that the potential of the present sales force might be more fully realized with additional compatible products.

Exhibit 1

SUPERB BISCUITS, INC.

Income Statement, Years Ending December 31
(Thousands of dollars)

	1956	1955	1954	1953	1952	1951	1950	1949	1948	1947	1946	1945
Net sales	$7,555	$7,001	$7,156	$7,508	$6,829	$6,374	$5,311	$4,841	$4,676	$4,933	$3,825	$3,704
Cost of goods sold	5,182	4,800	5,002	5,229	4,763	4,516	3,647	3,321	3,398	3,471	2,519	2,434
Gross profit	$2,373	$2,201	$2,154	$2,279	$2,066	$1,858	$1,664	$1,520	$1,278	$1,462	$1,306	$1,270
Selling, delivery and administration	2,199	2,029	1,990	2,036	1,814	1,672	1,469	1,389	1,289	1,148	946	899
Operating profit	$ 174	$ 172	$ 164	$ 243	$ 252	$ 186	$ 195	$ 131	$ ⟨11⟩	$ 314	$ 360	$ 371
Other income	23	29	10	10	4	17	14	15	13	4	9	⟨11⟩
Total income	$ 197	$ 201	$ 174	$ 253	$ 256	$ 203	$ 209	$ 146	$ 2	$ 318	$ 369	$ 360
Interest expense	11	5	10	20	22	13	16	22	21	7	8	19
Income before income tax	$ 186	$ 196	$ 164	$ 233	$ 234	$ 190	$ 193	$ 124	$ ⟨19⟩	$ 311	$ 361	$ 341
Federal income tax	$ 91	$ 95	$ 82	$ 119	$ 121	$ 95	$ 73	$ 47	$ ⟨5⟩	$ 119	$ 140	$ 246
Net profit	$ 95	$ 101	$ 82	$ 114	$ 113	$ 95	$ 120	$ 77	$ ⟨14⟩	$ 192	$ 221	$ 95
Preferred dividends	$ 40	$ 41	$ 42	$ 42	$ 43	-	-	-	-	$ 43	$ 21	-
Percentage Analysis												
Net sales	100.0%	100.0%	100.0%	100.0%	100.0%	100.0%	100.0%	100.0%	100.0%	100.0%	100.0%	100.0%
Cost of goods sold	68.6	68.5	69.9	69.6	69.7	70.9	68.7	68.6	72.7	70.4	65.9	65.7
Gross profit	31.4	31.5	30.1	30.4	30.3	29.1	31.3	31.4	27.3	29.6	34.1	34.3
Selling, delivery and administration	29.1	29.0	27.8	27.1	26.6	26.2	27.6	28.7	27.5	23.3	24.7	24.3
Operating profit	2.3	2.5	2.3	3.3	3.7	2.9	3.7	2.7	⟨0.2⟩	6.3	9.4	10.0
Other income	0.3	0.4	0.1	0.1	0.0	0.3	0.2	0.3	0.3	0.1	0.2	0.3
Total income	2.6	2.9	2.4	3.4	3.7	3.2	3.9	3.0	0.1	6.4	9.6	9.7
Interest expense	0.1	0.1	0.1	0.3	0.3	0.2	0.3	0.4	0.5	0.1	0.2	0.5
Income before income tax	2.5	2.8	2.3	3.1	3.4	3.0	3.6	2.6	⟨0.4⟩	6.3	9.4	9.2
Federal income tax	1.2	1.4	1.1	1.6	1.8	1.5	1.4	1.0	0.1	2.4	3.6	6.6
Net profit	1.3	1.4	1.2	1.5	1.6	1.5	2.2	1.6	⟨0.3⟩	3.9	5.8	2.6
Preferred dividends	0.5	0.6	0.6	0.6	0.6	-	-	-	-	0.9	0.6	-

Bracketed figures are negative

Source: Company records.

Exhibit 2

SUPERB BISCUITS, INC.

Balance Sheets, December 31
(Thousands of dollars)

Assets	1956	1955	1954	1953	1952	1951	1950	1949	1948	1947	1946	1945
Cash	$ 189	$ 160	$ 188	$ 134	$ 199	$ 120	$ 123	$ 93	$ 98	$ 149	$ 180	$ 268
Receivables - net	274	241	234	281	273	256	192	182	156	155	175	105
Inventories	983	753	608	572	449	518	375	326	317	332	306	205
Investments - restricted	-	-	-	119	109	100	92	82	74	64	56	52
Total current assets	$1,446	$1,154	$1,030	$1,106	$1,030	$ 994	$ 782	$ 683	$ 645	$ 700	$ 717	$ 630
Land, building & machinery	1,487	1,432	1,327	1,229	1,141	1,085	995	947	926	892	473	454
Reserve for depreciation	710	636	574	495	463	410	379	351	302	259	236	254
Net property	$ 717	$ 796	$ 753	$ 734	$ 678	$ 675	$ 616	$ 596	$ 624	$ 633	$ 237	$ 200
Prepayments	80	75	53	41	34	76	42	26	42	28	53	25
Goodwill	-	-	-	-	-	-	-*	450	450	450	450	450
Organization expense	-	-	-	-	-	-	-	-	-	-	88	88
Total assets	$2,303	$2,025	$1,836	$1,881	$1,742	$1,745	$1,440	$1,755	$1,761	$1,811	$1,545	$1,393
Liabilities												
Notes payable	$ 570**	$ 150	$ 75	$ 113	$ 38	$ 19	$ 22	$ 22	$ 11	$ 75	$ 30	$ 30
Accounts payable	206	235	205	175	173	238	139	124	232	158	104	89
Accruals	209	217	229	188	156	146	119	82	82	73	98	68
Federal income taxes	64	223	178	241	245	238	264	278	241	268	288	351
Total current liabilities	$1,049	$ 825	$ 687	$ 717	$ 612	$ 641	$ 544	$ 506	$ 566	$ 574	$ 520	$ 538
Notes payable - long term	-	-	-	281	319	356	244	266	289	300	150	180
Cumulative preferred stock ($.50 div. rate)	419	419	419	428	428	428	427	428	428	428	428	428
Common stock	122	122	122	122	122	122	122	122	122	122	122	122
Earned surplus	723	669	610	340	269	198	103	433	356	387	325	125
Total stock and surplus	$1,264	$1,210	$1,151	$ 890	$ 819	$ 748	$ 652	$ 983	$ 906	$ 937	$ 875	$ 675
Less: reacquired preferred stock	10	10	2	7	8	-	-	-	-	-	-	-
Net stock and surplus	$1,254	$1,200	$1,149	$ 883	$ 811	$ 748	$ 652	$ 983	$ 906	$ 937	$ 875	$ 675
Total liabilities	2,303	2,025	1,836	1,881	1,742	1,745	1,440	1,755	1,761	1,811	1,545	1,393
Net current assets (thousands of dollars)	$ 397	$ 329	$ 343	$ 389	$ 418	$ 353	$ 238	$ 177	$ 79	$ 126	$ 197	$ 92
Current ratio	138:1	140:1	150:1	154:1	168:1	155:1	144:1	135:1	114:1	122:1	138:1	117:1
Number of shares - preferred (1,000)	41	41	42	42	42	43	43	43	43	43	43	43
Earned per share - preferred	$ 2.26	$ 2.47	$ 1.98	$ 2.72	$ 2.70	$ 2.23	$ 2.81	$ 1.79	$ -	$ 4.49	$ 5.18	$ 2.24
Dividends per share - preferred	$ 1.00	$ 1.00	$ 1.00	$ 1.00	$ 1.00	$ -	$ -	$ -	$ -	$ 1.00	$ .50	$ -
Arrearages per share - preferred	$ 1.75	$ 2.25	$ 2.75	$ 3.25	$ 3.75	$ 4.25	$ 3.75	$ 3.25	$ 2.75	$ 2.25	$ 2.75	$ 2.75
Total arrearages (thousands of dollars)	$ 71	$ 92	$ 115	$ 136	$ 158	$ 182	$ 160	$ 139	$ 118	$ 96	$ 118	$ 118
Number of shares - common (1,000)	122	122	122	122	122	122	122	122	122	122	122	122
Earned per share - common	$ 0.44	$ 0.66	$ 0.51	$ 0.76	$ 0.75	$ 0.60	$ 0.81	$ 0.45	$ (0.29)	$ 1.39	$ 1.63	$ 0.61
Net tangible assets per share - common	$ 6.31	$ 5.70	$ 5.02	$ 2.67	$ 1.89	$ 1.13	$ 0.53	-	-	-	-	-
Per cent return on net worth (after tax)	7.5%	8.4%	7.2%	12.9%	13.9%	12.5%	18.4%	7.8%	(1.6%)	20.3%	25.3%	14.1%

*Goodwill was written off against earned surplus—now carried at $1.

**Short-term funds of $500,000 for seasonal inventory needs included.

Bracketed figures are negative.

Source: Company records.

Exhibit 3

SUPERB BISCUITS, INC.

Per Cent Changes in Sales and Profits
Three Large Biscuit Companies* and Superb Biscuits, Inc.

	Three Large Companies*				Superb Biscuits, Inc.			
Year	Sales (Millions)	% Change from Past Year	Net Profit (Millions)	% Change from Past Year	Sales (Millions)	% Change from Past Year	Net Profit (Millions)	% Change from Past Year
1956	$698.1	+ 9.8%	$31.1	+11.9%	$7.6	+ 8.6%	$.095	- 6.0%
1955	635.9	+ 3.8	27.7	-	7.0	- 2.8	.101	+21.9
1954	612.8	+ 2.6	27.7	- 2.1	7.2	- 4.0	.082	-28.1
1953	597.4	+ 4.8	28.3	+ 1.4	7.5	+10.3	.114	+ 0.9
1952	570.2	+ 2.5	27.9	+ 3.7	6.8	+ 6.2	.113	+18.9
1951	556.1	+13.5	26.9	-19.7	6.4	+20.8	.095	-20.8
1950	489.9	+ 2.0	33.5	- 3.7	5.3	+10.4	.120	+57.9
1949	480.1	- 1.3	34.8	+32.3	4.8	+ 2.1	.077	- } (negative basis)
1948	486.5	+10.9	26.3	+ 4.4	4.7	- 4.1	⟨.014⟩	- } (negative basis)
1947	438.5	+22.6	25.2	- 5.3	4.9	+28.9	.192	-13.1
1946	357.4	+ 8.4	26.6	+26.0	3.8	+ 2.7	.221	+132.6
1945	329.6	-	21.1	-	3.7	-	.095	

*National Biscuit Company, United Biscuit Company, Sunshine Biscuit Company, Inc.

Bracketed figures are negative.

Source: Compiled by Harvard Business School Research Staff from Moody's company records.

Exhibit 4

SUPERB BISCUITS, INC.

Per Cent Return on Net Worth over 12 Years

Typical Industry Performances and Superb Biscuits, Inc.

Company	Per Cent Return											
	1956	1955	1954	1953	1952	1951	1950	1949	1948	1947	1946	1945
National Biscuit Company	11.5%	10.7%	11.9%	11.5%	11.6%	10.8%	14.2%	15.3%	10.7%	12.4%	10.2%	15.9%
United Biscuit Company	8.2	8.1	4.2	9.8	11.2	12.3	14.7	17.2	26.7	32.4	37.4	15.7
Sunshine Biscuits, Inc.	12.5	12.0	12.2	12.8	12.8	14.3	17.9	20.6	20.4	15.4	24.0	11.2
Average of six large and medium companies (weighted average)	10.7	10.1	10.3	11.0	11.3	11.1	14.3	15.4	12.8	13.6	14.2	14.9
Superb Biscuits, Inc.	7.5	8.4	7.2	12.9	13.9	12.5	18.4	7.8	⟨1.6⟩	20.3	25.3	14.1

Relative Volume of Three Largest Biscuit Companies
(Selected years; Millions of Dollars)

Company	1956		1954		1951		1948		1945	
	Sales	%	Sales	%	Sales	%	Sales	%	Sales	%
National Biscuit Company	$410.4	59.0%	$376.4	61.5%	$329.9	59.5%	$296.2	61.0%	$205.0	62.2%
United Biscuit Company	137.1	19.7	117.2	19.4	107.2	19.1	87.7	17.9	50.6	15.4
Sunshine Biscuits, Inc.	150.6	21.3	119.2	19.1	119.0	21.4	102.6	21.1	74.0	22.4
Total	$698.1	100.0%	$612.8	100.0%	$556.1	100.0%	$486.5	100.0%	$329.6	100.0%

Note: Comparability is limited by the fact that the large companies have diversified or integrated their operations to some extent. For instance, NBC produces 80% of its own flour requirements and 50% of packaging supplies. NBC also produces bread and cake in the East. Similarly, Sunshine Biscuit and United Biscuit are engaged in comparable fields.

Bracketed figures are negative.

Source: Prepared by Harvard Business School Research staff.

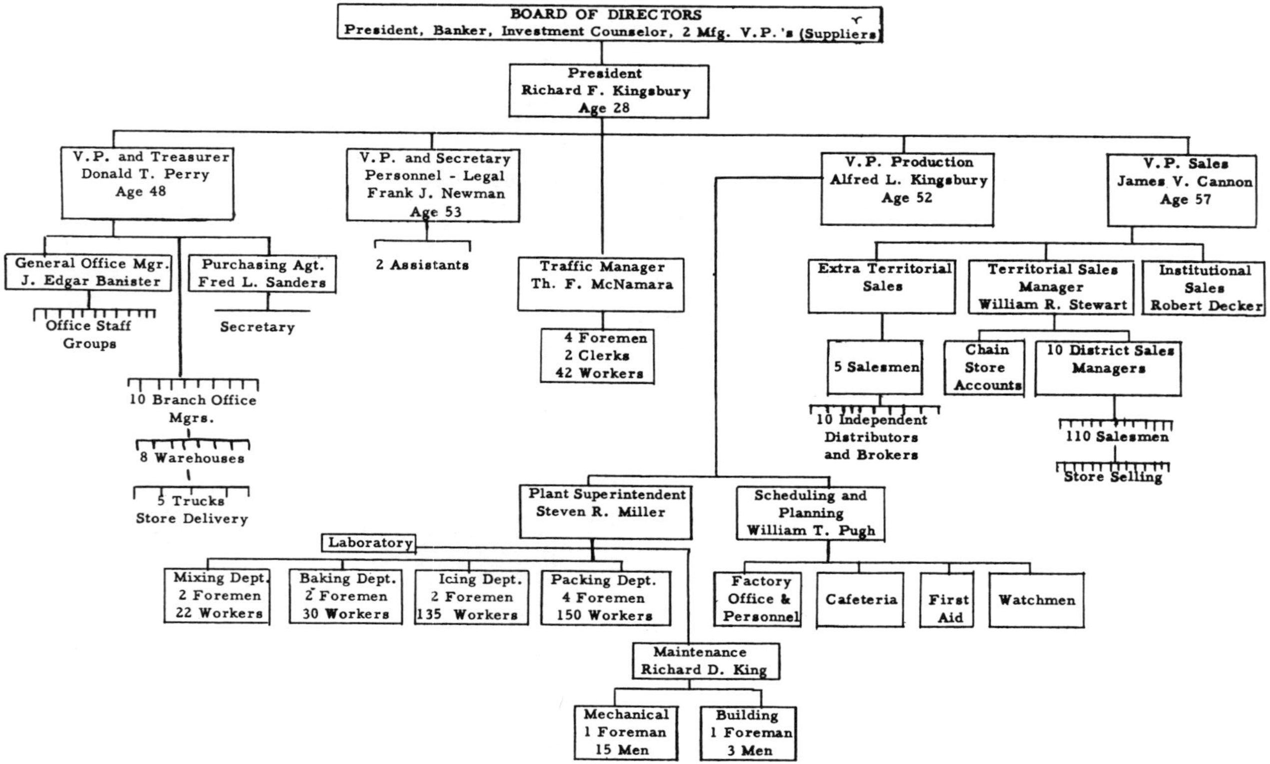

Source: Company officials.

Exhibit 5
SUPERB BISCUITS, INC.
Organization Chart

APPENDIX C

INDIAN HEAD MILLS INC.

POLICY MANUAL

INTRODUCTION[1]

Commenting on the policies and past record of Indian Head Mills, Inc., Mr. James E. Robison, president, stated in April 1961:

> In one year, 1956, we were going to expand our business by orthodox means. We did—from $20 million to $22 million—in the course of which we learned a lesson that I already knew, which is that you cannot take business from somebody else at a price that makes it worth having. We fell on our faces and we barely squeaked out at a profit. . . .[2]

Following the disappointing "orthodox" effort to expand sales through a major promotional campaign on piece goods in 1956,[3] and a parallel experience with a new product development (the first no-iron sheet) in 1958, executives of Indian Head had emphasized expansion through acquisition, adding eight companies from 1959 through March 9, 1961. Unlike two earlier acquisitions, these companies were purchased rather than merged (Exhibit 1).

As a result of its acquisition policy, Indian Head had expanded sales (Exhibit 2); gained substantial tax advantage and nonoperating profit (Exhibit 3); obtained experience in appraising assets (Exhibit 4); increased facilities and capacities (Exhibit 5); and expanded assets and income (Exhibits 6, 7 and 8). The company had also become diversified in the textile field. As outlined in a press release of February 1961, products and services were as follows:

> The company's growing range of textile products now includes woven fabrics of cotton, wool, silk and synthetic fibers in both greige and finished

[1]This introductory material and the exhibits are adopted from Aufrey T. Spront and E. P. Learned, *Indian Head Mills* (E), a case study (Boston: Harvard Business School, 1961).

[2]From an address by James E. Robison to the New York Collateral Group, National Association of Wool Manufactures, New York, April 5, 1961.

[3]For a complete account, see Indian Head Mills, Inc. EA-M 333, copyright 1957 by the President and Fellows of Harvard College.

states; commercial fishing nets, sports netting and cotton and synthetic threads and twines; and hand knitting yarns, art needlework, and decorative linens. Services performed for the textile industry include package dying of yarns of all fibers and commission finishing and printing operations.

Early in 1961, in the course of taking stock of the company's history and future, executives of Indian Head drew up two major documents: (1) an analysis of past acquisitions indicating the benefits to the owners of the companies acquired; and 2) the first edition of a Policy Manual, which was to be circulated among executives with a covering letter that read, in part:

> . . . the management of Indian Head Mills feels very strongly that the communication of management policies and objectives to the key people is extremely important. It will continue to be a deliberate policy of the company to over-inform rather than under-inform these key executives.
>
> . . . Remember—This is a First Edition and we are making this distribution not only because we want you to have it as a point of reference, but also because we want any comments or suggestions you, as a key executive, might have for further revisions of the Manual.

Presented below is a verbatim reproduction of the Policy Manual.

INDIAN HEAD POLICY MANUAL[4]

PRINCIPLES and GOALS

Objectives and Scope

Objective The objective of this company *is* to increase the intrinsic value of the common stock.

It *is not* to grow bigger for the sake of size, nor to become more diversified, nor to make the most or best of anything, nor to provide jobs, have the most modern plants, the happiest customers, lead in new product development, or to achieve any other status which has no relationship to the economic use of capital.

Any or all of these may be, from time to time, a means to our objective, but means and ends must never be confused. Indian Head Mills is in business solely to improve the inherent value of the common stockholder's equity in the company.

Scope The present basis of the company's earning power is a diversified textile business. Continued growth within the textile and related industries is contemplated, in part, because the nature of the industry at present seems to offer above average opportunities for expansion.

The company, however, is not committed irrevocably to this industry, particularly if the hazards to be overcome in achieving our objective outweigh the chances of success. There is no ultimate limit to the size of the corporation.

[4]Reprinted with permission of Mr. James Robison, President of Indian Head Mills. Mr. Robison requested that the reader keep in mind that policies change with business conditions and that what was true in 1961 for Indian Head does not necessarily represent company views today.

Special Problems of the Textile Industry

The textile industry offers special problems which must be overcome in order to reach the company's objective. The definition of these problems and the basic concepts which have been developed for solving them are an essential part of Indian Head Mills management philosophy.

It is the considered view of management that the textile industry in the United States is, at best, a static one. Although the market for textile and related products will grow with the expansion of population, the domestic textile industry and its owners are not likely to participate in this growth to any signficant degree and for the following reasons:

1. *Domestic productive capacity* is greater than the market can absorb at prices which provide a reasonable return on the capital employed in the industry.
2. *The equity capital invested* in the industry is undisciplined in that it is chronically employed at rates of return lower than those obtainable from prime debt securities.
3. *The rapidly expanding competitive power of foreign textile producers* cannot be held at bay by tariff and similar market restrictions against foreign goods. In addition, nontextile products, both domestic and foreign, are constantly encroaching upon American textile markets.
4. *An irrational public policy* with regard to the nation's agricultural problems aggravates these competitive problems by maintaining raw material cost (for cotton and wool) at greatly inflated levels relative to world markets. Federal tax rates on corporate income severely limit the power of business enterprise to retain profits for reinvestment to expand earning power to create more profits.
5. *The persistent advance of industrial wages,* re-enforced by minimum wage legislation, constantly forces employment costs up and is a factor in the steady advance of general operating costs.
6. *No Relief in Sight* It is believed that these problems will continue to dominate the textile industry for the foreseeable future, and the probability favors their becoming worse rather than better. While these problems are not unique to the textile industry, the narrowness of the profit margins on which the industry operates accentuates their impact because there is so little room for error.

Indian Head's Principles of Growth

Indian Head Mills has had to contend with these problems ever since its formation in 1953 and has grown in spite of them. This growth has been based on the following fundamental concepts, the application of which has enabled us to meet and successfully overcome these problems:

1. *Management* Management must have the intelligence, imagination and authority to cope with the problems of this difficult situation. To assure the best possible profit results for the stockholders, we believe that the interest of management should be identified as completely as possible with the interests of the stockholders. Compensation policies are keyed to this end.

2. *Organization* We believe that the operating divisions of the company are inescapably the profit centers. The company must be organized so that full responsibility for the profitable utilization of each division's assets rests with the division's General Manager.
3. *Pursuit of Profit* Profit must be pursued vigorously and without let-up in every area of operation, from the procurement of raw materials through the manufacturing and merchandising of the company's products and in the company's financial and administrative activities. The object is to maintain and enlarge operating earning power since this is the source of earnings per common share, which, in turn, build up the stockholders' equity.

It is a general company policy that no product, plant or program will be maintained which is clearly unable to produce a satisfactory return on the capital employed.

4. *Capital Turnover* Maximum turnover of capital is essential to the realization of a satisfactory return on investment. Idle assets, of whatever type and for whatever reason, must be put to profitable use or disposed of. The money invested in this company must work as hard as the people do. To apply this principle, it is necessary to seek the lowest investment consistent with sound operations, and to maintain the closest possible control of inventories.
5. *Leverage* The principle of leverage is utilized deliberately to maximize the growth of earnings per share and of stockholders' equity. Debt and preferred stock, in that order, are therefore the chosen instruments for financing the growth of the company. Borrowed funds, however, must earn enough to justify their cost and risk, because leverage works both ways.
6. *No Dilution of the Common Stock* It is a fundamental principle of the company not to dilute the common stock. The use of debt and preferred stock accomplishes this, in addition to providing leverage. Common stock will not be used to acquire other businesses. It is used, however, on a limited scale to complete the identification of Management interests with those of the stockholders.
7. *Growth by Acquisition* The Management of this company is convinced that it is too risky to expand operating earning power from within through major improvement programs for established operations or for new productive capacity. This conviction is based in part on the assessment of textile industry conditions cited earlier, and in part on the results of past efforts to set up new operations, through investment in inventories and personnel, to take volume away from competitors. The volume can be obtained, but not at costs or prices which permit reasonable profits. The growth potential from acquisitions is both more immediate and more certain, and opportunities for acquiring other businesses appear likely to exist indefinitely in the textile industry. This is due to the excess equity capital locked in at unreasonably low (often negative) rates of return. Unable to correct the problems from within, or to solve personal tax problems, the owners find the sale of the business is the most practical, and frequently the sole, alternative if they are to preserve their capital.

Summary

Five cardinal rules have been developed out of the company's experience which, when applied to any specific situation, should lead to the realization of our objectives:

1. Avoid catastrophe—but do not strive for the extra margin of safety which it is human nature to seek. Practice "Brinkmanship."
2. Maintain current operations at a profitable level.
3. Improve earning power, after satisfying rules 1 and 2 in that order.
4. In every phase of operation seek maximum return on minimum investment.
5. Play it straight. Whether in contact with the public, customers, stockholders, employees or any other individuals or groups, the only right way to deal with people is forthrightly and honestly.
   If any mistakes are made—admit them and correct them. Contracts should be honored and Indian Head has the right to expect the same performance from those people with whom it does business.

ACQUISITION POLICIES

Indian Head Mills will continue to seek opportunities to acquire textile businesses as the principal means to attain its objective of increasing the intrinsic value of the common stock. Specific goals of the Acquisition Program are:

To strengthen established divisions.
To provide profit stability through diversification.
To build future earning power by acquiring businesses which, when operated in accordance with Indian Head policies, can generate earnings sufficient to cover the cost of the money used to finance their purchase and yield a satisfactory return for the stockholders.

Policies developed to realize these goals are:

1. Acquisitions should be made as far as possible with cash or borrowed funds rather than stock, since the issuance of additional shares risks dilution of the earnings and equity value and reduction of the market price.
2. In seeking out potential acquisitions which can help build future earning power, the Management will be mainly interested in two types of situations:
   a) textile businesses which have proven earnings and growth potential, often with strong market positions and product acceptance;
   b) businesses which are not operating profitably, are losing ground to competition or are in need of management leadership.

   Sound and successfully operated textile businesses are available for purchase as going concerns from time to time because the owners of family or closely-held companies are interested in diversifying their investments for estate planning purposes or otherwise. These businesses can usually be taken over by the company in toto with a minimum of change in management and operations.
3. More common are the textile businesses which are so-called "problem children." The company will acquire such businesses if, by the application

of the policies outlined in this manual, it is felt they can be made profitable and can make a satisfactory return on our investment in them.

Profitability often results from integrating an acquired business with an existing division. This can have the effect not only of strengthening that division's operations but also increasing its profit potential.

Revitalization of an acquired business may, however, require the contraction of a portion of the business to preserve its inherently profitable operations. In these instances it may be necessary to consolidate operations in fewer locations or discontinue product lines which, even after the application of the company's basic operating policies, do not show a reasonable prospect of providing a fair return on the money and talent required to be devoted to them.

4. Potential nonrecurring profits are an important part of the analysis of a prospect for acquisition. With many textile securities selling at substantially less than book value it is frequently possible to acquire textile properties and inventories for less than book value and to realize nonrecurring profits from the sale of inventories purchased at a discount and from the disposition of plants and machinery which cannot be made productive.

   By and large the company is not interested in acquiring businesses which do not have the potential of providing future operating profits.

5. The company has established an Acquisition Committee whose members devote a substantial amount of their time to the investigation and evaluation of potential acquisitions.

FINANCIAL POLICIES

Covered in Goals:

Increased common stock equity
No dilution of common stock
Leverage—cash, debt and preferred for acquisitions
Capital turnover
Maximum return on minimum investment
Nonrecurring profits

Common Stock Dividends Cash dividends are not paid on the common stock because cash can be better utilized in the Acquisition Program to build up stockholders' equity. Dividends in stock have been paid from time to time to acknowledge the growth of the company's earning power.

Interdivisional Transactions No one division can look to another for uneconomic support or for any interdivisional transactions which is not competitive with the general market. All interdivisional contracts must be "arms length" transactions with market prices prevailing. Moreover there is no obligation on the part of one division to service another, even at market prices.

Factoring Accounts receivable are factored as a means of reducing investment and controlling overhead expense. Factoring increases corporate borrowing power, imparts additional leverage and hastens the realization of cash from the sale of products. Further, it speeds the turn-over of capital and relieves divisional and corporate personnel of credit problems.

Inventories For all operating analyses of inventories, actual cost or current market is the basis for valuing inventories. They provide the true definition of investment. LIFO is purely a tax device and must not be allowed to distort the picture of inventory investment or operating profit. Physical check of the inventory should be done at least once a year. If allowed to go overlong, the result is invariably bad. Relatively few situations are so neat and orderly that the books provide a true picture from day to day. Quarterly reviews therefore should not be resisted just because they're a nuisance. All obsolescent, slow-moving or unprofitable items must be cleaned out fast, and especially toward the year-end so as to provide a clean, realistic year-end balance sheet.

Fixed Assets The policy of the company with respect to fixed assets is to maintain plants and equipment capable of manufacturing products at cost levels which provide the most satisfactory return on investment.

Capital Expenditures In relation to the market value of textile securities, the bulk of fixed assets in the industry is valued at zero. The route preferred by Indian Head for improvement of plants and fixed assets is to acquire existing textile assets which can be purchased well below book value. Capital expenditures therefore:

a) Will be authorized only to increase potential return on investment through reduced labor cost.
b) Making possible the use of lower cost raw materials.
c) To support a new merchandising program.

In support of this policy the authority of Division Managers to make capital expenditures is deliberately limited. Individual ingenuity in making do with available equipment has been successful in the past and shows that survival does not depend on modernization nor does modernization assure survival.

Surplus Assets In line with the principle that the money must work as hard as the people do, any surplus or idle assets—plant, equipment, land, etc.—should be promptly disposed of. We would rather have live cash to work with than all the dead assets in the world. Even if we have to repurchase later at a higher cost, we will know when we do so that the acquired asset or material is going to be put to profitable use.

Own or Buy Decisions Whether to purchase or rent capital assets—buildings, equipment, autos, trucks, etc.—depends on the effect that ownership or rental would have on return on investment.

Fleet Leasing The general company-wide policy is to lease fleet cars rather than to buy them. Rare exceptions are made to this policy, and only on the basis of carefully worked out cost comparison. These exceptions should be reviewed at sufficiently frequent intervals to make sure that the policy objective is being met despite the exception.

Company Loans to Employees and Company Owned Houses The company does not make loans nor provide company owned houses to any employees. This is the policy. Exceptions to this policy must be approved by the President's office.

Expense Accounts Expense accounts are authorized for the purpose of reimbursing salesmen and other employees for all unusual costs of travel and maintenance incurred on behalf of the company, due to the character of their employment. It is not intended that ordinary every day expense incurred in normal work-day activity will be chargeable as a business expense.

The propriety and fairness of all charges will be considered in each individual case when approving expense vouchers. Details of allowable and excluded expenses are spelled out in administrative bulletins. As a general rule, expenses should be viewed like everything else in terms of their relation to profit and return on investment.

MANUFACTURING POLICIES

Efficiency, low labor cost, high quality, high volume, full schedules, minimum styles, and all of the conventional objectives of textile mill operations are acceptable to Indian Head, with one vital qualification:

"Only if consistent with maximum profits."

To achieve this, Indian Head's manufacturing policies are:

1. Coordination of manufacturing and merchandising is to be accomplished by assigning responsibility for both functions to one person, the Division General Manager. Manufacturing and merchandising executives will be in the same bonus plan as Division General Managers and top management.
2. Basic product specifications must be clearly defined and thoroughly understood throughout the organization concerned with their manufacture.
3. Complete cost analysis is mandatory, laying bare each element of cost for regular review. Emphasis is on *total cost*.
4. Flexibility will be expected. Swift adjustment to changing conditions, notably the shifting of cost elements, is vital to the maintenance of profits.
5. Manufacturing executives are responsible for and therefore must understand the economics of total cost.
6. Seek optimum efficiency and optimum quality *consistent with maximum profits.*
7. Do not accumulate inventories, even though to do so has the effect of reducing unit costs. Total costs are what count.

Labor Relations

1. Personnel policies are to be geared to local community custom and practice.
2. General company policies with regard to labor relations are:
   a) Compensation is to be related to performance, with emphasis to the fullest extent possible on incentive payment, i.e., piece rates.
   b) Length of service should have its proper place. It should not supersede quality or responsibility.
   c) The company is neither pro nor anti-union: . . . Where there are unions the objective is to get along with them—not to bust them. . . . Where there is no union, the objective is to stay nonunion.

MARKETING POLICIES

The basic policy of Indian Head is to produce goods and services which are needed and wanted enough to command prices which cover cost of production and yield a satisfactory profit for the stockholders who own the business.

The company's general marketing policy is to make maximum use of men, money, machinery and time. This requires high velocity of turnover and the maintenance of optimum inventory—neither the smallest nor the largest, but the one that permits the most effective marketing job to be done with the least utilization of capital investment. To this end the following policies have been developed:

1. Do not sell ahead at a loss.
2. No products are to be kept in the line which cannot be made to provide a profit. It is impossible to make enough on the winners to overcome losses on losers. It is not the policy of the company to have a complete line in order to keep a customer happy or provide extra service or convenience. Let competitors have the losers.
3. Do not build inventory without reasonable expectation of marketability. If orders are not in hand or reasonably foreseeable, production is to be curtailed. Do not produce inventories as a cushion for customer service. Inventories are produced to make a profit.
4. Keep all marketing people informed what inventory costs (real costs, not standards) relative to selling prices, including the cost of carrying slow-moving or unsalable merchandise.
5. Keep the corners swept out. It is company policy to have at least one annual housecleaning as an exercise in shrinking capital investment to minimum levels, and to get rid of unprofitable or slow moving merchandise. More frequent inventorying is highly recommended.

Claims On any question of claim where we are definitely in the wrong, we will admit that we are wrong and make certain the customer knows that we intend to conduct our business in such a way that he will have complete confidence in our products, our policies and our procedure. However, on questionable claims and unauthorized returns, we will stand absolutely firm and are quite prepared to go to arbitration before allowing a customer to take unreasonable advantage of us.

PERSONNEL POLICIES

Management Superior performance on the part of management is the single most important factor in the success of the company. Because of the special difficulties encountered in the textile industry and the unique nature of Indian Head Mills, the company must expect superior performance from its management personnel and expects to compensate this group accordingly. Compensation policies in turn must be conceived and administered so as to direct employee effort toward attaining the company's basic goal of increasing the equity value of the common stock.

Management Participation It is the policy of the company to seek the closest possible identification of the interests of its key employees with the interests of its stockholders. Incentive bonus plans, profit sharing retirement plans and stock options will be utilized for this purpose.

In order to focus profit responsibility in the operating divisions, incentive compensation programs will be established on a divisional basis to the fullest possible extent, so as not to dilute the return on investment concept which would occur if profit sharing and bonus programs were on a company-wide basis.

Corollary to this policy, however, is that if one of these incentive compensation devices is not working effectively within a division, the system will be re-evaluated and charged in order to obtain the desired result equitably.

Salary Administration It is the policy of the company to pay salaries and provide other benefits equal to or better than the industry or locality, so as to attract and hold employees of superior capabilities.

The company will not take a paternalistic point of view toward its employees. Employees will be compensated well, in return for which their full support and cooperation is expected. If terms of employment are not satisfactory, any employee is free to look elsewhere for more satisfactory arrangements.

The company wants superior personnel and will not settle for mediocrity. Length of service is of importance but not as important at Indian Head as is the quality of performance. Results, not effort count.

a) Salary commitments will not be made in a vacuum. Salaries of all employees will be reviewed as a group and adjustments made at regular semi-annual intervals to insure that rates are competitive.
General company policy permits free access to compensation information, through proper channels, as a means of assuring fair treatment throughout. Dissemination of salary information within division however, will be at the discretion of the Division Managers.
b) Interim salary adjustments are to be held to the absolute minimum.
c) Built-in cost rigidities are to be avoided. The policy of the company is to load up good men and pay them well, rather than drag along with several mediocre people who cost more to do a less effective job.
d) The effectiveness of management participation programs will also be reviewed and evaluated in connection with the salary reviews.

Indian Head will not pay unusually high salaries for specialized talents unless the total compensation arrangement is tied into the success of the business, through incentive compensation plans, commissions, and/or profit sharing. Key executives will be held responsible for their decisions which affect inventory control, merchandising, styling, purchasing and any other phase of the business that effects results on the "bottom line."

Advancement Opportunities Because of the growth of the company through successful operation of its Acquisition Program, constant opportunities are available to capable employees to advance into positions of broader responsibility. These opportunities are available to capable employees to advance into positions of broader responsibility. These opportunities are available alike to members of the present organization and to employees of companies acquired by Indian Head. In the former case, they benefit by the opportunities available in a dynamic, growing company. In the latter, they obtain the advancement opportunities which are characteristic of a larger and more diversified organization.

Management Development To assure that the company will have the management resources needed to continue its growth, the development of management talent is emphasized. Every executive is charged with the responsibility of insuring maximum development of his subordinate managers. Regular use is made of university-directed Advanced Management Programs and other management development programs outside of the company as a supplement to on-the-job development.

Interdivisional transfers are encouraged as a means of executive development.

Communications It is the policy of the company to keep employees fully informed of the company's plans and objectives and of its progress in accomplishing them. The widest possible distribution is to be given to financial data, minutes of planning meetings, etc., while policies and administrative procedures are to be communicated by means of bulletin series.

Encouragement of Initiative It is the policy of the company to encourage to the fullest extent the exercise of imagination and initiative on the part of its employees at all levels. Ease of communication between employees, supervisors and management is to be assured as a matter of company policy so that the free flow of ideas will not in any way be hindered.

Retirement Age The normal retirement age for all employees is 65. Persons continuing in the company's employ will do so only under special arrangements approved by the president's office.

Group Insurance As a general policy the company makes group insurance benefits available to all salaried employees. The specific coverage is controlled by the individual plans of the operating divisions. However, corporate policy provides that group insurance is terminated at retirement.

PUBLIC RELATIONS POLICIES

The basic objective of the company's public relations policies is to enhance its profit potential and return on investment. This requires the broadest possible acceptance of the company's goals, policies and procedures, and the fullest possible acceptance of its products and its personnel.

In pursuit of these objectives it must be realized throughout the company that public relations exist, whether one is aware of them or not. Indian Head stands well, or not well, with its stockholders, employees, customers, suppliers, plant towns and the business and financial communities. The attitude of these groups decides whether the company is permitted to continue doing business and affects the degree of success attained by any major activity of the company or any of its divisions.

The specific policies flowing from these concepts are:

Advance Preparation The public relations or publicity potential, for good or evil, of any action by a Division or the company as a whole will receive full consideration before the action is taken. This includes preparation in advance for the handling of typical emergencies.

Accessibility of Company Spokesmen A properly qualified spokesman is to be made available promptly and with no heel-dragging to handle questions from the press or any other individual or organization, PROVIDED the questioner is properly endowed with the power of enquiry.

Degree of Disclosure Accurate information sufficient to ensure understanding and acceptance of company behavior is to be made available as widely as necessary and with due care for propitious timing. Disclose all NECESSARY information to achieve this end, and do so with a willing and cooperative attitude.

Public reaction is governed not only by the action itself, but by the manner in which it is done.

Emphasize the Positive The company's function in the economy is a constructive one. Solid and substantial growth has been realized in a very short span of years. In every field in which it operates, the company has a good reputation for quality, style, service—products which meet the requirements of the customers at fair and reasonable prices.

Emphasize these positive and constructive results whenever possible. Steps must be taken which are bound to have a negative public relations impact. Emphasis should be placed upon what the company does to minimize the impact on the individuals concerned to ease a transition, etc.

Actively Explore Public Relations Opportunities Divisional and corporate public relations projects and programs which frequently can be undertaken at little cost should be actively explored as a means to increased sales volume, more profitable prices, improved relations with customers and suppliers within plant communities, etc.

Organization of the Public Relations Activity In keeping with the principle of decentralization and divisonal autonomy, the operating divisions will have the fullest possible latitude in the conduct of their public relations. Responsibility for developing a favorable over-all "corporate image" and for coordinating divisional and corporate public relations activities resides in the Corporate Public Relations Department. The latter is also available to advise and assist the operating divisions in the conduct of this activity.

Because no rule of thumb exists to determine with neatness and precision what is divisional and what is corporate in character, the Corporate Public Relations Department will be kept informed of all divisional public relations activities and, where doubt exists as to the purely divisional nature of the problem or program, it will be reviewed in advance whenever possible with the Corporate Public Relations office.

Similarly, the Corporate Department will not initiate or conduct public relations activities which impinge in any way on a division without prior consultation with the Division General Manager and the appropriate Group Vice President. General company policy with regard to the internal distribution of information will also be followed by the Corporate Department so that the possibility of learning about the company from outsiders will be minimized.

Contributions The policy with respect to contributions of money or goods to charitable organizations and activities is to limit them to the Red Cross and the Community Chest of the cities and towns in which the company operates plants. Exceptions to this policy may be made only by the President of the company.

The company's contribution policy should be like all other policies, directed to the achievement of Indian Head goals. Contributions should be made with a view to the benefit that the contribution will make to the company in the attainment of its goals or in the application of other policies.

Worthiness of the charity is not a relevant criterion. It is not incumbent on management to decide for the stockholders which charity is most deserving. It *is* management's function to determine whether and when the expenditure of corporate funds is in the best interests of the business. This includes charitable donations.

Contributions are to be budgeted as would any other expenditure of corporate or divisional funds.

PLANNING AND MEASUREMENT

For purposes of definition, long-range planning is taken to mean 10-to-20 years ahead. Intermediate-term planning covers the next 3-to-5 years. Short-term planning means the current year.

The nature of the industry makes long-range planning difficult, sometimes impossible. Indian Head Mills has been built on plans rarely looking more than six months to the future. The company's increased size and complexity have increased the need for planning, even though as the result of an acquisition-oriented growth policy, plans may have to be quickly altered. Planning is therefore considered desirable and will be encouraged wherever circumstances permit.

Long-term Planning The company's long-term plans are:

1. To continue to build an organization which can cope with the problems of a difficult situation.
2. To continue to build earning power and to stabilize earning power by acquiring existing textile assets.
3. To take advantage of factors in the import situation which might make possible the purchase of raw materials, semiprocessed or finished goods at advantageous cost or of the sale of products in world markets at satisfactory profit margins.
4. Profit opportunities in the textile industry will probably be better offshore than in the USA over the next 10-20 years. It is part of the company's long-term plan to investigate and develop any such opportunities which promise a return on investment at least commensurate with the risk involved.

Intermediate and Short-Term Planning

1. Forward planning must be done to "avoid catastrophe," such as being forced out of business by some radical change or new development. The impact of television on the movie industry is a case in point. The company must keep ahead of changing market conditions.
2. Planning which has as its goal the insulation of an operation from industry price or cost trends is encouraged in pursuit of profit stability and improved return on investment. It is recognized that this is extremely difficult to do in an industry where innovation is so easily pirated. Nonetheless, it is occasionally possible to create a position of strength, and Managers must be alert to seize these opportunities.
3. Short-term planning to accomodate the business cycle is absolutely essential for the preservation of profits and the maintenance of return on investment. All Managers are expected to anticipate the ups and downs of the cycle and to be prepared, in advance, to cope with falling markets, or to take fullest advantage of improving profit opportunities.

4. Profit planning is also essential to:
   a) Highlight potential trouble areas and assist management in focusing on the first area of responsibility, the avoidance of catastrophe.
   b) To provide a basis for formulating policies and determining objectives.
   c) To provide a target for management at all levels to shoot for.

Measurement All planning is to be backed up by concrete programs of action, timetables and priority schedules. These provide yardsticks against which to measure progress, evaluate performance and determine the validity of plans.

1. Plans are to be reveiwed at regular intervals, matched against accomplishment, creating the occasion for taking whatever corrective action may be required—either in future planning or in current operations.
2. A file of case histories will be maintained relating to events or programs which are most characteristic of the company, which particular emphasis on those activites, such as acquisitions, which typically contain a high disaster factor. Both models of success and monuments to failure will be collected in order to provide guidance in future policy formation.

Exhibit 1
INDIAN HEAD MILLS, INC. (E)
Acquired Companies, Prices, and Terms of Payment

	DATE	Method of Acquisition	Method of Payment	Number of Shares	Cash	Notes	Total
Naumkeag Steam Cotton Company	2/1955	Merger	$1.25 preferred*	246,055			
J. L. Stifel & Sons, Inc.	9/1957	Merger	$1.50 preferred**	204,960			
Franklin Process Company	12/1957	Purchase of substantially all assets	Cash		$ 5,831,080		$ 5,831,080
The Linen Thread Company and affiliates	2/1959	Purchase of stock	Cash & Notes***		1,035,000	$5,000,000	6,035,000
Textile Thread Company and affiliates	12/1959	Purchase of all outstanding common	Cash & Notes#		72,880	1,065,200	1,138,080
Hoosac Mills Corporation	2/1960	Purchase of stock	Cash		1,364,000		1,364,000
USF - Aspinook Finishing Division of Gera Corporation (Now USF - Arnold)	4/1960	Purchase of substantially all assets	Cash & Notes##		3,798,000	3,000,000	6,798,000
Bernhard Ulmann Co., Inc.	5/1960	Purchase of selected assets (not including real estate)	Cash		3,993,000		3,993,000
Bachmann Uxbridge Worsted Co.	8/1960	Purchase of selected assets	Cash		4,769,413		4,769,413
William Skinner & Sons	2/1961	Purchase of stock	Cash		4,348,000		4,348,000
TOTAL					$25,211,373	$9,065,200	$34,276,573

*Cumulative sinking fund preferred, call price $25, par $20, total par value approximately $4.92 million. Of the 246,055 shares authorized, 34,162 were originally subject to claims from dissenting stockholders who demanded $25 a share. The company appraised these shares at $12.69. Pending legal settlement, these shares (reduced in number to 33,662 by 1960) were treated as authorized but unissued.

**Cumulative sinking fund preferred, junior to the $1.25 issue, call price $25, par $20, total par value approximately $4.10 million.

***Indian Head Mills, Inc. agreed to buy from Linen Thread Ltd. the outstanding stock of its American subsidiary, Linen Thread Company, Inc. First a value of $12 million was established for the book net worth of approximately $19 million. The American subsidiary used its own cash to buy back 62,000 shares of stock from the parent company and cancelled the stock. Indian Head Mills, Inc. thus, actually paid a final purchace price of $6,035,000 for 63,000 shares of outstanding stock. The $5 million in notes drew interest at 5% and required a quarterly payment of $250,000.

#Seven per cent sinking fund notes of a subsidiary (guaranteed by the company) due in quarterly installments to 12/20/1964.

##Six per cent promissory not of subsidiary (guaranteed by the company), due in monthly installments to April 1, 1965.

Source: Company records.

Exhibit 2

INDIAN HEAD MILLS, INC. (E)

Contributions of new Acquisitions to Consolidated Net Sales, by Years

Fiscal Period Ended	Sales from Prior Year's Operations	Sales from New Acquisitions	Total
October 3, 1953	$ 8,863,000		$ 8,863,000
October 2, 1954	11,445,000		11,445,000
December 3, 1955	13,069,000	$ 7,039,000	20,108,000
December 1, 1956	21,986,000		21,986,000
November 30, 1957	20,627,000	1,871,000	22,498,000
November 29, 1958	21,874,000	21,301,000	43,175,000
November 28, 1959	44,969,000	11,185,000	56,154,000
December 3, 1960	56,291,000	25,637,000	81,929,000

Note:

1955 includes Naumkeag Steam Cotton Company for 12 weeks prior to merger on February 19, and 41 weeks of combined operations after merger.

1957 includes operation of J. L. Stifel & Sons, Inc. for 11 weeks following merger on September 13.

1958 includes operations of Franklin Process Company for 50 weeks following acquisition on December 10, 1957.

1959 includes operations of The Linen Thread Co., Inc. for 43 weeks following acquisition on February 3.

1960 includes operations of Hoosac Mills for 40 weeks following acquisition on February 29; USF-Arnold Finishing Company for 35 weeks following acquisition on April 1; Bernhard Ulmann Company for 29 weeks following acquisition on May 12; and Bachmann Uxbridge Worsted Company for 16 weeks following acquisition on August 15.

Source: Company records.

Exhibit 3

INDIAN HEAD MILLS, INC. (E)

Source of Tax Carry-Forward and Nonrecurring Income

Approximate Tax Carry-Forward*	
Naumkeag Steam Cotton Company	
Tax loss contribution	$ 3,200,000
J. L. Stifel & Sons Inc.	
Tax loss contribution	2,100,000
Glendale Mills	
Tax loss contribution	900,000
The Linen Thread Co. Inc.	
Tax loss contribution	2,300,000
Hoosac Mills Corporation	
Tax loss contribution	2,000,000
William Skinner & Sons	
Tax loss contribution	800,000
Total	$11,300,000
Nonrecurring Income	
52 weeks ending Nov. 30, 1957	
Discount on prepayment of long-term debt and refund of real estate taxes on property sold in prior year	$ 382,640
Year ending Nov. 28, 1958	
Profit on purchase of Franklin Process Company inventory	1,081,600
Loss on disposal of property, plant, and equipment	(195,799)
Year ending Nov. 28, 1959	
Profit on the purchase of The Linen Thread Co. Inc. inventory	1,534,491
Provision for loss on foreign receivables	(155,153)
Net loss on disposal of property, plant, and equipment	(517,831)
Year ended December 3, 1960	
Profit on sale of certain inventories of businesses acquired, less applicable expenses**	1,159,692
Provision for estimated expenses in discontinuance of certain facilities	(700,000)
Recovery on foreign receivables	107,081
Profit on sale of division acquired and sold during the year	71,314
Total	$ 2,768,035

*Amounts available at time of purchase plus amounts generated by losses on assets that the company planned to sell on acquisition.

**The inventories of the Bachmann Uxbridge Worsted Company were purchased at a substantial discount from their carrying values on the books of the predecessor company. The portion of the discount which was allocated to the surplus inventories, less applicable expenses, is included as a nonrecurring profit on the income statement. The portion of the discount which was allocated to the inventories of the continuing business was applied to the inventories by the adoption of the last-in, first-out method of valuing these inventories.

Source: Company records, Annual Reports.

Exhibit 4

INDIAN HEAD MILLS, INC. (E)

Analysis of Sales of Plant and Machinery and Equipment

Time of Acquisition	Year of Sale	Area in Square Feet	Previous Owner's Gross Cost	Previous Owner's Net Book Value	Proceeds to Indian Head: Gross Sales Price	Proceeds to Indian Head: Idle Plant Expense	Proceeds to Indian Head: Selling Commission	Proceeds to Indian Head: Net Proceeds	Gain or (loss) Based on Net Book Value
PLANT									
Naumkeag merger	1955	1,000,000	$ 3,397,263	$ 1,334,313	$ 500,000	$ 39,000	$20,000	$ 441,000	$ (893,313)
Stifel merger	1958	404,000	1,541,090	1,037,401	230,000	77,000		153,000	(884,401)
Franklin acquisition	1958, 1961	320,000	1,416,930	739,835	395,000	18,640	24,500	351,860	(387,975)
Linen Thread acquisition	1959	715,000	2,348,144	785,762	570,000		18,000	552,000	(233,762)
Textile Thread acquisition	1960	75,000	106,266	66,276	142,000			142,000	75,724
Bachmann Uxbridge acquisition	1960	651,300	4,319,858	2,735,841	837,500			837,500	(1,898,341)
Total		3,165,300	$13,129,551	$6,699,428	$2,674,500	$134,640	$62,500	$2,477,360	($4,222,068)
MACHINERY AND EQUIPMENT									
Naumkeag merger	1955		1,038,399	414,991	243,000		8,800	234,200	(180,791)
Stifel merger	1958		1,951,161	910,654	138,194			138,194	(772,460)
Franklin acquisition	1958,1961		721,000	240,000	46,357		2,105	44,252	(195,748)
Linen Thread acquisition	1959		3,913,542	1,187,863	402,829			402,829	(785,034)
Textile Thread acquisition	1960		594,624	188,899	112,319		2,384	109,935	(78,964)
Bachmann Uxbridge acquisition	1960		5,833,378	2,434,060	1,492,000			1,492,000	(942,060)
Total			$14,052,104	$5,376,467	$2,434,699		$13,289	$2,421,410	($2,955,057)
Grand Total			$27,181,655	$12,075,895	$5,109,199	$134,640	$75,789	$4,898,770	($7,177,125)

Note: Information not reproduced included net proceeds per square foot and as a per cent of book value and gross cost.

Source: Company records.

Exhibit 5

INDIAN HEAD MILLS, INC. (E)
PRODUCTION FACILITIES AND CAPACITIES
As of February 1, 1961

PLANTS	17
MANUFACTURING AND WAREHOUSE SPACE	3.5 Million Sq. Ft.
EQUIPMENT	
Spindles	161,490
Looms	3,784
Printing Machines	22
Yarn Dyeing Machines	107
EMPLOYEES	7,300

RAW MATERIAL CONSUMPTION (MILLIONS)

Cotton	74.7 Bales
Wool Tops	3.5 Pounds
Silk and Synthetic yarns	8.3 Bounds
Other Yarns	.6 Pounds

ANNUAL CAPACITIES (MILLIONS)

Cotton Fabrics	78.0 Yards
Worsted Fabrics	5.2 Yards
Silk and Synthetic Fabrics	34.6 Yards
Printing	95.0 Yards
Commission Finishing	26.0 Yards
Bleaching and Dyeing	27.5 Pounds
Threads and Twines	12.0 Pounds
Fish and Sports Nettings	2.5 Pounds

Source: Company records.

Exhibit 6
INDIAN HEAD MILLS, INC. (E)

Parent Company and Consolidated* Balance Sheets,
Showing the Division of Assets between Companies Acquired before and after 1958
(dollars in thousands)

	Parent Company (Includes business of the Finished Goods Division** The Greige and Industrial Fabrics Division***, and the Franklin Process Company)		Consolidated Company (Includes business of the parent company, The Linen Thread Company;# Hoosac Mills Division, the USF-Arnold Finishing Company, Bernhard Ulmann Company, and the Bachmann Uxbridge Worsted Company##)	
	November 28, 1959	August 27, 1960 (unaudited)	November 28, 1959	August 27, 1960 (unaudited)
Assets:				
Cash	$ 491	$ 725	$ 4,456	$ 1,815
Accounts receivable (net) (Note A)	5,867	2,118	8,316	4,563
Mortgages and notes receivable (net)	-	-	217	72
Inventories (Note B)	5,240	7,304	8,528	15,685
Prepaid expenses	73	12	165	101
Total current assets	$11,670	$10,158	$21,682	$22,236
Investments and advances (subsidiaries) (Note C)	6,270	7,869	100	100
Property, plant, equipment (net) (Note D)	2,281	2,198	3,824	9,190
Property, at amounts realized on sale (September 1960)	-	-		2,286
Mortgages and notes due after one year (net)	-	-	696	631
Other assets	585	569	704	684
Total assets	$20,806	$20,795	$27,007	$35,127
Liabilities & Capital:				
Balance, purchase price (Bachmann Uxbridge)	-	-	-	$ 3,769
Notes payable to banks	-	-	79	
Current installments, long-term debt	1,100	1,000	1,351	1,813
Accounts payable	2,066	1,615	2,635	3,102
Other (Note E)	2,003	2,710	2,647	3,284
Total current liabilities	5,169	5,325	6,712	11,968
Notes payable (Note F)	3,250	2,500	4,064	5,355
Accrued liabilities due	-	-	748	706
Total long-term liabilities	3,250	2,500	4,812	6,061
Preferred stock, $1.25 cumulative (Note G)	3,465	3,375	3,465	3,375
Preferred stock, $1.50 cumulative (Note G)	3,482	3,354	3,482	3,354
Common stock (Note H)	544	546	544	546
Capital surplus	2,285	2,264	2,285	2,264
Earned surplus (Note I)	2,609	3,431	5,706	7,561
Total capital stock & surplus	12,387	12,970	15,483	17,099
Contingent liability & leases (Note E,J)				
Total liabilities and capital	$20,806	$20,795	$27,007	$35,127

*Excludes Indian Head (Puerto Rico, Inc.)

**Comprises most of the business done originally by Indian Head Mills, Inc., the Naumkeag Steam Cotton Company; and commission sales.

***Comprises some business originally done by Indian Head Mills, Inc., and J. L. Stifel & Sons, Inc.

#Comprises the business of the Linen Thread Company and the Textile Thread Company and affiliates, organized as a subsidiary company.

##Comprises the business of the Hoosac Mills Division, the USF-Arnold Finishing Company, and the Bernhard Ulmann Company, and the Bachmann Uxbridge Company organized as a subsidiary company.

See notes to financial statements, pp. 00-00.

Source: Prospectus, November 19, 1960.

Exhibit 7

INDIAN HEAD MILLS, INC. (E)

Parent Company and Consolidated Statements of Income, Year Ended November 28, 1959, and Nine Months Ended August 27, 1960
(dollars in thousands)

	Parent Company		Consolidated Company	
	Year ended Nov. 28, 1959	Nine months ended Aug. 27, 1960 (Unaudited)	Year ended Nov. 28, 1959	Nine months ended Aug. 27, 1960 (Unaudited)
Net sales	$ 44,911	$ 31,880	$ 56,154	$ 52,010
Operating costs and expenses:				
Cost of sales	39,251	27,685	48,010	44,167
Advertising, selling and administrative expenses	3,478	2,493	5,069	5,077
	42,735	30,178	53,079	49,244
Operating profit	2,176	1,702	3,075	2,766
Other deductions (income):				
Interest on long-term debt	198	148	198	278
Other interest expense	106	135	100	138
Interest income	(13)	(12)	(88)	(48)
Contributions to profit sharing plans (Note L)	200	141	200	141
Provision for state income taxes	84	80	84	124
Miscellaneous - net	(36)	141	(59)	105
	538	633	435	738
Profit before nonrecurring items	1,638	1,069	2,640	2,028
Nonrecurring income (loss):				
Profit on disposal of inventories of business acquired (Note C)	--	--	1,535	--
Expenses applicable to profit on disposal of inventories (Note C)	(215)	--	--	--
Loss on disposal of property, plant and equipment (Note D)	(859)	--	(518)	--
Loss and recovery on foreign receivables	(155)	107	(155)	107
Profit on sale of division acquired and sold during period	--	--	--	74
	(1,229)	107	862	181
Net profit (no provision for federal income tax required - Note M)	$ 409	$ 1,176	$ 3,502	$ 2,209

See notes to financial statements, pp. 00-00.

Source: Prospectus, November 19, 1960.

INDIAN HEAD MILLS, INC. (E)

Notes to Financial Statements

A. ACCOUNTS RECEIVABLE:

At August 27, 1960 accounts receivable of the parent company are net of $3,731,406 advanced by a bank to which accounts receivable aggregating $5,871,539 have been assigned. Consolidated accounts receivable are net of $7,071,175 advanced by a bank to which accounts receivable aggregating $10,250,163 have been assigned. The bank has assumed the credit risk on the assigned accounts receivable.

At November 28, 1959 there were no advances against assigned accounts.

B. INVENTORIES:

The inventories used in the computation of the cost of sales for the three years and nine months ended August 27, 1960 were as follows:

	Parent Company	*Consolidated*
December 1, 1956	$3,884,519	$ 3,884,519
November 30, 1957	3,469,752	3,935,615
November 29, 1958	3,231,900	5,228,268
November 28, 1959	5,239,730	8,528,043
August 27, 1960 (unaudited)	7,303,522	15,684,900

Inventories have been stated at the lowest of standard costs approximating first-in, first-out costs, replacement market or estimated selling market after allowance for adminitrative and selling expenses. In pricing the inventories, allowance was made for obsolete, slow-moving and other irregular merchandise.

The portion of the purchase price allocable to the inventories of the Bernhard Ulmann Company, acquired on May 13, 1960, was approximately $685,000 less than their values (lower of cost or market) on the books of the predecessor company. No portion of this discount has been taken into income pending final determination of the method of valuing these inventories at the end of the 1960 fiscal year.

C. PRINCIPLES OF CONSOLIDATION AND INVESTMENTS IN SUBSIDIARIES:

The accompanying consolidated financial statements include the accounts of all subsidiaries except Indian Head (Puerto Rico) Inc., which company is not a significant subsidiary. The investment in this subsidiary is carried at cost, which approximates equity.

Intercompany accounts and transactons have been eliminated in preparing the consolidated financial statements.

The portion of the purchase price allocable to the inventories of the Franklin Process Company, which was acquired in December 1957 for cash and is operated as a division of the parent company, was $1,255,716 less than their book value. This discount, less applicable state income taxes and other expenses, was taken up as nonrecurring income when these inventories were sold.

The portion of the purchase price allocable to the inventories of The Linen Thread Co., Inc., which was acquired in 1959 and is operated as a subsidiary, was

$1,749,435 less than their book value. This discount, less applicable parent company expenses of $214,944, was taken up as nonrecurring consolidated income when these inventories were sold.

The consolidated balance sheet at November 28, 1959 gives effect to the purchase as of December 15, 1959 by a subsidiary of all of the stock of Textile Thread Company, Crywood Corporation and Herdmans Threads, Inc.

Operations of the businesses acquired during the periods are included in income from the dates of acquisition except that no amounts are reflected for the Bachmann Uxbridge Worsted Company, which was acquired on August 15, 1960.

The consolidated balance sheet at August 27, 1960 includes the assets purchased and the liabilities assumed on the acquisition of Bachmann Uxbridge Worsted Company. The inventories and plant and equipment were purchased at a substantial discount from their carrying values on the books of the predecessor company.

The company contemplates the use of the LIFO method of valuing inventories with respect to the portion of the business which will be continued and anticipates that there will be a nonrecurring profit on the disposal of surplus inventories acquired.

The company's equity in the net assets of its consolidated subsidiaries as shown by their books exceeded the investment in such subsidiaries by $4,719,452 at August 27, 1960. In consolidation, $4,129,182 has been credited to earned surplus, $513,520 to accumulated depreciation and $76,750 to accrued liabilities.

D. PROPERTY, PLANT AND EQUIPMENT:

In October 1959, the company sold for $2,000,000 the land, buildings, machinery and equipment comprising the Whitney and Glendale mills and leased them back for an initial period of five years with renewal options for an additional fifteen years. Annual rentals on these properties aggregate $464,040 through 1964 and $40,020 thereafter. The loss on the sale amounted to $981,880 which is included in the loss on disposal of property, plant and equipment in the 1959 income statement and is reflected in the Summary of Consolidated Earnings for the nine months ended August 29, 1959 since negotiations for the sale were in progress at that date.

Upon sale or retirement of property, plant and equipment the accumulated depreciation applicable thereto is removed from the reserve account and the profit or loss resulting from such sale or retirement is reflected in income, except that losses resulting from sales in 1959 of various surplus properties of The Linen Thread Co., Inc. were charged against reserves for losses on sales of properties established prior to its acquisition by the company.

Depreciation has been provided generally on the straight-line or declining balance basis at annual rates based on the estimated remaining useful lives of the depreciable assets as follows:

Land improvements	3% to 5%
Buildings and building improvements	2 ½% to 6 ⅔%
Machinery and equipment	4% to 12 ½%
Leasehold improvements	Over life of lease

Maintenance, repairs and renewals of a minor nature are generally charged to income as incurred. Betterments and major renewals which extend the useful life of fixed assets are capitalized.

E. PROVISION FOR APPRAISAL CLAIMS:

On February 16, 1955, Indian Head Mills, Inc. (a Rhode Island corporation) was merged with and into Naumkeag Steam Cotton Company (a Massachusetts corporation) which assumed all the assets and liabilities of the former company and changed its name to Indian Head Mills, Inc.

There are outstanding demands of four former holders of 33,862 shares of Naumkeag Steam Cotton Company capital stock, who voted against the merger, for payment of such shares. These demands aggregate $846,550 at the demand price of $25.00 per share. The company has offered $12.69 per share to these claimants and on this basis the Board of Directors has authorized the establishment of a reserve to be used for such purpose in the amount of $429,709. Where the parties fail to agree, Massachusetts law provides that the value of these former shares be ascertained by three disinterested appraisers. The company regards its offer of $12.69 as fair. The status of shares of preferred stock otherwise issuable to these four claimants is not clear under Massachusetts law, but for purpose of simplification the company treats them as authorized but unissued.

F. LONG-TERM NOTES PAYABLE:

Long-term notes payable, exclusive of amounts due within one year, consist of the following:

	November 28, 1959	*August 27, 1960 (Unaudited)*
Parent Company:		
5% promissory note, due in quarterly installments of $250,000 to February 1, 1964	$3,250,000	$2,500,000
Subsidiaries:		
7% sinking funds notes, due in quarterly installments to December 20, 1964	814,470	654,690
6% promissory note, due $50,000 monthly to April 1, 1965	—	2,200,000
Total consolidated	$4,064,470	$5,354,690

At August 27, 1960, the payments required on the above indebtedness, due after one year are:

	Parent Company	*Consolidated*
Three months ended Nov. 30, 1961	$ 250,000	$ 453,260
Fiscal year ended:		
1962	1,000,000	1,813,040
1963	1,000,000	1,813,040
1964	250,000	1,017,565
1965	—	257,785
	$2,500,000	$5,354,690

In September 1960, a subsidiary of the Company entered into a loan agreement with banks under which it borrowed $5,500,000 on its 5% notes, due in installments to October 1961.

The notes of subsidiaries are guaranteed by the parent company as to payment of principal and interest.

G. PREFERRED STOCK:

The following is a summary of preferred stock at August 27, 1960:

	Shares	
	$1.25 *Cumulative*	$1.50 *Cumulative*
Authorized	207,233	174,124
Issued	173,271	174,124
Held for retirement	4,523	6,438
Outstanding	168,748	167,686

At November 28, 1959 there were outstanding 173,271 shares of $1.25 cumulative preferred stock and 174,124 shares of $1.50 cumulative preferred stock.

The holders of $1.25 cumulative preferred stock are entitled to $25.00 per share and accrued dividends on liquidation of the company or on redemption of the stock at the option of the company. This stock has the benefit of a sinking fund which requires the company to deposit $30,756 quarterly with the transfer agent, which fund is to be used for the purchase of $1.25 cumulative preferred stock tendered by holders at prices not in excess of $25.00 per share.

Subject to the prior rights of the $1.25 cumulative preferred stock, the holders of $1.50 cumulative preferred stock are entitled to $25.00 per share and accrued dividends on liquidation of the company or on redemption of the stock at the option of the company. This stock has the benefit of a sinking fund which requires the company to deposit $51,240 quarterly with the transfer agent, which fund is to be used for the purchase of $1.50 cumulative preferred stock tendered by holders at prices not in excess of $25.00 per share. Any shares of $1.50 cumulative preferred stock outstanding on November 15, 1982, may, prior to May 15, 1983, be converted, at the option of the holder, into 3.3 shares of common stock (subject to adjustment to protect against dilution).

H. STOCK OPTION AGREEMENTS:

At August 27, 1960, 131,274 shares of common stock were reserved for stockholder approved restricted stock options described elsewhere in this Prospectus under the heading "Employee Benefit Plans," including 124,074 shares reserved for outstanding options of which 112,574 were exercisable at that date. Details of the outstanding options are as follows:

Fiscal Year Granted	*Number of Shares*	*Option price*		*Market price at dates of grant*	
		Per Share	*Total*	*Per Share*	*Total*
1954	53,174	$4.55	$241,942	$239 and $3.30	$148,447
1955	52,800	6.37	336,336	6.19	326,832
1956	4,400	5.46 and 7.27	28,028	4.66 and 5.11	21,494
1958	2,200	7.50 and 10.23	19,503	7.50 and 10.23	19,503
1959	5,500	21.82 and 30.91	160,006	20.00 to 30.45	154,990
1960	6,000	41.00 to 49.00	256,000	41.00 to 49.00	256,000
	124,074		$1,041,815		$927,266

Options which became exercisable and those exercised during the three fiscal years and nine months ended August 27, 1960 are summarized below:

	Number of	Option price		Market price	
Exercisable	*Shares*	*Per Share*	*Total*	*Per Share*	*Total*
				At dates first exercisable	
1957	55,000	$6.37	$350,350	$7.05	$387,750
1958	5,500	$5.46 and $ 7.27	36,036	$ 7.95 and $13.07	60,621
1960	2,200	$7.50 and $10.23	19,503	$31.50 and $41.50	80,300
	62,700		$405,889		$528,671
Exercised				*At dates exercised*	
1958	4,620	$4.55	$ 21,021	$13.18 and $13.41	$ 61,499
1959	36,300	$4.55 to $7.27	172,172	$18.18 to $29.55	763,516
1960	1,540	$4.55	7,007	$33.50 and $39.50	59,510
	42,460		$200,200		$884,525

The excess of the proceeds over par value of shares issued has been credited to capital surplus. No charges have been made to income with respect to these options.

The options granted, exercisable and exercised, as shown above, together with option prices and market prices, have been adjusted to give effect to the two-for-one stock split and the 10% stock dividend in 1959.

I. EARNED SURPLUS:

See "Description of Common Stock" elsewhere in this Prospectus for comments on provisions in the company's charter restricting purchase of its common stock and the payment of cash dividends and other distributions thereon. At August 27, 1960, $240, 575 of the company's earned surplus was restricted by these provisions.

As indicated in Note 7, the redemption price of the preferred stock, $25.00 per share, is $5.00 per share in excess of par value, or a total of $1,682,170 at August 27, 1960. In the opinion of Company's counsel, this does not constitute a restriction on earned surplus of the company.

J. LONG-TERM LEASES:

Annual rentals payable under long-term leases in effect at August 27, 1960 covering office space, buildings, machinery and equipment are approximately $600,000 for the parent company and $1,100,000 on a consolidated basis. Under certain of these leases the lessee is also required to pay for insurance, taxes and repairs.

In general, these leases are for five year terms with renewal options at reduced rentals. One lease of office space, with an annual rental of $100,000, expires in 1973.

K. RETIREMENT PLANS:

Information with respect to the company's Profit Sharing Retirement Plan is contained under the caption "Employee Benefit Plans" elsewhere in this Prospectus. Amounts shown in the statement of income exclude $120,178 in 1958 and $174,944 in 1959 applicable to profit on disposal of inventories of businesses acquired.

Trusteed retirement plans of the Franklin Process Company and The Linen Thread Co., Inc. have been assumed and continue in effect for the benefit of certain salaried employees who are not eligible for benefits under the Indian Head plan. Annual costs under these trusteed plans aggregate approximately $105,000.

L. FEDERAL INCOME TAXES:

No provision for federal income taxes was required for the three fiscal years ended November 28, 1959 and the nine months ended August 27, 1960 as the operating loss carryover from prior years exceeded taxable income for these periods.

Information as to unused federal tax loss carryovers is set forth under the caption "Summary of Consolidated Earnings—Tax Loss Carryover" contained elsewhere in this Prospectus.

Source: Prospectus, November 19, 1960.

Exhibit 8

INDIAN HEAD MILLS, INC. (E)

Financial Highlights, an Eight-Year Summary

	1953 (8 Months)	1954	1955 (C)	1956	1957 (B)	1958 (B)	1959 (B)	1960 (B)
Sales (thousands)	$ 8,863	$ 11,444	$ 20,108	$ 21,986	$ 22,498	$ 43,175	$ 56,154	$ 81,930
Net profit (thousands)(A)	-	184	593	363	1,911	2,331	3,502	3,604
% Profit to sales (before nonrecurring income & provision for federal income tax)	-	1.6%	2.9%	1.7%	6.8%	3.3%	4.7%	4.0%
% Net profit to average net worth	-	46.3	18.4	6.3	22.5	19.6	24.9	21.4
Net profit per common share (D):								
Before nonrecurring income	-	$ .35	$ .78	$ .22	$ 2.36	$ 1.74	$ 3.76	$ 4.37
Nonrecurring income	-	-	-	-	.72	1.66	1.51	1.11
TOTAL	-	$ .35	$ .78	$ .22	$ 3.08	$ 3.40	$ 5.27	$ 5.48
Working capital (thousands)	$ 1,454	798	3,521	3,343	5,110	6,917	14,971	13,239
Total assets (thousands)	5,163	3,548	9,689	9,227	13,688	16,013	27,007	34,673
Long-term debt (thousands)	3,857	1,594	1,895	1,666	250	100	4,064	4,851
Net worth:								
$1.25 preferred stock (thousands)	-	-	4,027	3,882	3,732	3,587	3,465	3,344
$1.50 preferred stock (thousands)	-	-	-	-	3,874	3,666	3,482	3,312
Common equity (thousands)	170	625	1,784	1,921	3,549	5,405	8,536	11,593
TOTAL	$ 170	$ 625	$ 5,811	$ 5,803	$ 11,155	$ 12,658	$ 15,483	$ 18,249
Preferred dividends:								
$1.25 preferred stock (thousands)	-	-	$ 181	$ 248	$ 239	$ 229	$ 221	$ 214
$1.50 preferred stock (thousands)	-	-	-	-	41	285	270	256
TOTAL			$ 181	$ 248	$ 280	$ 514	$ 491	$ 470
Common Stock (D):								
Number of shares outstanding	392,700	528,990	528,990	528,990	528,990	533,841	571,174	571,687
Book value per share - preferred at par	$ .43	$ 1.18	$ 3.37	$ 3.63	$ 6.71	$ 10.12	$ 14.94	$ 20.28
% Increase per share in common stock equity	-	174.4%	185.6%	7.7%	84.8%	50.8%	47.6%	35.7%
Number of options outstanding	-	102,957	160,707	165,096	160,476	157,935	125,594	131,327

(A) No federal income tax required for 1955-1959 because of the availability of loss carry-forward. $325,000 provided for federal income tax in 1960 and $215,000 in 1954.

(B) Includes operations of companies acquired from date of acquisition as follows: J. L. Stifel & Sons, Inc., September 13, 1957; Franklin Process Company, December 10, 1957; The Linen Thread Co., Inc., February 13, 1959; Hoosac Mills Corporation, February 29, 1960; USF-Arnold Finishing Company, April 1, 1960; Bernhard Ulmann Co. Inc., May 13, 1960; Bachmann Uxbridge Worsted Company, August 15, 1960.

(C) Includes Naumkeag Steam Cotton Company (Pequot Mill) for 12 weeks prior to merger on February 19, 1955 and 41 weeks of combined operations after merger.

(D) Years prior to 1960 have been adjusted for two-for-one stock split and 10% stock dividend in 1959 and 5% stock dividend in 1960.

Source: Annual Report, 1960.

Exhibit 9

INDIAN HEAD MILLS, INC. (E)

Comparative Ranking of the 16 Textile Companies Listed in *Fortune* Magazine's Directory of the Nation's 500 Largest Industrial Companies (Rank Number in Parentheses is Rank Among the 16 Textiles Listed)

Company	Sales (Millions)		Ranks	Profit as % of Sales %		Ranks	Assets (Millions)		Ranks	Profit as % of Invested Capital* %		Ranks	Capital Times	Turnover Ranks
Burlington Industries	$912.9	(1)	48	3.9	(7)	285	$606.4	(1)	63	9.8	(4)	219	1.5	(4)
Stevens (J.P.)	512.6	(2)	90	3.0	(12)	344	358.4	(2)	108	6.6	(10)	356	1.4	(5)
United Merchants & Mfrs.	468.2	(3)	98	3.1	(11)	340	314.7	(3)	123	9.7	(5)	228	1.5	(4)
Lowenstein (M) & Sons	253.3	(4)	190	2.0	(14)	408	194.6	(4)	188	6.0	(11)	383	1.3	(6)
Cannon Mills	202.9	(5)	232	6.4	(2)	146	163.2	(8)	223	9.3	(6)	245	1.2	(7)
Cone Mills	188.5	(6)	248	2.0	(15)	410	164.3	(7)	220	3.2	(16)	446	1.1	(8)
Springs Cotton Mills	187.6	(7)	250	10.0	(1)	51	188.5	(5)	192	11.4	(2)	152	.99	(9)
Dan River Mills	162.8	(8)	271	4.5	(5)	244	167.9	(6)	217	7.6	(8)	311	.97	(10)
West Point Manufacturing	156.9	(9)	278	5.2	(3)	197	97.2	(9)	324	10.5	(3)	186	1.6	(3)
Kendall	111.6	(10)	365	4.6	(4)	236	80.6	(11)	374	9.0	(7)	254	1.4	(5)
Pepperell Manufacturing	100.2	(11)	388	3.5	(9)	311	57.3	(14)	449	6.8	(9)	344	1.7	(2)
Mohasco Industries	96.5	(12)	404	3.4	(10)	319	96.7	(10)	327	4.6	(14)	424	.99	(9)
Riegel Textile	90.7	(13)	423	2.6	(13)	365	61.4	(13)	436	5.4	(13)	399	1.5	(4)
Indian Head Mills	81.9	(14)	467	4.4	(6)	248	34.6	(16)	494	19.8	(1)	26	2.4	(1)
Bibb Manufacturing	80.3	(15)	473	3.9	(8)	286	56.6	(15)	452	5.9	(12)	386	1.4	(5)
Bigelow-Sanford	74.2	(16)	489	2.0	(16)	412	64.1	(12)	432	8.3	(15)	441	1.4	(7)
Industry Average for companies in the 500:				3.9										

*Net worth at year's end.

Source: Company records.

INDIAN HEAD MILLS, INC. (E)
INCENTIVE COMPENSATION PLAN, PURPOSE AND PRINCIPLES

Purpose

The purpose of the plan is to reward eligible "officers and employees' with cash bonus payments based on "contribution to profit results."

Principles

(1) Separate funds, based on earnings, are established for each division and/or department, plus a fund for corporate management "based on over-all results" after division bonuses are paid.

(2) Administration of the plan is through a board committee composed of nonparticipating members. The board has power to modify the plan, but stockholders must ratify any change that would increase aggregate payments in any fiscal year to a figure "in excess of 20% of the company's net earnings before taxes in excess of $1 million."

(3) The funds to be set up and the amounts payable into each are determined annually by the committee in accordance with a predetermined, detailed formula (as opposed to a purely descretionary basis). The committee annually designates individual participants in each plan.

(4) In computing the bonus fund, a deduction is made from profits to cover dividend requirements on preferred stock plus (in the case of the corporate fund) 15% on the common stock equity, or (in the case of divisional and departmental plans) 15% of average net worth.

(5) Payments into the bonus funds are made on the basis of a sliding scale; that is, the higher the proportion of net earnings to company equity or divisional/departmental net worth, the higher the percentage of net earnings paid into the bonus fund.

(6) For the purpose of determining amounts payable into the bonus funds, the term "net earnings" is precisely defined. By and large, income and expenses over which management has little or no control (for example, Federal income tax, idle plant expense, and gains or losses from the sale of capital assets) are excluded from the definition of net earnings.

(7) Bonus payments to individual participants are figured as a percentage of salary, with no bonus exceeding 100% of this base. All payments are current rather than deferred, and are made in cash rather than in stock or phantom stock units. (Selected corporate and divisional executives receive stock options under a separate incentive plan.)

(8) Bonus participants are divided into four classes, respectively eligible to receive maximum bonuses of 100%, 75%, 50% and 25% of salary. In 1961 only five officers, all at the corporate level, were in the top, or 100% maximum, class.

(9) Bonuses, like bonus funds, are on a sliding scale. At the corporate level, payment of maximum bonuses depends on net earnings (after provision for preferred dividends) reaching 40% or more of the common stock equity. Otherwise bonuses are scaled down, dropping to a minimum of 15% of maximum, provided any bonus at all is paid. (See principle 4 above.)

At the divisional level, there is no fixed minimum bonus percentage, but if money in the fund is insufficient to provide for maximum payments, then each participant receives a pro rata portion of his maximum.

Source: Prepared by case writers from a company document entitled, "Incentive Compensation Plan, Fiscal 1961."

Exhibit 10

INDIAN HEAD MILLS, INC. (E)

CORPORATE MANAGEMENT GROUP
1961 EXECUTIVE INCENTIVE COMPENSATION PLAN

PROFIT REQUIRED FOR VARIOUS PER CENTS OF MAXIMUM BONUS

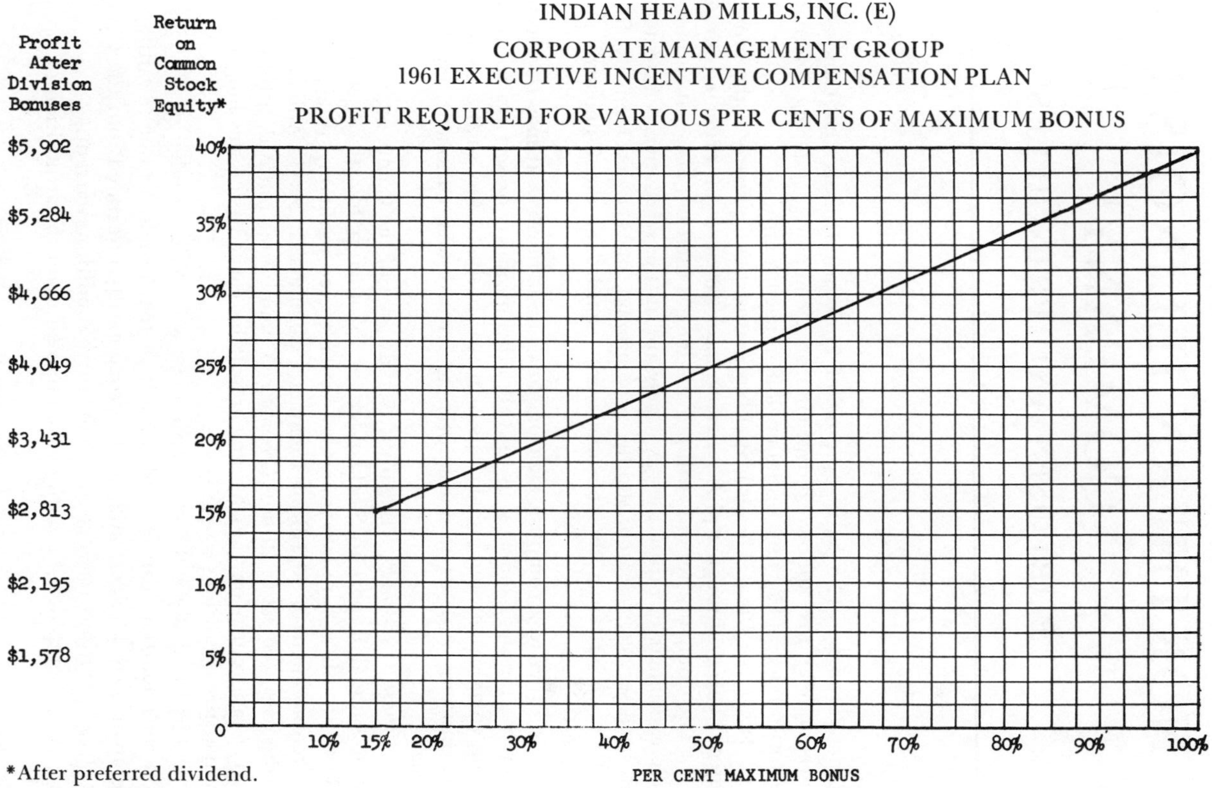

*After preferred dividend.

Source: Company records.

APPENDIX D

NORTHERN ILLINOIS GAS COMPANY[1]

PURPOSES AND PRINCIPLES

Basic Purpose: The basic purpose of Northern Illinois Gas Company is to perpetuate an investor-owned, free enterprise company, rendering a needed, satisfactory service and earning optimum, long-range profits.

What We Do: The principal business of the Company is the provision of gaseous energy through a pipe system to meet the needs of ultimate consumers.

The Company not only will provide the gas itself but also will encourage and help consumers to utilize the gas widely and in the safest, most efficient manner. All such service, research, supply, promotional, market development, financing and similar activities for consumers are regarded as the Company's principal business.

In order to accomplish the Company's basic purpose, it may be necessary or desirable for the Company to provide other products or services which supplement, complement and enhance its principal business. Any such activities should be consistent with its responsibilities to its investors, customers, employes and others.

Where We Do It: The utility service area of the Company is shown in the latest Annual Report to Stockholders or in other publications. Service will be offered in this area to everyone who can be served profitably, in accordance with the requirements of the Illinois Commerce Commission. Service will also be offered in this area, subject to Illinois Commerce Commission approval, if indications are that a fair return on the investment will be earned over the long term, or if competitive conditions warrant.

The Company will seek to acquire or will construct other gas systems whenever such additions can be made on a basis that promises to be rewarding to the Company's stockholders and can be economically integrated into the Company's existing operations, or whenever competitive conditions warrant.

No geographical limitations are imposed upon the acquisition of gas and its

[1]Reprinted with permission of the Northern Illinois Gas Company.

transportation to the service area nor upon supplementary and complementary activities into which the Company may enter.

How We Do It: The Company will conduct its business in full recognition of its responsibilities, as set forth hereafter, to the several elements of the community upon which its operations have an impact. The Company believes that in general, over the long run, the interests of all these elements are compatible.

INVESTORS

The Company will:

A. Strive to provide to its owners, the holders of its common stock, a growing per share value, measured in terms of both income and appreciation, and to be the maximum, in the long run, consistent with the Company's responsibilities to its customers, employes and the public.

B. Seek to continue to hold the interest of its broad, diversified, well-balanced and stable family of stockholders, and to attract others who will maintain this balance.

C. Provide for its stock a ready, convenient and technically sound market to ensure optimum flexibility for its owners.

D. Keep present and potential investors in the Company and their representatives well informed about the Company and its prospects, in order that they may make their investment decisions with full knowledge and that the Company's securities are appraised fairly.

E. Keep its books in accordance with accepted accounting principles and practices.

F. Safeguard and soundly employ Company funds and property.

G. Maintain a sound, conservative capital structure to support the quality of all of its securities, assure its ability to attract new capital when needed, provide good protection to the investors in its senior securities, and, coupled with strong earnings, assure optimum preservation of the investments of both the stockholds and senior security holders.

H. Develop strong earnings. To accomplish this *the Company will:*

1. Promote agressively the use of its product through the sale of gas and the sale of appliances and equipment utilizing the product.
2. Maintain a close control over expenses, and constantly seek means to reduce them.
3. Recover, as an operating expense, a realistic allowance for depreciation.
4. Engage in and support research to improve the utilization of gas, develop new uses, provide a substitute when needed and find better ways to transport, store, deliver, measure, bill and collect for it.
5. Provide capable, well-trained and enthusiastic managers, with adequate replacements ready when needed.
6. Engage in other activities than its principal business which supplement, complement and enhance such business.

I. Pay to the holders of its common stock in dividends a reasonable proportion of earnings, after annual review, bearing in mind the desirability of maintaining dividend stability so far as possible even if economic, regulatory or other developments become adverse.

J. Promote private enterprise and endeavor to minimize municipal or other governmental ownership of business.

CUSTOMERS

The Company will:

A. Deliver to its gas customers, safely and dependably, a gas of uniform heating value that will burn cleanly and efficiently.

B. Provide this gas at a fair and reasonable price, as low as possible consistent with prompt, courteous and dependable service, and consistent with its responsibilities to its investors, employes and the public.

C. Provide an adequate and dependable supply of gas over both the short- and long-range.

D. Provide prompt, courteous, dependable and economical service on customer appliances and equipment, or assure itself that satisfactory service is otherwise available to customers and that they have been so informed.

E. Publicize vigorously the advantages of its product.

F. Respect the right of every customer to use the form of energy which he prefers and, to that end, support energy competition so that a freedom of choice will be available to each customer.

G. See to it that better, even more modern appliances and equipment utilizing its energy are developed and brought to the Customer's attention.

H. Keep abreast of technological change.

I. Seek and utilize innovations and improvements to hold down and reduce costs.

J. Maintain its facilities and equipment well from the viewpoints of both operation and appearance.

K. Provide qualified personnel who are friendly, neat, courteous, well-informed, helpful and promptly attentive in a fair and just manner to the customer's individual problems.

EMPLOYES

A. *The Company will*, without discrimination as to race, creed, national background, age, sex, or physical handicaps not detrimental to performance or general health:

1. Hire employees with good appearance, attitude, and at least a high school or equivalent education.
2. Fill vacancies above starting levels from within the Company whenever possible.
3. Promote on the basis of ability, performance, and experience, not solely on length of service.
4. Provide job training and educational opportunities to help employes perform better in their jobs and prepare for advancement.

B. *The Company will*, in return for the fulfillment by employes of their responsibilities as outlined later:

1. Pay fair and just compensation comparable to what others are paying for like work.

2. Increase compensation from time to time as merited by improved productivity or performance.

C. *The Company will* provide:

1. Job security to the greatest extent possible, subject to continued satisfactory performance and adherence to Company work rules.
2. A comprehensive, modern benefit program.
3. Safe and, as far as possible, pleasant working conditions and practices. Tools and equipment will be safe and efficient.
4. An opportunity for employes to become stockholders in the business.

D. *The Company will* bargain fairly and realistically with recognized representatives of employes engaged in physical and clerical work.

E. *The Company will* administer discipline to all employes fairly, equitably, and firmly.

F. *The Company will*:

1. Seek to promote a working climate in which all employes understand and accept the Company's objectives and management's decisions, and are motivated to accomplish and implement them in a fully coordinated team effort.
2. Keep employes informed of matters of interest to them pertaining to their jobs, the Company, its product and service.
3. Endeavor to merit the pride of all employes in the Company, its management and policies.
4. Provide good, well-trained supervisors at all levels, with respect both for the individual and the need to get the job done properly, economically, and safely.
5. Provide its managers with a sound organization structure and clearly defined duties.
6. Delegate responsibility and authority as nearly as possible to the point of action.
7. Encourage self-reliance, creativity, initiative and decision-making.
8. Urge supervisors to discuss matters freely with their subordinates and encourage employes to feel free to discuss problems with their supervisors.
9. Encourage the search for new, more efficient ways of conducting its business, in order to reduce costs, increase productivity, and free manpower from the tasks of greatest drudgery to those more challenging and better paying.
10. Strive to utilize every employe on required work to his maximum capability in the long run.
11. Inform each employe what is expected of him and how well he is doing it.

G. *The Company will expect each employe to*:

1. Do a fair day's work for a fair day's pay.
2. Be quick to suggest improvements and be adaptable to change.
3. Uphold the highest standards of integrity.
4. Be loyal, supporting Company objectives and policies.
5. Be a good-will ambassador of the Company, pleasant and courteous in all customer and public contacts.
6. Be enthusiastic about the Company's business and promote it diligently.

7. Use Company-recommended safety equipment properly for his own personal well-being and for that of his fellow employes and of the public generally.
8. Be a good citizen, and participate in community activities of his choice, consistent with Company polices.

PUBLIC

The Company will foster and strive to maintain a sense of public interest. In discharging its responsibility to the public, it will endeavor to be a good citizen in every way, constantly seeking means to be of service and to deserve and enjoy the highest measure of public confidence and esteem.

The Company will:

A. Keep its properties and equipment in good condition and appearance.

B. Plan ahead so that its operations will be performed with a minimum of public inconvenience.

C. Inform the public of construction to be performed by it and the reasons therefor.

D. Restore property if disturbed.

E. Maintain a safe system.

F. Provide adequate capacity for the present needs of the communities it serves and be ready to meet their growth.

G. Promote the development of the area it serves.

H. Pay its fair share of taxes.

I. Encourage its employes to be leaders in community and civic activities to the extent consistent with Company policies.

J. Contribute to worthwhile community activities, to a reasonable extent considering its public utility status.

K. Keep the public informed of its problems and achievements which affect the public.

L. Be nonpartisan but speak out on issues where interests of the business, its investors, employes or customers are seriously affected.

SUPPLIERS

The Company will:

A. Deal fairly with its suppliers.

B. Place its orders strictly on the basis of ethical and sound business considerations after competitive bidding whenever appropriate.

C. Enter into no agreements with others to apportion business, maintain prices or otherwise restrain trade.

D. Instruct its employes to refuse gifts of immoderate entertainment from present or prospective suppliers.

COMPETITORS

The Company will:

A. Compete vigorously but fairly and ethically.

B. Enter into no agreements with others to apportion business, maintain prices or otherwise restrain trade.

GOVERNMENT

The Company will:

A. Encourage the selection of regulators and other government officials who are able, intelligent, conscientious, experienced and cognizant of the rights of investors as well as consumers.

B. Endeavor through proper channels to keep its regulators and other government officials well informed of the Company's position and problems.

C. Deal with these officials frankly, openly and in good faith.

D. Accept reasonable and farsighted regulation.

E. Make its position known when its interests may be adversely affected.

GAS INDUSTRY

The Company will:

A. Carry its fair share of well-conceived and well-executed gas industry activities.

B. Establish itself as an industry leader and set an outsanding example to others.

APPENDIX E

VARIAN ASSOCIATES

BASIC OBJECTIVES AND GENERAL POLICIES

The basic objectives and general policies of Varian Associates stated below are intended to provide the framework upon which both the long-range and day-to-day operations are to be based. These objectives have developed over a period of time, stemming from the basic philosophy agreed upon by the founders of the Company and have evolved as the Company matured. Changes in objectives must be developed carefully and the objectives should not be neglected for the purpose of everyday expediency.

PREMISES

This statement of objectives is conceived as a mechanism for the examination and appraisal of working policies. The objectives are based on the following five major points:

a. The Company must be operated as a profitable enterprise, and must serve the needs of its customers, shareholders, and employees. It is our responsibility to think of the profits in terms of complex responsibilities involving the shareholders (dividends, stock appreciation), employees (salaries, benefits, working conditions), and the customer quality product, fair price, good service).
b. The character of the Company is determined by its decision to operate in highly specialized fields, and to carry a large burden of pioneering in new fields of applied science.
c. The rarest commodities in the world are human intelligence and ingenuity. These must not be wasted, neglected, or allowed to stagnate.
d. The best of scientific and engineering talent must be employed and placed in an environment which will facilitate the proper utilization of knowledge, intellect, and skill.

[1]Reprinted with permission of Varian Associates.

e. The operations of the Company are to be led by a management group which must have the respect of the organization for its business ability, integrity, fairness, and human approach to everyday problems.

Based upon these premises, the basic Company objectives are as follows:

OBJECTIVES

1. Purpose

The prime objective is to conduct a strong, well-balanced, stable, well-managed research, engineering, and manufacturing international enterprise organized to return maximum benefits to employees, customers, and stockholders.

2. Nature of Enterprise

The Company shall strive to be a highely competent, profit-minded, technically oriented enterprise engaging in research, engineering, and manufacturing to meet the needs of the world markets. The Company shall operate in those fields in which its research and development talents are required for business success. The Company shall endeavor to exploit its talents in establishing new techniques and, through them, new products for commercial, industrial, and defense applications.

3. Fields of Interest

The Company shall be engaged in the fields of microwave tubes and components; vacuum systems, instruments, and components; in fields exploiting recent contributions to science, including radio-frequency spectroscopy and instrumentation resulting therefrom; and other fields of science which may produce products useful for industrial, commercial, and defense needs.

4. Diversification

In recognition of the usual business cycles, the Company shall develop new products and enter new product areas or activities as may properly diversify, balance, and profitably strengthen the Company's economic position.

The Company shall endeavor to broaden and strengthen its product lines or fields of interest by sponsoring research and engineering programs, by purchase of patent rights, or by acquisition in part or in whole of other companies.

The diversification and growth of the Company shall be tempered with full consideration of its impact upon those who form the Company structure and careful consideration of financial stability and the danger of overextension.

5. Business Stability

The Company shall endeavor to optimize profits, stabilize employment, and develop a sound financial position by:

a. Good management practices
b. Long-range planning
c. Product diversification

d. Balanced commercial, industrial, and defense programs
e. Strong research and engineering efforts
f. Strong financial control
g. Efficient, low-cost organization and economical procedures

6. Planning

The Company shall prepare management programs looking several years in advance to permit prudent program decisions, and to permit analysis and criticism by the Board of Directors, the management, and others.

7. Patents

The Company shall maintain a strong patent position by obtaining patent protection for the inventions made by members of its staff, by acquiring patents from others, and by entering into licensing agreements with others. It shall encourage inventiveness of its employees by financial awards, publication, and other means.

8. Product Lines

The Company shall develop a balanced line of profitable products which lend themselves to Varian techniques of engineering, manufacturing, and distribution, and which serve diversified markets having either a continuing profit potential or showing promise of becoming profitable in the future.

In recognition of the importance and obligation of its role in the defense efforts of the United States, the Company shall undertake research and development contracts from the government on a larger scale than is needed for the Company's manufacturing programs.

9. Financial

The Company shall strive to establish a stable financial structure, tightly controlled, with ample capitalization to operate the business efficiently and to permit necessary expansion and product diversification and to permit the Company to take advantage quickly of changing conditions.

10. Stock Policy

The Company shall encourage employee participation in the ownership of the Company.

11. Organization

The Company shall establish and maintain a sound structure and plan of organization which is necessary to meet the present and future Company objectives.

The Company shall be organized on a product line basis, with full profit accountability at the product division level. Methods of research, engineering, manufacturing, and marketing shall be adapted to the product areas. Corporate management will be responsible for binding these diverse products into the whole, and corporate staff functions shall supply those services not provided by line functions.

Management personnel shall be so developed and guided as to insure able and efficient performance of their duties. It is the Company's policy to hold each executive, manager, and supervisor responsible for the wholehearted and effective execution of its principles and objectives.

The Company shall adopt such principles of personnel administration as will improve the mutual understanding and increase the effectiveness of the staff.

GENERAL POLICIES

In conformance with its objectives, the Company shall adopt general administrative policies, including the following:

I. Organization

The Company shall so administer the organization as to make possible and to induce the highest possible productive efforts by:

a. Expecting above-average performance from employees and supervisors.
b. Coupling responsibility with authority, and reaching an understanding with those concerned before changing the scope of any responsibility.
c. Providing that no person shall be given directions by more than one person.
d. Assuring that all directions to an employee come from the immediate supervisor.
e. Assuring that no difference of opinion between supervisors or between employees as to authority or responsibility shall be considered too trivial for prompt and painstaking attention.
f. Assuring that a supervisor will counsel his employees, and will keep them informed on the nature of their performance.

II. Principles of Supervision

The Company shall conduct its supervision so as to emphasize respect for the personality and dignity of the individual. The policy of consultation up and down the organization lines of authority and channels of communication shall be encouraged, as well as:

a. Giving consideration to an employee's views before reaching decisions materially affecting his job and interests.
b. Encouraging employees to express their views on matters affecting their jobs and interests.
c. Freely explaining all matters affecting employee relations.
d. Attempting to understand the other person's point of view, and assuming that he too wants to do a good job.

III. Employment

The Company shall recruit and maintain the highest caliber staff possible to fill all positions, whether scientific, administrative, clerical, or of the skilled trades, and will do so by:

a. Selecting applicants on the basis of character, ability, skill, experience, and training, and without reference to age, sex, race, or creed.
b. Giving careful consideration to the promotion of employees to vacancies which occur, with the understanding that the strength of the Company's organization must be protected.
c. Giving consideration to employees who request job changes, and attempting to place each employee in the work for which he is best suited.
d. Maintaining a planned management development program to assure maximum performance by supervisors.

IV. Wages and Compensation

The Company shall establish a balanced compensation program for all employees, clearly related to job requirements of skill, responsibility, education, and experience, as demanded in current job descriptions.

The Company shall pay rates of pay, and establish rate ranges for all jobs, that are at least as good as those prevailing for similar work under similar conditions, and will maintain an equitable program for the granting of merit and promotional salary increases.

In recognition of the principle that scientific and technical contributions are as important as those made by management personnel, the Company will make the higher salaries available to top technical personnel without requiring them to shift to management occupations.

V. Working Conditions

The Company shall create and maintain working conditions in offices and factories so that they are safe, clean, attractive, and generally conducive of high productive effort.

VI. Grievances

The Company shall assure employees that they are free to express themselves and without prejudice as to matters discussed. The Company will also insure that the supervisory staff will try to remove promptly any source of dissatisfaction, and failing prompt and satisfactory adjustment, to provide for submission of the case to the Personnel Office for review and settlement in consultation with management.

VII. Benefit Plans

The Company shall make provisions for vacations, sick leave, and holidays with pay; install such insurance plans as will afford financial protection to the individual and his dependents in time of illness, injury, or death; and provide, at the employee's discretion, for the planned accumulation of funds sufficient to assure retirement benefits.

EVALUATION

The Company shall periodically appoint an advisory committee to assess the progress towards achievement of the Objectives and General Policies.

LIST OF BOOKS CITED

Abramson, Adolph G., and Mack, Russell H. *Business Forecasting in Practice.* New York: John Wiley and Sons, Inc., 1956.

Ackoff, Russell L. *A Concept of Corporate Planning.* New York: John Wiley and Sons, Inc., 1970.

Ackoff, Russell L., and Rivett, Patrick. *A Manager's Guide to Operations Research.* New York: John Wiley and Sons, Inc., 1963.

Aguilar, Francis F. *Scanning the Business Environment.* New York: The Macmillan Company, 1967.

Allen, Louis A. *Management and Organization.* New York: McGraw-Hill Book Company, Inc., 1958.

Ammer, Dean S. *Materials Management.* Homewood, Illinois: Richard D. Irwin, Inc., 1968.

Ansoff, H. Igor. *Corporate Strategy: An Analytic Approach to Business Policy for Growth and Expansion.* New York: McGraw-Hill Book Company, Inc., 1965.

Anthony, Robert N. *Planning and Control Systems: A Framework for Analysis.* Boston: Division of Research, Graduate School of Business Administration, Harvard University, 1965.

Anthony, Robert N., Dearden, John, and Vancil, Richard F. *Management Control Systems: Cases and Readings.* Homewood, Illinois: Richard D. Irwin, Inc., 1965.

Argenti, John. *Corporate Planning: A Practical Guide.* Homewood, Illinois: Richard D. Irwin, Inc., 1969.

Argyris, Chris. *The Impact of Budgets on People.* New York: Controllership Foundation, Inc., 1952.

Argyris, Chris. *Integrating the Individual and the Organization.* New York: John Wiley and Sons, Inc., 1964.

Argyris, Chris. *Personality and Organization.* New York: Harper and Row, Publishers, 1957.

Argyris, Chris. *Understanding Organizational Behavior.* Homewood, Illinois: The Dorsey Press, Inc., 1960.

Barish, Norman. *Economic Analysis for Engineering and Managerial Decision Making.* New York: McGraw-Hill Book Company, Inc., 1962.

Bassie, V. Lewis. *Economic Forecasting.* New York: McGraw-Hill Book Company, Inc., 1958.

Bennis, Warren G. *Changing Organizations: Essays on the Development and Evolution of Human Organization.* New York: McGraw-Hill Book Company, Inc., 1966.

Bergen, Garret L., and Haney, William V. *Organizational Relations and Management Action: Cases and Issues.* New York: McGraw-Hill Book Company, Inc., 1966.

Bierman, Harold, Jr., *et al. Quantitative Analysis for Business Decisions.* Homewood, Illinois: Richard D. Irwin, Inc., 1965.

Bonini, Charles P. *Simulation of Information and Decision Systems in the Firm.* Englewood Cliffs, N.J.: Prentice-Hall, Inc., 1963.

Bowman, Donald M., and Fillerup, Francis M. *Management: Organization and Planning.* New York: McGraw-Hill Book Company, Inc., 1963.

Branch, Melville C. *The Corporate Planning Process.* New York: American Management Association, 1962.

Branch, Melville C. *Planning: Aspects and Applications.* New York: John Wiley and Sons, Inc., 1966.

Branch, Melville C. *Selected References for Corporate Planning.* New York: American Management Association, 1966.

Bratt, Elmer Clark. *Business Cycles and Forecasting.* Fifth ed. Homewood, Illinois: Richard D. Irwin, Inc., 1961.

Bridges, Francis J., and Olm, Kenneth W. *Business Policy: Cases, Incidents, and Readings.* Boston: Allyn and Bacon, Inc., 1966.

Brooks, Frederick P. Jr., and Iverson, Kenneth E. *Automatic Data Processing.* New York: John Wiley and Sons, Inc., 1963.

Butler, William F., and Kavesh, Robert A. *How Business Economists Forecast.* Englewood Cliffs, N.J.: Prentice-Hall, Inc., 1966.

Cannon, J. Thomas. *Business Strategy and Policy.* New York: Harcourt, Brace and World, Inc., 1968.

Carvel, Fred J. *Human Relations in Business.* New York: The Macmillan Company, 1970.

Carzo, Rocco, Jr., and Yanouzas, John N. *Formal Organization: A Systems Approach.* Homewood, Illinois: Richard D. Irwin, Inc., 1967.

Chamberlain, Neil, *Public and Private Planning.* New York: McGraw-Hill Book Company, Inc., 1965.

Cleland, David I., and King, William R. *Systems Analysis and Project Management.* New York: McGraw-Hill Book Company, Inc., 1968.

Cohen, Jerome B., and Robbins, Sidney M. *The Financial Manager: Basic Aspects of Financial Administration.* New York: Harper and Row, Publishers, 1966.

Collier, James R. *Effective Long-Range Business Planning.* Englewood Cliffs, N.J.: Prentice-Hall, Inc., 1968.

Controllership Foundation. *Planning, Managing and Measuring the Business.* New York: Financial Executives Institute, 1955.

Cooper, William H., Leavitt, Harold J., and Skelly, Maynard W. III. *New Perspectives in Organization Research.* New York: John Wiley and Sons., Inc., 1964.

Costello, Timothy W., and Zalkind, Sheldon S. *Psychology in Administration.* Englewood Cliffs, N.J.: Prentice-Hall, Inc., 1963.

Croxton, Frederick E., Cowden, Dudley J., and Klein, Sidney. *Applied General Statistics.* Third ed. Englewood Cliffs, N.J.: Prentice-Hall, Inc., 1967.

Dauten, Carl A. *Business Cycles and Forecasting.* Second ed. Cincinnati: South-Western Publishing Company, 1961.

Davis, Gordon B. *An Introduction to Electronic Computers.* New York: McGraw-Hill Book Company, Inc., 1965.

Dearden, John. *Computers in Business Management.* Homewood, Illinois: Dow Jones-Irwin, Inc., 1966.

Dearden, John and McFarlan, F. Warren. *Management Information Systems: Text and Cases.* Homewood, Illinois: Richard D. Irwin, Inc., 1966.

Drucker, Peter. *The Practice of Management.* New York: Harper and Row, Publishers, 1954.

Dubes, Richard C. *The Theory of Applied Probability.* Englewood Cliffs, N.J.: Prentice-Hall, Inc., 1968.

Due, John F., and Clower, Robert W. *Intermediate Economic Analysis: Research Allocation, Factor Pricing and Welfare.* Fifth ed. Homewood, Illinois: Richard D. Irwin, Inc., 1966.

Emory, C. William and Niland, Powell. *Making Management Decisions.* Boston: Houghton Mifflin Company, 1968.

Ewing, David W. *The Human Side of Planning.* New York: The Macmillan Company, 1965.

Ewing, David W. *Long-Range Planning for Management.* Rev. ed. New York: Harper and Row, Publishers, 1964.

Ewing, David W. *The Practice of Planning.* New York: Harper and Row, Publishers, 1968.

Fayol, Henri. *General and Industrial Management.* New York: Pitman Publishing Corporation, 1949.

Ferrell, Robert W. *Customer-Oriented Planning.* New York: American Management Association, 1964.

Finley, Robert E., and Ziobro, Henry R. *The Manufacturing Man and His Job.* New York: American Management Association, 1966.

Forrester, Jay W. *Industrial Dynamics.* Cambridge, Mass.: The M.I.T. Press, 1961.

Glans, Thomas B., Grad, Burton, Holstein, David, Meyers, William E., and Schmidt, Richard N. *Management Systems.* New York: Holt, Rinehart and Winston, Inc., 1968.

Goetz, Billy E. *Quantitative Methods: A Survey and Guide for Managers.* New York: McGraw-Hill Book Company, Inc., 1965.

Gray, Edmond. *Readings in Business Policy.* New York: Appleton-Century-Crofts, 1969.

Greene, James H. *Production Control.* Homewood, Illinois: Richard D. Irwin, Inc., 1965.

Greenlaw, Paul S., Herrow, Lowell W., and Randon, Richard H. *Business Simulation in Industrial and University Education.* Englewood Cliffs, N.J.: Prentice-Hall, Inc., 1962.

Greenwood, James. *EDP: The Feasibility Study—Analysis and Improvement of Data Processing.* Washington, D.C.: Systems and Procedures Association, 1962.

Greenwood, William T. *Management and Organizational Behavior Theories: An Interdisciplinary Approach.* Cincinnati: South-Western Publishing Company, 1965.

Gross, Alfred and Gross, Walter. *Business Policy: Selected Readings and Editorial Commentaries.* New York: The Ronald Press, 1967.

Gross, Bertram M. *Organizations and Their Managing.* New York: The Macmillan Company, 1968.

Haire, Mason. *Organization Theory in Industrial Practice: A Symposium.* New York: John Wiley and Sons, Inc., 1962.

Hall, John F. *Psychology of Motivation.* Chicago: J. B. Lippincott Company, 1961.

Hardwick, C. T., and Landuyt, B. F. *Administrative Strategy and Decision Making.* Second ed. Cincinnati: South-Western Publishing Company, 1966.

Hargrove, Merwin M., Harrison, Ike H., and Swearington, Eugene L. *Business Policy Cases with Behavioral Science Implications.* Rev. ed. Homewood, Illinois: Richard D. Irwin, Inc., 1966.

Hastings, Delbert C. *The Place of Forecasting in Basic Planning for Small Business.* Minneapolis: University of Minnesota Press, 1961.

Henry, Harold W. *Long-Range Planning Practices in 45 Industrial Companies.* Englewood Cliffs, N.J.: Prentice-Hall, Inc., 1967.

Hicks, Herbert G. *The Management of Organization.* New York: McGraw-Hill Book Company, Inc., 1967.

Higginson, M. Valliant. *Management Policies, Vol. I: Their Development as Corporate Guides.* New York: American Management Association, 1966.

Higginson, M. Valliant. *Management Policies, Vol. II: Source Book of Statements.* New York: American Management Association, 1966.

Hillier, Frederick S., and Lieberman, Gerald J. *Introduction to Operations Research.* San Francisco: Holden-Day, Inc., 1967.

Hunt, Pearson, Williams, Charles M., and Donaldson, Gordon. *Basic Business Finance: Text and Cases.* Homewood, Illinois: Richard D. Irwin, Inc., 1966.

Hutchinson, John C. *Organizations: Theory and Classical Concepts.* New York: Holt, Rinehart and Winston, 1967.

James, John H., and Milroy, Robert R. *Long-Range Planning for Small Business.* Bloomington, Indiana: Bureau of Research, Graduate School of Business, Indiana University, 1964.

Jamison, Charles L. *Business Policy.* New York: Prentice-Hall, Inc., 1953.

Jerome, William Travers III. *Executive Control—The Catalyst.* New York: John Wiley and Sons, Inc., 1961.

Johnson, Richard A., Kast, Fremont E., and Rosenzweig, James E. *The Theory and Management of Systems.* New York: McGraw-Hill Book Company, Inc., 1963.

Jones, Manley Howe. *Executive Decision-Making.* Rev. ed. Homewood, Illinois: Richard D. Irwin, Inc., 1962.

Kantrowitz, M. J. *Dynamic Priorities.* Little Neck, N.J.: Hazeltine Corp., 1968.

Kepner, Charles H. and Tregoe, Benjamin B. *The Rational Manager: A Systematic Approach to Problem Solving and Decision-Making.* New York: McGraw-Hill Book Company, Inc., 1965.

Kolosa, Blair J. *Introduction to Behavioral Science for Business.* New York: John Wiley and Sons, Inc., 1969.

Koontz, Harold and O'Donnell, Cyril. *Principles of Management.* Fourth ed. New York: McGraw-Hill Book Company, Inc., 1968.

Lawrence, Paul R. and Lorsch, Jay W. *Organization and Environment.* Homewood, Illinois: Richard D. Irwin, Inc., 1969.

Lawrence, Paul R., *et al. Organization Behavior and Administration.* Homewood, Illinois: Richard D. Irwin, Inc., 1961.

Learned, Edmond P., *et al. Business Policy: Text and Cases.* Homewood, Illinois: Richard D. Irwin, Inc., 1965.

LeBreton, Preston P., and Henning, Dale A. *Planning Theory.* Englewood Cliffs, N.J.: Prentice-Hall, Inc., 1961.

Levin, Richard I., and Kirkpatrick, Charles A. *Planning and Control with PERT/CPM.* New York: McGraw-Hill Book Company, 1966.

Levin, Richard I., and Kirkpatrick, Charles A. *Quantitative Approaches to Management.* New York: McGraw-Hill Book Company, Inc., 1965.

Likert, Rensis. *New Patterns of Management.* New York: McGraw-Hill Book Company, Inc., 1961.

MacDonald, Jr., Morgan, B. *Appraising the Market for New Industrial Products.* New York: The National Industrial Conference Bond, 1967.

Magee, John F. *Industrial Logistics.* New York: McGraw-Hill Book Company, Inc., 1968.

Malcolm, Donald G., and Rowe, Alan J. *Management Control Systems.* New York: John Wiley and Sons, Inc., 1960.

March, James G., and Simon, Herbert A. *Organizations.* New York: John Wiley and Sons, Inc., 1958.

Martin, E. W. Jr., *Electronic Data Processing: An Introduction.* Homewood, Illinois: Richard D. Irwin, Inc., 1965.

Marting, Elizabeth. *New Products, New Profits: Company Experiences in New Product Planning.* New York: American Management Association, 1964.

Maslow, Abraham H. *Motivation and Personality.* New York. Harper and Row Publishers, 1965.

McCarthy, E. Jerome, McCarthy, J. A., and Humes, Durward. *Integrated Data Processing Systems.* New York: John Wiley and Sons, Inc., 1966.

McNichols, Thomas J. *Policy Making and Executive Action: Cases on Business Policy.* Third ed. New York: McGraw-Hill Book Company, Inc., 1967.

Merchant of the Millions—A Brief History of the Origin and Development of Sears, Roebuck and Company. Chicago: Sears, Roebuck and Company, National Public Relations Department, 1967.

Michigan Business Review. March, 1968.

Michigan Business Review. May, 1968.

Miller, Ben. *Managing Innovation for Growth and Profit.* Homewood, Illinois: Richard D. Irwin, Inc., 1970.

Miller, David W., and Starr, Martin K. *Executive Decisions and Operations Research.* Rev. ed. Englewood Cliffs, N.J.: Prentice-Hall, Inc., 1969.

Miller, Ernest C. *Advanced Techniques for Strategic Planning.* New York: American Management Association, 1971.

Miller, Ernest C. *Marketing Planning: Approaches of Selected Companies.* New York: American Management Association, 1967.

Mockler, Robert J. *Circulation Planning and Development for the National Observer: A Research Study on Business Applications of Management Planning and Control Principles.* Atlanta: Georgia State College, 1967.

Mockler, Robert J. *The Management Control Process.* New York: Appleton-Century-Crofts, 1971.

Mockler, Robert J. *Putting Computers to Work More Effectively in Business Publishing.* New York: American Business Press, 1969.

Mockler, Robert J., and Easop, Harrison. *Guidelines for More Effective Planning and Management of Franchise Systems.* Atlanta: Georgia State College, 1968.

Mooney, James D., and Reiley, Alan C. *Onward Industry!* New York: Harper and Brothers, 1931.

Moore, Geoffrey H. *Business Cycles Indicators.* Princeton: Princeton University Press, 1961.

Moreno, Ignacio Garcia. *Top Management Long-Range Planning.* New York: Vantage Press, 1963.

Newell, William T. *Long-Range Planning Policies and Practices: Selected Companies Operating in Texas.* Austin, Texas: Bureau of Business Research, The University of Texas, 1963.

Newman, William H., and Logan, James P. *Business Policies and Central Management.* Fifth ed. Cincinnati: South-Western Publishing Company, 1965.

Newman, William H., and Summer, Charles E. Jr. *The Process of Management:*

Concepts, Behavior and Practice. Second edition. Englewood Cliffs, N.J.: Prentice-Hall, Inc., 1967.

Papoulis, A. *Probability, Random Variables, and Stockatic Processes.* New York: McGraw-Hill Book Company, Inc., 1965.

Payne, Bruce. *Planning for Company Growth: The Executives Guide to Effective Long-Range Planning.* New York: McGraw-Hill Book Company, Inc., 1963.

Pessimier, Edgar A. *New Product Decisions: An Analytical Approach.* New York: McGraw-Hill Book Company, 1966.

Pigors, Paul, Meyers, Charles A., and Malm, F. T. *Management of Human Resources.* New York: McGraw-Hill Book Company, Inc., 1964.

Planning for Future Growth: A Small Company Must. New York: The Research Institute of America, 1967.

Pratt, R., Raiffa, H., and Schlaifer, R. *Introduction to Statistical Decision Theory.* New York: McGraw-Hill Book Company, Inc., 1965.

Prince, Thomas R. *Information Systems for Management Planning and Control.* Homewood, Illinois: Richard D. Irwin, Inc., 1966.

Pritzer, Robert A., and Gring, Robert A. *Modern Approaches to Production Planning and Control.* New York: American Management Association, 1960.

Richards, Max D., and Greenlaw, Paul S. *Management Decision Making.* Homewood, Illinois: Richard D. Irwin, Inc., 1966.

Rubenstein, Albert H., and Haberstroh, Chadwick J. *Some Theories of Organization: Readings.* Homewood, Illinois: Richard D. Irwin, Inc., 1966.

Rudwick, Bernard H. *Systems Analysis for Effective Planning.* New York: John Wiley and Sons, Inc., 1969.

St. Thomas, Charles E. *Practical Business Planning: A Manager's Guide.* New York: American Management Association, 1965.

Schlaifer, Robert. *Probability and Statistics for Business Decisions.* New York: McGraw-Hill Book Company, Inc., 1959.

Schoderbek, Peter P. *Management Systems.* New York: John Wiley and Sons, Inc., 1967.

Schnelle, Kenneth E. *Case Analysis and Business Problem Solving.* New York: McGraw-Hill Book Company, Inc., 1967.

Scott, Brian W. *Long-Range Planning in American Industry.* New York: American Management Association, 1965.

Scott, William G. *Organization Theory: A Behavioral Analysis for Management.* Homewood, Illinois: Richard D. Irwin, Inc., 1967.

Schuchman, Abe. *Scientific Decision Making for Business: Readings in Operations Research for Non-Mathematicians.* New York: Holt, Rinehart and Winston, Inc., 1963.

Simon, Herbert A. *The New Science of Management Decision.* New York: Harper and Row, Publishers, Inc., 1960.

Solomon, Irving I., and Weingart, Laurence O. *Management Uses of the Computer.* New York: Harper and Row, Publishers, Inc., 1966.

Spencer, Milton H., Clark, Colin G., and Hoguet, Peter W. *Business and Economic Forecasting: An Econometric Approach.* Homewood, Illinois: Richard D. Irwin, Inc., 1961.

Sproat, Audrey T., and Learned, E. P. *Indian Head Mills.* Harvard Graduate School of Business Administration, 1961.

Steiner, George A. *Managerial Long-Range Planning.* New York: McGraw-Hill Book Company, Inc., 1963.

Steiner, George A. *Top Management Planning.* New York: Macmillan Company, 1969.

Steiner, George A. *Strategic Factors in Business Success.* New York: Financial Executives Research Foundation, 1969.

Steiner, George A., and Cannon, Warren M. *Multi-National Corporate Planning.* New York: The Macmillan Company, 1966.

Stieglitz, Harold. *Organization Planning.* New York: National Industrial Conference Board, 1962.

Sweet, Franklin H. *Strategic Planning . . . A Conceptual Study.* Austin, Texas: Bureau of Business Research, The University of Texas, 1964.

Tannenbaum, Arnold S. *Control in Organizations.* New York: McGraw-Hill Book Company, Inc., 1968.

Taylor, Frederick W. *Scientific Management.* New York: Harper and Row, 1947.

Terry, George R. *Principles of Management.* Fourth ed. Homewood, Illinois: Richard D. Irwin, Inc., 1964.

Thompson, Stewart. *How Companies Plan.* New York: American Management Association, 1962.

Vazsonyi, A. *Scientific Programming in Business and Industry.* New York: John Wiley and Sons, Inc., 1958.

Von Bertalanffy, Ludwig. *Problems of Life: An Education of Modern Biological and Scientific Thought.* London: C. A. Watts and Company, Ltd., 1952.

Wadia, Maneck S. *Management and the Behavioral Sciences: Text and Readings.* Boston: Allyn and Bacon, Inc., 1968.

Warren, E. Kirby. *Long-Range Planning: The Executive Viewpoint.* Englewood Cliffs, N.J.: Prentice-Hall, Inc., 1966.

Weber, Max. *The Theory of Social and Economic Organization.* New York: Oxford University Press, 1947.

Weston, J. Fred, and Brigham, Eugene F. *Managerial Finance.* New York: Holt, Rinehart and Winston, 1962.

Wiener, Norbert. *The Human Use of Human Beings: Cybernetics and Society.* Boston: Houghton Mifflin Company, 1950.

Wolf, Herbert T. *Policy Development and Implementation in a Large Retail Chain.* New York: St. John's University, 1968.

Wolfe, Harry Deane. *Business Forecasting Methods.* New York: Holt, Rinehart and Winston, 1966.

Ziegler, Raymond J. *Business Policies and Decision Making.* New York: Appleton-Century-Crofts, 1966.

INDEX